FEDERAL RESERVE POLICY
REAPPRAISED, 1951–1959

FEDERAL RESERVE POLICY

REAPPRAISED, 1951–1959

by Daniel S. Ahearn

COLUMBIA UNIVERSITY PRESS
New York and London

This study, prepared under the Graduate Faculties of Columbia University, was selected by a committee of those Faculties to receive one of the Clarke F. Ansley awards given annually by Columbia University Press.

COPYRIGHT © 1963 BY COLUMBIA UNIVERSITY PRESS

First printing 1963
Second printing 1965

LIBRARY OF CONGRESS CATALOG CARD NUMBER: 63–10522
PRINTED IN THE UNITED STATES OF AMERICA

To My Mother and Father

ACKNOWLEDGMENTS

THIS STUDY was written during a leave of absence from the First National City Bank of New York. For that opportunity I wish to express gratitude to the Bank and to Dr. Norris O. Johnson, vice-president in charge of the Economics Department. The ideas presented and the conclusions drawn are, of course, entirely my own and the Bank had no responsibility whatsoever for them. I am indebted to Professor James W. Angell, who supervised this dissertation, for penetrating yet tolerant and sympathetic criticism of ideas which in many cases differed widely from his own. I wish also to mention the stimulation and helpful criticism received from members of the faculty of the University of Pennsylvania. In particular, Professor Charles R. Whittlesey gave generous amounts of time and encouragement while critically reading large parts of the manuscript. Professor Ervin Miller was ever ready to engage in discussion of difficult points, and Professor Lawrence Klein gave needed expert advice on the foray into multiple correlation analysis in Chapter XII. Mr. Joel Popkin carried out the multiple correlation analysis with a keen awareness of theoretical niceties. I am also grateful for the courtesy and help given to me by the staff of the Federal Reserve Bank of Philadelphia, particularly Dr. Clay Anderson, economic adviser, Dr. David Eastburn, vice-president in charge of Research, and Miss Doris Zimmerman and her staff in the library.

D. S. A.

CONTENTS

Part III. THE FEDERAL RESERVE'S CONTROL OVER FINANCIAL VARIABLES

Part IV. SUMMARY

TABLES

CHARTS

FEDERAL RESERVE POLICY
REAPPRAISED, 1951–1959

INTRODUCTION

The restoration of flexibility to United States monetary policy in 1951 reflected the revival of belief that monetary policy would prove to be a highly useful tool of national economic policy. The Douglas Committee *Report* of January, 1950, which laid the groundwork for the move, expressed the prevailing view when it said:

an appropriate, flexible, and vigorous monetary policy, employed in co-ordination with fiscal and other policies, should be one of the principal methods used to achieve the purposes of the Employment Act. Timely flexibility toward easy credit at some times and credit restriction at other times is an essential characteristic of a monetary policy that will promote economic stability rather than instability.[1]

Yet, after ten years of experience, another Congressional committee, also headed by Senator Douglas, took a rather critical view of flexible monetary policy measures that had actually been applied. In a report dated January, 1960, the committee said:

Just as the preaccord policy promoted artificially low interest rates, the policies pursued, particularly since 1953, have brought interest rates to levels higher than they should or need be. In other words, while the accord created the conditions under which monetary policy could do a better job, and while some improvement has been made, the full potential of monetary policy to promote stability and economic growth has not been realized.[2]

Some critics went much further and questioned whether any monetary policy had potential to be useful. On the one hand it was argued that the "real" economy had become unresponsive to monetary con-

---

[1] U.S. Congress, Joint Committee on the Economic Report, Subcommittee on Monetary, Credit, and Fiscal Policies, *Monetary, Credit, and Fiscal Policies, Report,* 81st Cong., 2d Sess., 1950, pp. 1–2. Cited hereafter as Douglas Committee, *Report.*

[2] U.S. Congress, Joint Economic Committee, *Employment, Growth, and Price Levels, Report,* 86th Cong., 2d Sess., 1960, p. 30. Cited hereafter as Joint Committee, *1959 Employment Report.*

trols because of widespread market imperfections. For example, monetary policy was said to have been ineffective in dealing with inflation of the types which can be ascribed to cost-push, wage-push, administered prices, or shifts in the composition of demand. Other critics asserted that monetary policy was ineffective because the financial environment had become less sensitive to Federal Reserve controls as a result of the vast increase in holdings of liquid assets, the rapid growth of nonbank credit-granting financial intermediaries outside the direct sphere of Federal Reserve influence, and the ability of individuals and business to speed up the turnover or velocity of the existing money supply. While some critics suggested that monetary policy could have been made effective by suitable modifications, others argued that it was inherently defective and needed to be replaced by more reliance on direct controls on various types of economic activity.[3]

The issue is clearly important. It seems to me that before flexible monetary controls are relegated to a secondary place, serious consideration should be given to the possibility that the alleged deficiencies of monetary policy might have been due to the way in which they were applied rather than to any inherent defect. The effectiveness of monetary policy, after all, was the end result of a number of interrelated steps: (1) the monetary authorities' vigor, resourcefulness, and flexibility in making use of policy instruments; (2) the impact of policy instruments on the supply of money, interest rates, the availability of credit, and the financial markets generally; and (3) the influence of monetary magnitudes and of conditions in the financial markets on economic activity. A criticism that the economy was insensitive to monetary influences involves only the final step in the chain; it is misdirected if the real fault was that the monetary variables and the financial markets were affected insufficiently, or with poor timing, because of lack of vigor or poor choice of instruments on the part of the central bank.

Accordingly, this study attempts to evaluate monetary policy's effectiveness in influencing monetary variables and the financial mar-

[3] For a broad discussion of recent criticisms of monetary policy see U.S. Congress, Joint Economic Committee, *Staff Report on Employment, Growth, and Price Levels*, 86th Cong., 1st Sess., 1959, pp. 315–408. Cited hereafter as Joint Committee, *1959 Staff Report*.

kets from 1951 to 1959. If monetary policy was unsuccessful here, in its immediate area of impact, it was not likely to have had significant impact on economic decisions in the economy at large. Moreover, the financial sector deserves special emphasis because much of the case for the revival of a flexible monetary policy in 1951 rested on the new view that its effectiveness would derive from its impact on lenders, the availability of credit, and liquidity generally, that is, on the financial sector, rather than from its influence on borrowers through changes in the cost of credit. Finally, much of the controversy about monetary policy followed in recent years has turned on conflicting views of its efficacy in affecting the financial sector, of the uses to be made of the various instruments of policy, of the importance of the growing volume of money substitutes, and of the implications of the growing importance of financial intermediaries.

Thus, the basic issue to be investigated is whether the views of monetary policy held by the Federal Reserve, and the actions taken on the basis of those views, significantly impaired the monetary authorities' ability to influence the money supply, interest rates, the availability of credit, and financial institutions and markets generally. Or, to put it another way, could a somewhat different central banking approach have produced more appropriate behavior of monetary and financial variables?

Part I discusses the general background in which Federal Reserve policies were formulated from 1951 to 1959. Chapter I discusses the significant aspects of the revival of belief in a flexible monetary policy from 1945 to 1951. Chapter II presents Robert V. Roosa's theory, the so-called "New York Bank view," of how a "new monetary policy" might be most effective. Chapter III sets out the different view which seems to have governed the Federal Reserve Board's application of monetary policy from 1951 to 1959.

Part II makes a detailed survey of the history of the Federal Reserve's use of its monetary policy instruments over the ten years from 1951 to 1959. Chapters IV, V, and VI are devoted to the policy of confining open market operations to "bills only," because this stimulated the most controversy and because open market operations are widely considered to be the most important policy instrument. There is also extended discussion of discount policy (Chapter VII), changes in reserve requirements (Chapter VIII), and the failure to use selective controls on consumer and real-estate mortgage credit (Chapter IX).

Part III examines the over-all impact of the Federal Reserve's policy on monetary magnitudes and the financial markets. Chapter X investigates whether the money supply has been influenced appropriately, and also takes up a number of criticisms which have asserted that interest rates, liquidity, financial intermediaries, or general liquidity, are more important variables for the central bank to control than the money supply. Chapter XI discusses the behavior of the velocity of money and assesses its significance for monetary policy. Chapter XII attempts to test empirically Robert V. Roosa's thesis that rising yields and falling prices of U.S. Government securities make financial institutions more willing to hold government securities and less willing to sell them, and accordingly affect the willingness of these institutions to extend credit to private borrowers.

Part IV contains the conclusions reached in the study. Briefly summarizing them:

(1) Continuous adherence to the "bills only" policy was and is undesirable. Throughout 1953–1959, this self-imposed restriction on the Federal Reserve's freedom of action reduced its ability to influence long-term interest rates and bond prices, reduced its area of direct contact with nonbank financial institutions, and resulted in the creation of excessive liquidity in recessions.

(2) The discount mechanism should be used essentially as a defensive weapon of monetary policy, and except in 1952–1953, the authorities have so used it.

(3) Increases in reserve requirements might well be used as a tool of credit restraint in order to achieve a quicker and more widely spread impact on bank reserve positions and the money supply.

(4) Selective credit controls on consumer and mortgage borrowing might prove useful at times when demand in these sectors is expanding rapidly and general credit controls are already so restrictive that further tightening would have unduly harsh effects on the economy.

(5) The Federal Reserve has been successful in promptly influencing the volume of demand deposits in New York City and other weekly reporting member banks. The bulk of the rest of the

money supply, demand deposits in all other commercial banks, responded to the Federal Reserve's monetary policy actions promptly in recessions, when reserve requirement reductions were used, but only slowly in periods of expansion. The use of reserve requirement increases in periods of business expansion might help to control deposit volumes in these banks more promptly. Control of the money supply is essential to any effective monetary policy since it is intimately related to the level of interest rates and comprises a major part of any of the liquidity constructs which have been proposed as alternative control variables. However, monetary policy might have been more effective if the Federal Reserve had recognized that interest rates and liquidity are, to some degree at least, partially independent variables which could usefully have been influenced directly.

(6) Increases in the income velocity of money were a substantial offset to restraint on the money supply from 1951 to 1959 but are not likely to be as much of a problem in the future. The ability of business corporations, at least, to economize on cash in response to the high interest rates associated with restrictive monetary policy seems to have lessened.

(7) Holdings of government bonds of some financial institutions, mutual savings banks and life insurance companies, appear to be positively related to changes in yields on such bonds. This implies that the "bills only" policy, eschewing any direct influence on long-term government bond yields, probably reduced the influence of monetary policy as a whole on these institutions. However, the willingness of commercial banks, fire, marine and casualty insurance companies, and pension funds to hold long-term government securities, does not seem to have been closely related to their yields.

These findings are almost all critical in some degree of the Federal Reserve's administration of monetary policy in the 1951–1959 period. It is impossible to avoid the conclusion that the Federal Reserve authorities' conception and application of monetary policy was tradition-bound too long to permit maximum effectiveness. On the other hand fairness compels the observation that Federal Reserve policy in these years was markedly successful in contributing to the avoidance of major inflation or deflation while simultaneously making a difficult transition from a pegged bond market to one which was free to respond to private market forces. Moreover, since 1959, the

Federal Reserve has abandoned the "bills only" policy and also given other evidences of a more flexible, less doctrinaire approach to the achievement of the goals it has set for itself—the promotion of economic stability and growth, the maintenance of the value of the currency, and the protection of the nation's foreign exchange and gold reserves.

Part I

THE BACKGROUND
OF THE RETURN TO
FLEXIBLE MONETARY POLICY

I

THE REVIVAL OF BELIEF IN

FLEXIBLE MONETARY POLICY:

1945–1951

MONETARY POLICY could hardly have been in lower esteem than it was at the close of World War II. Few economists or financial observers thought that it would have any significant role to play in the postwar years. Alvin Hansen spoke for many when he wrote in 1945 that "on grounds of both experience and general theoretical analysis, it is now widely accepted that the interest rate is a very poor instrument" to "effectively control a speculative boom." [1] Even the highest echelons of the Federal Reserve System itself were dubious about the postwar usefulness of flexible monetary policy. Marriner Eccles, chairman of the System's Board of Governors, told Congress in 1947, "Control of interest rates on Government securities . . . is not an effective instrument for achieving monetary objectives." [2]

This deep-seated pessimism reflected a variety of considerations. The failure of extremely easy money conditions and low interest rates to stimulate any substantial recovery from the Great Depression was still fresh in mind. Since there was widespread fear that another depression would be precipitated by a cessation of wartime armament expenditures, it was natural for economists to feel that monetary policy would also be ineffective in the postwar period. Moreover, skepticism about the influence of monetary policy was reinforced by the results of several surveys of the effect of interest costs on business investment decisions in the late 1930s. These surveys suggested that

[1] Alvin Hansen, "Stability and Expansion," in *Financing American Prosperity*, ed. by Homan and Machlup, p. 251.
[2] *Federal Reserve Bulletin*, XXXIV (January, 1948), 16.

businessmen were little affected by interest rates.[3] In any case, no one thought interest rates would be free to fluctuate in the postwar period; during World War II rates had been stabilized at low levels by the Federal Reserve in order to facilitate war financing, and the general expectation was that this imposed stability would continue into the postwar years. Even those who considered the possibility of releasing the Federal Reserve from its wartime commitment to stabilize Treasury security prices and yields rejected this alternative because of fear that fluctuations in interest rates and security prices might adversely affect the willingness of investors to continue to hold the vastly swollen public debt. Finally, there was not too much interest in monetary policy because many economists thought the newly discovered weapon, fiscal policy, promised all the economic control that public policy makers would need.

In 1945 these ideas, assumptions, and presumptions constituted a new orthodoxy. However, the realities of the postwar world gradually led to recognition that skepticism about the usefulness of flexible monetary policy had been overdone and that in any case an inflexible monetary policy involved difficulties of its own. This awakening involved a number of influences but three seem especially significant: (1) The major postwar problem turned out to be inflation rather than deflation as had been anticipated; (2) Both theory and practice revealed fiscal policy to be less of a panacea than had been thought in 1945; and (3) Inflexible monetary policy, that is, holding interest rates stable, proved to involve far more difficulties than had been expected.

SIGNIFICANCE OF POSTWAR INFLATION

The fact that inflation, not deflation, turned out to be the major problem of the postwar period revived interest in monetary policy for two reasons. First, as noted earlier, much of the pessimism about monetary policy's usefulness had been based on the assumption that monetary policy is ineffective in dealing with depression. However

[3] H. D. Henderson, "The Significance of the Rate of Interest," J. E. Meade and P. W. S. Andrews, "Summary of Replies to Questions on Effects of Interest Rates," and P. W. S. Andrews, "A Further Inquiry into the Effects of Rates of Interest," in *Oxford Studies in the Price Mechanism*, ed. by Wilson and Andrews, pp. 16–27, 27–30, and 51–67. Also J. F. Ebersole, "The Influence of Interest Rates upon Entrepeneurial Decisions in Business," *Harvard Business Review*, XVII (Autumn, 1938), 35–40.

true one might believe this to be, the postwar inflation made it an irrelevant consideration. Second, inflation is widely believed to be a monetary phenomenon; its occurrence naturally induced a search for monetary cures.

Thus attention soon turned to money and liquid asset accumulations. Writing in December, 1951, James Tobin noted that "a striking characteristic of monetary theory has been the revival of interest in holdings of assets as determinants of the flow of spending." [4] To be sure, not all economists agreed with the redirection of emphasis toward money, liquidity, and asset holdings as influences on expenditure. But it is significant that even those who remained critical were inclined to give more importance to monetary factors than had been fashionable a few years earlier.[5]

Economists also took another look at the prewar surveys of the influence of interest rates which had been so important in creating skepticism about the value of monetary policy. The result, more often than not, was a revision of the original verdict against interest rates to a less skeptical "not proven" on the grounds that the surveys were not well designed to elicit the information sought and that in any case the abnormal circumstances of the Great Depression invalidated the results for more normal periods.[6] Even R. S. Sayers, who in 1939 had summarized the results of one of the surveys as indicating that "the potency of that weapon [the rate of interest] in a constantly changing world must, I think, be described as very low," [7] in 1951 was willing to grant that "changes in the interest rate may have considerable effect on business activity through their effects on both capital outlay and consumption outlay" [8] subject to the continuing proviso that this influence may diminish in the future.

In addition, economists emphasized the availability of credit as an influence on ability to borrow and spend. The concept of the availability of credit was not new—Keynes had referred to it in a discussion

---

[4] Tobin, "Asset Holdings and Spending Decisions," *American Economic Review*, XLII (May, 1952), 109. A good selection of the discussions to which Tobin had reference is set out in the footnotes to an article by Morris Cohen, "Liquid Assets and the Consumption Function," *Review of Economics and Statistics*, XXXVI (May, 1954), 202–11.

[5] Tobin, *American Economic Review*, XLII, 122.

[6] R. S. Sayers, "The Rate of Interest as a Weapon of Economic Policy," in *Oxford Studies*, pp. 1–16.

[7] *Ibid.*, p. 5.   [8] *Ibid.*, p. 15.

of "the fringe of unsatisfied borrowers" [9]—but the postwar discussion gave it new importance. As Ellis described it:

The price of credit, unlike prices in most markets for goods and services, does not separate buyers from non-buyers, since with a sufficient assumption of risk by the lender, any amount of capital could be lent at any interest rate. All potential lenders (and most significantly all commercial banks) both in boom and depression must somewhere draw a line because of insufficient "credit-worthiness" of potential borrowers. Those borrowers who could pay the required rate of interest but who are excluded by the lender's credit standards have been called the "unsatisfied fringe" to distinguish them from borrowers (or from excluded buyers on other markets) who cannot demand because the price is too high; the process of applying the decisive credit standards has been called "credit-rationing"; and its effect on the supply of credit (on money in a broad sense) has been designated as its "availability," to distinguish this factor from the limitation imposed by the rate of interest.[10]

In common with a number of other economists Ellis concluded, "Availability is probably more important as a determinant of the supply of investable funds than the interest rate." [11]

Thus the postwar inflation had the effect, among many others, of redirecting attention to the role of money, liquidity, and interest rates. In the broad, it led many economists to feel that they had been over-hasty in completely dismissing the importance of money, but it left open the question of whether a flexible monetary policy could be a powerful tool.

SECOND THOUGHTS ABOUT THE POWER OF FISCAL POLICY

Gradual disappointment of the early optimistic expectations of what might be expected of fiscal policy also helped revive the idea that monetary policy might still have a useful role to play. Fiscal policy—government use of expenditure and tax policies to influence general economic activity—had caught the imagination of economists

[9] Keynes, *A Treatise on Money*, II, 364–67.

[10] Ellis, "The Rediscovery of Money," in *Money, Trade, and Economic Growth*, p. 255. For useful discussions of the availability doctrine, see Ira Scott, Jr., "Monetary Policy, the Theory of Assets, and the Availability of Credit" (Unpublished Ph.D. dissertation, Harvard University, 1953); John Kareken, "Lenders' Preferences, Credit Rationing, and the Effectiveness of Monetary Policy," *Review of Economics and Statistics*, XXXIX (August, 1957), 292–302; Donald Hodgman, "In Defense of the Availability Doctrine: A Comment," *Review of Economics and Statistics*, XLI (February, 1959), 70–74; and Guttentag, "Credit Availability, Interest Rates, and Monetary Policy," *Southern Economic Journal*, XXVI (January, 1960), 219–28.

[11] Ellis, in *Money, Trade, and Economic Growth*, p. 255.

after Keynes had focused attention on it.[12] While not denying some
influence to monetary magnitudes, Keynes put the major emphasis on
the possibilities for government to influence the economy through direct investment and tax policies. Government, he argued, could thus
inject or withdraw income from the economy, and such injections or
withdrawals would have a multiplied effect on income because people
ordinarily respend the greater part of additions to income and save
only a fraction.

The key term in the Keynesian analysis was the consumption function or propensity to consume, "a fundamental psychological law" on
the basis of which "men are disposed, as a rule and on the average,
to increase their consumption as their income increases, but not by as
much as the increase in their income." [13] In the short run, Keynes
argued that the propensity to consume "may be considered a fairly
stable function." [14] He went on to point out that income is made up
of consumption expenditures and investment expenditures so that any
change in income, denoted as ΔY, must always equal the sum of the
change in consumption, ΔC, and the change in investment, ΔI. If
investment is assumed exogenous, these relationships can be solved
to show that $\Delta Y = \dfrac{1}{(1-k)}\Delta I$, where k is the proportion of a change
in income which is spent on consumption. In a community which nor-
mally consumes 75 percent of additional dollars of income, any given
change in investment would produce a change of $\dfrac{1}{(1-.75)}\Delta I$ in income or four times the change in investment.

This simple relationship seemed to hold out the prospect of easy
control of the level of national income. Public investment spending
could be varied, if necessary, to stimulate total income by a multiple
of itself. Taxation could have the same powerful effects in the opposite direction, if necessary. The leverage or multiplier of a given
amount of investment or taxation would depend on the community's
marginal propensity to consume but would almost always be large
enough to make this way of affecting economic activity attractively
powerful. Even if monetary policy had been regarded as effective at

---

[12] Keynes, *The General Theory of Employment, Interest, and Money.* Cited
hereafter as *General Theory.*
[13] *Ibid.,* p. 96.   [14] *Ibid.,* p. 95.

the close of World War II, it could hardly have competed with this powerful yet simple instrument of economic control. As Schumpeter has said:

Before the appearance of the *General Theory,* economics had been growing increasingly complex and increasingly incapable of giving straightforward answers to straightforward questions. The *General Theory* seemed to reduce it once more to simplicity, and to enable the economist once more to give simple advice that everybody could understand.[15]

Unfortunately fiscal policy proved not to be as facile a tool for manipulating the economy as had been thought in the first flush of enthusiasm. The consumption function turned out, on closer examination and in practice, to be much less simple than some of Keynes' more enthusiastic followers had assumed.

Perhaps the major shock to economists who had regarded the consumption function and fiscal policy as a philosopher's stone for economic policy-makers was the failure of postwar economic forecasts based on Keynesian models. Part of the answer was the inability of forecasters to anticipate the rapidity with which demobilization slack would be taken up and the consequent underestimation of postwar production levels. But what most upset the forecasters was the evidence that the prewar relation of consumption to income used in making the forecasts was not holding in the postwar years. Consumption was higher in relation to income than had been expected. After the fact, there were a number of explanations, including, belatedly, some that Keynes had warned of in 1936. In 1947, Harris, a leading Keynesian, concluded:

it is generally agreed that we must allow for the effects of changing distribution of income, accumulation of liquid assets, cyclical variations in relationships, lags in the adjustment of spending to income, population changes, relative price changes, etc., etc. The danger now is that the models may become so complicated as to become useless.[16]

No one ever again had quite the same faith in a simple unchanging relation of consumption to income, nor in the precisely calculable effects of a change in Government spending.

At the same time, it was becoming evident that fiscal policy was

[15] Schumpeter, "Keynes, the Economist," in *The New Economics,* ed. by Seymour Harris, pp. 99–100.
[16] Harris, "Keynes' Influence on Public Policy," in *The New Economics,* pp. 19–20.

also subject to practical difficulties. To be sure, the early postwar Federal budgets produced sizable cash surpluses, a welcomed anti-inflationary contribution. But this was largely an automatic development, reflecting the fact that expenditures dropped to half their wartime levels with the end of hostilities while tax collections, though reduced, remained close to the wartime peaks. Thus the surpluses were not a particularly good indication of the success of a purposeful fiscal policy. Indeed, it was in this period that the difficulties of achieving cyclical variations in Government spending, to compensate for fluctuations in private spending, became apparent.

Expenditure increases, politically attractive to groups benefiting from them, were relatively easy to put in force. But expenditure reductions were another matter entirely. The limits of fiscal policy through purposeful manipulation of Government spending were indicated as early as August, 1946, when President Truman attempted to cut expenditures to reduce inflationary pressures. He was able to pare only $2 billion from a $40 billion budget. And even this amount was achieved only by stern determination in the face of substantial political opposition. The balance of the budget was regarded as inflexible, either because specific programs were held to be too important to cut or because expenditures on them were called for by basic authorizing legislation and could not be cut by administrative action. The nature of the problem was pointed out in 1955 by the Bureau of the Budget when it stated that only 13 percent of that year's budget was available as a target for budget cutters; of the remaining 87 percent, 61 percent was allocated to national defense and 26 percent to programs under which expenditures were made automatically according to formulae or criteria set out in the authorizing legislation.[17]

Flexible tax policies could also influence the economy, of course. But they also ran into difficulties. Congress, which under the Constitution is charged with responsibility for tax laws, was and is still reluctant to delegate any of its powers to the Executive which presumably could move more rapidly in raising or lowering tax rates in response to changes in economic conditions. Congress itself is slow in dealing with tax matters because of the importance of taxes to

[17] U.S. Executive Office of the President, Bureau of the Budget, *Review of the 1956 Budget*, August 25, 1955, pp. 5–6.

individuals and businesses who naturally object to any change that would put them at a disadvantage. Moreover, political considerations have bulked large in tax policy, as in expenditure policy. In 1948, an election year, Congress cut taxes at a time of acute inflationary pressure, despite opposition by most economists and President Truman.

Thus fiscal policy proved more difficult to use for economic stabilization purposes than had been expected in 1945. The conclusion many economists drew was that it had been decidedly premature to feel that monetary policy was no longer needed.

DIFFICULTIES OF INFLEXIBLE MONETARY POLICIES:
BREAKDOWN OF PEGGING

Meanwhile, the conduct of an inflexible monetary policy, that is, one devoted to the stabilization of the wartime pattern of interest rates, was proving to be a troublesome problem in the postwar years. During the war, yields and prices of Treasury securities had been stabilized in a situation in which investors had few or no alternative outlets for their money. But in the postwar years business was booming and opportunities for investment were widespread. In this atmosphere, pegging Government securities prices and yields not only prevented the Federal Reserve from using its powers to limit inflation but actually became a substantial inflationary force itself. The pegging policy made the entire marketable debt, regardless of stated maturity, convertible on demand into cash at the option of the holder and therefore practically as liquid as money. Moreover, so long as all Treasury maturities were supported at fixed prices or yields, control of the money supply passed over to the holders of Government securities; the Federal Reserve had to buy to maintain support-price levels regardless of what happened to the money supply.

The inflation potential created by the pegging commitment naturally made Federal Reserve officials uneasy. But two considerations counseled, or at least permitted, delay in attempting to withdraw from it. First, the Federal Reserve no less than the Treasury felt it vitally important that the swollen public debt remain in its holders' hands and not be thrown upon the market by panicky sellers fearful of price declines. Second, as noted earlier, the Federal budget produced substantial cash surpluses in the early postwar years, permitting retirement of bank-held Treasury debt and reduction of the money supply, and thus to some degree at least offset the inflationary potential of the pegging process.

As time went on, of course, these latter considerations dwindled in importance. The public debt diminished in size relative to the national income and to private debt, reflecting retirement of maturing securities as well as, and more importantly, the fact that the national income and private debt were growing rapidly in the inflationary, high-employment postwar atmosphere.[18] Moreover, by 1948 when Congress reduced tax rates well below the wartime levels, it had become clear that the period of large, almost automatic cash budget surpluses was over. Thus the public debt gradually came to seem less of an inhibiting factor to a flexible monetary policy while the approaching disappearance of the federal cash surplus made the monetary weapon seem more important.

The Federal Reserve began to move cautiously toward a somewhat greater degree of flexibility as early as 1946.[19] The approach was to withdraw gradually from the commitment to buy short-term Treasury securities at pegged prices and yields. This opened up at least the hope that the Federal Reserve need not lose control of the money supply if holders of the still-supported, long-term Treasury obligations began to unload them on the Federal Reserve at the support prices. Free from concern about short-term yields, the Federal Reserve could sell short-term Government securities to recapture the reserve funds it released when it purchased long-terms. As things turned out, this proved a wise precaution. The next development the Federal Reserve had to deal with was massive sales of nearly $11 billion long-term Government bonds in the year ended November, 1948, by insurance companies, banks, and other investors who

[18] The gross public debt declined from 128.1 percent of the gross national product in 1946 to 90.1 percent in 1950. The net Federal debt declined from 57.8 percent of all net public and private debt in 1946 to 44.6 percent in 1950 (net means elimination of duplicating intergovernmental and intercorporate debt).

[19] For a more detailed discussion of the events mentioned in this paragraph, see Henry Murphy, *The National Debt in War and Transition* (New York, McGraw-Hill, 1950), Ch. 17; Charles Abbot, *The Federal Debt, Structure and Impact* (New York, The Twentieth Century Fund, 1953); and U.S. Congress, Joint Committee on the Economic Report, Subcommittee on General Credit Control and Debt Management, *Monetary Policy and the Management of the Public Debt, Replies to Questions and Other Material*, 82nd Cong., 2d Sess., 1952, Pt. I, pp. 52–64. Cited hereafter as Patman Committee, *Compendium*.

were raising cash for higher-yielding private loans and who were also protecting themselves against the possibility that the Federal Reserve would be unable, or unwilling, to support long-term Government bond prices indefinitely.

Had the Federal Reserve not already taken the precaution to free short-term interest rates, so that it was able to make offsetting sales of short-term Government securities, the full impact of these $11 billion bond purchases would have caused a corresponding rise in bank reserves and an even larger increase in the money supply. But as it was, the sales of short-term Government securities offset the effects of the purchases of long-terms. Indeed, since the Treasury was retiring securities out of its cash surplus, Federal Reserve holdings of Government securities actually declined during this period.

Nevertheless, the 1947–1948 experience left a residue of lasting concern in the minds of Federal Reserve officials. Had the torrent of sales of long-term bonds gone on for another year at the same rate, it would have exhausted the Federal Reserve's holdings of short-term Governments which were being sold to prevent the expansion of bank reserve positions and the money supply. It was only a coincidence that the 1949 recession developed to slow credit demands and sales of bonds by lending institutions. Another time—the Federal Reserve authorities might well worry—things might not turn out so well. Also, although the Reserve authorities had prevented their purchases of long-term Government bonds from increasing the money supply, they had not been able to prevent the private sector from substantially increasing its liquidity by the swap of long-term bonds for the short-term obligations sold by the Federal Reserve.

Moreover, 1949 provided further evidence that a policy of stabilizing Government bond prices and yields was inconsistent with a credit policy directed at economic stability. For as the 1949 recession deepened, bond prices rose, and in line with the policy of maintaining orderly conditions in the Government securities market, the Federal Reserve authorities felt impelled to sell bonds to limit the extent of the price rises and decline in yields. But this meant withdrawal of bank reserves at a time when credit ease was called for to combat recessionary conditions in the general economy. Thus, the pegging policy dictated action in recession which was no more appropriate in terms of the general economic situation than had been the support purchases of bonds in inflationary circumstances. Facing up to the dilemma, the Federal Open Market Committee on June 28, 1949, announced that, "it will be the policy of the Committee to direct purchases, sales, and exchanges of Government securities by the Federal Reserve Banks with primary regard to the general business and credit situation." [20] In other words, bonds would not be sold just to prevent a rise in their prices.

It was against this general background that the Congressional Joint Economic Committee on the Economic Report launched its now historic investigation of monetary, credit, and fiscal policies. In January, 1950, the Committee concluded that:

> an appropriate, flexible and vigorous monetary policy, employed in coordination with fiscal and other policies, should be one of the principal methods used to achieve the purposes of the Employment Act. Timely flexibility toward easy credit at some times and credit restriction at other times is an essential characteristic of a monetary policy that will promote economic stability rather than instability.[21]

This expression of Congressional support for flexible monetary policy undoubtedly strengthened the resolve of the Federal Reserve authorities to free themselves from the commitment to support Treasury bond prices. The occasion arrived in June, 1950, when the outbreak of the Korean War stimulated a vast wave of inflationary borrowing and spending. The result was a behind-the-scenes struggle between the Federal Reserve and the Treasury which involved the highest officials of both agencies, key Congressional committee chairmen and even the President of the United States. The issue was whether the long-term Government bond market should continue to be supported on a 2½ percent yield basis. Finally, faced with a sizable prospective budget deficit and corresponding need to borrow large amounts of new money and with about $50 billion of maturities requiring refunding in 1951, the Treasury decided to modify its previously unyielding stand.[22] Representatives of the Treasury and the Federal Reserve started work on a compromise solution in mid-Feb-

[20] *Federal Reserve Bulletin*, XXXV (July, 1949), 776.
[21] Douglas Committee, *Report*, p. 1.
[22] For an excellent description of these events from the Treasury's point of view, see Patman Committee, *Compendium*, Pt. I, pp. 66–74; and for the Federal Reserve's views, pp. 346–51 and 362–68.

ruary, 1951. The result was the Treasury-Federal Reserve Accord
of March 3, 1951:

The Treasury and the Federal Reserve System have reached full accord
with respect to debt-management and monetary policies to be pursued in
furthering their common purpose to assure the successful financing of
the Government's requirements and, at the same time, to minimize monetization of the public debt.[23]

However cryptic this language appears, no market participant
doubted that it meant that the Federal Reserve was being freed to
conduct flexible monetary and credit policies as needed to influence
appropriately the general economic situation.

IMPLICATIONS OF THE 1945–1951 PERIOD
FOR FUTURE FLEXIBLE MONETARY POLICY

The return to a flexible monetary policy gave the Federal Reserve
freedom to use its powers as it saw fit to achieve and maintain economic stability and growth. But this did not mean that any particular path had to be taken. In fact, the 1945–1951 experience afforded justification for two widely different views of monetary policy.

On the one hand, it was possible to draw from the 1945–1951 experience a number of reasons why a flexible monetary policy might
best be confined to a rather limited role. For one thing, the revival
of belief in monetary policy in those years had not reflected any new
discoveries about the efficacy of monetary policy but rather recognition that the early postwar skepticism about its effectiveness had
been overdone. To some degree, the adoption of the flexible monetary policy reflected a belief that the failure of fiscal policy to live
up to expectations made even a modest contribution toward stability
from monetary policy worthwhile. In addition, the willingness to restore flexibility to monetary policy reflected in considerable degree
recognition that an inflexible monetary policy—that is, the policy of
stabilizing Government security yields and prices—had destabilized
the economy, rather than a strong conviction that a flexible monetary policy would be a powerful stabilizer. Finally, it could be argued
that monetary policy had become most useless, in terms of appropriately influencing the economy, during the pegging period. Such
an interpretation of the 1945–1951 years would lead to the convic-

[23] *Ibid.,* p. 74.

tion that monetary policy might make its greatest contribution to economic stability if it simply kept money from being a destabilizing factor.

On the other hand, there were a number of elements in the 1945–1951 experience which could be cited to justify a more active and positive role for a flexible monetary policy. The broad distribution of a large public debt, earlier considered an obstacle to an effective monetary policy, could be looked at as a sensitive part of the economic structure which monetary policy could influence through changing interest rates, that is, the terms on which debt instruments can be converted into cash. Moreover, in its endeavor to meet its pegging commitment without destabilizing the economy, the Federal Reserve had gained substantial experience in extending the scope of open market operations and also had developed new types of monetary instruments such as selective controls on consumer and real estate credit. Imaginative use of the experience gained with the new techniques and instruments, it could be argued, might powerfully increase the capabilities of a flexible monetary policy.

II

THE NEW THEORY OF MONETARY MANAGEMENT:
THE ROOSA DOCTRINE

THE optimistic view of the potentialities of a flexible monetary policy was sometimes called the new theory of monetary control, and was associated with the economists of the Federal Reserve Bank of New York, particularly with one of its officers, Robert V. Roosa. In the pages which follow this shall be referred to as the Roosa doctrine. Roosa suggested:

The securities and credit markets have become much more susceptible than they were years ago to any given change in interest rates. May it not also be significant that the presence of a substantial volume of Government securities in the debt structure, at all maturity periods, gives the central bank a medium through which it can directly influence the prices and yields on securities and credits of all terms? Is it not possible now that relatively small changes in interest rates, initiated or permitted by a central bank capable of reaching any segment of the rate structure, may give general credit policy an influence which it could not exert in the past? [1]

The Roosa doctrine was a fresh analysis of the way in which monetary policy works as well as a reinterpretation of the significance of the postwar financial and economic environment for the effectiveness of monetary policy. It stressed the importance of lenders and security underwriters rather than of borrowers or savers; the advantages of a large public debt as a fulcrum on which monetary policy could operate; and the increased institutionalization of savings as a factor making financial markets more sensitive to central bank policy. Finally it implied full use of all that had been learned about monetary instruments—and particularly open market operations—to make monetary policy effective in this environment.

[1] Roosa, "Interest Rates and the Central Bank," in *Money, Trade, and Economic Growth*, p. 271.

LENDERS AND THE AVAILABILITY OF CREDIT

Roosa's optimism about a flexible monetary policy stemmed directly from his view that much of the earlier pessimism had been based on a misinterpretation of the way monetary policy worked. In 1950 he said:

Economists and central banking theorists long believed that the significance of market rates of interest, and of central banking efforts to vary these rates, lay in the effects produced upon *borrowers,* and upon *savers.* Little if any attention was given to *lenders;* their function was considered that of automatic response to central bank action, without any meaningful independent influence on economic behavior.[2]

But, Roosa contended, this entire view of the workings of monetary policy was incomplete. Monetary policy could exert substantial influence on the economy, above and beyond its influence on borrowers or savers, by affecting lenders' willingness to make credit available. And the central bank could influence lenders through relatively modest changes in interest rates.

Roosa argued that upward changes in interest rates would make lenders less willing to extend credit. This is a rather paradoxical position on the face of it. The interest rate, after all, is the price of money, and price increases are usually considered to draw out an increased supply, not to limit supply. But Roosa had a number of ingenious arguments to support his position, although, as we shall see later, they left many economists unconvinced.

Most of Roosa's case hinged on the fact that lending institutions ordinarily carry substantial proportions of their loan resources in the form of interest-bearing investments, particularly U.S. Government securities. These can be turned into cash for lending only as they mature, or as they can be sold in the open market. Whether lenders would sell their Governments securities in order to increase loans to private borrowers depends on the capital loss which they might suffer and also on the yield differential they would gain by switching to private loans. Rising interest rates on Government securities would, Roosa contended, narrow the yield differential in favor of private loans, at least initially, and also increase prospective capital losses for sellers of Governments, both effects tending to reduce lenders' willingness to make credit available.

[2] *Ibid.,* pp. 271–72.

These effects would be reinforced by the influence of interest rate increases on expectations, particularly since many loan rates, and notably bank lending rates, are conventionally determined and "sticky." If increases in the more flexible open-market rates of interest gave rise to expectations of an eventual rise in lending rates, lenders might well be encouraged to hold funds off the market in anticipation of better returns at some future date. This would be true even with respect to cash reserves of loan funds, if the anticipated rise in rates was great enough to compensate lenders for the anticipated loss of income over the period when the funds would be held idle.

Moreover, Roosa argued that rising interest rates introduce uncertainty into the financial markets, causing a re-evaluation of the riskiness of private loans and turning investors toward the relative security of short-term Government securities. Private securities, which are subject to credit risk (the risk of the borrower's failure to make interest payments and/or repay principal at maturity) as well as to market risk (the risk of changes in prices of debt instruments because of interest rate changes), would lose liquidity faster than Governments when estimates of credit risk rise.

The practice of making "forward commitments" of loan funds, which had developed, especially among the insurance companies, to ensure steady employment of their inflow of investable funds, also was cited as an influence making lenders sensitive to interest rate movements. In the era of the pegged Government securities market, lenders had been willing to make future loan commitments which exceeded their anticipated inflow of new investable funds; they counted on sales of Government securities to make up the difference. Flexibility in prices and yields of Government securities could be a powerful deterrent to this practice. Increases in interest rates would raise the possibility of greater declines in bond prices than could be foreseen at the time a forward loan commitment was arranged and thus might be quickly reflected in a reduced willingness to make forward commitments.

In addition to these possibly temporary influences, proponents of the Roosa doctrine argued that some institutional investors might display an increased demand for U.S. Government securities after their yields had increased even though yields on private investments and securities had gone up as much or more. This rather surprising conclusion—for private securities would then be relatively more attractive than Governments on a straight-yield basis—rested on the allegation that insurance companies, mutual savings banks, and pension funds seek investments of maximum quality and safety consistent with a yield sufficient to cover contractual obligations to policyholders, depositors, and pensioners. Thus when yields on U.S. Governments, the safest available investment, are low, necessity to earn some minimum average return on portfolio forces these investors to seek riskier but higher-yielding private securities. Should increases in interest rates raise the return on Governments up to, or beyond, the minimum earnings rate need to satisfy contractual obligations, institutional investors might increase their demand for Governments even though yields on private investments had increased even more.

Finally, the institutional arrangements for the marketing of new security issues, the Roosa doctrine argued, made security underwriters peculiarly sensitive to the impact of monetary policy. Investment bankers' small capital positions—often only 5 or 10 percent of commitments undertaken—meant substantial exposure to risk of losses arising out of changes in the level of bond prices. A rise in long-term bond yields of only .05 percent would mean a decline of one point in the price of a 30- to 40-year bond (common in public utility financing which makes up the bulk of publicly underwritten new debt issues) bearing a 3 or 4 percent coupon. Since underwriters often operate on a one-point gross-profit margin on new offerings (that is, they underwrite at 100 and reoffer to the market at 101), a one-point loss could wipe out their gross profit and probably inflict a net loss when their costs were considered. A further .05 percent rise in long-term yields might impose a net loss of more than one point. This is significant; it might well wipe out 1/10 or even 1/5 of their total equity capital. Thus, changes in interest rates might be expected to find a quick response in the readiness or lack of readiness of underwriters to undertake the marketing of new issues.

Thus the argument of the Roosa doctrine was that central banking policy could still exert considerable influence on the economy through lenders and underwriters, even if one was skeptical of its influence on borrowers or savers.

SIGNIFICANCE OF THE PUBLIC DEBT

The Roosa doctrine stressed the importance of the large, widely distributed public debt as an aid to the effectiveness of monetary policy, which was in sharp contrast to the view generally taken earlier in the postwar years. Then, interest rate changes had been feared because of the possibility that they might produce unsettling changes in the capital value of the public debt, which had assumed an important place in the portfolios of the financial institutions of the country.

The new approach emphasized the fact that fluctuations in the capital value of the widely-held debt could insure maximum response to even modest monetary control actions. It was argued that a widely distributed public debt makes the transmission of credit ease or stringency from one sector of the capital market to another a faster and less uncertain affair than in the prewar period. With major lenders and investors operating in more than one sector and holding appreciable amounts of U.S. Treasury securities, a tendency for credit demands to outrun the supply of funds in the market for corporate bonds, for example, would soon be reflected in increased sales of U.S. Government securities as lenders raised additional funds in this manner. But these sales would depress U.S. bond prices, making their sale less attractive and eventually contracting the supply of funds for other borrowers.

Moreover, this view continued, a large, actively traded public debt would give the market earlier and more accurate notice of changes in underlying credit conditions. This is because Treasury obligations are free of credit risk and homogeneous in quality. Changes in market yields of corporate securities are not as good a guide to underlying credit conditions because they may reflect shifts in the credit rating or economic position of a particular company. Furthermore, the homogeneity of the public debt means that successive trades, even if not in precisely the same maturity, could be given, approximately at least, the same significance.

A final argument was that a big public debt could contribute to more effective monetary control because the Federal Reserve authorities historically have concentrated their open market purchases and sales in U.S. Treasury obligations and have made little or no use of their powers to buy and sell municipal warrants, etc.

Thus, a large, widely distributed public debt not only could quicken the transmission of the effects of credit policy actions into other markets but also could increase the direct impact of purchases and sales of Treasury securities on the portfolios of investors.

ROLE OF INSTITUTIONAL INVESTORS

Part of the case for believing that effective credit control might have become possible with only small changes in interest rates was based on the idea that:

The channeling of loanable resources into highly specialized investment concerns, had made lenders acutely sensitive to slight changes in the yield differentials among alternatives, both short and long. A steadily growing popular insistence on "security"—the avoidance of loss, at the expense of accepting lesser yields—had favored the growth of conservative, intermediary institutions, operating on relatively narrow margins, and alert to small changes among the yields on debt instruments that would have been considered trivial a few decades earlier.[3]

Institutional investment managers were regarded as having an extreme distaste—"phobia" is the word Roosa used—for capital losses on security sales. Roosa acknowledged that this attitude might change over in time, but he pointed out that as long as it persisted "a slight rise in yields on Governments may 'freeze in' many current holders who would readily have shifted from Governments into new loans or investments had the yield on Governments been pegged."[4] Consequently he argued

rate flexibility is not likely at any time to mean wide gyrations in rates; small changes will do what is needed provided they can be made at the right time, and provided there are no rigidly specified limits on the range of movement which would take away the powerful reinforcement of "uncertainty."[5]

OPERATIONS IN LONG-TERM BONDS

The central bank might count on the sensitivity of lenders and investment bankers to its actions to assure significant influence on the economy. It might expect that the widely held public debt would transmit its actions throughout the credit structure to all lenders. It might hope that the increased importance of professional investment

[3] Roosa, in *Money, Trade, and Economic Growth*, p. 278.
[4] *Ibid.*, p. 290.
[5] Roosa, "The Revival of Monetary Policy," *Review of Economics and Statistics,* XXXIII (February, 1951), 32.

managers would increase the sensitivity of response to its actions. But the central bank was still left with the responsibility of implementing its policy so that it took effect promptly and efficiently.

Roosa suggested that to achieve maximum effectiveness the central bank should buy and sell long-term Government bonds to exert direct influence on interest rates and yields in all maturity sectors of the securities market:

It is no longer sufficient to consider the effects of the discount rate upon commercial bank borrowing from the central bank, the effects of that borrowing upon bank rates and the money supply, and the effects of those in turn upon the entire level and structure of interest rates. For open market operations in Government securities bring the central bank into contact not only with the volume of available bank reserves, but also with the portfolios of all classes of lenders. . . . the central bank may also exert its influence directly on the prices of long-term securities.[6]

Such a policy, Roosa argued, would keep the central bank in direct contact with the capital market. A rise in long-term rates of interest would be particularly likely to exert a restraining influence on business expansion based on longer-term financing. It would strike directly at the salability of new long-term security issues, causing at the very least a greater spacing-out of new issues in comparison to the flow that would otherwise have occurred. Perhaps the sharpest influence was expected to be on lenders' attitudes toward mortgages and accordingly on the availability of mortgage credit.

Moreover, it is through operations in long-term bonds that the central bank could have the greatest effect on capital values. Advocates of the Roosa doctrine tended to claim considerable effect for relatively small changes in long-term interest rates because of the increased impact on capital values. Roosa observed, "Already the postwar experience suggests that yield changes of scarcely ⅛ percent for the longest-term bonds have considerable market effects." [7] But this was not an essential part of the Roosa view and some of its advocates conceded: "It is too early to be sure that lenders and borrowers will not become hardened to small rate changes, and reassured as to their possible extent." [8]

[6] Roosa, in *Money, Trade, and Economic Growth*, pp. 280, 288.
[7] *Ibid.*, p. 288.
[8] Sproul, "Changing Concepts of Central Banking," in *Money, Trade, and Economic Growth*, p. 324.

The significant argument for operations in long-term securities was more modest. It stated simply:

Properly guided—not with central bank pinpointing of rates, but with central bank action at critical junctures to bring about changes in the direction and pace of rate movements—the long-term market can, by spacing the flow of funds into longer-term investment opportunities, make a positive contribution toward lessening the amplitude of booms and depressions.[9]

Moreover, Roosa asserted that the Federal Reserve could not escape responsibilities for long-term rates regardless of its own wishes in the matter.

The choice is not between central bank control and "free market prices," but among alternative uses of the inherent power imposed upon the central bank by the existence of the large public debt. That power will be exercised whether consciously or unconsciously; and whether by the Treasury or the Federal Reserve. The need is for purposeful direction, based upon an understanding of the influences which changes in long-term rates may bring about.[10]

SOME CRITICAL RESERVATIONS

Roosa's analysis was a challenging presentation of the possibilities inherent in a flexible monetary policy vigorously administered to take full advantage of special circumstances in the postwar environment. But no one doubted that he had painted an optimistic picture. Some economists, more skeptical, questioned some steps in the analysis and also suggested that certain aspects of the postwar environment were less favorable for the success of monetary policy than Roosa had asserted. Some of the criticisms are mentioned below, but statistical analysis of the major premise of the Roosa doctrine—that rising interest rates deter sales of Government securities by institutional investors—is deferred until Chapter XII.

Critics were most puzzled by Roosa's allegation that increases in interest rates would reduce lenders' willingness to extend credit. Robertson pointed out that it is not clear why in every case rising interest rates (and the falling Government bond prices which accompany them) should slow an institutional investor's advances to private borrowers or retard sales of Government securities to finance such advances. Robertson argued that if an institutional lender expected a

---

[9] Roosa, in *Money, Trade, and Economic Growth*, p. 291.
[10] *Ibid.*, p. 288.

further rise in interest rates, it might well be spurred to accelerate sales of Governments in order to avoid even bigger capital losses after the expected rise in interest rates had taken place.[11] While there is little question that both reactions are possible and have occurred, the analysis in Chapter XII suggests that Roosa's conception seems somewhat more in accord with the experience of the post-1951 years.

Robertson also observed that the Roosa doctrine seemed to imply that a rise in interest rates would lead lenders to expect a continued increase but would lead borrowers to expect lower interest rates in the future. To Robertson it seemed "paradoxical to suppose that lenders and borrowers should consistently draw opposite inferences from the fact of an accomplished rise in [interest] rates." [12] If they did not, of course, an increased demand for credit from borrowers, to avoid higher loan rates later, might offset the lessened willingness of lenders to make credit available. According to Robertson, Roosa explained (in an unpublished letter) the apparent paradox by agreeing "that borrowers will share the 'elastic' expectations of lenders" but argued that borrowers nevertheless "will not, in the most important cases, be in a position to act upon them by rushing in to borrow now; i.e. borrowers will be more affected by the actual rise in the rate of interest, and lenders by its expected further rise." [13] But as Robertson reiterated, it is far from clear what keeps borrowers from borrowing ahead, though possible congestion in the new issue market or lessened availability of credit from banks, insurance companies, and other lenders are obvious possibilities.

However, insofar as lessened credit availability hinges on the "stickiness" of loan rates in the face of rising open market rates of interest, it can be argued that it is only a transitional phenomenon. Bankers and other lenders will not indefinitely rely on nonprice rationing of their funds; it is less profitable and harder to explain to customers than is an upward adjustment in loan rates. But if loan rates are adjusted upward the focus returns to interest rate rather than availability of credit.[14] But this criticism of the Roosa doctrine

---

[11] Robertson, *Economic Commentaries*, pp. 69–70.
[12] *Ibid.*   [13] *Ibid.*
[14] See Samuelson's testimony in U.S. Congress, Joint Committee on the Economic Report, Subcommittee on General Credit Control and Debt Management, *Monetary Policy and the Management of the Public Debt, Hearings*, 82nd Cong., 2d Sess., 1952, pp. 695–97.

is itself open to question. Even a transitional slowing of the rate of credit extension could have important economic effects. And there is some reason to believe that nonprice rationing of credit—in the form of compensating balance requirements, eligibility requirements for the prime loan rate, stricter mortgage credit terms—persists even after interest rates have been increased.[15]

Some further possible reservations were expressed about the implications of the institutional factors. The widespread public debt, for example, could be viewed as a stimulant to velocity-increasing shifts of idle funds into Government securities. The growing importance of financial institutions and professional portfolio managers could reduce, not increase, the "locked in" effect of capital losses: professionals, presumably less subject to irrational behavior than amateurs, might be more likely to take their losses before they grew larger. Also, it could be argued that the forward commitment process would reduce the economy's sensitivity to the *current* impact of monetary policy. Forward commitment activity might be cut back in response to credit stringency but current lending and spending would go on to fulfill commitments made in the past.

The criticisms of the Roosa doctrine made it clear that in some respects at least it was overoptimistic in its assessment of the power of a flexible monetary policy. In particular, few economists, even in 1950–1951, believed that monetary policy could effectively control the economy with interest rate changes of as little as ⅛ percent. But even after these defects were granted, it was difficult to escape the conclusion that Roosa's analysis had opened a promising path for a flexible monetary policy. Only actual application would be an adequate test of the controversial aspects. But the possibilities of success seemed real enough to warrant trying it out.

[15] Guttentag, "Credit Availability, Interest Rates, and Monetary Policy" *Southern Economic Journal,* XXVI (January, 1960), 220.

III

THE FEDERAL RESERVE BOARD'S CONCEPTION

OF MONETARY MANAGEMENT: A RETURN TO

ORTHODOXY AND TRADITION IN PRACTICE

ROOSA'S conception of how a new monetary policy could have greater influence in the changed economic and financial environment never really was tested by experience. Soon after the March, 1951, Treasury-Federal Reserve Accord had restored freedom to conduct a flexible monetary policy, it became apparent that the monetary authorities intended to use the new freedom conservatively. While much of Roosa's analysis of how monetary policy worked in the postwar environment was accepted, his proposals to employ open market operations in long-term Government securities to exert a direct effect on long-term interest rates and bond prices—and thus on the nonbank financial intermediaries which dominated the capital market—were rejected. Instead, the Federal Reserve authorities decided to restrict themselves to what they deemed the traditionally appropriate scope of monetary policy: affecting the reserve positions of commercial banks and thus the volume of money through open market operations in short-term Government securities and through extension of loans or advances to banks under the discount mechanism.

This traditional approach also excluded reliance on selective control of specific credit areas, such as Regulation W governing consumer credit and Regulation X governing real-estate mortgage credit, though both of these had been in effect under Federal Reserve administration at the time of the Accord. Moreover, it apparently meant only limited use of the authority to vary member bank reserve requirements, which had been granted by the Banking Acts of 1933 and 1935. After 1951 this authority was used only to lower reserve requirements; and statements by Federal Reserve officials made it clear that increases in reserve requirements had been ruled out as an appropriate tool of restrictive credit policy.

This narrowing of the range of weapons available to the Federal Reserve authorities had a number of grounds. It seems clear that the authorities believed that a monetary policy restricted to the control of bank reserve positions and of the money supply would be adequately effective. But this approach to monetary control also fitted in with other aims of the central bank which had little to do with the effectiveness of monetary policy. For example, it kept Federal Reserve policy actions relatively remote from the borrowers and investors they influenced, shielding the Reserve System, in some degree at least, from resentment against monetary restraint. It also left to free market forces the major role in the setting of interest rates and thus guarded the Reserve System from being criticized for interest rate movements or pressured into returning to pegging interest rates.

EMPHASIS ON BANK RESERVES AND THE MONEY SUPPLY

Federal Reserve Board spokesmen soon made it clear that in their view the only proper function of a central bank was to control the volume of bank reserve funds and the volume of money (defined as currency outside banks and demand deposits, adjusted, in the hands of the public). Although not unchallenged within the Federal Reserve System and largely rejected by academic economists, this was the view which governed Federal Reserve policy as evidenced by statements made in testimony before Congress, speeches by officials, expositions in Federal Reserve publications, and—most importantly— the use or nonuse of Federal Reserve policy instruments.

It is perhaps worthy of comment—in view of the vast changes that had taken place—that this view was practically the same as that held in 1949, when the commitment to support Treasury bond prices and yields made the power to vary interest rates unavailable. At that time Reserve Board Chairman Thomas B. McCabe told the Douglas Committee:

Federal Reserve policies influence the supply, availability, and cost of money by adding to or subtracting from the supply of funds available to banks for extending credit or for meeting currency needs without depleting their reserves below the required level.[1]

[1] U.S. Congress, Joint Committee on the Economic Report, Subcommittee on Monetary, Credit, and Fiscal Policies, *Monetary, Credit, and Fiscal Policies,*

Some broadening of this narrow view was visible to any close observer in the Board's reply to the Patman Subcommittee's investigation, prepared in 1951, when Roosa's analysis still had freshness and influence. Commenting on the scope of Federal Reserve policy, the Board included as a secondary tool "collaterally . . . influencing the supply of funds available to other lending agencies and investors:"

System operations affect the supply, availability, and cost of money primarily by making reserve funds more or less readily available to banks for extending credit or meeting credit needs and *collaterally by influencing the supply of funds available to other lending agencies or investors.*[2]

But this concession to Roosa's enlarged conception of the scope of monetary policy was only temporary. The traditional view re-emerged in the February, 1953, *Federal Reserve Bulletin,* which reprinted the System's replies to the Patman Subcommittee in a modified form. This article stated:

an essential preface to the study of credit and monetary policy is a consideration of the meaning of money and of the factors influencing the quantity of money. . . .

It is the function of reserve banking, by regulating the volume of bank reserves, to counteract the tendency for excessive swings in the volume of money.[3]

There is little evidence that criticisms of this point of view made any lasting impression on the majority of the Federal Reserve Board. So far as their policy actions went, they continued to concentrate on affecting bank reserve positions and the money supply. Reserve Board public statements continued to display what Shaw called "an immaculate, high church and 19th century view of its responsibilities." [4] There was no retreat from the view that, as one high official put it early in 1960:

Compendium, 81st Cong., 1st Sess., 1949, p. 22. Cited hereafter as Douglas Committee, *Compendium.*

[2] Patman Committee, *Compendium,* Pt. I, p. 213.

[3] "The Monetary System of the United States," *Federal Reserve Bulletin,* XXXIX (February, 1953), 98, 108 ff. To be sure, some other effects of monetary policy are conceded. For example, on p. 109, "capital values are affected by changes in conditions in the security markets which accompany changes in credit policies, and thus the liquidity of major sectors of the economy is increased or reduced. . . ." But this admits only indirect central bank influence on capital values, the procedure Roosa had criticized as "roundabout."

[4] U.S. Congress, Joint Committee on the Economic Report, Subcommittee on Economic Stabilization, *United States Monetary Policy: Recent Thinking and Experience, Hearings,* 83d Cong., 2d Sess., 1954, p. 46. Cited hereafter as Flanders Committee, *1954 Hearings.*

The appropriate scope of monetary regulation is relatively narrow compared with all the factors that can influence economic growth and stability and the structure of interest rates. That scope is to make possible the extension of credit by commercial banks in amounts sufficient to provide the cash balances that the public needs and is willing to hold.[5]

A formal statement of this position was made in 1958 to the British Radcliffe Committee, which had solicited views of foreign central banks to aid it in assessing the proper role of British monetary policy. The Federal Reserve's memorandum to the Radcliffe Committee set out a view of its proper function in terms that hardly differed from those used back in 1949 by Reserve Board Chairman McCabe:

The primary responsibility of the Federal Reserve System is to determine the volume of member bank reserves. These reserves serve directly as the base for the deposits and asset-acquiring functions of member banks and indirectly for those of non-member banks. Those commercial banks that are members of the Federal Reserve System hold about 85 percent of the deposits of all commercial banks. By regulating the volume of member bank reserves, the Federal Reserve thus exerts a dominant influence on the size of the money supply and on the flow of commercial bank loans and investments.[6]

There have been, of course, some vigorous criticisms of the idea that the Federal Reserve has done all that it should do to achieve the goals of monetary policy when it adds or subtracts reserves from the banking position. Significantly, some of the most forceful opposition came from Allan Sproul, president of the Federal Reserve Bank of New York. His views carry special weight because of his stature as a central banker and his long leadership in the fight to free the Federal Reserve of its pegging responsibility. Sproul stated in 1954:

It has been my view that a central banking system does not discharge its responsibilities and complete its functions in the best possible manner in our present day economy by directing its open market operations solely toward putting reserves into or taking reserves out of the commercial banking system. I believe that the central banking system should retain freedom of action to assist or promote, directly and under appropriate circumstances, changes in the availability and cost of funds throughout the money and capital markets.[7]

Enlarging on this theme in a 1955 speech, Sproul referred to the

[5] Thomas, "The Controversy over Interest Rates," p. 24.
[6] Great Britain, Committee on the Working of the Monetary System, *Memoranda of Evidence* (London, 1960), Vol. I, p. 299. Cited hereafter as Radcliffe Committee, *Memoranda*.
[7] Sproul, "Central Banks and Money Markets."

impact of changes in interest rates on capital values, which Roosa had argued could be so important. Mr. Sproul said:

And I had supposed that this would mean central bank action to help the market in determining the significant characteristics of the maturity structure of interest rates implied by the kind of credit policy being pursued—not to try to set decimal points on daily quotations, nor to peg a curve, but to nudge the market in the direction sought by credit policy. And finally I had supposed that the effects of increases or decreases in capital values, arising from changes in long-term rates of interest, were becoming more and more important in an economy in which public as well as private debts have become so large a part of our so-called assets, and that some direct intervention in this area might at times be appropriate.[8]

Other economists granted that interest rates were no longer the powerful regulators of economic activity that they were once thought to be, but they still regarded them as important, both as a cost for some industries and, more notably, as an influence on and measure of credit availability and liquidity.[9]

Still others would have put the main stress of central bank policy on interest rate control and very little on control of the money supply or bank reserve positions.[10] In other words, they would have taken exactly the opposite tack from the course adopted by the Federal Reserve Board and Open Market Committee. This point of view found vigorous expression in the *Report* of the British Radcliffe Committee on the Working of the Monetary System.

The authorities thus have to regard the structure of interest rates rather than the supply of money as the centre-piece of the monetary mechanism. This does not mean that the supply of money is unimportant but that its control is incidental to interest rate policy.[11]

Actually it is misleading to make a sharp demarcation between control of interest rates and control of the volume of money. The truth lies in between the extremes. The supply of money has important influence on interest rates, but the relation is not precise and it

---

[8] Sproul, "Reflections of a Central Banker."

[9] As expressed, say, by R. S. Sayers, "The Rate of Interest as a Weapon of Economic Policy," in *Oxford Studies in the Price Mechanism,* ed. by Wilson and Andrews, pp. 1–16; and Sayers, *Modern Banking,* 4th ed., pp. 185–86.

[10] See, for example, R. F. Kahn and Nicholas Kaldor, Memoranda Nos. 19 and 20, in Radcliffe Committee, *Memoranda.*

[11] Great Britain, Committee on the Working of the Monetary System, Report (London, 1959), p. 135. Cited hereafter as Radcliffe Committee, *Report.*

is most imprecise for long-term rates. Money supply and interest rates are perhaps best regarded as related but partially independent influences on the economy. Even if the money supply is controlled closely, effective monetary restraint or ease is not likely to be achieved until interest rates have changed appropriately and thus affected capital values as well as lenders' and borrowers' behavior. On the other hand, actions to raise or lower interest rates are not likely to be effective so long as the biggest single source of liquidity in the economy —the money supply—is unaffected.

But the Federal Reserve tended to ignore the possibility that the effectiveness of monetary policy would be increased if it directly influenced *both* the volume of reserves and money *and* the level and structure of interest rates.

REJECTION OF DIRECT INFLUENCE ON INTEREST RATES

While the Federal Reserve frequently stressed the importance of affecting bank reserves and the volume of money, it made no statements suggesting the desirability of affecting interest rates. On the contrary, the few explicit Federal Reserve statements on the subject specifically rejected direct influence on interest rates. This reflected a number of reasons.[12] Among the most important, however, seem to be a belief that any direct Federal Reserve influence on interest rates would be equivalent to pegging rates; and a conviction that central bank interference with the forces of the free market should be held to a minimum.

FEAR OF A RETURN TO PEGGING. Apparently the Federal Reserve's reluctance to influence interest rates directly stemmed from the fear that any such action would degenerate into rigidly fixing yields and prices on U.S. Government securities. In defending its decision to confine open market operations to "bills only" and thus to concentrate on affecting bank reserves, the Federal Reserve told the Flanders Subcommittee investigating monetary policy in 1954:

monetary actions would be much more difficult if the Federal Reserve were to make itself responsible not only for adding to and withdrawing marginal amounts of reserve funds from the money market, but also for

[12] Federal Reserve objections to dealing with interest rates directly are enumerated and discussed in much greater detail in the following chapters on the policy of confining open market operations to "bills only."

making continuous markets and establishing interest rates and prices prevailing in all sectors of the security markets.[13]

The implication of this statement is that Federal Reserve influence on interest rates in a purposeful way would mean "establishing interest rates and prices prevailing in all sectors of the security markets" or, in other words, "pegging." Although it is quite clear that influencing interest rates need not mean pegging and that this is not what Roosa had in mind when he suggested a direct influence on long-term rates of interest, Reserve Board Chairman Martin told the Flanders Subcommittee in 1954:

> Now, if we should operate directly in all maturities, we could, perhaps, be wise enough to know just what the relationship between the prices of different securities ought to be at all times. But . . . I think that is a step towards pegging.[14]

However, as Sproul said repeatedly, there is a middle ground between the extremes of rejecting any direct influence over interest rates on the one hand and the "post war approach of pegged prices and detailed control over the whole interest rate curve, on the other." [15] In a 1954 exposition of this point of view, Sproul said:

> the approach I prefer has nothing to do with price pegging, nor with trying to establish and maintain a particular pattern of interest rates, nor with other practices which during the war and earlier post war years destroyed or handicapped monetary policy. There is a natural and justified aversion to these practices, but this aversion is quite beside the point I am discussing. The issue is not whether to peg or not to peg, but whether at all times and in all circumstances (except for disorderly markets) the System should confine itself to shoving reserves in or taking them out. . . . The issue is whether there will not be times when direct operations in other areas will be appropriate and more effective. Almost everyone is agreed, I think, that our intervention in the market should not be to impose a fixed pattern of prices and yields on the market.[16]

In fact, pegging is only one, and the most extreme, kind of influence on rates that a central bank may exercise. Moreover, foreign central banks have successfully exercised direct influence on interest rates without pegging them.[17] Ironically, the Radcliffe Committee *Report* holds up the era of pegged markets in the United States as a horrible

[13] Flanders Committee, *1954 Hearings,* p. 25.
[14] *Ibid.,* p. 235.
[15] Sproul, "Central Banks and Money Markets," p. 5.
[16] *Ibid.,* p. 7.
[17] Radcliffe Committee, *Memoranda,* No. 7.

example of how interest rates should *not* be controlled,[18] at the same time that it recommends a greater degree of control over interest rates by the central bank.[19]

Nevertheless, the Federal Reserve Board apparently remained convinced that effective direct influence over interest rates would either mean, or quickly lead to, pegged interest rates. Accordingly, it did everything it could to minimize its direct influence on interest rates, including most importantly the restriction of its open market operations to dealings in very short-term securities. The detailed arguments for and against this policy, including a more thorough discussion of the pegging issue, are presented and analyzed in succeeding chapters.

FREE MARKET THEORY OF CREDIT POLICY. A key element in the Federal Reserve Board's 1953–1959 conception of the proper role of a central bank was the idea that a central bank should reduce its interference with the free forces of the private credit markets to a minimum. This conception, along with the fear of pegging, would seem to provide a large part of the explanation for the decisions to concentrate on affecting the reserve base and money supply and to leave interest rates to be determined by free market forces. Thus Reserve Board Chairman Martin told the Flanders Subcommittee in 1954:

Now that does not mean that we are not interested in interest rates or that we are not influencing interest rates. It does mean that we confine ourselves to supplying and absorbing reserves in the shortest area of the market and let the processes of the market channel those reserves throughout all the other areas and maturity sectors of the market. . . . It is my conviction that we do the most service . . . consonant with the concept of private competitive enterprise by giving the play of the market the maximum influence that it can have without disruptive effects.[20]

This attitude colored Federal Reserve policy actions in the succeeding years, and in 1959 Chairman Martin reiterated the importance of giving maximum freedom to private market forces in the following words:

No one here would deny that free markets are essential to the vital and vigorous performance of our economy. . . . few would advocate Government interference with the market process as a general principle. On the contrary, nearly everyone would agree that such developments are injurious to the best use of our resources, that they distort the equitable

[18] Radcliffe Committee, *Report,* p. 176.
[19] *Ibid.,* pp. 177–78.
[20] Flanders Committee, *1954 Hearings,* p. 229.

distribution of final product, and that they interfere with economic progress.[21]

It is indisputable, as a general statement, that free markets are important to the effective functioning of a competitive economy. But it is also true that restrictions on freedom in some areas may sometimes actually increase the over-all area of free action.[22] The real issue is whether a general bias for freedom should be interpreted to mean, as the Federal Reserve has seemed to interpret it, that the central bank should place major emphasis on making the money market as free as possible.[23] The historical experience is that unregulated free banking and money markets led to inflation and financial and industrial crises.[24] Accordingly, it was recognized generations ago by believers in free markets that maintaining freedom in the markets for materials, products, and labor might require considerable restriction of freedom in the money and credit market.[25] Indeed, Chandler has pointed out:

Central banks exist because we are not willing to allow the total supply of money and credit, and the cost of credit, to be determined by the unregulated forces of private supply and demand. The basic function of a

[21] U.S. Congress, Joint Economic Committee, *Employment, Growth, and Price Levels, Hearings*, 86th Cong., 1st Sess., 1959, Part 6A, pp. 1231–32. Cited hereafter as Joint Committee, *1959 Employment Hearings*.

[22] A classic illustration is automobile traffic controls. They restrict the freedom to drive as one pleases but they increase everyone's freedom to drive safely and effectively.

[23] The Federal Reserve Board's view that free-market forces should have a maximum role in the money market, particularly in setting interest rates, has sometimes been expressed in such sweeping terms that it has excited incredulity on the part of Congress. Thus in 1956, testifying before a Joint Economic Subcommittee, Chairman Martin replied to a plea for lower interest rates from Senator O'Mahoney as follows: "Well, again I return, Senator, to the fact that I do not think we make the interest rates. . . ." Senator O'Mahoney then asked whether it was not true that the Reserve authorities set the discount rates of the Reserve Banks and was met with the reply: "We fix it in accord with supply and demand. . . ." At this point Senator O'Mahoney said: "Why don't we close up the Federal Reserve Banks if you don't have any part in it? . . ." Mr. Martin thereupon conceded that the Federal Reserve had an influence on interest rates. See, U.S., Congress, Joint Economic Committee, Subcommittee on Economic Stabilization, *Monetary Policy: 1955–56, Hearings*, 84th Cong., 2d Sess., 1957, p. 91. Cited hereafter as Joint Committee, *1956 Monetary Policy Hearings*.

[24] See, for illustrations, Rodkey, *Legal Reserves in American Banking;* Hawtrey, *The Art of Central Banking;* and Rist, *History of Monetary and Credit Theory*, particularly pp. 390–402 and 412–13.

[25] Sproul, "Reflections of a Central Banker," p. 8; also Rist, *History*, pp. 390–402 and 412–13.

central bank is to regulate the total supply of money and credit and the terms on which they are made available.[26]

Once central banks exist, with their large powers over money and credit, is it possible to speak of a "free" money market? Can the market be free so long as there is a Federal Reserve System with a Government securities portfolio running into the tens of billions of dollars which affects money conditions continually? Moreover, even if the Federal Reserve System were to withdraw completely from the money market, could one say that free private demand and supply were ruling the market when the U.S. Treasury is by far the biggest single borrower with demands for new money and refinancing totaling more than $100 billion a year?

Sproul has concluded that "we haven't had a free market in money and credit at least since the Federal Reserve System was established." [27] Martin conceded that formation of the Federal Reserve infringed on the freedom of the private credit market but he argued, "we seek to reduce that infringement to the minimum." [28] In fact, he said, "If we make the controlling influence we are not performing our function, as I understand it." [29] This view would seem to deny the very purpose of central banking. For if the central bank is not to control the money markets in the interests of its monetary policy goals and the national welfare, what reason is there for its existence? Again, Martin seems to be confusing the desirability of freedom in general with the desirability of a money market in which the central bank has consciously relinquished the "controlling influence." Exercising a "controlling influence," one suspects, is regarded as equivalent to pegging. But this is, as we have pointed out, a mistaken view.

Moreover, the Federal Reserve sometimes seems to imply that the decisions of private market participants are per se always right, and therefore they should not be altered by the central bank.[30] One does

[26] Flanders Committee, *1954 Hearings,* p. 46.
[27] Sproul, "Central Banks and Money Markets," p. 6.
[28] Joint Committee, *1959 Employment Hearings,* Pt. 6A, p. 1280.
[29] Joint Committee, *1956 Monetary Policy Hearings,* p. 91.
[30] See for example, Flanders Committee, *1954 Hearings,* p. 25; U.S. Senate, Committee on Finance, *Investigation of the Financial Condition of the United States, Hearings,* 85th Congress, 1st Sess., 1957, Vol. 3, p. 1269 (cited hereafter as the Byrd Committee, *1957 Hearings.*); Thomas, "The Controversy Over Interest Rates," pp. 32, 34; Young and Yager, "The Economics of 'Bills Preferably'," *Quarterly Journal of Economics,* LXXIV (August, 1960), 358, 362. Occasionally, Reserve System spokesmen recognize the difficulties of this

not have to be a believer in a centrally planned economy to reject this view outright. Private decisions are often wrong, even from the viewpoint of the individuals or institutions concerned. Furthermore, since private decisions are made on the basis of the advantage or disadvantage to particular private persons or institutions, they may diverge from what is desirable from the standpoint of the national welfare even when they achieve private aims. At least since Wicksell, economic opinion has held that the market rate of interest set by private transactions can and does diverge from the natural rate which would balance savings and investment and maintain economic stability. Indeed, as noted earlier, it is the belief that private market forces are not adequate to maintain consistency between monetary conditions and stable employment, prices, and production which underlies the entire theory of countercyclical monetary policy to which the Federal Reserve itself subscribes.

It is hard to escape the conclusion that the Federal Reserve's emphasis on the virtues of maximum scope for free market forces was a mistake. The money market cannot be really free with a powerful central bank and a large public debt. Moreover, the basic reason for the existence of a central bank is to "manage" money conditions in such a way as to achieve monetary policy goals, such as, high-level economic stability and growth. The important issue is not whether actions impose some limitation on the freedom of market forces, but whether they are inconsistent or consistent with policy objectives. As Chandler urged before the 1954 Flanders Subcommittee:

The Federal Reserve's mistake during the pegging period was not that it controlled interest rates; the mistake was in stabilizing interest rates—in making stability of interest rates an overriding objective and in sacrificing all other objectives. To be successful in promoting economic stability and growth, the Federal Reserve should use its powers to control interest rates . . . to bring about, those changes in interest rates which will best promote its purposes.[31]

CONCLUSION ON FEDERAL RESERVE BOARD'S
CONCEPTION OF MONETARY MANAGEMENT

There was clearly a substantial contrast between the conceptions of monetary management held by Roosa and those which were actu-

---

view but it has been much more common both in statements and policy actions to imply that there is something sacrosanct about the free market's decisions.
[31] Flanders Committee, *1954 Hearings,* p. 46.

ally put into practice by the Federal Reserve Board and the Federal Open Market Committee. Roosa's ideas were open to criticism on a number of points, and particularly on the ground that they were overoptimistic in their assessment of the possible efficacy of monetary policy. But Roosa's ideas were also imaginative, eclectic and daring in the way they held out new possibilities for the use of the instruments of monetary policy. Emphasis was placed on extracting the maximum of effectiveness from the instruments at hand. The ambitiousness of Roosa's aims for monetary policy was matched by his willingness to make full use of all available means of making policy effective.

The Federal Reserve Board, however, while putting forth fully as ambitious a set of goals for monetary policy as had Roosa, was much less willing to make full use of the monetary policy instruments at its disposal. Thus at the same time that the Board enlarged its assignment, it voluntarily limited the means by which it could achieve the broadened program of monetary-policy goals. The Reserve Board's concept of monetary management seemed to place most emphasis on preventing central bank actions from interfering with or disrupting decisions of the private credit markets, and relatively little on using the powers of the central bank in a positive way to achieve its objectives.

It seems apparent that this approach to monetary management could have important implications for the ability of the Federal Reserve to affect the financial markets and through them the flow of economic activity. If the money managers have doubts about the legitimacy of "managing," it is hardly likely that the central banking function will be performed as well as it might otherwise be. The chapters which follow examine the use made of the various instruments of monetary policy under the Federal Reserve's general philosophy of monetary management.

Part II
THE FEDERAL RESERVE'S USE
OF MONETARY INSTRUMENTS

IV

OPEN MARKET OPERATIONS AND THE POLICY
OF DEALING IN "BILLS ONLY"

Both the Federal Reserve and its critics are agreed that open market operations in Government securities are its most flexible and powerful instrument of monetary control. Purchases and sales of Government securities affect the volume of bank reserves and money, the level and structure of interest rates, the prices of Government securities, and indirectly the capital value of all marketable debt and equity instruments; and through these avenues affect the liquidity and net worth of the economy. It is not surprising then that the major controversy concerning Federal Reserve policy has centered on the Federal Open Market Committee's decision in March, 1953, —only two years after the Accord had restored full freedom over open market operations—to give up a part of this freedom and confine open market transactions to dealings in short-term securities, preferably Treasury bills, in what has come to be called the "bills only" policy.[1]

The "bills only" policy was unveiled to the public in a speech, "The Transition to Free Markets," [2] in 1953 by Chairman Martin. The rationale behind the adoption of this policy is evident from the title. A free market in Government securities was defined in the 1953 *Annual Report* of the Board of Governors of the Federal Reserve System as:

[1] The Federal Reserve System has objected to the designation, "bills only." See, Young and Yager, "The Economics of 'Bills Preferably'," *Quarterly Journal of Economics*, LXXIV (August, 1960), 341. But in practice almost all open market transactions from late 1952 through late 1960 were in "bills only."

[2] Martin, "The Transition to Free Markets," *Federal Reserve Bulletin*, XXXIX (April, 1953), 333.

one in which the allocation of available funds among various uses is effected through competition in the market. Borrowers offer interest rates and other terms that enable them to obtain the funds they require, and lenders bid for loans and securities in accordance with their appraisals of risks, yields, and their portfolio needs, and with their estimate of current Federal Reserve actions.[3]

While such a definition need not rule out Federal Reserve open market operations to exercise direct influence on interest rates, both long- and short-term, the Board went on to say, "In such a market Federal Reserve purchases and sales would be solely for the purpose of influencing the volume of bank reserves in order to promote economic stability and growth." [4]

The 1953 *Annual Report* also revealed that the "bills only" policy had been adopted after a special study of the Government securities market by an Ad Hoc Subcommittee of the Federal Open Market Committee and that there had been a sharp divergence of opinion between the majority ·of the Open Market Committee and Mr. Sproul as to the wisdom of· accepting the Ad Hoc Subcommittee's recommendations.[5] The arguments for and against the "bills only" policy were set forth more fully in December, 1954, when the Flanders Subcommittee of the Congressional Joint Economic Committee invited both Martin and Sproul to testify, and published, as part of the record of its hearings, the papers developed and assembled by the Ad Hoc Subcommittee.[6]

The principles which governed open market operations under the "bills only" policy were three: (1) Open market operations were limited to those necessary for "providing or withdrawing reserve funds in amounts and at times appropriate to the general economic situation." [7] (In other words the Federal Reserve ordinarily would not intervene to prevent fluctuations in prices or yields of Government securities, although it specifically excepted actions needed to "correct a disorderly situation in the Government securities market." [8]) (2) Open market operations were limited to short-term securities,

---

[3] Board of Governors of the Federal Reserve System, *Annual Report,* 1953, p. 6.
    [4] *Ibid.*   [5] *Ibid.,* pp. 89, 99–100.
    [6] Flanders Committee, *1954 Hearings,* pp. 257–331.
    [7] *Ibid.,* p. 21.
    [8] Board of Governors of the Federal Reserve System, *Annual Report,* 1953, pp. 86–90.

preferably, and in practice, Treasury bills. (3) As follows from the first two principles, Treasury refundings were not supported by open market operations in "rights" (the maturing Treasury obligations), when-issued securities (the new securities offered which were traded for delivery "when-issued"), or securities comparable in term to the new issues the Treasury offered.[9]

How well the Federal Reserve succeeded in applying these principles and eliminating open market transactions in Treasury certificates, notes, and bonds is shown in Table 1. The figures for annual

TABLE 1

FEDERAL RESERVE PURCHASES (+) AND SALES (−)
OF TREASURY CERTIFICATES, NOTES, AND
BONDS, 1953–1959

($ million)

Calendar Year	Certificates	Notes	Bonds	Total
1953	− 100	− 10	− 25	− 135
1954				
1955	+ 167			+ 167
1956				
1957	− 70	− 83		− 153
1958	+ 1,090	+ 10	+ 165	+ 1,265
1959				

Blanks indicate that there were no transactions.

Source: Computed from data in Board of Governors of the Federal Reserve System, "Weekly Statements of Condition of the Federal Reserve Banks," for years 1953–1959.

transactions in these categories should be considered in the perspective of operations (excluding repurchase agreements) in Treasury bills running from $4.5 to $8 billion a year from 1957 to 1959.[10] Apart from the figures for 1957 to 1959, the Federal Reserve has not published data on its total transactions in Treasury bills; accordingly, they are excluded from the table.

The $167 million of certificates bought in 1955 reflect when-issued purchases to facilitate a large-scale Treasury refunding at a time of stringent money market conditions not foreseen when the terms of the Treasury refunding were decided upon.[11] This represents an exception to the "bills only" policy since the market was

[9] *Ibid.*

[10] Young and Yager, *Quarterly Journal of Economics*, LXXIV, 351.

[11] Board of Governors of the Federal Reserve System, *Annual Report*, 1955, pp. 8, 109–10.

not described as "disorderly." The sales of certificates and notes in
1957 were evidently made because the Federal Reserve was running
low on bills to sell. The $1,265 million of certificates, notes, and
bonds bought in 1958 represent the Federal Reserve's response to
the first disorderly market situation since the "bills only" policy was
adopted. With the exceptions of the 1955 and 1958 purchases—
both involving Treasury financing operations and both in difficult if
not disorderly market conditions—the Reserve System held its operations in certificates, notes, and bonds to perhaps 1 percent of its
total open market transactions.[12]

TECHNICAL CASE FOR "BILLS ONLY": IMPROVING
THE GOVERNMENT SECURITIES MARKET'S PERFORMANCE

It is significant that the Federal Reserve's initial justification for
the "bills only" policy was largely concerned with improving the
technical functioning of the Government bond market. To be sure,
this was desired because an effectively working bond market is necessary for the effective application of monetary policy. But the whole
force of the initial justification and defense of "bills only" was spent
on supporting what is essentially a *means* for credit policy, and the
implications of "bills only" for the effective prosecution of monetary policy itself were explored only indirectly and in response to
questions and objections. It was not until much later that Reserve
Board spokesmen defended the economics of "bills only." [13] These
will be dealt with later in Chapter V.

The tone of the Federal Reserve's initial justification of the "bills
only" policy is perhaps best given by some citations from its reply
to the Flanders Subcommittee. The Ad Hoc Subcommittee report of
the Federal Open Market Committee put even more emphasis on the
importance of encouraging development of the Government bond
market and similar technical concerns, but this was after all a technical document.

[12] Assuming that bill transactions in 1953–1956 were similar in magnitude to
those shown for 1957–1959 by Young and Yager.

[13] The System's major defenses of the economics of "bills only" did not appear until 1958 and 1960. See, W. Riefler, assistant to the chairman of the Board
of Governors of the Federal Reserve System, "Should the Federal Reserve Buy
Long-Term Securities," a paper delivered at the Money and Banking Workshop
of the Federal Reserve Bank of Minneapolis, May 3, 1958; Riefler, "Open Market Operations in Long-Term Securities," *Federal Reserve Bulletin*, XLIV
(November, 1958), 1260–74; Young and Yager, *Quarterly Journal of Economics*, LXXIV, 341–73.

Setting out the reasons for the adoption of the new principles for open market policy, the Federal Reserve said:

These three decisions did not change basic policy objectives. They were taken after intensive re-examination in 1952 of the techniques then employed in System open market operations with particular reference to the potential impact of such techniques on market behavior. Their purpose was to foster a stronger, more self-reliant market for Government securities. Improvement in this market was desired (1) in order that the Federal Reserve might better implement flexible monetary and credit policies, (2) to facilitate Treasury debt management operations, and (3) to encourage broader private investor participation in the Government securities market.

The decisions were taken to remove a disconcerting degree of uncertainty that existed at that time among market intermediaries and financial specialists. The market was uncertain, first, with respect to the limits the Federal Open Market Committee had in mind in its directive to "maintain an orderly market in Government securities." A second uncertainty pertained to the occasions when the System might decide to operate directly in the intermediate and long-term sectors of the market to further its basic monetary policy objectives, i.e., to ease intermediate and long-term interest rates in periods of economic slack or to firm these rates in periods of exuberance.

Both of these uncertainties related solely to transactions initiated by the System outside the short end of the market, transactions which had as their immediate objective results other than a desire to add to or absorb reserves from the market. The effect, however, was to limit significantly the disposition of market intermediaries and financial specialists to take positions, make continuous markets, or engage in arbitrage in issues outside the short end of the market.[14]

It was the Ad Hoc Subcommittee which condensed these and other similar criticisms of the Government securities market before adoption of the "bills only" policy into the contention that the market lacked "depth, breadth, and resiliency." [15] The Subcommittee defined these terms as follows:

In strictly market terms, the inside market, i.e., the market that is reflected on the order books of specialists and dealers possesses depth when there are orders, either actual orders or orders that can be readily uncovered, both above and below the market. The market has breadth when these orders are in volume and come from widely divergent investor groups. It is resilient when new orders pour promptly into the market to take advantage of sharp and unexpected fluctuations in prices.[16]

At the same time, the Subcommittee removed operational content from its definitions, making it impossible to measure improvement

[14] Flanders Committee, *1954 Hearings,* p. 16.
[15] *Ibid.,* p. 265.
[16] *Ibid.*

or deterioration in the market by these standards, when it qualified its statement:

The subcommittee is not referring to the degree of fluctuation that has characterized prices in the market for Government securities since the Accord. Considering the pressure on the economy and on the supply of savings, the range of price fluctuation in the market for Government securities has been moderate. The subcommittee refers rather to the psychology that still pervades the market, to the confusion among professional operators in the market with respect to the elements they should take into consideration in the evaluation of future market trends, and to their apprehension over the attitude toward prices in the market on the part of the Federal Open Market Committee and of its representatives on the trading desk. This psychology would not characterize a market that possessed real depth, breadth and resiliency.[17]

Thus, the Federal Reserve was proposing to make important changes in its credit policy powers on the basis of subjective evaluations of the state of mind of dealers and other market participants. Since "depth, breadth, and resiliency" were not so defined as to be objectively determinable, it is not surprising that there has been considerable difference of opinion as to whether "bills only" improved the situation even after years of experience.

On the one hand, Chairman Martin told the Flanders Subcommittee in December, 1954, that the "bills only" policy had improved the functioning of the market.

This is particularly true of operating experience since June 1953. Without any intervention from the Federal Open Market account, except in the short end, the market for United States Government securities has become progressively broader, stronger, and more resilient throughout all maturity ranges.[18]

On the other hand, Allan Sproul, president of the New York Reserve Bank, where the System's open market operations are conducted, told the Subcommittee:

It is my information and observation that the market for longer term securities has remained at least as "thin," under existing open market procedures [bills only], as it was before these procedures were adopted. I think it has lost depth, breadth and resiliency, whether you view it in terms of dealer willingness to take position risks, volume of trading, or erratic price movements.[19]

---

[17] *Ibid.*   [18] *Ibid.*, p. 16.

[19] *Ibid.*, p. 226. The main burden of the New York Reserve Bank's objections to the "bills only" policy, however, was that it would hamper the administration and effectiveness of monetary policy. But these economic aspects of "bills

STATISTICAL EVIDENCE. Empirical measurement of whether the "bills only" policy improved the performance of the Government bond market—its depth, breadth, and resiliency—has proved extremely difficult because of the vagueness of these terms and the lack of relevant data. Thus, information on the volume of trading in Government securities and dealer positions (both possible measurements mentioned by Sproul) has not been publicly available for a period sufficiently long to compare the experience before and after the adoption of the "bills only" policy.[20] At no time did either of the contending parties within the Federal Reserve System support its allegations about improvement or lack of improvement in the functioning of the Government bond market with statistical evidence.

There have, however, been a few attempts by economists outside the Federal Reserve System to appraise the "bills only" policy in terms of its effect on the functioning of the Government securities market in spite of the scarcity of data. A study by Edward Marcus attempted to discover whether there had been measurable influence on fluctuations in the Treasury bill rate but failed to uncover any clearly significant findings.[21]

Louise Freeman attempted another approach, a study of the fluctuations in the daily closing price of the 2½ percent Treasury bonds of December 15, 1967–1972, before and after the adoption of "bills only," to see whether extreme changes in prices were less frequent since 1953. (While the Ad Hoc Subcommittee stated that it was not concerned about price fluctuations since the Accord,[22] Chairman Martin mentioned the fact that long-term bond prices had fluctuated widely in response to small orders prior to 1953.[23]) Freeman's study, for 1951 to 1956 by calendar years, found that the

only" will be taken up in succeeding chapters. Here, in the interest of clarity of exposition, only the technical case for "bills only" is discussed.

[20] Figures on positions of Government security dealers were developed and shown for October 31, 1957, to December 31, 1958, by weeks in the joint study of the Government securities market made by the Treasury and the Federal Reserve. But, although suggestive, this does not cover a long enough period for analysis. See, U.S. Treasury Department and Board of Governors of the Federal Reserve System, *Treasury-Federal Reserve Study of the Government Securities Market*, 1959–60, II, pp. 138–139. Cited hereafter as Treasury-Federal Reserve, *Study*.

[21] Edward Marcus, "The Federal Reserve and the Treasury Bill Market," *The Commercial and Financial Chronicle*, January 20, 1955.

[22] Flanders Committee, *1954 Hearings*, p. 265.

[23] *Ibid.*, p. 21.

frequency of large price changes in periods "when credit policy is manifestly restrictive" was not reduced by the "bills only" policy but that there may have been some lessening of fluctuations in periods of less active restraint, that is, in years such as 1955.[24]

Thus Freeman's findings tended to confirm the New York Reserve Bank's view that "fear of adverse [price] trends, or uncertainty as to what the trend is likely to be, is the predominant reason for thin markets, rather than apprehensions concerning System intervention in particular sectors to limit price movements." [25] It may be noted here, too, that Chairman Martin's view that the market's depth, breadth, and resiliency had been improved was based on the experience from July, 1953, to November, 1954, generally a period of credit ease.[26]

In another study,[27] Dudley Luckett argued that in a "deep" market dealers could safely narrow the "spread" between their quoted bid and asked prices for Government securities. Luckett found that the dealers' spreads actually had widened rather than narrowed after 1953 and concluded that the market had not become deeper. This conclusion was consistent with indications that the dealers' readiness to stand behind their quotations and do business in some amount without further question has declined in recent years.[28] On the other hand, the observed widening of spreads may be related to a desire to increase earnings (for the dealers' spreads are major sources of income for these merchants in securities) rather than to fear of uncertain or adverse price trends. To whatever extent this is true, the increased spreads would not indicate a decrease in the depth of the market.[29] Finally, in general comment on the use of spreads as a

[24] Louise Freeman, "The 'Bills Only' Policy: An Aspect of the Federal Reserve's Relationship to the United States Government Securities Market," pp. 26–28. Miss Freeman pointed out that this procedure is far from ideal: it covered only one bond, it failed to measure perhaps sizable fluctuations within days, it did not examine the frequency and size of price movements lasting more than a day, and the periods studied were calendar years rather than periods of different types of credit restraint.

[25] Flanders Committee, *1954 Hearings*, p. 310.

[26] *Ibid.*, p. 16.

[27] Luckett, " 'Bills Only': A Critical Appraisal," *Review of Economics and Statistics,* XLII (August, 1960), 301–6.

[28] Treasury-Federal Reserve, *Study,* Pt. I, pp. 17–21.

[29] Dealers have complained for years about the rising cost of bank financing, which is recent years often has exceeded what they could earn on positions in Treasury bills and even longer-term securities. This has led them to seek

surrogate measure of depth, it is perhaps relevant to note that dealers' spreads were smaller during the period of pegged markets than they were before or since, but this reflected the market's belief in the Federal Reserve's ability and willingness to maintain prices rather than any real depth.

Luckett also tried to evaluate "breadth" by examining changes over time in the percentage distribution of Treasury securities due after five years among the six investor groups shown in the Treasury survey of ownership data. Excluding the Federal Reserve and commercial banks, he found evidence of declining breadth in the fact that the proportion of bonds due after five years held by life insurance companies, fire, marine and casualty insurance companies, and mutual savings banks has declined since 1953. He rejected the rise in the proportion held by the category of "all others" (including individuals, pension funds, savings and loan associations, etc.) as evidence of increased breadth because this category declined in 1953. This seems to be an inadequate evaluation. Certainly the broad public response to the high-coupon Treasury issues of 1959 (most notably to the "magic" 5 percent notes due in November, 1964) argues for greater breadth.

Luckett's conclusion on "resiliency" also seems open to question, though he admittedly did not take a firm stand because he recognized that resiliency is not an operational concept. He said only that the two near-panics in the bond market in recent years (May–June, 1953, and June–September, 1958) took place under the "bills only" policy, and left the implication that the occurrence of these crises suggests lack of resiliency. It might equally well be argued that the ability of the market to withstand these crises and to function in the face of really substantial price and yield swings in 1953–1960 implies a great deal more resiliency than even optimists would have hoped for in 1950–1951. But this is not to say that the "bills only" policy had any responsibility for this.

These attempts, however, by no means exhaust the ways in which the performance of the Government securities market might be tested.

---

cheaper financing from corporations by means of repurchase agreements and might well also have encouraged some offsetting widening in spreads. See, Aubrey G. Lanston's comments, Flanders Committee, *1954 Hearings*, p. 112; Rudolf Smutny, "Effects Upon the Bond Market of a Restrictive Credit Policy," *The Commercial and Financial Chronicle*, June 21, 1956.

For example, it can be argued that persistent wide fluctuations in Government bond prices and yields are a sign of a poorly functioning "thin" market. To be sure, occasional wide fluctuations may reflect basic economic changes to which bond yields should and do adjust. But in such cases, one would expect a large fluctuation to be followed by a return to narrow fluctuations around a new norm. On the assumption that persistent wide variations in yield, then, may be taken as indicative of a poorly functioning market, we have tested the behavior of Government bond yields from 1951 to 1959 to see whether there had been appreciably more variation after 1953 than there was before the "bills only" policy was adopted.

To avoid influences that might be peculiar to one bond issue, the test is of variations in an average of long-term yields, the Federal Reserve's average of yields on long-term Government bonds due or callable in ten years or more. To avoid erratic influences, we have averaged the weekly figures published by the Federal Reserve for each month and accordingly tested the amount of variation from one monthly average yield to the next. Table 2 presents the results of this analysis: a frequency distribution of such changes in monthly average yields by size of change for each year from 1951 to 1959.

Extreme fluctuations in long-term Government bond yields were more frequent in the years under the "bills only" policy. Before 1953 there were no fluctuations exceeding .10 percent; while in, and after, 1953 there were no less than 14 beyond this figure and some ran as much as .27 percent. Moreover, the total yield variation, that is, the sum in each year of all changes in yield from one month to the next, during 1956 to 1958 was more than double the variation for 1951 and 1952 when bond yields were free to fluctuate and the Federal Reserve had not yet adopted the "bills only" policy. Even if similar years are compared as far as economic conditions and Federal Reserve policy are concerned, the recent years under "bills only" show greater variation. Thus 1957 shows 102 basis points of variation compared with 64 for 1953; 1958 shows 102 compared with 58 for 1954.

This test, while far from conclusive, does not support the Federal Reserve's contention that the performance of the Government bond market improved during the years under "bills only" open market operations. On the contrary, if it means anything, it means that the functioning of the Government bond market deteriorated under "bills only."

To be sure, each one of these, and indeed any, statistical measures of how the "bills only" policy affected the Government bond market

TABLE 2

SIZE DISTRIBUTION OF MONTHLY CHANGES IN LONG-TERM GOVERNMENT BOND YIELDS BY CALENDAR YEAR, 1951–1959

(*yield changes in hundredths of a percentage point*)

Yield Change	NUMBER OF MONTHS								
	1951	1952	1953	1954	1955	1956	1957	1958	1959
0–2	4	3	3	4	5	1	1	4	6
3–4	1	6	2	2	3	4	3	0	0
5–6	3	1	2	2	1		3	3	
7–8	2	1	2	2	1	2	2		1
9–10	1	1	1	2	2	3		1	2
11–12							1		
13–14				1		1		1	
15–16				1				1	2
17–18						1	1	1	1
19–20									
21–22									
23–24									
25–26								1	
27–28							1		
Total yield variation [a]	48	45	64	58	56	91	102	102	81

[a] The sum in each year of all month to month yield changes, calculated from original data not shown in table.

Source: Based on data in Board of Governors of the Federal Reserve System, Table "Bond and Stock Yields," *Federal Reserve Bulletin* for the period from February, 1951, to December, 1959.

is subject to criticism on several counts. First, none of them do, or can, measure the state of mind of dealers or investors; and as noted earlier this is what the Ad Hoc Subcommittee had in mind when it talked of improving the "depth, breadth, and resiliency" of the market. Second, the results of any statistical test will inevitably reflect the influence on the bond market of factors other than the "bills only" policy. Thus changes in the liquidity of the economy, fluctuating demands for capital and credit, the effect of Federal Reserve credit policy on the supply of loanable funds—all could produce significant changes in the volume of trading, prices, yields, and dealers' spreads.

Nevertheless, it seems significant that practically all of the statistical measures examined suggest that the functioning of the Government bond market did not improve under "bills only" but rather deteriorated. If random influences are responsible for this result, they have acted in a singularly systematic way. These findings gain plausibility since they are in general supported by a study for the Congressional Joint Economic Committee which concluded

the absence of any upward trend in dealer bond positions and the decline in transactions in the over five-year maturity class seem to imply that the "bills only" policy has failed to provide the much advertised "depth, breadth, and resiliency" in the long-term market for Government securities.[30]

Moreover, the statistical results are supported by the judgment of dealers, investors, and Government bond market observers—all have expressed criticism of the performance of the Government bond market in recent years.

JUDGMENTS OF GOVERNMENT SECURITY DEALERS, INVESTORS, AND MARKET ADVISORY SERVICES. It is pertinent in an examination of the functioning of the Government bond market under "bills only" to consider the views of Government security dealers, investors, and other expert observers of the bond market. The daily transactions in which they engage or which they observe *are* the market. Indeed, when one considers the difficulties of interpreting the available statistical data, the value of direct evidence provided by the experiences and views of market participants is apparent.

Dealers, investors, and market advisory services repeatedly criticized the thinness or artificiality of the long-term Government bond market, particularly, though not exclusively, in periods of credit restraint when bond prices were falling. One widely respected bond advisory service told its clients in September, 1956:

The United States Government securities market is highly unstable, painfully thin, and dismally unreceptive of offerings. The volume of trading

[30] U.S. Congress, Joint Economic Committee, *A Study of the Dealer Market for Federal Government Securities*, 86th Cong., 2d Sess., 1960, p. 36. Cited hereafter as Joint Committee, *A Study of the Dealer Market.*

is a mockery of the Federal Reserve's and Treasury's hopes for re-estab-
lishment of a broad, receptive market.[31]

By November, 1956, the same service found it necessary to reassure clients by denying the imminence of panic conditions in the
bond market.[32] In December, with conditions little better, much the
same comment as had been made in September was deemed appropriate again:

The size of this market mocks those who had hopes for the development of a broad, receptive long-term Government market. Instead, it has
become narrow, thin, erratic.[33]

In April, 1957, the bond market was still in poor condition as the
Treasury approached a refinancing. The weekly comment this time
was:

Debt management in this era is no simple task. The market to which the
Treasury must appeal is sloppy, painfully thin. Its "base" is so uncertain
that it fades away under even slight pressure. The action of all top-grade
markets in the past few weeks—corporates, municipals and Governments
—has given confidence another rude shaking.[34]

These views were broadly confirmed by the *Treasury-Federal Reserve Study of the Government Securities Market* which, though focused on the bond market crisis of June–September, 1958, provided
a great deal of information on investors' and dealers' opinions and
transactions generally. Thus while the *Study* reported "general satisfaction" on the part of investors doing business with government
security dealers, it also conceded that it took "a little patience" to
"complete orders of reasonable size at reasonable prices." [35] The
Study also reported a feeling on the part of some investors that
"dealers have become less willing to make markets in certain maturity areas" and noted "at least a tacit recognition that the ability
of the customer to trade has declined relative to most previous years
because of the special pressures under which the market has been
operating since last June." [36]

Particularly interesting in the *Study* were the indications that in

[31] Porter, *Reporting on Governments,* September 28, 1956.
[32] *Ibid.,* November 23, 1956.   [33] *Ibid.,* December 21, 1956.
[34] *Ibid.,* April 19, 1957.
[35] Treasury-Federal Reserve, *Study,* Pt. I, p. 17.
[36] *Ibid.,* p. 18.

the long-term area, dealers were becoming brokers—the fate from which the "bills only" policy had been intended to save them. The *Study* gave both investors' and dealers' views on the allegations of market thinness and broker rather than dealer behavior. Both sides suggested that the broker approach was spreading, as the following citation indicates:

a consultant who deals mostly in long term bonds reported that in this sector dealers have become little more than brokers, seldom being willing in practice to undertake substantial transactions at quoted prices.

In dealer comments on the allegation of market thinness, a distinction was made between different types of customers. On the one hand, it was stated, there are customers who work closely with a dealer, placing their problems in his hands and giving him time to work out trades at agreed prices or spreads [and permitting him to function essentially as a broker]. On the other hand, there are customers who are sharp traders and seek to accomplish their ends by hitting bids of various dealers without giving thought to resulting price consequences. In periods of rapid price change, dealers are wary in quoting firm prices to the latter type of customer, who therefore is likely to complain of inadequate [dealer] service, while customers of the first type may still be accommodated [by broker-type service] to their satisfaction.[37]

Another study, *Employment, Growth, and Price Levels,* the Congressional Joint Economic Committee's 1959 investigation, included some specific questions to Government security dealers about the value of "bills only." All the dealers who commented were in favor of "bills only" but their testimony was far from clear as to whether it had brought more "depth, breadth, and resiliency" to the bond market. Moreover, some who thought it had increased these attributes of the market clouded the usefulness of this judgment by indicating that drastic and rapid bond price declines from 100 down to as low as 20 would be consistent with their conception of a deep, broad, and resilient Government bond market.[38]

Perhaps the typical view of dealers and investors with respect to "bills only" was given by Girard Spencer, partner of Salomon Brothers and Hutzler. Spencer stated "the market benefits from a 'bills only' policy," but when asked if he believed that the "bills only" policy had resulted in an increase in the "depth, breadth, and resiliency" of the long-term market, he replied, "No, sir; I do not." [39]

[37] *Ibid.*
[38] Joint Committee, *1959 Employment Hearings,* Pt. 6B, pp. 1594, 1604.
[39] *Ibid.,* pp. 1570, 1575.

He went on to explain the apparent inconsistency by saying, "I do think any other policy might have even decreased the breadth and resiliency of the market." [40]

Another way of explaining dealers' support for "bills only" at the same time that they are critical of the performance of the market is simply that like participants in any market they are reluctant to subject themselves to outside interference which Federal Reserve operations in long-term securities would represent. But, in any case, the Government security dealers' general bias for the "bills only" policy gives their adverse opinions about the performance of the Government bond market particular weight; just as the testimony of a witness who testifies against his own interest is given particular credence in a court of law. Accordingly, special interest attaches to the following indictment of the thinness and artificiality of the Government bond market which was expressed in early 1960 in the weekly market letter of Aubrey G. Lanston & Co., a Government securities dealer whose principals had been and remain outspoken advocates of the "bills only" policy.[41] The Lanston market letter commented as follows:

How do you measure "going market rates" at the present time? For example, as of closing prices last Thursday, issues outstanding with a 1969 maturity showed yields as follows: The 2½s of June 1969/64 were offered . . . to yield 4.65 per cent (to maturity) and the 2½s of December 1969/64 were offered . . . to yield 4.61 per cent (to maturity) while the 4s of October 1969 were offered . . . to yield 4.28 percent. We, therefore, have a situation where two issues yield an average of .35 percent more than the third one. How does this happen?

The answer is inactivity. In the first place, there are few buyers for such securities. The "captive" funds (those who are required to invest solely in Treasury securities) have become fewer and fewer in number. . . .

While no one wants to buy the 4s of 1969, sellers are infrequent too. The issue is small. . . . It isn't even worthwhile for dealers to try and arbitrage the securities (by selling the 4s "short" and going "long" the 2½s). . . . In existing market inactivity such arbitrage is a tough way to make money.

Not many people realize that dealers can go day after day without being asked either to bid or offer reasonable amounts of issues of this kind and frequently they find themselves at a loss as to how to respond when such requests are made. Take the case of the State of Michigan

---

[40] *Ibid.*, p. 1575.

[41] Flanders Committee, *1954 Hearings*, pp. 102–28; Lanston, "Address Delivered by Aubrey G. Lanston before the Investment Group of Hartford."

last December: When it became known that legislation was being sought to approve the sale of $37 million of securities such as the 2½s of June and December 1972/67, the market price of these issues dropped 3 points or thereabouts without developing any real buying interest. The story is that the bonds were taken off the market by the Treasury for its accounts. As far as we know, no other buyers existed.

The same kind of situation exists in the so-called long-term bonds— the 3¼s of 1983/78, the 3¼s of 1985, the 3½s of 1990, and the 3s of 1995. Last Thursday the first three mentioned issues sold to yield 4.25 percent or thereabouts; the 3s of 1995 offered a yield of only 3.92 percent. But there are practically no buyers! . . . If . . . anyone wished to sell any large amounts then, as in the case of the State of Michigan, a downward price adjustment of several points probably would occur— without assurance that adequate buying power would develop.[42]

It seems clear that these market participants did not believe that they had been dealing in a market which was functioning adequately, much less one which could be described as deep, broad, and resilient.

CONCLUSION ON TECHNICAL CASE FOR "BILLS ONLY"

The available statistical evidence and the view of market participants suggest that, despite the "bills only" policy and contrary to Chairman Martin's assertions, the Government bond market in recent years has been thin and artificial. Thus the "bills only" policy would seem to have failed in one of its main purposes.[43]

Moreover, it can be argued that the technical argument for "bills only"—the assertion that it was needed to strengthen dealer and investor confidence and improve the functioning of the Government bond market—was misguided in the first place. As the Federal Reserve Bank of New York has pointed out, and as will be discussed at greater length in the next chapter, there have been, and will be, occasions when the functioning of the Government securities market *should be impaired* by monetary policy in order to check the conversion of debt instruments into cash for spending.[44] Thus the failure of "bills only" to achieve its technical objective may have been a setback for the Federal Reserve Board and the majority faction in the

[42] Aubrey G. Lanston & Co., "Weekly Market Letter," February 29, 1960.

[43] It may be, of course, that the Government bond market has performed better under "bills only" than it would have if the Federal Reserve had conducted open market operations in all maturities. But this is "what might have been reasoning" and not susceptible of proof.

[44] Flanders Committee, *1954 Hearings,* p. 309.

Open Market Committee but not necessarily for monetary policy. The real questions to be answered about the "bills only" policy concern not whether it helped the Government securities market but whether it facilitated or hindered the Federal Reserve's application of appropriate monetary policies and achievement of its objectives; in other words they concern the economics of "bills only."

V

THE CONTROVERSY ABOUT "BILLS ONLY" AND

THE EFFICACY OF MONETARY POLICY

THE CONTROVERSY over the implications of "bills only" for the effective conduct of monetary policy has been essentially a dispute between those who believe that the central bank must take a broad view of its responsibilities and functions if it is to be effective, and those who, like the Federal Reserve Board and Open Market Committee, believe that a central bank policy of minimum intervention is not only most consistent with free markets but is also most effective. By far the vast majority of economists rejected "bills only" as an unwarranted restriction on the powers of the central bank.[1] If the central bank is to achieve its goals of promoting economic stability and noninflationary growth, economists have argued, it must be free to affect not only bank reserve positions, the money supply, and short-term interest rates but also long-term interest rates, bond

[1] See, for example, Hansen, "Monetary Policy," *Review of Economics and Statistics,* XXXVII (May, 1955), 110–19; Sidney Weintraub, "Monetary Policy," *Review of Economics and Statistics,* XXXVII (August, 1955), 292–96; Carson, "Recent Open Market Committee Policy and Techniques," *Quarterly Journal of Economics,* LXIX (August, 1955), 321–42; Elmer Wood, "Recent Monetary Policies," *Journal of Finance,* X (September, 1955), 314–25; Sayers, *Central Banking After Bagehot,* pp. 144–45; Angell, "The Monetary Standard: Objectives and Limitations," *American Economic Review,* XLVIII (May, 1958), 76–87; Albert G. Hart, "Making Monetary Policy More Effective," in *United States Monetary Policy,* pp. 171–95; Henry C. Wallich, "Postwar United States Monetary Policy Appraised," *United States Monetary Policy,* pp. 91–117; Luckett, " 'Bills Only': a Critical Appraisal," *Review of Economics and Statistics,* XLII (August, 1960), 301–6; "Controversial Issues in Recent Monetary Policy: A Symposium," *Review of Economics and Statistics,* XLII (August, 1960), 245–82; Whittlesey, "Monetary Policy and Economic Change," *Review of Economics and Statistics,* XXXIX (February, 1957), 31–39; Miller, "Monetary Policy in a Changing World," *Quarterly Journal of Economics,* LXX (February, 1956), 23–43.

prices, and capital values generally; and through these, the liquidity and net worth of the entire economy.

Both the critics and the Federal Reserve presented a wide variety of arguments to support their positions. However, despite their diversity, the arguments for and against the "bills only" policy can be classified into two main categories: (1) Those which consider the implications of "bills only" or open market operations in all maturities for the Government securities market; and (2) Those which focus on the implications of "bills only" or its alternative for effective central bank influence over interest rates.

"BILLS ONLY" AND THE GOVERNMENT SECURITIES MARKET

The preceding chapter concluded that "bills only" open-market operations did not improve the functioning of the Government securities market. The first part of this section focuses on the question whether the objective of improving the performance of the Government securities market was consistent with the Federal Reserve's economic stabilization responsibilities. Thereafter the discussion focuses on the Federal Reserve's assertions that: (1) Open-market operations in all maturities would destroy the private market in Government securities and leave a market in which the Federal Reserve alone sets prices and yields; (2) Difficult market conditions would make it unlikely that the Federal Reserve would be able to sell long-term Government bonds in periods of credit restraint; (3) The Federal Reserve should not sell long-term Governments to enforce credit restraint because it would suffer losses on such sales and thus reduce its income; and (4) Federal Reserve sales of long-term Governments at a time when the Treasury was not selling long-term bonds would be undesirable because the market might think there was a dispute between the two agencies.

DOES IMPROVING THE MARKET CONFLICT WITH MONETARY POLICY OBJECTIVES? The first issue concerning "bills only" is whether the goal it sought to achieve—a Government securities market that is deep, broad, and resilient at all times and thus able to take Federal Reserve credit policy actions in its stride with only minor price reactions—is compatible with monetary policy's objective of achieving effective credit restraint or ease. Sizable price changes and difficulty in selling securities—both conditions which would not exist in a market with depth, breadth and resiliency—may at times be of great help in achieving credit policy objectives.[2]

It will be recalled that Roosa's analysis of how monetary policy could be most effective had leaned heavily on prospective capital losses on securities and difficulties of selling in thin markets as essential parts of the mechanism which reduces the willingness of financial institutions to sell from their Government portfolios in order to raise funds for loans to private borrowers. As has been noted, Roosa was wrong in thinking that such capital losses could be very small and still be effective in curbing selling by financial institutions. But this does not mean that larger changes in bond prices and long-term yields could not be effective. The one certainty is that if the Government securities market can always absorb large volumes of sales with only minor price changes, this weapon of credit control has been lost.

In this connection it seems worth noting that two major criticisms of monetary policy in recent years (to be dealt with in Chapters X and XI) have been (1) that nonbank financial institutions have been largely free of effective control by the Federal Reserve and (2) that the ability of the Government securities market to turn securities into cash without appreciable price declines has made it possible for the economy to escape Federal Reserve restraint on the money supply by drawing existing idle balances into use and thus increasing the velocity of the existing money supply. A Government securities market that was more, not less, responsive to Federal Reserve policy actions—that is, a market in which depth, breadth, and resiliency would vary depending on credit policy—would enable the authorities better to control the sales of Governments by both nonbank financial intermediaries and by anyone else seeking to draw idle balances into use for active spending or lending.

These objections seem well taken. However, the Federal Reserve's spokesmen have not explicitly recognized any inconsistency between the stated goal of improving the Government securities market's depth, breadth, and resiliency under all circumstances and general credit policy objectives. The explanation would seem to be that the Federal Reserve authorities felt that curbing institutional selling of

[2] Flanders Committee, *1954 Hearings,* pp. 309–10.

securities and controlling the rise in the income velocity of money are only peripheral objectives, and that so long as they have control of bank reserve positions and the money supply, they have control of the important monetary magnitudes. As the balance of this study indicates, this is an overly complacent view.

Excessive concern by the central bank for the welfare of the Government securities market can, moreover, be inconsistent with an effective monetary policy in still other ways. Thus dealers have requested still further special consideration, above and beyond the restriction of open market operations to "bills only," from the central bank in order to help the bond market work well. They would like preferential financing through access to Federal Reserve repurchase agreements at low interest rates whenever they desire in order to help them carry their security positions in periods of restrictive credit policy and high interest rates.[3] More important, despite the "bills only" policy, dealers' continued concern about the size of the Federal Reserve's portfolio and possible open market operations (concern which the Ad Hoc Subcommittee thought would be greatly reduced if not eliminated by "bills only") led at least one dealer to suggest that effective functioning of the Government securities market might require that the Federal Reserve disclose to dealers confidential credit policy decisions and objectives. As Rudolf Smutny, then partner of Salomon Brothers & Hutzler, said

we dealers are continuously over a barrel, due to the discrepancy in interest income between what we are long and the rate of interest we have to pay to carry our position. And, of course, our position can be made untenable without warning by an Open Market Committee operation. Today we are painfully aware of the heavy overhead cost of conducting increasingly profitless business in short-term securities, and of needless inventory losses occasioned by the Open Market Committee's indifference to dealer problems.

We're all playing on the same money market team—the banks, the Treasury, and ourselves, with the Fed's Open Market Committee at quarterback. If we dealers are to continue to function in the future on the same basis as we have in the past, we're going to have to ask for a little more teamwork from the other members of the money market team than we are now getting. We're going to have to get bank loaning rates suitable for the carrying of short-term inventory, and our quarterback will have to give up whispering his signals.[4]

[3] Treasury-Federal Reserve, *Study*, Pt. I, pp. 35–36.
[4] Rudolf Smutny, "Effects Upon the Bond Market of a Restrictive Credit Policy," *The Commercial and Financial Chronicle*, June 21, 1956, p. 32. Allan

It seems clear that the welfare of the Government securities market cannot be made an important objective of Federal Reserve policy without conflicting with and frustrating the aims of general credit policy. As Louise Freeman observed:

If this objective is pursued apart from credit policy objectives, it could lead to the adoption of policies on the revealing of information to dealers and on the financing of dealers which were clearly incompatible with credit policy.[5]

And this was no mere theoretical possibility. The Federal Reserve had already actually gone through something very like it. Back in the 1920s the Federal Reserve was perhaps even more solicitous about developing a healthy, self-reliant acceptance market than it has been recently about developing "depth, breadth, and resiliency" in the Government securities market. And the abuses and interference with the objectives of general credit policy which accompanied this attempt to nurture the acceptance market became notorious.[6] One observer pointed out how the Reserve System's "paternalistic support accorded the bankers' acceptance market by low buying rates" [7] resulted in Federal Reserve credit being channeled into the stock market, at a time when one of the objectives of general credit policy was to curb stock market credit.[8] Seymour Harris' study of Federal Reserve policy in the 1920s led him to the judgment that "credit policy has sometimes been jeopardized by the assumed need of protecting the acceptance market," [9] and he cited "numerous failures to

---

Sproul must have smiled when he read Smutny's comment about the indifference of the Open Market Committee to dealer problems. He had pointed out that "bills only" would hamper the effective administration of credit policy without satisfying the dealers. Indeed, the New York Reserve Bank had predicted, in a sense, Mr. Smutny's speech in its critical comments on the Ad Hoc Subcommittee report: "Dealers, of course, would very much like the Federal Reserve System to telegraph its intended actions in advance so that they could conduct their affairs in such a manner as to maximize their profits and minimize their losses. They would like to be in the position of 'shooting fish in a bucket'." Flanders Committee, *1954 Hearings*, p. 313.

[5] Freeman, "Bills-Only," p. 25.

[6] A striking description of some of the abuses of the Federal Reserve's indulgence of the acceptance market is afforded in Beckhart, *Discount Policy of the Federal Reserve System*, pp. 441–51. See also Hardy, *Credit Policies of the Federal Reserve System*, Ch. XII.

[7] Lawrence Clark, *Central Banking Under the Federal Reserve System* (New York, The Macmillian Co., 1935), p. 378.

[8] *Ibid.*, p. 384.

[9] Harris, *Twenty Years of Federal Reserve Policy*, I, 428.

carry through an acceptance policy consistent with other . . . policies of reserve banks," [10] including most particularly the release of a substantial amount of funds to acceptance dealers in late 1928.

It is hard to escape the conclusion that the goal of building a Government bond market which would be deep, broad, and resilient at all times is inconsistent with the objectives of general credit policy. Difficulties in completing security transactions and in financing dealer positions—in a word, impairment of the bond market's ability to function, temporarily at least—are an essential part of a restrictive credit policy. Thus the "bills only" policy was not only poorly designed to achieve its purpose; its very purpose was wrong.

POSSIBLE ADVERSE MARKET REACTIONS TO FEDERAL RESERVE OPERATIONS IN LONG-TERM SECURITIES. The Federal Reserve argued on a number of occasions that the private segment of the securities market would be so sensitive to intervention by the Federal Reserve in the long-term sector of the market that almost as soon as this intervention took place all private participants—dealers, traders, portfolio managers—would "either withdraw from active trading or endeavor to operate on the same side of the market as they believed, rightly or wrongly, that the System was operating.[11] Chairman Martin stated this position in 1959 before the Congressional Joint Economic Committee. Martin went on to add:

If the professionals in the market did the former, the Federal Reserve would become in fact the price and yield administrator of the long-term Government securities market. If they did the latter, the total effect might be to encourage artificially bullish or bearish expectations as to prices and yields on long-term securities. This could lead to unsustainable price and yield levels which would not reflect basic supply and demand forces. The dangerous potentialities of such a development are illustrated by the speculative building and liquidation of mid-1958, described in detail in the Treasury-Federal Reserve study.[12]

Riefler called these possibilities a "major reason for the System's policy of non-intervention in the intermediate and long-term sectors of the market." [13] And, it will be recalled, this was also a favorite theme of the Ad Hoc Subcommittee and the Goverment security

[10] *Ibid.,* p. 326.
[11] Joint Committee, *1959 Employment Hearings,* p. 1234.
[12] *Ibid.,* p. 1235.
[13] Riefler, "Open Market Operations in Long-Term Securities," *Federal Reserve Bulletin,* XLIV (November, 1958), 1264.

dealers in making a case for "bills only." As one dealer put it to the 1954 Flanders Subcommittee: "When the Reserve moves in to intervene in the market for Treasury securities, the public market has no option but to begin to move out." [14] No one could categorically deny that these undesirable results *could* follow Federal Reserve intervention in the long-term markets. As has already been noted, the dealers have tended to move out of difficult markets even at times when the Federal Reserve resolutely held to its promise not to intervene. But there were reasons, even before the abandonment of "bills only" in 1960 and 1961, for believing that Federal Reserve intervention in long-term markets would not bring about the disappearance or collapse of the private market in Government securities any more than the withdrawal of Federal Reserve support for Government bond prices in 1951 did, although similar evil consequences were feared then.

Consider, first, the possible immediate effects of Federal Reserve intervention. This could either moderate price swings in the long-term markets, as Hansen [15] and Whittlesey [16] believe and prefer, or it could bring somewhat greater, if less erratic, price fluctuations in the course of making monetary policy effective, as Hart has suggested.[17] If price swings were moderated (but basic forces of supply and demand were still permitted to express themselves), then Government securities presumably would become more attractive to those investors, institutional and otherwise, who have become less interested in Treasury bonds because of their instability in price. Dealers, too, would have less reason to fear erratic swings that might imperil their capital. Thus, if some members of the private market "moved out," the presumption is that at least part of the slack would be taken up by others "moving in."

If on the other hand bond price fluctuations proved to be greater, risks would rise but profit opportunities would also increase for those able to outwit the market. The chances of success in this endeavor presumably would be greatest for those most expert in the market's

[14] Flanders Committee, *1954 Hearings,* p. 113.

[15] Hansen, *Review of Economics and Statistics,* XXXVII, 113.

[16] U.S. Congress, Senate, Committee on Finance, *Investigation of the Financial Condition of the United States, Compendium,* 85th Cong., 2d Sess., 1958, p. 730. Cited hereafter as Byrd Committee, *1958 Compendium.*

[17] Albert G. Hart, "Some Inconsistencies in Debt Management," *Review of Economics and Statistics,* XLII (August, 1960), 257–58.

behavior, that is, for the Government securities dealers. To be sure, the risk of loss and capital impairment would be a considerable deterrent to dealers and might well result in their reducing their positions in long-term Governments even further. But dealers' holdings of long-term bonds are already rather small so even their complete elimination would not unduly harm the market's performance.[18]

It is much more unlikely that the major investing institutions and the general public, which held $21 billion of the 24.6 billion Government bonds due in ten years or more on December 31, 1959,[19] would move out of the Government securities market if price fluctuations increased. Portfolio managers of the great financial institutions might not like a market of large price fluctuations but, it may be asked, with billions of dollars of intermediate and long-term Treasuries in their portfolios, just *how* are they going to move out of the Government bond market? Moreover, if prices swung unusually low (and yields high), it might be expected that both portfolio managers and the general public would be attracted back into the Government bond market.

As a matter of fact, there was dramatic evidence of the power of high yields on Government securities to attract buyers in the latter half of 1959 when the Treasury offered coupons of 4¾, 4⅞, and 5 percent on note issues. These rates were the highest offered since 1929 and, particularly in the case of the 5 percent rate, made front-page news, stimulated a number of magazine articles, and were mentioned on national radio broadcasts.[20] The result was an unprecedented public interest in Government securities. The $2 billion offering of 5 percent notes, the so-called "magic fives," attracted 108,000 separate subscriptions for $25,000 or less for a total of $941 million,[21] and

---

[18] Dealer positions in Treasury bonds due after five years have run well under $100 million since 1955, at least for the dates on which data are available, and this is to be compared with a total volume of such securities outstanding of some $48 to $64 billion during this period. See Treasury-Federal Reserve, *Study*, Pt. II, pp. 138–39; Joint Committee, *A Study of the Dealer Market*, p. 37; *Federal Reserve Bulletin*, XLVI (April, 1960), 405 and XLII (February, 1956), 153. Data on dealer positions in bonds over ten years are not available over most of this period.

[19] *Federal Reserve Bulletin*, XLVI (April, 1960), 405.

[20] See, for example, *The New York Times*, October 2, 1959, p. 1 and October 3, 1959, p. 1; *Wall Street Journal*, October 2, 1959, p. 2 and October 10, 1959, p. 1; *U.S. News and World Report*, October 19, 1959, pp. 113–15.

[21] *Treasury Bulletin*, October 1959, p. A-1.

the Treasury indicated that some $805 million was taken by individuals and others than commercial banks and savings institutions.[22] This was a massive demonstration of the power of attractive yields to increase public interest in Government securities. Thus it is not at all clear that wider swings in Government securities' prices and yields would narrow the market.

To be sure, it is sometimes argued that private investors and dealers might view Federal Reserve operations in long-term Gorevnment bonds as "capricious." But, as noted earlier, if such long-term dealings were directed at achievement of the same goals as short-term dealings—economic stability, growth, and stable price levels—as they presumably would be, dealers and investors generally could make reasonable estimates of the probability of their occurrence by appraisal of the state of the economy in general and of the capital investment sector in particular. Just as the Federal Reserve does not ease or tighten the short-term markets arbitrarily but rather with reference to the state of business, prices, employment, etc., so it presumably would not intervene arbitrarily in the long-term markets. And as Whittlesey noted: "The entire history of the Federal Reserve indicates that it can be counted on to act carefully, with circumspection, and on the basis of full analysis of factual information." [23]

It is perhaps also worth noting, although circumstances naturally differ from country to country, that a number of foreign central banks have operated directly in the long-term sectors of their bond markets without driving the private sector of the market out of existence. This is true of Canada, for example, as Sproul indicated when he quoted the Governor of the Bank of Canada in a 1954 speech:

As part of our programme to improve and broaden the money market for the benefit of lenders and borrowers and of our financial structure as a whole, the Bank of Canada has been a constant trader in Government of Canada securities since we opened our doors in 1935. While the total amount of our holdings of Government securities is necessarily determined by considerations of monetary policy, we have endeavored to help make a market for all Government issues and have been very substantial buyers and sellers.[24]

The Bank of England has also been a steady participant in the United Kingdom's long-term Government securities market in its

[22] *The New York Times,* October 11, 1959, sec. 3, p. 1.
[23] Whittlesey, *Review of Economics and Statistics,* XXXIX, 32–33.
[24] Sproul, "Central Banks and Money Markets," p. 5.

role as agent for the British Treasury. The Radcliffe Committee described the procedure in its *Report*.

These operations in the gilt-edged market are conducted through a firm of stockbrokers, whose representative is "the Government broker," to whom instructions to buy or sell are given by the Bank of England. Again, the Bank does not itself enter the Stock Exchange, but its operations are generally identifiable by their immediate origin and other circumstances.[25]

The Reserve Bank of South Africa also has operated in all maturity sectors of the South African money and bond market, in part for the same reasons as the Bank of Canada: to nurture and develop a private market. The South African Reserve Bank has in general permitted the forces of market supply and demand to express themselves in the prices and yields at which it trades Government securities but on occasion the Bank has actively brought about large changes in yields when it felt these were necessary to accomplish its purposes.[26] Nevertheless, this has not frightened the private trader or investor out of the market. This point was discussed before the Radcliffe Committee in the following exchange between Lord Radcliffe and Governor M. H. De Kock of the South African Reserve Bank:

Lord Radcliffe: Your bank can set the pattern of interest rates and can at any time take a decision to shift the yield; and any investor in the market would find the capital value of his investment at any one time was affected by your decision. It could be said that that would scare him away. Have you any comment on that?

Governor De Kock: I do not think it would scare him any more than if it was market forces that did it. Market forces would probably do it more violently with greater fluctuations. The market always overdoes any movement. If it goes upwards it goes too far for a time, and then there is some slide backward before it goes up again. I have reason to believe that in South Africa there is greater confidence in the gilt-edged market because of the Reserve Bank's operations. In the first place, there are far fewer fluctuations than there would otherwise be in the market; secondly, they consider the Bank must have a pretty good reason for doing what it does; and thirdly, it does not change too frequently. It does keep the position for at least some time; and many institutions must invest. . . . Even if they think that in six months' time there is going to be another change, it pays them to make the investment now. So I would say, I

[25] Radcliffe Committee, *Report,* p. 341.
[26] Great Britain, Committee on the Working of the Monetary System, *Minutes of Evidence* (London, 1960), Question 9325 and Reply. Cited hereafter as Radcliffe Committee, *Minutes of Evidence.*

hope correctly, that we are a stabilizing force, not only in the market but in the minds of investors.[27]

Foreign experience also does not support the Federal Reserve's contention that market participants would stampede to either buy or sell bonds in company with the central bank and thus cause a market crisis. But all of these foreign markets are considerably smaller, more tightly organized, and thus, perhaps, more subject to suasion by the central bank. Therefore, it is time to analyze briefly the Federal Reserve's contention on its own terms.

Chairman Martin and Messrs. Riefler, Young, and Yager cite the 1958 speculative rise and collapse in the bond market as an illustration of what could occur as a result of the market's reaction to Federal Reserve purchases of long-term bonds. Perhaps the first point that needs to be made is that the 1958 speculation had nothing to do with Federal Reserve operations in the bond market for the simple reason that there were none at that time. If anything, the 1958 speculation points up the fact that so long as there is a central bank with power to affect money conditions—no matter how indirectly exercised—it will be watched closely by market participants seeking to make profits or avoid losses by anticipating its actions. Thus, whether it deals in "bills only" or in all maturities, a central bank and its policies are crucial parts of the calculations of any market participant.

If, however, the central bank detects overreaction on the part of market participants to its own actions—say, to purchases of bonds— the remedy would seem simple enough; it need merely backtrack a little and sell some bonds. Indeed, in the relatively narrow long-term market, a small volume of sales presumably would suffice to chill speculative enthusiasm without tightening reserve positions more than negligibly. And if larger bond sales were required, they could be accompanied by purchases of Treasury bills to keep bank reserve positions and the money supply unchanged at the substantial levels appropriate to recession conditions. Such flexibility is available only if open market operations are conducted in all maturities, of course. In the actual conditions of 1958, the authorities were operating under "bills only" and, even if they had wanted to backtrack, they could not have done so without tightening bank reserve positions and re-

[27] *Ibid.*, Question 9338 and Reply.

ducing the money supply; both actions were inconsistent with the policy of credit ease which had been adopted to combat the recession.

It seems fair to conclude, on the basis of this discussion, that the possibility of the private Government securities market disappearing or collapsing in crisis as a result of Federal Reserve open market operations in long-term Government securities has been overdramatized. No discussion could rule out the possibility. But the likeliest eventuality even before the Federal Reserve authorities began to deal in long-term securities in 1961, was that the Government securities market could learn to live with a central bank which operated in all maturities. This, rather than a market collapse, is in fact what has happened since the abandonment of "bills only."

WOULD THE FEDERAL RESERVE BE ABLE TO SELL LONG-TERM GOVERNMENT BONDS? However, still another line of argument as to why Federal Reserve operations in long-term securities would not be feasible has been expressed by Young and Yager. They contend that the inability of the Treasury to sell long-term bonds during periods of prosperity in recent years, an explicitly expressed debt-management goal, has made it "self evident or almost so" [28] that efforts of the Federal Reserve to sell bonds as a part of its monetary policy would be similarly unsuccessful.[29] Young and Yager argue:

As pointed out above, the Treasury in its financing decisions each year deals with many tens of billions of maturing issues. In terms of dollar amounts alone, the Federal Reserve in any conceivable program of transactions in outstanding securities could not expect to reverse, or alter much, the impact on the debt structure of these large Treasury financing operations. . . . Thus, if the Treasury should find it disruptive to the Government securities market to issue several billions of new long-term bonds, it is also likely that the Federal Reserve, faced with the same market conditions, would find it unfeasible to offer a comparable amount of bonds from its portfolio, assuming that it had them. Also, it would seem questionable for the Federal Reserve, as a public body, all of whose net income now flows into the Treasury, to sell bonds at declining prices and

[28] Young and Yager, "The Economics of 'Bills Preferably'," *Quarterly Journal of Economics*, LXXIV (August, 1960), 371.

[29] It is worth pointing out in passing the fact that the Treasury *did not* sell long-term bonds in periods of prosperity does not prove or mean that it was *unable* to do so. A willingness to offer more attractive yields (most of the time the legal 4¼ percent bond rate limit was well above what might have had to be paid) *might* have attracted appreciable demand, though at the cost of diverting funds away from private borrowers.

severe losses at times when the Treasury finds that long-term interest rates are high enough to preclude a Treasury bond offering.[30]

These arguments do not seem convincing. For one thing, the case for having the Federal Reserve rather than the Treasury influence the long-term market is precisely that it *can operate more delicately,* sell smaller amounts of bonds, and time its operations more precisely in relation to credit policy needs, since it, unlike the Treasury, is constantly in the market.[31] No one except perhaps Riefler, Young, and Yager has suggested that the Federal Reserve would offer several billions of bonds from its portfolio as a regular part of open market operations in all maturities.

It is beside the point to argue that Federal Reserve dealings in long-terms would be useless because they could not "reverse, or alter much" the impact on the debt structure of Treasury debt management decisions. This may be granted, and it is unfortunate if the impact of debt management should be counter to the aims of monetary policy. But should the central bank not do what it can in the interests of a sound monetary policy? After all, one rarely hears Federal Reserve officials suggesting that monetary policy be given up as hopeless because it cannot completely reverse the impact of unsound budget, tax, wage, and price policies. Moreover, it may be unduly pessimistic to assume that Treasury debt management will always affect the debt structure in ways adverse to monetary policy. When debt management and monetary policy are working in the same direction, the Federal Reserve's continual presence in the market and greater flexibility could be an invaluable supplement to the more powerful but blunter weapon of debt management.

So far as Young and Yager's concern about the effect on Federal Reserve earnings of sales of bonds at losses goes, this is not a serious objection. The achievement of economic stability, growth, and a stable value for the currency are the paramount goals for a central bank, not profit. As a matter of fact, Reserve Board Chairman Martin said just this in replying in 1959 to a suggestion by Congressman Henry Reuss that Federal Reserve earnings could be increased

[30] *Ibid.*
[31] Flanders Committee, *1954 Hearings,* p. 74; also, Hart, *Review of Economics and Statistics,* XLII, 257.

by buying bonds rather than lowering bank reserve requirements whenever the Federal Reserve wished to increase the supply of available bank reserves. Martin said:

Mr. Reuss, we do not ever operate the System account, and never should in my judgment, to make money for the Treasury Department or the Federal Reserve. We are trying to exercise our influence in the money stream in terms of the public welfare of the country.[32]

Apart from the arguments so far presented, Young and Yager argue that there is an additional drawback to Federal Reserve operations in long-term securities in possible market reactions. They said:

about the only interpretation that the market could place on a Federal Reserve attempt through its own portfolio operations to change the maturity composition of the publicly-held debt is that the Federal Reserve and the Treasury disagreed on a matter which is primarily the Treasury's concern.[33]

This seems far too pessimistic a view of market reaction. In the first place, the market is likely to be aware that on many occasions such operations would simply reflect the fact that the Federal Reserve can sell small amounts of bonds which it would not be practical for the Treasury to market. Second, the market may be expected to learn in time, if not immediately, that even disagreements reflect the differing responsibilities of the two agencies in an area which, contrary to Young and Yager, is of concern to both. Thus, the market eventually would judge operations in long-terms as a part of general credit policies aimed at economic stabilization and growth. As Hart has said: "The public can be made to see the objectives of a policy move in terms of effects on business activity, prices, etc.—or more immediately of effects on owned reserves—rather than of goals definable in security prices." [34] Reason for confidence in the market's ability to learn is afforded by experience. Back in August, 1950, when the Federal Reserve authorities raised the discount rate just before a Treasury refunding, it was regarded as evidence—and was—of a deepseated dispute between the two agencies. Now, with flexible credit policies accepted, discount rate changes are regarded as routine aspects of monetary policy.

[32] Joint Committee, *1959 Employment Hearings*, Pt. 6A, p. 1244.
[33] Young and Yager, *Quarterly Journal of Economics*, LXXIV, 371.
[34] Hart, *Review of Economics and Statistics*, XLII, 258.

Thus, the arguments presented against operations in long-term securities—by Martin, Riefler, Young, and Yager—were open to serious question.

"BILLS ONLY" AND CONTROL OVER INTEREST RATES

Much of the controversy over "bills only" has centered on the proper relation of the Federal Reserve to interest rates. The critics of "bills only" have presented a relatively straightforward case: (1) Interest rates are important tools of monetary policy and therefore should be controlled or effectively influenced by the central bank; (2) Long-term rates are particularly important; (3) Arbitrage between the short- and long-term markets is imperfect; (4) Hence, "bills only" is not an effective way for the Federal Reserve to exercise control over interest rates and particularly long-term rates.

The Federal Reserve's defense of "bills only," on the other hand, has seemed to be the following series of related but not always convincing arguments: (1) The central bank's business is to control bank reserves and the money supply and it is the business of free market forces to set interest rates which "bills only" best permits them to do; (2) If interest rates are important for the central bank to control, then it can be said that—so far as we really know—short-term rates are just as important as long-term rates, and "bills only" gives influence over short-term rates; (3) If long-term rates really are important for the central bank to influence, then market arbitrage can be counted on to transmit central bank actions in the short-term market to the long-term market; (4) In any case the central bank's open market operations have their main impact on security yields through their effect on bank reserve positions. "Bills only" operations have just as much of an impact on bank reserve positions as do bond dealings. Therefore long-term dealings are unnecessary. Moreover, direct dealings in bonds or "swaps" of bonds for short-term securities which do not affect reserve positions cannot appreciably affect long-term yields or the structure of interest rates.

INFLUENCED VERSUS FREE MARKET RATES OF INTEREST. To the critics of "bills only," the Federal Reserve's decision to confine open market operations to short-term securities seemed to confirm that the central bank intended to abdicate most, if not all, of its responsibility for the cost and availability of credit, particularly in the long-term markets. As noted in Chapter III, there was basis for this fear in the pronouncements and basic philosophy of responsible Federal Reserve officials. To be sure, Chairman Martin had stated that the Federal Reserve was not "absolving itself from concern with developments in the longer-term sector of the market" [35] but on the other hand the Federal Open Market Committee was on record as having said "confining operations to short-term securities would allow adequate flexibility in open market operations with a minimum of disturbance to prices and yields on longer-term securities." [36] However one might define "concern," there was no suggestion here of long-term interest rates being used as active instruments of monetary policy.

Many economists were highly critical of the Federal Reserve's opinion that interest rates, and particularly long-term rates, would be determined to the maximum extent possible by free market forces if open market operations were confined to "bills only." After all, the Federal Reserve would still be exerting decisive influence on money conditions through its operations in the bill market. Moreover, a number of the critics charged that the Federal Reserve's withdrawal from the long-term market seemed only to hand over control of long-term interest rates to the Treasury. Edward Shaw told the Flanders Subcommittee:

The Federal Reserve has bowed off on the long market. It will no longer manipulate relative market supplies of long-term and short-term securities. That function passes to the Treasury. The Treasury proposes to push out long securities, at relatively high rates of interest, when excess liquidity is contributing to cyclical boom. It will borrow short, at low rates of interest, when more liquidity may soften a cyclical recession. Debt management is stepping into the market arena from which the Federal Reserve has withdrawn. [37]

Hansen labeled the arrangement an "informal cartel" in which the Federal Reserve influences the volume of credit and the Treasury the cost. [38]

While all this may underrate the influence of the volume of credit available on its cost, there can be little doubt that Treasury debt-management decisions to offer short- or long-term securities affect at

[35] Flanders Committee, *1954 Hearings*, p. 16.
[36] Board of Governors of the Federal Reserve System, *Annual Report, 1953*, p. 89.
[37] Flanders Committee, *1954 Hearings*, p. 74.
[38] Hansen, *Review of Economics and Statistics*, XXXVII, 113.

least the structure of interest rates, and, in this writer's opinion, even on occasion the absolute level of interest rates. The critics granted that the Treasury may be closely cooperating with the Federal Reserve by issuing types of securities appropriate to current credit policy but suggested that the Federal Reserve, not the Treasury, is better fitted to have responsibility for the interest rate structure. Shaw remarked, "Treasury techniques for managing the rate structure are less agile than central banking techniques." [39]

Most of the critics of "bills only" therefore asserted that the central bank and Treasury cannot avoid substantial influence on interest rates and argued that such influence should be exercised purposefully toward the ends of a stable and growing economy. Chandler described the Federal Reserve's task:

In some cases it may succeed in doing this solely by regulating the volume and cost of bank reserves; in others it may need to exert a direct effect on the prices and yields of long-term securities by purchasing and selling them.[40]

But the Federal Reserve has argued that open market transactions in long-term securities would destroy the usefulness of the long-term market as an indicator of pressures of credit demand and supply, of savings and investment. For, in the words of Young and Yager, "Price and yield quotations then would no longer index the state of equilibrium in the savings-investment process; they would reflect, rather, market expectations of, or response to, Federal Reserve decisions about what prices and yields are desirable for the market to have." [41] Monetary policy, they asserted, would be correspondingly hampered, for the Federal Reserve now uses movements in long-term yields as indicators of the effectiveness of policy and as guides to needs for action.[42]

Perhaps the first comment on this view is that market decisions are not always correct and hence may be an unreliable guide for central bank action.[43] Indeed, it has long been recognized that precisely one objective of central bank policy should be to influence market

[39] Flanders Committee, *1954 Hearings,* p. 74.
[40] *Ibid.,* p. 46.
[41] Young and Yager, *Quarterly Journal of Economics,* LXXIV, 362.
[42] *Ibid.,* pp. 357–58.
[43] Wallich, *United States Monetary Policy,* pp. 106–08. Young and Yager recognize the problem, but elsewhere Federal Reserve spokesmen have tended to lose sight of such qualifications.

expectations and behavior. As a matter of fact even under the "bills only" policy, the long-term market reacted to both its own demand and supply and to what the Federal Reserve was currently doing in the short-term market.

But accepting that long-term interest rates are useful guides to the monetary authorities, it can be argued that they would continue to be so even if the Federal Reserve intervened from time to time in the long-term market. The point is that so long as the Federal Reserve is aware of its own actions in the market (and it will always be in full knowledge of this) it can allow for them and hence arrive at judgments of what the residual, or private, market is doing. Consider, for example, how the authorities might allow for their own actions in interpreting market movements following an open market purchase of bonds: (1) A rise in yields could indicate that private credit demand was outstripping private credit supply, for yields rose *despite* the extra funds supplied by the Federal Reserve; (2) Steadiness in yields could indicate that private credit demand was somewhat greater than private credit supply since the extra funds supplied by the Federal Reserve were needed to satisfy demand without a rise in yields; (3) A decline in yields might have several interpretations. A small decline would indicate that private credit supply just about equaled private credit demand, for the extra funds supplied by the Federal Reserve were just enough to raise supply above demand and cause a yield decline. A large yield decline could have two interpretations: it might suggest that even without the funds supplied by the Federal Reserve private credit supply would have exceeded credit demand; or it might mean that Government security dealers had interpreted the Federal Reserve's purchases to indicate a new policy and were adjusting prices and yields accordingly.

There are a number of reasons for thinking that the Federal Reserve could intervene in the long-term market and still use market movements as a guide: (1) Even during the pre-1951 years when the Federal Reserve was supporting, not merely intervening in, the Government securities market and minimizing fluctuations in yields, it was able to judge the relative strength of private credit demand and supply from the amount of securities it had to buy or sell to stabilize yields; (2) The Federal Reserve has used yield movements in the short-term market, in which the authorities are constantly intervening, as "guides . . . to current supply and demand tendencies in the money market," [44] and, (3) Officials of central banks which operate in all sectors of the money and bond markets have testified that they are still able to judge basic trends in credit supply and demand from market movements.[45]

IMPORTANCE OF LONG-TERM RATES OF INTEREST. The critics of "bills only" have been particularly concerned that effective control be maintained over long-term rates of interest. Federal Reserve spokesmen, on the other hand, have tended to downgrade the importance of directly influencing the long-term market. The Ad Hoc Subcommittee justified its recommendations for "bills only" in part by saying: "Traditional principles of central banking made no provision for operations in the intermediate or long maturities of any borrower." [46] Young and Yager, in their defense of "bills only," argued that if some economic theories stressed the importance of long-term rates of interest, there was one which placed importance on short-term rates. Moreover, they stated that there is litttle empirical evidence on the relative elasticities of demand for short- and long-term loans and therefore no adequate basis for proposals that the Federal Reserve try to affect long-term rates any differently than it affected short-term rates.[47]

Against these contentions, the critics of "bills only" brought up a battery of citations. Opposing the argument based on tradition, Sayers warned against narrow reliance on tradition which was not suited to contemporary conditions [48] and suggested "a disposition to discover novelties and to be versatile in technique" is the "cardinal virtue of the central banker." [49] He recommended that a broad view of the central banking function is the most satisfactory.

The business of a central bank is to influence the behaviour of the country's financial institutions in the interest of the broad economic policy of the government. The most appropriate way for it to function depends on

---

[44] Young and Yager, *Quarterly Journal of Economics*, LXXIV, 357.

[45] See, for example, the very interesting testimony and memorandum of M. H. De Kock, Governor of the South African Reserve Bank, in Radcliffe Committee, *Memoranda of Evidence*, Vol. 1, p. 287, par. 15 and *Minutes of Evidence*, Question No. 9325 and Reply.

[46] Flanders Committee, *1954 Hearings*, p. 267.

[47] Young and Yager, *Quarterly Journal of Economics*, LXXIV, 365.

[48] Sayers, *Central Banking*, p. 33.

[49] *Ibid.*

the nature of the financial institutions it is called upon to influence, and the economic policy whose furtherance is its ultimate purpose.[50]

The New York Federal Reserve Bank pointed out that one of the major monetary policy questions which developed during the inter-war period concerned the ability of central banks to achieve desired degrees of ease or restraint solely through reliance on traditional operations in the short-term market.[51] Thus, Keynes said in 1930:

The main direct influence of the Banking System is over the short-term rate of interest. But when it is a question of controlling the rate of investment, not in working capital but in fixed capital, it is the long-term rate of interest which chiefly matters.[52]

Keynes concluded at that time that only under special circumstances might it be necessary to "impose on the Central Bank the duty of purchasing bonds . . . " [53] but a few years later he went much further.

Perhaps a complex offer by the central bank to buy and sell at stated prices gilt-edged bonds of all maturities, in place of the single bank rate for short-term bills, is the most important practical improvement that can be made in the technique of monetary management. . . . The monetary authority often tends in practice to concentrate on short-term debts and to leave the price of long-term debts to be influenced by belated and imperfect reactions from the price of short-term debts.[54]

Another indication of the drift of economic thought on the subject is the fact that both of the great investigations of monetary policy and practices in the United Kingdom in the past generation have recommended central bank influence over long-term markets. The Macmillan *Report* included among its recommendations on the Bank of England's policies the proposal that the bank undertake

deliberate exchanges between the Bank's holdings of long-dated and of short-dated securities respectively, with the object of influencing the margin between the market rate of interest on the two types of securities [and thus] . . . regulating the rate of investment. . . . We think that the policy of bringing to bear such influence as the Bank may possess for widening or narrowing the margin between long-term and short-term rates of interest in different sets of circumstances, with a view to encouraging fixed investment or liquidity as the case may be, should be frequently considered and should sometimes form the basis for action.[55]

[50] *Ibid.*, p. 47.
[51] Flanders Committee, *1954 Hearings*, pp. 311–12.
[52] Keynes, *A Treatise on Money*, II, 352.
[53] *Ibid.*, p. 371.   [54] Keynes, *General Theory*, p. 206.
[55] Great Britain, Committee on Finance and Industry, *Report*, p. 154.

The Radcliffe Committee *Report* in 1959 also put the emphasis on the long-term rate of interest as the more promising avenue for central bank influence in a number of scattered references. Thus, the Committee concluded

it is at fixed capital that the rate of interest must strike if it is to have any direct impact, and for this purpose the longer rates are relevant. . . . The authorities should not aim at complete stability of interest rates, but should take a view as to what the long-term situation demands and be prepared by all the means in their power to influence markets in the required direction.[56]

It is true, as Young and Yager maintained, that the theory that long rates are the important rates has competition from a theory that short rates are the significant factor. But the implication that the two views enjoy anything like the same standing is completely unfounded. The view that short rates are the important rates is generally identified with R. G. Hawtrey, who related short rates to traders' demands for inventories and built a theory of cycle causation upon this. But the drift of economic opinion has been away from this view and it would be hard to identify a prominent economist, apart from Hawtrey, who holds it. On the other hand, a number of leading economists favor emphasis on the long rate.[57]

The reasons for believing that the long rate is, in Robertson's words, "the senior partner" [58] are mainly theoretical but they have an empirical basis. Theoretically, it is possible to demonstrate that interest costs gain increasing importance with the length of duration of the loan, that is to say, with the durability of the capital asset purchased and the certainty and calculability of the expected return. Short-term interest rates charged on loans to carry inventory have lesser influence, in part because of the shorter period to which they apply and also because, as Sayers puts it:

There are many other costs of holding stocks—warehousing, insurance, allowance for perishing, and above all, the risk that the price of the commodity will fall while it is being held. These various charges vary very much from one commodity to another but in most cases they are suffi-

[56] Radcliffe Committee, *Report,* pp. 175, 177.

[57] To give a few names: J. M. Keynes, R. F. Harrod, D. H. Robertson, F. A. Lutz, G. L. S. Shackle, A. G. Hart, P. A. Samuelson and practically all critics of the "bills only" policy.

[58] D. H. Robertson, "Some Notes on the Theory of Interest," in *Money, Trade and Economic Growth,* p. 208.

cient to swamp any but the most extreme changes in [short-term] interest rates.[59]

Empirical studies of the effect of interest rates on economic behavior have generally agreed that if economic activity is influenced by interest rates at all, it is the long-term rate which is important.[60] The Oxford inquiries found "almost universal agreement that short-term rates of interest do not directly affect investment either in stocks [inventories] or in fixed capital" but did find some influence for the long-term rate in housing, public utility, and transportation investment.[61] Klein found that bond yields had a significant effect on investment in the railroad and electric utility industries.[62] Gehrels and Wiggins found that they influenced investment in manufacturing.[63] Even studies which found that the interest rate was not a significant determinant of investment focused on the long-term rate as the variable to be studied.[64]

The long-term rate of interest has also gained in importance from the increased attention paid to the influence of changing bond prices (directly related to long-term interest rates) on the willingness of financial institutions to make credit available. Sayers has emphasized

it is important for the central bank to affect the bond market even if the main objective is to influence the behavior of the commercial banks because the banks' substantial holdings of investments could permit them to raise cash for lending by sales of securities even if their reserve positions were under pressure.[65]

This happened in the United States during 1946.

[59] Sayers, *Modern Banking*, p. 168.

[60] For surveys of such studies, see White, "Interest Inelasticity of Investment Demand—The Case from Business Attitude Surveys Re-examined," *American Economic Review*, XLVI (September, 1956), 565–87; and U.S. Congress, Joint Economic Committee, *Staff Report on Employment, Growth, and Price Levels*, 86th Cong., 1st Sess., 1959, pp. 368–78. Cited hereafter as Joint Committee, *1959 Staff Report*.

[61] *Oxford Studies*, pp. 28–30, 51–67.

[62] Lawrence Klein, "Studies in Investment Behavior," in *Conference on Research in Business Cycles* (New York, National Bureau of Economic Research, 1951), pp. 233–303, particularly 250, 253, 276.

[63] Gehrels and Wiggins, "Interest Rates and Manufacturers' Fixed Investment," *American Economic Review*, XLVII (March, 1957), 79–92.

[64] Avram Kisselgoff and Franco Modigliani, "Private Investment in the Electric Power Industry and the Acceleration Principle," *Review of Economics and Statistics*, XXXIX (November, 1957), 363–79.

[65] Sayers, *Central Banking*, p. 144.

Although there is not a great deal of statistical evidence bearing directly on the relative importance of short and long rates of interest, what there is tends to support theoretical reasoning which stresses the importance of long-term rates of interest. And this is the point of view which the great body of authoritative economic opinion also takes. Young and Yager, then, have been distinctly in the minority in their view that long-term rates of interest are not clearly important enough to justify exerting direct influence on them.

CONTROVERSY ABOUT THE EFFECTIVENESS OF ARBITRAGE. Although the Federal Reserve authorities have felt that the free market should be mainly responsible for long-term interest rates and also have doubted that long-term rates are enough more important than short-term rates to justify directly influencing them, they nevertheless have maintained that they exercise adequate, though indirect, influence over long-term rates through their control of the short-term market. Riefler, in a 1958 review of the experience with "bills only," concluded that although there is *sometimes* "a sluggish response in the long-term markets to changes in the availability of funds in the short-term markets," [66] *in general* "the response . . . has been anything but lethargic." [67] And Young and Yager have gone considerably further:

Changes in supply or demand in one sector of the Government securities market have tended to be transmitted promptly to other sectors of that market. A high degree of correspondence has consistently been shown by the direction of change in market yields on short and long-term Treasury securities. . . . This transmission process, which helps diffuse the effects of change throughout the market, reflects the ready substitutability in investor portfolios of issues in adjacent maturity sectors as well as arbitrage activity on the part of market professionals.[68]

These views have been challenged vigorously by economists who say that there are important lags and imperfections in the transmission of impulses in the short-term sector of the market to the long-term sector. As Sayers put it:

Even in the most highly developed financial systems, supplies and demands do not switch with perfect ease from one part of the market to another, and in most countries the imperfection is substantial. . . . Moreover, there is the very important fact that the relationship between short

[66] *Federal Reserve Bulletin*, XLIV, 1266.
[67] *Ibid.*, p. 1260.
[68] Young and Yager, *Quarterly Journal of Economics*, LXXIV, 345.

and long rates depends largely on expectations about the future course of rates. A wide movement of short rates causes hardly a ripple in long rates if it is thought purely ephemeral.[69]

Thus the critics of "bills only" have argued that in ordinary circumstances arbitrage and substitutability between the different sectors of the market is not good enough to be relied on to translate movements in short-term yields into effective influence on long-term rates of interest.[70] And some have pointed out that on important occasions the reaction of long-term yields to changes in short-term yields could even be perverse.[71]

The statistical evidence of movements in short- and long-term security yields from 1951 to 1959 tends to support critics of the "bills only" policy, not its Federal Reserve defenders. The Federal Reserve spokesmen have in their favor the fact that the broad, longer-range sweeps of short, intermediate, and long-term interest rates have usually been in the same direction. But it is the relationships over relatively short periods which are important for monetary policy and consequently for judging the effectiveness of "bills only" operations in influencing long-term rates of interest. In short periods the relationship between short- and long-term rates has varied widely, not only in timing and extent of movement but also in direction of movement.

Thus from 1951 to 1959 the coefficient of correlation between yields on 91-day Treasury bills and long-term Treasury bonds, averaged monthly, was 0.7901. While this indicates a very definite degree of relationship, it nevertheless suggests that some 38 percent of the variation in bond yields was *not* associated with changes in bill yields. To be sure, effectiveness for a "bills only" policy would not require perfect correlation between bill yields and bond yields, or invariance in the term structure of interest rates. But *some* stability and predictability in these relationships would seem to be necessary. Yet, as Luckett pointed out, there is substantial variation in the degree of relationship.[72] A study by this writer of changes in monthly average

[69] Sayers, *Modern Banking,* p. 308.
[70] Angell, *American Economic Review,* XLVIII, 78–79.
[71] Flanders Committee, *1954 Hearings,* pp. 311–12; also, Carson, *Quarterly Journal of Economics,* LXIX, 338.
[72] Luckett, *Review of Economics and Statistics,* XLII, 301–06. Luckett found the Federal Reserve's "control" through "bills only" operations to be deficient in the most basic sense: the same bank reserve position was found to be asso-

yields on 91-day bills and long-term government bonds during 1951–1959 showed that even when bond yields moved in the same direction as bill yields, the degree of response varied widely and unpredictably and ran as high as 7½ times and as low as 0.03 of the change in bill yields.

Most damaging, however, to the case for "bills only" as an effective means of influencing long-term Government bond yields is the surprisingly large number of times in which Government bond yields behaved perversely in response to changes in Treasury bill yields. Table 3 shows that monthly average yields on Government bonds

TABLE 3

MOVEMENTS IN MONTHLY AVERAGE YIELDS ON
91-DAY TREASURY BILLS AND LONG-TERM
U.S. GOVERNMENT BONDS, 1951–1959

Year	Same Direction	Opposite Direction	No Response in Bond Yield	Change in Bond Yield and No Change in Bill Yield
1951	4	5	1	2
1952	4	7	1	
1953	7	5		
1954	6	6		
1955	7	5		
1956	8	4		
1957	8	4		
1958	9	3		
1959	6	5	1	
Total	59	44	3	2

moved in a direction opposite to the direction of change in average 91-day Treasury bill yields in from three to six months of every year from 1951 to 1959. For the period as a whole bond yields moved opposite to bill yields in 44 of the 108 months, showed no response to changes in bill yields in 3 months, and changed in 2 months when bill yields were steady.

It seems apparent that this experience does not support the view that yield movements in the short-term market are transmitted quickly to the long-term market.

Thus, the critics of "bills only" have considerable reason for assert-

---

ciated with widely differing levels of Treasury bill yields (p. 304). Moreover, he found that the sensitivity of long-term yields to movements in bill yields varied sharply in different periods of time (pp. 305–06).

ing that arbitrage and linkage between the short- and long-term sectors of the money and capital market are imperfect and that slippage or perhaps unwarranted intensity in the transmission of credit policy actions in the short-term sector is a likely occurrence. Such slippage and intensification of credit policy actions have had serious impact on the effectiveness of monetary policy. This subject will be discussed in Chapter VI; now a few additional Federal Reserve arguments against open market operations in all maturities must be considered.

ALLEGED INABILITY OF THE FEDERAL RESERVE TO AFFECT LONG-TERM YIELDS DIRECTLY. Winfield Riefler, speaking for the Federal Reserve System, argued that Federal Reserve dealings in bonds, as such and apart from the related impact on bank reserve positions or expectations, would not have appreciable effects on long-term bond yields or on the structure of yields.[73] He contended that open market sales (the process would be reversed for purchases) would affect interest rates through two channels: (1) They would increase the supply of securities in the market, lowering their prices and raising their yields; and (2) They would contract bank reserve positions, which would reduce banks' demand for securities or lead to bank selling (if reserves were reduced below required levels) and this also would result in lower prices and higher yields. The latter of these two channels, Riefler asserted, would clearly be the more powerful since the ability of a fractional reserve banking system to acquire or discard assets is a multiple of any change in its reserve base. Moreover, he said that since the effects of open market operations on bank reserve positions would be directly "dispersed over all types of assets commonly found in bank portfolios," [74] the impact on yields in any sector of the market would be largely due to the change in reserve positions. Riefler argued that with the ratio of required reserves to demand deposits at about 7 to 1 for all member banks in 1958 "something like seven-eighths of any resulting effect on market yields" [75] of an open market operation "should reflect the change in the volume of reserves available to the banks and only one eighth" [76] the fact that the operation was executed in any particular type of security and thus changed the market supply of that type of security. Since "bills only" operations would have $\frac{7}{8}$ of the impact of operations in bonds but would not

---

[73] *Federal Reserve Bulletin*, XLIV, 1260–74.
[74] *Ibid.*, p. 1263.   [75] *Ibid.*, p. 1269.
[76] *Ibid.*

give rise to unsettling market reactions, "bills only" would be preferable.

We have already indicated in the preceding section that experience with "bills only" and analysis of the effectiveness of market arbitrage shows that the impact of "bills only" operations on bond yields is highly uncertain, in timing, extent, and direction. The issue here is the contention that pure operations in bonds (excluding effects on reserves and expectations) can do very little to affect yields or the structure of yields. In support of this contention Riefler cited the Treasury refunding of February, 1958, which shifted some $5 billion of securities from the very short sector of the market to the intermediate and long-term sectors without affecting reserve balances or market expectations about the course of future Federal Reserve policy. Comparing the yield curve on Treasury securities as of January 13, 1958, before the refunding was announced, with that for February 5, after it was completed, Riefler found very little change in relative yields of long- and short-term securities. Summarizing, he said:

that the effects on yields of the redistribution of maturities among the various sectors of the market was noticeable but still limited considering the magnitudes involved . . . is indicated by the fact that bill rates did not drop even to 1½ percent and remained much above levels that usually prevail when member banks have $500 million of free reserves. Long-term bond yields, which had also been dropping rapidly, concurrently leveled off and then rose somewhat. . . . There was, however, no sharp upward reaction.[77]

On the basis of this illustration which, he argued, confirmed his theoretical expectation, Riefler concluded

the Federal Reserve System would have to undertake very large swapping operations indeed if it wished to use this device to affect appreciably the availability of funds as among the short, the intermediate, and the long-maturity sectors of the market.[78]

The first question which arises with respect to Riefler's analysis and conclusion is simply, How large an impact on relative long- and short-term yields would Riefler require before he admitted that a swapping operation did "affect appreciably" the structure of yields and relative availabilities of long- and short-term funds? For the change in the yield structure which accompanied the February refunding, although dismissed by him as "noticeable but still limited,"

[77] *Ibid.,* p. 1272.   [78] *Ibid.*

was really quite large. The chart, showing the yield curves before and after the Treasury refunding, which he used in his discussion, shows that Treasury bill yields dropped approximately 1 percentage point, from about 2⅝ percent to about 1⅝ percent, while long-term Treasury bond yields rose something like ⅛ percentage point, from around 3⅛ percent to something like 3¼ percent.[79] Thus, the refunding, or "swap," widened the spread between bill yields and long-term bond yields from about ½ percent on January 13, 1958, to about 1⅝ percent on February 5. If it means anything, this tripling of the yield spread is surely evidence of the *power* of swap operations to affect the structure of yields, not evidence of their inability to do so.

Moreover, it deserves emphasis that this large change in the yield structure, lowering short-term yields and raising long-term yields, was achieved at a time when the demand for long-term securities probably was increasing faster than the demand for short-term obligations, a consideration which would have worked toward *narrowing* of the bills-bonds yield spread. Demand for long-terms was spurred by hopes for capital gains arising out of expectations that the recession and the Federal Reserve's easy money policy would lower interest rates further as well as by the banks' willingness to extend maturities in order to "nail down" the going interest return for an extended period and thus protect income if the recession and low interest rates should continue for a protracted period. Demand for short-terms on the other hand was being held back by the sharp decline in rates (particularly because of the sensitivity of foreign investors to short-term yield levels) as well as by the recession-induced shrinkage in the cash flow of corporations which are the largest holders of Treasury bills.[80] Riefler seemed to assume unchanged relative demand for long- and short-term securities since he admitted into his analysis only the effects of a change in relative supply, but in view of the above considerations this seems unrealistic.

Thus, the considerable widening of the yield spread between long and short obligations was achieved in the face of demand considerations which otherwise might have narrowed it, abstracting as Riefler

[79] *Ibid.*

[80] Corporate profits before taxes in the first quarter of 1958 were running at the annual rate of $32.0 billion, $7.4 billion below their rate in the last quarter of 1957 and $11.5 billion below the rate in the first quarter of 1957 according to Department of Commerce estimates.

has from impacts on reserve positions. The implication of this is that credit policy swaps would have greater impact on the yield spread between short-term and long-term securities because credit policy swaps presumably would for the most part be aimed at working with the broad movements of long- and short-term interest rates, and not against them. Thus, in recession the central bank is most likely to attempt to extend and perhaps accelerate an already declining pattern of long-term yields by purchases of bonds.[81] If the central bank is working in the direction of current interest-rate movements, it is much more likely to achieve its goals. It is the attempts to defy basic economic forces, such as the Dalton drive for a 2½ percent long-term rate in Great Britain in 1946 when demands for capital and credit were great, that require herculean efforts and even so may fail.

Finally, it should be pointed out that Riefler's analysis of the short-term/long-term yield structure is couched in terms of changes in the *total supply* of long-terms relative to the *total supply* of short-terms. Looked at in this way, it would seem plausible that very large changes in relative supplies would be necessary to get appreciable effects if only because the totals outstanding are so large. But the prices and yields of both short- and long-term securities—and particularly long-term—are not set by transactions involving all such securities outstanding but rather by a relatively small volume of transactions which equate marginal demand and supply. Thus, although there were $57.8 billion of marketable Treasury securities maturing in more than five years outstanding on June 30, 1958, transactions in Treasury obligations due in more than five years averaged less than $150 million a day in 1958, and the volume of transactions in the long maturity area was probably well under this figure.[82] If the problem of affecting long-term yields is looked at in terms of affecting these marginal flows of funds and securities, rather than the totals outstanding, it begins to appear much more manageable.

To sum up: Riefler's argument that direct dealings in bonds and swaps are not likely to be effective in achieving any appreciable changes in the relative structure of short- and long-term yields seems

---

[81] A situation in which the central bank might want to work against the market—to slow the rise in bond yields during June-September, 1958 for example—is not impossible but is likely to be infrequent. Any attempt to give the Treasury yields on its new financing much below the market would however require such operations on a large scale.

[82] Treasury-Federal Reserve, *Study*, pp. 140–41.

incorrect. Both logic and the evidence presented by him and the Treasury-Federal Reserve study of the Government securities market suggest that exactly the opposite is more likely. In other words open market operations in bonds and swaps could be an effective and powerful tool of monetary policy. They could afford closer control over long-term interest rates and accordingly more direct influence over fixed capital investment sensitive to interest rate movements. They could supplement the Federal Reserve's control over bank reserve positions by limiting banks' ability to raise loan funds by sale of securities. Swaps could permit some degree of differential impact on short- and long-term interest rates, thus increasing the ability of the Federal Reserve to discriminate, if necessary, between the needs of the domestic business situation, the bond market, and the balance of payments. Moreover, dealings in bonds and swaps could also be used to affect the availability, as well as the cost, of long-term credit.[83]

TREASURY FINANCE AND PRESSURES FOR PEGGING. The Federal Reserve's attachment to the "bills only" policy can be plausibly explained by a deep-seated fear that operations in all maturities will bring a return to the discredited practice of pegging prices and yields of Treasury securities. If this objective again became paramount, the central bank would no longer be able to make economic stability and growth the main criteria by which it decided to supply or withdraw money from the economy; it would have to supply funds in whatever measure was necessary to stabilize security prices, regardless of the state of the economy at the time. Theoretical reasoning and experience have shown that a return to pegging would not be likely to result from a complete disappearance or collapse of the private Government

[83] Apart from affecting lenders' willingness to sell Government bonds to raise funds for private lending, in the way Roosa suggested, Federal Reserve dealings in bonds could affect the availability of credit in another way. Some capital market investors, such as state and local government retirement funds, regularly invest a proportion of accruing funds in long-term Treasury bonds, and are little affected by Federal Reserve open market operations in the short-term market. But if the Federal Reserve offered long-term Treasury bonds from its portfolio at slightly below the ruling market price, it would in effect be absorbing the cash which such retirement funds normally make available to the market. The result would be that private borrowers and institutions which had been raising funds for lending by sales of Government bonds would find that the supply of long-term money available to them had shrunk. While would-be sellers of Government bonds could reduce their offering prices and attempt to attract buyers from other sectors of the market, this would mean that they had to accept larger capital losses and that they, rather than the Federal Reserve, would have to depend upon the imperfect arbitrage and uncertain linkages between sectors of the market.

securities market following a Federal Reserve decision to operate in all maturities of Government securities. But the Federal Reserve authorities have envisioned another avenue by which operations in all maturities could lead to pegging.

This fear—perhaps the most realistic of the Federal Reserve's objections to operating in all maturities—is that if the Federal Reserve were to deal in notes, intermediate-term bonds, and long-term bonds it would obviously be affecting the terms on which the Treasury could finance itself. It would be showing that it had the power to influence Treasury borrowing rates considerably at the same time that, in a period of credit restraint, it was raising interest costs for the Treasury. The feared result would be that pressures would arise—if not from the Treasury, then from Congress and the public—to compel the Federal Reserve to use its powers not to raise interest rates against the Treasury, but to lower them. Thus, when Federal Reserve spokesmen consider the argument that the Federal Reserve should affect the maturity structure of interest rates they tend to view it as a proposal that would eventually lead the System to peg interest rates and keep them low regardless of economic stabilization necessities. Chairman Martin made a characteristic statement before the Joint Economic Committee in 1959 when he said:

> Any attempt to use System operations to influence the maturity pattern of interest rates to help debt management would not, in my opinion, produce lasting benefits—I emphasize the word "lasting"—and would produce real difficulties. If an attempt were made to lower long-term interest rates by System purchases of bonds and to offset the effect on reserves by accompanying shifts of short-term issues, market holdings of participants would shift by a corresponding amount from long-term securities to short ones. This process could continue until the System's portfolio consisted largely of long-term securities. Accordingly, the System would have put itself into a frozen portfolio position.
>
> The effect of thus endeavoring to lower long-term yields, without affecting bank reserves, would be to increase the overall liquidity of the economy. Not only would the supply of short-term issues in the market be increased, but also all Government bonds outstanding would be made more liquid because they could be more readily converted into cash. The problem of excess liquidity in the economy, already a serious one, would be intensified.[84]

There is no denying that the Federal Reserve has reason to fear pressures to use its money creation powers to assure low, or at least reasonable, borrowing rates for the Treasury. Few economists or

[84] Joint Committee, *1959 Employment Hearings*, Pt. 6A, p. 1234.

public men of prominence now share Congressman Wright Patman's continued belief that the Government securities market should be rigidly pegged by the Federal Reserve System. But a considerable and influential group of Congressmen and some economists feel that the System should use its powers to lower Treasury borrowing rates and to keep them as low as possible.[85] A considerable number of the Congressional investigations of monetary policy since the unpegging of the bond market have given substantial prominence to the idea that money had become too tight and interest rates too high. This feeling went so far in 1959 that the President's request for elimination of the 4¼ percent legal limit on rates the Treasury could pay on new bond issues (which was preventing the Treasury from issuing new bonds) was refused unless the Federal Reserve agreed to give up the "bills only" policy and buy bonds to hold down long-term interest rates.[86] Thus, the 1960 *Report* of the Joint Economic Committee included, among others, the following conclusions:

We need a less restrictive monetary policy within the framework of a more effective fiscal policy. Specifically, the money supply should grow in line with the growth in output. Interest rates could then be lower and would support a more adequate rate of growth and investment without inflation.[87]

The *Report* then went on to specific recommendations in the area of monetary policy and debt management:

In summary, our major recommendations are—
The Federal Reserve should—
   (a) abandon its discredited "bills only" policy,
   (b) agree to build up its portfolio of long-term bonds, and
   (c) use open market operations rather than lowering reserve requirements as the means of bringing about the secular expansion of credit which the Federal Reserve and the banks desire.[88]

While denying any intent to peg security prices and interest rates, the Joint Committee made it plain that it thought the Federal Reserve could peg rates and was pegging them at undesirably high levels.

[85] See *Journal of Commerce,* March 15, 1960, the letter by 21 Senators. Among economists, see Hansen, *The American Economy,* pp. 51–55, and "A High and Rising Rate of Interest," *Review of Economics and Statistics,* XXXIX (August, 1957), 345.

[86] For this controversy see, U.S. Congress, House, Committee on Ways and Means, *Public Debt Ceiling and Interest Rate Ceiling on Bonds, Hearings,* 86th Cong., 1st Sess., 1959.

[87] U.S. Congress, Joint Economic Committee, *Report on the January 1960 Economic Report of the President,* 86th Cong., 2d Sess., 1960, p. 2.

[88] *Ibid.,* p. 16.

We do not seek a policy of pegging Government bond prices at artificially high prices and low yields. We do seek abandonment of policies aimed at pegging Government bonds at artificially low prices and high yields.

It is for these reasons that, pending reforms in fiscal, monetary, and debt management policies, we have opposed the elimination of the present 4¼ percent statutory ceiling on the rate which may be offered on Federal Government debt instruments with a maturity of more than 5 years.[89]

These few citations are relatively restrained in giving the flavor and the intensity of the drive for cheaper money which is expressed most vigorously, perhaps, in Congressional debate and can be found scattered throughout the *Congressional Record* for dates beginning with June 8, 1959.

Nevertheless, it is possible to argue that the Federal Reserve's fears of a return to pegging were unfounded and that in any case it was selecting the wrong battleground when it made the "bills only" policy its main line of defense against pegging.

In the first place, it is significant that the Joint Economic Committee *Report* specifically disclaimed any desire to peg Government security prices and yields. The Joint Committee obviously felt that pegging, as such, was not defensible. Senator Douglas, chairman of the Joint Committee and a leader in the fight against eliminating the 4¼ percent bond rate limit, went to pains during the debate on the Senate floor to deny any attempt at pegging and to disassociate himself from Congressman Patman's views. Moreover, the vast majority of economists also have rejected pegging. In reply to a Joint Economic Subcommittee questionnaire sent out in September, 1958, only 14 economists of 615 queried, or 2.3 percent, expressed the opinion that the Federal Reserve should "subordinate other considerations to 'pegging' the Government bond market (as was done prior to 1951)." [90] Thus, there is considerable reason to accept the judgment of Arthur Burns, former chairman of the President's Council of Economic Advisers, that "any return to the pegging of yields on government securities, which contributed materially to the sharp rise in the general price level during the years immediately after the war, has today become almost unthinkable." [91]

[89] *Ibid.*, p. 17.
[90] U.S. Congress, Joint Economic Committee, Subcommittee on Economic Stabilization, *Economic Policy Questionnaire*, 85th Cong., 2d Sess., 1958, p. 7.
[91] *Prosperity Without Inflation*, p. 35.

On the other hand, there was, and is, no such general feeling that "bills only" is a desirable policy or that operations in all maturities inevitably will lead to pegging. The discussion in the preceding pages has suggested that the Federal Reserve's case for "bills only" was not a strong one. The same group of economists who almost unanimously rejected pegging in their reply to the Joint Economic Subcommittee also rejected "bills only," and by almost as large a margin: 523 to 46.[92]

In view of these attitudes, the question arises whether the best way to protect against pressures for pegging was for the Federal Reserve to stake its prestige on a "bills only" policy which impaired the effectiveness of monetary policy, which enjoyed little support among informed observers, and which developed an image of the Federal Reserve authorities as being doctrinaire and intractable on a policy which seemed almost indefensible to many. An earlier willingness to conduct open market operations in all maturities, on the other hand, could have improved the effectiveness of monetary policy, might well have sharply reduced the ranks of the critics of Federal Reserve policy and produced a more understanding climate for the policy to operate in, and yet have left the Federal Reserve equally well prepared to resist resolutely any pressures for pegging should they arise. Indeed, the elimination of such a peripheral and dubiously defensible issue as "bills only" would have permitted the Federal Reserve to concentrate its force on the inherently strong arguments against pegging, which is after all the crucial issue, and the one on which it would enjoy the widest support.

CONCLUSIONS ON FEDERAL RESERVE'S POLICY OF OPERATING IN "BILLS ONLY"

To recapitulate a rather extended discussion, the Federal Reserve's policy of conducting open market operations in "bills only" was justified in a wide variety of not always convincing ways. First, there were the positive cases expressed in the assumptions: (1) "Bills only" would improve the functioning of the Government securities market because dealers would have less reason to fear sizable impact on prices of long-term bonds; and (2) A "bills only" policy would provide ample influence, through the normal linkage of markets and arbitrage, on

[92] Joint Committee, *1958 Questionnaire,* p. 7.

all maturity sectors and would therefore be sufficient to make monetary policy fully effective. Next, there were the more or less passive objections to the alternative of open market operations in all maturities: (3) Open market operations in all maturities were not needed because long-term interest rates could not be shown to be clearly more significant to monetary policy than short-term rates; and (4) In any case operations in all maturities could have had little more impact on long-term rates and the structure of rates than "bills only" operations. Finally, there were the vigorous objections that operations in all maturities, and particularly in the long-term markets, would have a number of positively harmful effects: (5) They would seriously impair, if not destroy, the usefulness of the Government securities market as an indicator of private credit demand and supply trends; (6) They would destroy the private market in Government securities, either through the withdrawal of private participants or through a massive crisis following explosive waves of private buying and selling in imitation of Federal Reserve operations in the long-term market; (7) Federal Reserve pegging would result from a policy of operating in all maturities either because (a) the private market had withered away, or (b) the private market had required massive support in crisis, or (c) the simple presence of the Federal Reserve in the long-term market had created demands that it use its powers to create receptive markets for Treasury financing.

It is not necessary to have recourse to sophisticated analysis or the facts of experience to see a basic inconsistency in the first two points of the Federal Reserve Board's case. The argument that "bills only" would improve the functioning of the Government securities market because it minimized direct impacts of monetary policy on long-term bond prices and yields implied poor linkage between the short- and long-term sectors of the market and tardy transmission of credit policy impulses in the short-term sector. Yet the argument that "bills only" operations could quickly and effectively influence long-term bond prices and yields implied just the opposite about linkage between the short and long sectors of the market. Whatever the true state of linkage was, it could not have been both good and bad at the same time.

An examination of the entire Federal Reserve case for "bills only" revealed that many of the assumptions and expectations on which it was founded were either unfounded or exaggerated. The Government securities market did not become stronger as a result of "bills only." Due to imperfect market arbitrage, "bills only" impaired the Federal Reserve's ability to influence long-term interest rates. Theory and experience indicate that long-term rates of interest are probably more important than short-term rates in influencing investment behavior. Far from indicating that operations in all maturities would have little significant effect on the interest-rate structure, the data presented by Federal Reserve spokesmen strongly suggested that they could have significant and powerful effects. So far as the dangers of operating in long-term securities go, it must be said that even though such dangers could not be completely ruled out in advance, the probabilities of their occurring were greatly exaggerated. Experience since the abandonment of "bills only" has shown this to be true. Even with the Federal Reserve operating occasionally in long-term securities, the Government securities market has been able to serve as an indicator of private credit demand and supply. Logic and experience have lent little support to the idea that the private market in Government securities would either wither away or collapse as the result of Federal Reserve intervention in the long-term area. The threat of a return to pegging is probably not as great as the Reserve authorities fear, but in any case it would be best met directly, not indirectly on the poorly defensible issue of "bills only."

The conclusion, on the basis of this analysis, must be that the "bills only" policy could only be justified as a pledge to the market that the Federal Reserve believes in allowing market forces to express themselves. But it was needed for that purpose for only a limited period. Attachment to "bills only" thereafter seemed to be mainly a reflection of attachment to traditional principles of central banking, and a belief that by minimizing its intervention, the central bank could reduce the likelihood of public objection to its presence in the markets. But these were unacceptable grounds for the retention of the "bills only" policy once it was recognized that it could significantly impair the effectiveness of monetary policy.

VI

THE RECORD OF "BILLS ONLY" IN THE

APPLICATION OF MONETARY POLICY

THE "BILLS ONLY" POLICY concentrated the initial impact of monetary policy in the short-term market and on short-term yields. Yet the importance of capital investment in a modern economy strongly suggests that the capital market and long-term interest rates should also be influenced by monetary policy. The Federal Reserve authorities counted on arbitrage and the normal linkage between sectors of the market to ensure that their actions in the short-term sector would be transmitted with relatively little delay to the bond market. But imperfect arbitrage and loose linkage between sectors of the market made it probable that the "bills only" approach to monetary control would involve a number of difficulties.

Credit-easing policies involving "bills only," for example, worked by saturating the short-term markets with liquidity and relying on the seepage of some of this liquidity into longer-term markets to produce appropriate responses in long-term yields and in the availability of long-term credit. But bringing down long-term rates indirectly by easing short-term money involved the possibility of the creation of excessive ease in the short-term markets, and this in turn could lead to a flow of funds abroad or to difficulties for the central bank in controlling the economy in the next expansion phase. Moreover, even if long-term rates declined in response to declines in short-term rates, the response could have been slow or inadequate in extent. Finally, in circumstances where short-term rates of interest were already near zero it would clearly be very difficult to achieve reductions in long-term rates by lowering short-term rates further.

Policies to restrain credit through "bills only" operations, on the other hand, could have been hampered if the long-term markets and interest rates reacted either too slowly and too little or too quickly and too much to increased interest rates and lowered liquidity in the short-term markets. The former reaction would have meant lack of effectiveness; the latter could have brought on panic in the bond market and perhaps even recession. Faulty arbitrage and consequent slippage in the transmission of credit policy actions in the short-term markets to the long sectors of the market could imply a consistently inadequate influence over capital market borrowing and lending. Efforts to make up for lack of influence on capital market institutions by intensifying pressure on the short-term market could have developed resentment on the part of commercial bankers as well as political opposition to extremes of credit restraint. The result could have been an easier monetary policy than was desirable on strictly economic grounds.

Thus there were a number of ways in which the "bills only" policy could have impaired the effectiveness of monetary policy. The remainder of this chapter will examine the experience of the seven years under "bills only" to see whether the Federal Reserve's effectiveness was seriously handicapped in any of these ways.

RECORD OF "BILLS ONLY" IN PERIODS OF CREDIT EASE

Examination of the record of "bills only" during periods of credit ease suggests that the major problem was the creation of excessive liquidity in the short-term markets. While there have been criticisms that long-term rates did not decline enough in recessions, such criticisms do not find support in the facts. And in the circumstances of recent years there were no occasions when it was impossible to lower long-term rates because short-term rates were already at or near zero. We turn now to discuss each of these situations.

FAILURE OF LONG-TERM RATES TO DECLINE. Many critics of "bills only" focused on the possibility that when short-term rates were already very low, further reductions would not be effective or possible as a means of lowering long-term rates. Reference was usually made to conditions in the Great Depression when yields on 91-day Treasury bills were often close to zero and sometimes even negative, banks had billions of dollars of excess reserves, and, despite all this ease in short-term money, yields on long-term Treasury bonds remained well above 2 percent.

Under such circumstances, the critics argued, the central bank could reduce long-term yields only by direct purchases of bonds. The New York Federal Reserve Bank, in its critique of the Ad Hoc Subcommittee report, pointed out that when the outbreak of war in 1939 unsettled the bond market, only this approach would have worked because of the Depression circumstances.[1]

But such extremes of liquidity were not a feature of the years in which "bills only" was in force as an operative policy. Moreover, from the general tenor of Federal Reserve defenses of "bills only," it may be safe to assume that such depression-type circumstances would be regarded as ample justification for its suspension.[2] If this is so, then there would be no need to be concerned about "bills only" hampering the conduct of monetary policy in emergency circumstances.

INADEQUATE RESPONSE OF LONG RATES TO SHORT-TERM EASE. The response of long-term interest rates to easing actions by the Federal Reserve in the short-term markets in the 1954 recession was regarded as adequate even by critics of "bills only."[3] But there was considerable criticism that in the 1958 recession long-term rates did not come down far enough in response to the Federal Reserve's easy credit policy.[4] While yields on long-term Treasury bonds fell about ⅝ of a percentage point in both the 1954 and 1958 recessions (from 3.13 percent in June, 1953, to 2.48 percent in April, 1954, and from 3.73 percent in October, 1957, to 3.12 percent in April, 1958), this represented only about one-quarter of the percentage point decline in yields on 91-day Treasury bills in 1958 (from 3.59 percent to 1.13 percent in April) compared with about one-half in 1954 (when bill yields declined from 2.23 percent in June, 1953, to 1.01 percent in April, 1954). Had bond yields been as sensitive to changes in bill

---

[1] Flanders Committee, *1954 Hearings*, p. 311.

[2] Young and Yager, "The Economics of 'Bills Preferably'," *Quarterly Journal of Economics*, LXXIV, 341, 358, 360, 363.

[3] Hansen, *The American Economy*, p. 61.

[4] The President of the United States commented during his press conference, May 28, 1958, that he would like to see long-term interest rates ¼ or ½ percent lower to encourage business recovery; see *The New York Times*, May 29, 1958, pp. 1, 12. Even Reserve Board Chairman Martin, testifying before a Congressional committee in 1959, revealed that he had been surprised that long-term rates had not come down more in response to the very great degree of ease in the short-term markets; see Joint Committee, *1959 Employment Hearings*, Pt. 6A, pp. 1285–86. Note also Senator Paul H. Douglas' remarks in the course of the same Hearings, pp. 1427–29.

yields in 1958 as they were in 1954, they would have declined no less than 1⅛ percentage points and the absolute level of long-term Treasury bond yields in April, 1958, would have been closer to 2⅝ percent than the 3.12 percent actually recorded.

However, as the defenders of "bills only" pointed out, even though the 1958 decline in bond yields was relatively small (compared to the decrease in Treasury bill yields), it was *effective* in terms of stimulating and accommodating a very large volume of borrowing by state and local governments and corporations.[5] Net state and municipal bond issues in the first six months of 1958 totaled $3.5 billion,[6] a record for the period, and net new issues of bonds and notes by corporations amounted to $3.2 billion, second only to the record set in the first six months of 1957 when $3.3 billion were issued.[7] While it took somewhat longer for the easier conditions to have their full effect on the mortgage market, the net increase in mortgage debt in the first six months of 1958 totaled $6 billion, compared with $5.9 billion and $5.1 billion in the comparable periods of 1957 and 1954.[8] These facts are based on the information given in Table 4. Thus, in this instance credit policy would appear to have been effective in easing the long-term markets even though its point of impact was on the short-term market.

However, it must be pointed out that "bills only" was as successful as it was in bringing down long-term yields only because there was a great deal of speculative buying of bonds in 1958. While the speculation led to the bond market collapse in June, 1958, and has therefore been roundly criticized, it was the speculators who provided the demand for bonds which the Federal Reserve, by sticking to "bills only," refused to supply. Without the speculative bond purchases, it is possible to argue, long-term yields would have come down even less and perhaps would not have attracted the volume of borrowing that helped stem the recession. Moreover, without the speculators there would not have been sufficient long-term funds available to absorb the bonds sold by borrowers. In the longer per-

[5] Young and Yager, *Quarterly Journal of Economics*, LXXIV, 367.
[6] *Federal Reserve Bulletin*, XLV (August, 1959), 1048.
[7] United States Securities and Exchange Commission tabulation, "Net Change in Corporate Securities Outstanding," April, 1960.
[8] *Federal Reserve Bulletin*, XLI (July, 1955), 797; XLV (January, 1959), 53; XLV (August, 1959), 1021.

TABLE 4

SECURITY YIELDS AND NEW SECURITY ISSUES, QUARTERLY, 1953–1959

| | | YIELDS | | | | | NEW ISSUES | | |
| | | (average in percent) | | | | | (total in $ billion) | | |
		Treas-ury Bills	Long-term Treas-ury Bonds	New Corpo-rate Bonds	FHA Mort-gages	Munic-ipal Bonds	Corpo-rate Bonds	Munic-ipal Bonds	All Mort-gages
1953	I	2.04	2.84	3.28	4.43	2.54	1.0	0.9	2.0
	II	2.20	3.07	3.72	4.58	2.81	1.6	0.8	2.8
	III	2.02	3.03	3.55	4.90	2.93	0.9	1.1	2.6
	IV	1.49	2.84	3.15	4.87	2.66	1.3	1.1	2.3
1954	I	1.08	2.61	2.87	4.72	2.47	0.8	1.2	2.1
	II	0.81	2.52	2.90	4.59	2.48	1.0	1.4	3.0
	III	0.87	2.49	2.96	4.55	2.29	1.3	0.9	3.5
	IV	1.04	2.57	2.88	4.55	2.34	0.7	1.0	3.8
1955	I	1.26	2.74	3.07	4.57	2.43	0.9	1.0	3.7
	II	1.51	2.82	3.12	4.62	2.40	0.9	0.5	4.6
	III	1.86	2.93	3.27	4.67	2.57	0.9	1.0	4.3
	IV	2.35	2.89	3.20	4.74	2.51	1.5	1.0	3.6
1956	I	2.38	2.89	3.17	4.70	2.51	0.9	1.4	3.5
	II	2.60	2.99	3.53	4.77	2.65	1.3	0.6	4.0
	III	2.60	3.13	3.85	4.87	2.79	1.4	0.6	3.9
	IV	3.06	3.30	4.16	5.04	3.11	1.1	0.6	3.2
1957	I	3.18	3.27	4.20	5.32	3.10	1.7	1.3	2.8
	II	3.16	3.43	4.48	5.34	3.27	1.6	1.0	3.1
	III	3.38	3.63	4.68	5.46	3.49	2.0	1.3	3.3
	IV	3.34	3.53	4.44	5.62	3.28	1.8	1.1	2.9
1958	I	1.84	3.25	3.74	5.55	3.00	2.1	1.9	2.5
	II	1.02	3.15	3.65	5.40	2.95	1.1	1.6	3.5
	III	1.71	3.57	4.27	5.41	3.33	1.2	1.3	4.1
	IV	2.79	3.75	4.42	5.59	3.37	1.4	0.8	4.4
1959	I	2.80	3.91	4.32	5.59	3.36	0.9	1.3p	4.1
	II	3.02	4.06	4.72	5.64	3.56	1.0	1.4p	4.4
	III	3.53	4.15	4.94	5.83	3.67	1.0	1.8p	5.2
	IV	4.30	4.17	5.11	6.18	3.61	1.4	0.4p	4.5

Source: Treasury bill and Treasury bond yield, Board of Governors of the Federal Reserve System, *Federal Reserve Bulletin;* New corporate bond yield, Economics Department, First National City Bank of New York; FHA mortgage yield, Federal Reserve Board series carried back before June, 1955, by assuming same relative changes as shown in the monthly mortgage yield series computed by J. M. Guttentag of the Federal Reserve Bank of New York and reproduced in Leo Grebler, *Housing Issues in Economic Stabilization Policy* (New York, National Bureau of Economic Research, 1960), Occasional Paper No. 72, p. 117; Municipal bond yield, *The Daily Bond Buyer;* Net new issues of corporate bonds, Securities and Exchange Commission; Net issues of municipal bonds and all mortgages, Board of Governors of Federal Reserve System, "Flow-of-Funds Accounts."

spective, it would seem unwise for the central bank to depend on speculators to do its work for it. As Culbertson has pointed out, "Things may be different next time; speculation is an unreliable servant." [9]

Some critics of "bills only" argued that the excessive ease created in the short-term markets in 1958 encouraged the financing of speculative positions in bonds and thus contributed to the ensuing bond market collapse. The suggestion has been made that "this development could probably have been prevented or at least mitigated by appropriate operations in long-term securities." [10] "Appropriate operations" must be construed as purchases of bonds because sales of bonds would have kept bond yields up at or above the criticized levels. But if purchases of bonds are meant, difficulties arise. It is true that bond purchases would have brought long-term yields down while permitting less downward pressure on bill yields, thus narrowing the yield spread and creating less short-term ease. But Federal Reserve bond purchases surely would have reinforced speculators' convictions that bond prices were going still higher and thus would have encouraged the speculative demand for bonds. It is not clear that there would have been less bond speculation in 1958 if the Federal Reserve had bought some bonds rather than "bills only." However, the contention that "bills only" led to excessive ease in the short-term market in 1958 focused on a critical objection to "bills only."

TENDENCY OF "BILLS ONLY" TO DEVELOP EXCESSIVE LIQUIDITY There is considerable reason to believe that with arbitrage imperfect, "bills only" operations may require an excessive amount of ease in short-term markets in order to achieve a desired response in the long-term market. Appropriate money conditions in the capital market are an important objective if such key sectors of the economy as plant and equipment investment, home building, and state and local government public works are to be influenced so as to contribute to economic stability. But influencing long-term interest rates indirectly by easing bank reserve positions, increasing the money supply, and lowering short-term interest rates is precisely most difficult when the need is greatest—that is, when market conditions are disturbed, con-

[9] Culbertson,"A Positive Debt Management Program," *Review of Economics and Statistics,* XLI (May, 1959), 91, footnote 4.

[10] Warren Smith, "Monetary Policy, 1957–1960: An Appraisal," *Review of Economics and Statistics,* XLII (August, 1960), 271.

fidence is low, and liquidity preference is accordingly increased. Under such circumstances, it may require a great deal of money creation and exceedingly low short-term rates of interest before liquidity preference is satisfied and the availability of funds is increased for long-term borrowers.

The New York Federal Reserve Bank suggested, for example, that the use of "bills only" open-market purchases in May–June, 1953, to calm incipient panic in the bond market resulted in the creation of a much easier bank reserve position than was necessary, and that direct purchases of bonds would have reassured the market more effectively and more economically. This criticism seems well taken.[11]

The most important practical aspect of the tendency for "bills only" purchases to create excessive liquidity, however, has to do with Federal Reserve efforts to combat recession. If "bills only" purchases resulted in the creation of too much liquidity in recessions, the Federal Reserve could have considerable difficulty in applying credit restraint in the next business recovery. All or most of the excess liquidity then would have to be absorbed before borrowers and lenders felt the "bite" of monetary restraint. In this way, "bills only" would be striking at the Federal Reserve's effectiveness in one of its most important objectives: economic stabilization.

It is, therefore, highly significant that there seems to be a substantial measure of agreement that a "bills only" monetary policy did create too much liquidity in combating the recessions of 1954 and 1958. With regard to 1954, one major money market bank commented in late April of that year:

> The stabilizing trends in the business situation, and the active absorption of credit in construction, led some observers to question the wisdom of another shot of easy money at this time.
>
> It is a question whether, in trying to make money still easier, long-run dangers do not counterbalance short-term benefits. . . . The law of diminishing returns applies to repeated dosages of easy money. And surplus

[11] The Federal Reserve Board has argued in rebuttal that in May-June, 1953, the markets had had little experience with, or understanding of, the "bills only" policy and thus implied that with more experience of "bills only" the market might have been calmed with more moderate bill purchases. Flanders Committee, *1954 Hearings*, p. 16. It is significant, however, that two and one-half years later when the money market tightened unexpectedly in December, 1955, during a Treasury refunding, the Federal Open Market Committee departed from "bills only" and supported the market by buying the new Treasury issue (2⅝ percent certificates) directly on a when-issued basis with the proviso that the volume of funds to be so supplied should not exceed what was already scheduled to be released on credit policy grounds.

funds are easier to put in than to take out, as the experiences of 1927–29, 1933–37, and 1942–53, so well demonstrate.[12]

Warren Smith, reviewing the 1953–1954 experience several years later, concluded:

During the 1953–54 recession, the banking system was supplied with a very large quantity of reserves—more than was really necessary, in my opinion. The excessively liquid condition of the banking system—especially the large holdings of short-term Government securities—proved to be a severe handicap to the Federal Reserve in the ensuing period of inflation. If the banks had been somewhat less liquid than they were at the end of 1954, it is possible that the Federal Reserve would have been more effective in restraining the expansion of bank loans in 1955–57.[13]

Even the Federal Reserve admitted that excessive liquidity was created in 1954. The twelve Federal Reserve Bank presidents, in their joint reply to the Senate Finance Committee's investigation of the financial condition of the United States in 1957, said:

There is some question . . . whether the policy of ease was carried too far in 1954, when a combination of open market operations and reductions in discount rates and reserve requirements pushed available reserves of member banks to high levels and short-term interest rates to exceedingly low levels.[14]

Reserve Board Chairman Martin was more emphatic in making the same point in his testimony:

In the inventory recession of 1953–54, we pursued a policy . . . of adjusting promptly, to make the inventory adjustment as orderly as possible, by easing money.

By the end of 1953 and the early part of 1954, I personally think that we were overdoing it a bit. We were using the phrase "active ease." . . . and I think in retrospect that one of the errors we made was that in 1954, when the adjustments that were being made by the market were cumulating and the base was being laid for the recovery that we had, we got a little bit enthusiastic about increasing the money supply, and we lowered our discount rate in February of 1954 from 2 to 1¾ percent; and then we lowered it again to 1½ per cent in April of that year.[15]

With regard to excessive liquidity in 1958, *The Treasury-Federal Reserve Study of the Government Securities Market* reported that many respondents to its questionnaire were "critical of the Federal

[12] First National City Bank of New York, *Monthly Letter*, May, 1954, pp. 53, 55.

[13] U.S. Congress, Joint Economic Committee, *The Relationship of Prices to Economic Stability and Growth, Compendium*, 85th Cong., 2d Sess., 1958, p. 511. Cited hereafter as Joint Committee, *1958 Prices Compendium*.

[14] Byrd Committee, *1958 Compendium*, p. 44.

[15] Byrd Committee, *1957 Hearings*, Pt. III, pp. 1304–5.

Reserve System for creating a degree of ease in bank reserve positions in the spring of 1958 that they regarded as excessive." [16] Reserve Board Chairman Martin told the Congressional Joint Economic Committee in 1959 that he too thought short-term yields had been eased too much in 1958.

> Talking about the money supply, money supply for several months in there was rising at the rate of 8 per cent and 12 per cent, if you include time deposits in it. We were doing everything we could, so far as the money stream was concerned, to facilitate the stabilization of and assistance to the economy.
>
> I think the bill rate got too low during that period. We cannot set those rates.[17]

In the course of the same Congressional hearings, Roosa, representing the Federal Reserve Bank of New York, expressed the opinion that only the fact that the Treasury had been simultaneously funding short-term debt into long-term maturities had prevented an even more excessive degree of liquidity from developing.

> I . . . believe, sitting here now with the benefit of all the hindsight that that permits, that the result of that Treasury action [long-term debt issues] was useful, that it prevented an excessive spreading of liquidity at a time when the System was putting in too much. . . . The fact that they [Treasury officials] were issuing them provided the offsetting pressure in the long-term market which avoided an undue seepage of liquidity through the economy that might otherwise have left us with a residue that would have been very hard to manage when the recovery came about.[18]

There seems to be very little doubt that monetary policy did create too much liquidity in the 1954 and 1958 recessions and that the policy of "bills only" was a major reason why this happened. For, as noted earlier, the way "bills only" works is to saturate the short-term markets with funds and then allow some of the excess liquidity to seep into all other sectors of the market. And it is also clear that much of the difficulty which monetary policy had in imposing restraint on the economy in a timely fashion can be traced to the necessity to absorb such excess liquidity before restrictive measures could take effective hold.

Thus while open market operations, restricted to "bills only," were able to ease the capital markets sufficiently to stimulate long-term borrowing and spending and to reverse recessionary trends, the price

16 *Ibid.*, Pt. I, p. 10.
17 *1959 Employment Hearings*, Pt. 6A, pp. 1285–86.
18 *Ibid.*, p. 1297.

was the creation of so much liquidity as to severely impair the ability of monetary policy to restrict credit in succeeding periods of business recovery and expansion.

EXCESSIVE LIQUIDITY AND THE GOLD OUTFLOW. Toward the end of the 1953–1959 period there was a new concern that "bills only" might not only complicate Federal Reserve efforts to control the economy in recovery periods but also limit its ability to combat recession. The problem arose out of the change in the international position of the United States, which brought substantial balance of payments deficits and new record amounts of short-term dollar balances held by foreign central banks, treasuries, businesses, and individuals. In these circumstances, the excessive liquidity and exceedingly low short-term rates of interest associated with "bills only" efforts to combat economic recession in the United States could adversely affect the willingness of foreign investors to keep their funds invested in short-term dollar investments or to put new dollar earnings into such short-term investments. The alternative for these foreign investors is to demand gold for their dollar earnings.[19] And when the United States gold stock declines, other things equal, member bank reserve balances are reduced correspondingly, thus tightening reserve positions at a time when, in the interests of combating recession, they should be eased. Moreover, apart from the direct impact on bank reserve positions, any substantial outflow of gold from the United States stimulates talk of dollar devaluation and, whether justified or not, this has adverse psychological effects on confidence both in the United States and abroad.[20]

The Federal Reserve can act to offset the gold drain's impact on bank reserve positions and thus maintain a given degree of ease in the domestic money market. But if the needed reserve funds are supplied by purchases of "bills only" the result would be to put further downward pressure on Treasury bill and other short-term yields and thus make short-term dollar investments even less attractive to

[19] Actually, only central banks and treasuries may demand gold but if private holders of dollar balances sell them in the exchange markets, the practice of keeping the dollar exchange rate within some fixed limits results in the acquisition of the dollars by the foreign central bank or treasury.

[20] The effects can be more than psychological, of course. The typical predevaluation behavior of foreign businessmen—to pay slowly but to require payment for their shipments extra rapidly—can build up a nation's balance of payments deficit extremely rapidly in the short-term.

foreign investors. This in turn risks increasing the drain of gold abroad.

The dimensions of the problem became evident in 1958 when the sharp drop in short-term rates of interest was accompanied by a gold outflow which began in mid-February and which totaled no less than $2.3 billion by the end of the year. In 1959, with interest rates much higher, the gold outflow tended to slow down, though there was some acceleration in the middle six months which may have reflected foreign fears that Congressional desires for low interest rates might lead to adoption of unsound monetary policies by the Federal Reserve. Renewal of a substantial rate of gold outflow came in mid-1960 when, with the economy slowing down, the Federal Reserve lowered its discount rate from 4 to 3½ percent at about the same time the Bank of England raised its discount rate from 5 to 6 percent. Reflecting investors' dissatisfaction with short-term yields here, and the pull of 5 to 6 percent bill rates in England, the gold outflow increased from a nominal $134 million in the first six months of 1960 to almost $1 billion from June to October.

Although it had retained "bills only" during the 1958 gold drain, the Federal Reserve acted quickly in 1960 once it became clear that another major gold movement was underway. In the week ending November 2, 1960, the Federal Open Market Committee made its third major departure from "bills only" since the policy was adopted in 1953. To supply needed reserve funds, the Open Market Committee bought, in addition to $315 million Treasury bills, $12 million certificates, $5 million notes, and $57 million short-term bonds. An official revealed that all the securities purchased had maturities within one year. While these purchases were not large and no purchases of long-term Government securities were involved, this was clearly a move away from a long-established policy.

While the Federal Reserve made no public announcement of the reasons for the departure from "bills only," news reports, evidently based on discussions with informed officials, said:

Indications are that the System broadened the range of its security purchases in the open market in order not to drive down bill yields, which would tend to stimulate the outflow of gold. . . . A further decline in bill yields, observers noted, would tend to increase the already wide disparity between short-term interest rates here and in Europe. The higher rates obtainable in London and other overseas centers has encouraged a flow of investment money out of the U.S., thus accelerating the outflow of U.S. gold to foreign lands.[21]

On February 20, 1961, the Federal Reserve announced officially:

The System Open Market Account is purchasing in the open market U.S. Government notes and bonds of varying maturities, some of which will exceed five years.

Authority for transactions in securities of longer maturity has been granted by the Open Market Committee of the Federal Reserve System in the light of conditions that have developed in the domestic economy and in the U.S. balance of payments with other countries.[22]

This brief review of experience with "bills only," in periods when the aim of monetary policy was to ease the credit markets, lends strong support to the critics' view that "bills only" importantly hampered the effectiveness of monetary policy. The indirect way in which it affected the long-term markets led to the creation of excessive liquidity in the short-term markets in order to get adequate response in the long-term area. This in turn made the Federal Reserve's task of controlling the expansions which follow recession substantially more difficult. In recent years the presence of a large United States balance of payments deficits and substantial foreign short-term dollar balances, which are sensitive to short-term interest rates, made "bills only" and the excessive liquidity which it tends to create especially inappropriate.

RECORD OF "BILLS ONLY" IN PERIODS OF CREDIT RESTRAINT

It is possible to find a number of instances in which "bills only" open market operations directed toward credit restraint either had inadequate influence over long-term rates of interest or had too much impact. In either case, monetary policy did not achieve the effects it sought. In reviewing the experience during periods of credit restraint, it must be borne in mind that the issue is whether the long-term Government securities market responded to what current monetary policy *was,* not what it *should have been.* This reminder is necessary because there have been periods, such as June, 1954, to December, 1954, when Treasury bond yields showed almost no response to sub-

---

[21] The *Wall Street Journal,* November 4, 1960, p. 26.
[22] *Federal Reserve Bulletin,* XLVII (February, 1961), p. 165.

stantial rise in yields on Treasury bills, but these have also been periods when the Federal Open Market Committee had not yet decided to impose credit restraint.

The first illustration of an apparently faulty response of long-term Government bond yields to increased restraint in the short-term market is provided by the entire year of 1955. During the first five months of the year the economy was still recovering from the 1954 recession, and the Open Market Committee, while allowing credit demands to tighten the markets somewhat, was still aiming at encouraging the recovery rather than at credit restraint. Consistent with this moderate approach, yields on Treasury bills rose 0.32 percentage points (from 1.17 in December, 1954, to 1.49 percent in May, 1955). However, the reaction of long-term Treasury bond yields was not at all moderate, and they rose 0.22 percentage points (from 2.59 to 2.81 percent), or two-thirds of the increase in bill yields. While this percentage rise in yields may not seem large, it was equivalent to a four point drop in price on a seventeen year 2½ percent bond. It seems questionable that so large an impact on the bond market was consciously intended by the authorities.

For the balance of the year and into January, 1956, however, the long-term Treasury market showed almost no response to substantial increases in Treasury bill yields, even though the Federal Open Market Committee had decided in May that recovery had been achieved and that credit restraint was thereafter appropriate. The discount rate was raised from 1¾ percent to 2½ percent by the end of the year, and bank reserve positions were tightened substantially (the position going from free reserves of $212 million in May, 1955, to net borrowed reserves of $255 million in January, 1956), and these actions were reflected in a rise of almost 1 percentage point in Treasury bill yields (from 1.49 percent in May, 1955, to 2.46 percent in January, 1956). But long-term Treasury bond yields rose only 0.07 percentage points (from 2.81 to 2.88 percent) in the same period.

Thus, in 1955 there was the curious spectacle of monetary policy having a large impact on the bond market in the early months of the year when policy was still relatively easy and having only a small impact later in the year when definite credit restraint was being sought. It is hard to avoid the conclusion that such erratic reactions to policy are not consistent with the achievement of policy goals. It should be noted that the failure of the bond market to tighten in the latter part of 1955 permitted savings banks and insurance companies to sell $716 million Government securities from May, 1955, to January, 1956, the proceeds being used to extend credit to private borrowers.

The first half of 1956, from January to July, was a period in which monetary policy tended to temporize, influenced by fears that business was weakening. Accordingly, the existing policy of restraint was modified to "take into account any deflationary tendencies in the economy." [23] Treasury bill yields declined about ⅛ percentage point (from 2.46 to 2.33 percent) while long-term Government bond yields rose ⅛ (from 2.88 to 3.00 percent). While probably both these reactions could be regarded as consistent with a monetary policy which essentially was marking time, the downward drift of 91-day bill yields presumably reflected more closely the intentions of the Open Market Committee. The rise in long-term yields essentially reflected the impact of the continuing heavy sales of Governments by banks and insurance companies. To this extent, it might be said that "bills only" had failed to transmit credit-policy intentions effectively to the long-term markets.[24]

The second example of ineffective control of the bond market through "bills only" open market operations is provided by the period from June, 1956—when the Open Market Committee took a definite stand to the effect that significantly increased restraint would be necessary to control inflation—to September, 1957—when the Open Market Committee decided that further intensification of restraint would be unwise.[25] It was in this period that the bond market's sensitivity to credit restraint suddenly seemed to increase substantially. Indeed, it surprised and alarmed the members of the Open

[23] Board of Governors of the Federal Reserve System, *Annual Report,* 1956, p. 19.

[24] With benefit of hindsight it is, of course, fortunate that bond yields did not fall in the first half of 1956. This would have given sellers of securities an even more receptive market than they had, at a time when the economy was only pausing in its upward thrust. But from the standpoint of effective credit policy, the question is whether the authorities can effectuate their best judgment, not whether they are right.

[25] Board of Governors of the Federal Reserve System, *Annual Report,* 1956, pp. 35–36 and 1957, pp. 50–51.

Market Committee who, perhaps, had expected the insensitivity of late 1955 and early 1956 to persist.[26] Thus, while yields on 91-day Treasury bills rose 1.05 percentage points (from 2.53 to 3.58 percent) from June, 1956, to September, 1957, long-term Treasury bond yields moved up 0.73 percentage points (from 2.93 to 3.66 percent), corporate bond yields (new issues) rose 1.12 percentage points (from 3.56 to 4.68 percent) and municipal bond yields (tax exempt) increased 0.99 percentage points (from 2.55 to 3.54 percent). These yield increases meant price declines of something like 8 points on a seventeen-year Treasury 2½, 18 points on a thirty-year public utility 3½, and 9 points on a ten-year tax exempt state or municipal 3 percent obligation. Capital losses and yield increases of these dimensions were evidently more than was sought so late in the expansion period (industrial production stopped rising in June, 1957, and turned down in September), for the authorities took action late in 1956 to cushion the impact on the capital market.[27]

However, the Open Market Committee's attempt to relax pressure temporarily in the money and capital market in the fall of 1956 was unsuccessful. "Bills only" proved incapable of exercising the quick influence which is extremely important in periods of crisis. As Riefler admitted, "many rates remained firm despite an easing in the reserve position." [28] The member bank net borrowed reserves position was eased from a figure of $195 million (borrowings from the Federal Reserve Banks beyond excess reserves held) in October, 1956, to only $37 million in December, 1956, but yields on 91-day Treasury bills rose from 2.96 percent to 3.23 percent, and long-term Treasury bond yields rose from 3.20 to 3.40 percent. It was not until the second half of December and early January that the tension in the capital markets subsided, and then only because "free" excess reserves (excess reserves above borrowings from the Federal Reserve Banks) running into the hundreds of millions had appeared for several successive weeks. At this point the market swung from fears of panic to expectations of easier credit policies, higher bond prices and economic recession. The authorities then had to spend some

[26] *Ibid.,* 1956, pp. 42, 44, 45.
[27] *Ibid.,* pp. 43–44.
[28] Riefler, "Open Market Operations in Long-Term Securities," *Federal Reserve Bulletin,* XLIV, p. 1269.

months regaining the desired climate of restraint. In this case, it was "bills only," not the absence of it, which gave rise to unsettling and unwarranted market expectations and complicated the task of monetary policy.

The third time "bills only" was called into question as an effective tool of credit restraint began in June, 1958, when the bond market collapsed under the weight of speculation and sagged almost continuously into September. The decline became so rapid as to be characterized as a "disorderly market" and the Open Market Committee on July 18 made its second major departure from "bills only" in order to steady the market. However, of the $1,265 million securities other than Treasury bills purchased in this operation, $1,200 million were short-term issues directly connected with a Treasury refunding of certificates and bonds maturing August 1 and September 15. Only $65 million of the purchases were longer-term in nature and by July 24 the Open Market Committee had re-established the "bills only" policy even though bond prices continued to decline into September.

From June to September, yields on long-term Treasury bonds rose more than ½ percentage point (from 3.19 percent in June to 3.75 percent in September), an increase unequalled in any other comparably short period. Yet it deserves emphasis that during the first two months of the period, the Federal Open Market Committee's policy was not devoted to restraint but rather to "contributing further by monetary ease to resumption of stable growth in the economy." [29] Some shift away from "ease" came in late July and August but in the Open Market Committee directive of August 19 the aim was still "fostering conditions in the money market conducive to balanced economic recovery." [30] The question asked by a number of observers was, of course, whether such a sharp rise in bond yields was consistent with these objectives. Warren Smith commented:

It seems to me that it was foolhardy to have permitted interest rates to rise to such high levels so early in the period of recovery, when investment had shown no signs of revival. It is interesting to note that the pickup in plant and equipment expenditures during the present recovery

[29] Board of Governors of the Federal Reserve System, *Annual Report,* 1958, pp. 48–56.
[30] *Ibid.,* pp. 57–63.

period has been noticeably less rapid than during the recoveries of 1950 and 1954–55. One wonders if this is due to the sharp rise in interest rates early in the recovery period.[31]

It seems apparent that the "bills only" policy created a dilemma for the authorities that they could not solve. The recovery in business called for some restraint on bank reserve positions but the concurrent near-panic drop in bond prices called for some easing action to reassure the bond market. The compromise adopted—delaying restraint on bank reserve positions—permitted the banks and the economy to retain the excessive liquidity which had been built up by "bills only" credit-easing actions but did little to help the bond market. The direct purchases of bonds that were made after suspension of "bills only" came too late and were too modest to be effective.

Although it did not seem feasible to the Open Market Committee, there was a possibility of slowing the rise in bond yields while at the same time recapturing reserve funds from the market. The avenue was to use a massive swap operation, buying intermediate and long-term bonds while at the same time selling a slightly larger amount of Treasury bills. This would probably have been considerably more effective than the actual purchases of $1,200 million one-year certificates, when issued, and $65 million notes and long-term bonds when "bills only" was suspended. Indeed, if investors had been given reason to think that the Federal Reserve was concerned about rates rising too rapidly, the Treasury's refunding offer of 1⅝ percent certificates might have seemed reasonably attractive and might not have required the massive direct support which nevertheless left it a failure. But any such operation was precluded by the commitment to "bills only." As Sproul had pointed out in 1954:

Among other things, this excludes offsetting purchases and sales (even swaps) of securities which have the effect of altering the maturity pattern of the System's portfolio, and excludes purchases (and sales) which might be made at times of Treasury financing in direct furtherance of an integrated program of debt management and credit policy.[32]

It may be noted that some of the bonds that might have been added to the Federal Reserve's portfolio in such a swap operation could have been released back into the market in the final months of 1958 and first six or nine months of 1959. In a sense, the goal

[31] Warren Smith, *Review of Economics and Statistics*, XLII, 271.
[32] Sproul, "Central Banks and Money Markets," p. 4.

would have been to redistribute the rise in yields over time, not to prevent it. As it actually happened Treasury bond yields held steady around 3¾ percent in the final quarter of 1958, even though bill yields rose from 2.48 percent in September to 2.81 percent in December. And in 1959 the inability of the Treasury to issue long-term bonds because of the legal limit prohibiting payment of more than 4¼ percent interest sheltered the Treasury bond market to some degree, and provided a natural opportunity for Federal Reserve bond sales in some moderate amounts.

In 1958, as in the earlier periods of recovery and expansion, the response of the long-term market to "bills only" operations was almost the opposite to what it should have been. Bond yields rose relatively most in periods when credit policy was still expansive or neutral and showed little or no response to impulses in the short-term markets at times when credit policy was actively restrictive, and when some greater degree of restraint in the capital markets would hence have been desirable.

EQUITY CONSIDERATIONS. "Bills only" may also have increased the inequity in the impact of credit restrictive measures as between banks and nonbank financial intermediaries, reduced the ability of general monetary controls to reach the nonbank intermediaries, and thus reduced the effectiveness of credit restraint. There has been considerable criticism that the growing importance of nonbank financial intermediaries, which create credit in competition with the banking system but which are not subject to direct control by the Federal Reserve, has left monetary policy with direct influence over only a shrinking portion of the financial mechanism, the commercial banks. Therefore, the argument goes, monetary policy either must lose overall effectiveness or must be applied with unusual and discriminatory severity on the banks. Gurley and Shaw said:

> The authorities today limit the growth of a relatively diminishing segment of this system, making the job of regulating terms of lending correspondingly more difficult.
>
> We are not arguing that general monetary controls cannot do the job at all, simply that the job has to be done with outmoded instruments. The situation today in monetary policy would be similar to that of fiscal policy if long ago we had imposed an income tax only on the agricultural sector of the economy. The shrinkage of the agricultural sector relative to other sectors of the economy would render this control a decreasingly efficient instrument of fiscal policy. Rapid expansion of spending by

other sectors would necessitate higher tax rates on an agricultural sector that was of diminishing importance relative to the whole. The job could be done perhaps, but the growth of the agricultural sector would have to be greatly slowed down to balance the rapid growth elsewhere.[33]

This criticism gained all the more force, of course, when the Federal Reserve was limiting itself to a policy of "bills only." Open market operations in all maturities could have brought monetary policy into direct contact with the nonbank financial intermediaries via their portfolio operations in the capital market. This was part of Roosa's conception in suggesting a broad scope for open market operations, and Shaw recognized the promise of this approach before the Flanders Subcommittee.[34]

Commercial bankers echoed the Gurley-Shaw criticism and expressed resentment at being singled out as the main direct target of credit restraint because it impaired their competitive position vis a vis the relatively immune nonbank lenders. S. Clark Beise, president of the Bank of America, said in 1956 that a restrictive monetary policy "has tended to drain business away from the banking system . . . and has tended to deflect it to institutions that are not directly subject to such [credit policy] decisions." [35] Beise went on to suggest that nonbank financial intermediaries be subjected to reserve requirements similar to those imposed on commercial banks, that tax treatment of all financial institutions be made more uniform, and that borrowings by savings and loan associations from the Federal Home Loan Banks "be governed by the same ground rules and policies as commercial bank borrowings from the Federal Reserve Banks." [36]

"Bills only," by concentrating the impact of monetary policy on the banks and the short-term money market, increased the likelihood that bankers would object on grounds of inequitable discrimination at the same time that it required great pressure in the short-term market (because of reliance on imperfect market arbitrage to transmit policy actions from short to long-term markets). Whether this

[33] Gurley and Shaw, "Financial Growth and Monetary Controls," pp. 16–17.

[34] *Ibid.* Later in the "bills only" period, Shaw came to believe that direct controls on nonbank intermediaries may be a requirement for effective monetary control of their activities.

[35] S. Clark Beise, Remarks before the Economic Club of New York, as reported in the *Wall Street Journal* and the New York *Herald Tribune,* November 20, 1956.

[36] *Ibid.*

built-in dilemma made the Federal Reserve authorities oversensitive to criticisms of excessive tightness in the short-term markets and impairment of the competitive position of commercial banks is impossible for an outside observer to say. However, two things are clear. First, most observers agreed that there was inadequate control over nonbank financial intermediaries and the capital markets. Angell said

[the nonbank financial] institutions involved, which are now the biggest collectors and investors of capital funds, can and do escape in appreciable degree, at least for substantial periods, from the types of restraint which the Federal Reserve has sought to impose at intervals since 1951. The effect has certainly been to retard and even prevent contractions in the monetary demand of their customers for investment goods, which might otherwise have taken place; and I believe the effect has also been positively expansionary.[37]

Second, whatever the reason, Reserve Board Chairman Martin on several occasions expressed the opinion that Federal Reserve policies had not made money tight enough in periods of credit restraint; that in general the Federal Reserve had erred on the side of ease. He told the House Ways and Means Committee in June, 1959, "I do want to point out that in eight years of experience in the Federal Reserve System, I am convinced that our bias, if anything, has been on the side of too much money rather than too little." [38] This repeated at greater length an opinion he had given to the Joint Economic Committee in January, 1957. At that time he said:

If we had the whole period to go through again, I think I would be inclined toward having a little bit more restriction in monetary policy from the latter part of 1954 to date. If we had been more restrictive, we would have had more influence, not that monetary and credit policy is the only thing, but it would have been a more stabilizing force in the economy.[39]

CONCLUSION: "BILLS ONLY" AND EFFECTIVENESS
OF MONETARY POLICY

Given imperfect arbitrage in the securities markets, there were a number of theoretical reasons why confining open market operations

[37] Byrd Committee, *1958 Compendium,* p. 528.
[38] U. S. Congress, House, Committee on Ways and Means, *Public Debt Ceiling and Interest Rate Ceiling on Bonds, Hearings,* 86th Cong., 2d Sess., 1960, p. 185.
[39] U.S. Congress, Joint Economic Committee, *Hearings on the January 1957 Economic Report of the President,* 85th Cong., 1st Sess., 1957, p. 257.

to "bills only" could have made monetary policy less effective than it could and should have been. In fact, the years of experience with "bills only" provide a number of illustrations of how the effectiveness of monetary policy was impaired. First, and perhaps most important, the "bills only" policy resulted in the creation of excessive liquidity during recessions, hampering the effectiveness of restrictive credit policy in the ensuing recoveries. Second, as large balance of payments deficits resulted in substantial and growing foreign holdings of short-term dollar investments sensitive to interest rate movements, the Federal Reserve was unable to take adequate credit easing measures to combat recession through "bills only," operations because of the extreme declines in short-term interest rates which this policy involved. Third, the "bills only" policy denied the central bank the ability to influence long and short-term interest rates to different degrees, or to influence them in different directions. This was a serious restriction when a crisis in the bond market called for action different from what was needed to deal with general business conditions or when international considerations limited the ability to manipulate short-term rates of interest. Fourth, in periods of credit restraint, incomplete market arbitrage led to several instances in which the behavior of bond yields was inappropriate when judged by current credit policy actions in the short-term market via "bills only." Reactions were sometimes perverse or inadequate; bond yields rose most, relative to changes in bill yields, during periods when only moderate effects were apparently being sought, and least when real restraint seemed to be the goal. Finally, the policy of concentrating pressures on the short-term market via "bills only" operations gave rise to complaints of inequity and possibly led the Federal Reserve authorities to moderate monetary policy more than would have been appropriate on purely economic grounds.

In short, it is difficult to escape the conclusion that the "bills only" policy was responsible for a significant impairment of the effectiveness of monetary policy. Its abandonment in the autumn of 1960 and winter of 1961 was long overdue.

VII

THE USE OF THE DISCOUNT MECHANISM

AT THE SAME TIME that the Federal Reserve Board was narrowing the scope of open-market operations, it was attempting to make the discount mechanism a major tool of monetary policy.[1] The contrast meant no contradiction in basic policy, however. Both decisions were consistent with the Federal Reserve Board's preference for restricting itself to traditional methods of credit control, for giving free market forces maximum scope, and for affecting the volume rather than the cost of credit. Discounting, after all, was the traditional way in which central banks had exerted influence over the money market. Moveover, since discounting is done at the request of member banks, it gives private market forces the primary initiative. And, in at least the early stages of the post-Accord revival of the discount mechanism, the Federal Reserve authorities evidently envisaged its main importance as lying in the volume of funds borrowed rather than in the rate charged on the borrowings.

The Federal Reserve soon found that its ambitious conception of

[1] Under the discount mechanism the Federal Reserve Banks make short-term loans to their member banks on the security of eligible commercial paper or (more important in recent years) on the security of Treasury securities at a rate of interest—the discount rate—which is changed from time to time in accordance with the economic situation and credit conditions. See, Board of Governors of the Federal Reserve System, *The Federal Reserve System, Purposes and Functions* (Washington, D.C., 1954), Ch. III. When the Federal Reserve Act was enacted in 1913 the discount mechanism and rate were regarded as the principal, if not the only, instrument of monetary policy. During the 1920s, discounting remained important though open market operations assumed increasing prominence. However, during the Great Depression of the 1930s discounting dropped to negligible levels, reflecting the shrinkage of credit demands and the vast rise in banks' excess reserves which accompanied the heavy gold inflow from abroad. Discounting remained insignificant during World War II, since the Federal Reserve's readiness to buy or sell Treasury bills on a ⅜ percent yield basis gave banks access to all the reserve funds they needed, and showed only slight increase in the postwar years up to 1951 when the Accord freed the Federal Reserve from its obligation to support Treasury bond prices.

the discount mechanism was not consistent with an effective execution of monetary policy, and it adopted a more modest view of the role discounting could fill. However, a number of academic economists rejected this solution; their conceptions of the discount mechanism's position ranged from the idea that it ought to be the most important weapon of monetary policy to the idea that discounting should be abolished entirely. The balance of this chapter describes the post-1951 experience with the discount mechanism and the varying conceptions of discounting, evaluates the experience and theoretical proposals, and draws conclusions as to the proper role of the discount mechanism in the central bank's array of monetary instruments.

FEDERAL RESERVE ATTITUDES TOWARD DISCOUNTING

Almost as soon as the 1951 Accord enabled it to pursue a flexible monetary policy, the Federal Reserve moved to rehabilitate the discount mechanism.[2] The records of the Federal Open Market Committee reveal that by March, 1952

the [Federal Reserve] System contemplated that principal reliance for additional Federal Reserve credit, to support increased bank loans and investments, would be placed on member bank borrowings from the Federal Reserve Banks and that open market operations would be limited as much as possible to supplying such additional demands as might be necessary to avoid undue restraint.[3]

That this was no momentary aberration is apparent from the Federal Reserve Board's *Annual Report* for 1953 which commented:

During the preceding two years, the Federal Reserve has moved toward greater reliance on influencing the cost, availability, and supply of credit through the discount mechanism, that is by making it necessary for member banks to borrow from the Federal Reserve Banks a portion of the additional reserves required to meet credit growth. This mechanism limits credit expansion, puts pressure on banks, and makes them more responsive to changes in the discount rate.[4]

Giving the results of this approach, the Board commented:

The general level of [bank] borrowings rose from less than half a billion dollars in the first half of 1952 to more than a billion dollars during the

[2] The Accord itself provided for revival of the discount mechanism since it envisaged that "banks would depend upon borrowing at the Federal Reserve to make needed adjustments in their reserves." See Patman Committee, *Compendium*, Pt. I, p. 75.

[3] Board of Governors of the Federal Reserve System, *Annual Report*, 1952, p. 91.

[4] *Ibid.*, 1953, p. 87.

last half of the year. Average borrowing in December (1.6 billion dollars) was the largest since 1921.[5]

While the Federal Reserve authorities were taking action to insure that discounting became more important, their policy statements put so much emphasis on the discount mechanism as to make it appear that the more powerful tool of open market operations had importance only as a means of forcing member banks to borrow at the discount window. Federal Reserve Board Chairman Martin described the two instruments in April, 1953, as follows:

Open market operations and the discount rate are again being used . . . as twin reserve banking measures, each complementing the other in affecting the availability, volume, and cost of credit.

Primary reliance is once more placed upon the discount mechanism as a means for supplying the variable short-term needs of individual banks for reserves. . . .

Open market operations can be employed when needed to condition the current tone in credit markets and the general availability of credit. By these operations the Federal Reserve can tighten or ease the pressure on member bank reserve positions and thus cause banks to borrow or enable them to reduce borrowings at the Reserve Banks. Subsequently, this tightness or ease is transmitted and magnified in money and credit markets.[6]

This early view of the discount mechanism leaned heavily on the volume of borrowing and relatively little on the discount rate itself as the significant factor in making credit restraint effective. When the volume of borrowing is high, some students have argued, credit restraint is increased because member banks are reluctant to be indebted and therefore immediately take steps to repay their borrowings. These steps may involve sales of portfolio securities, less willingness to make new loans, or (rarely) demands for repayment of old loans; but in every case the result is either decreased availability of credit or increased interest rates, and hence increased credit restraint. The discount rate was granted some importance as a means of making borrowing more expensive or of signaling a change in credit policy, but these were secondary considerations. As Roosa put it in 1952:

the very existence of a substantial volume of discounting becomes in time a powerful cause of bank credit restraint. It is in this way, rather than through the solitary fact of an increase in discount rate itself, that the

[5] *Ibid.*, p. 82.
[6] *Federal Reserve Bulletin*, XXXIX (April, 1953), 334.

discount mechanism has been restored to first rank importance in the methodology of U.S. central banking.[7]

Thus, Simmons has commented: "It is quite clear that in reactivating the discount mechanism a deliberate choice was made to rely heavily on nonprice rationing to control the amount of lending by the central bank." [8]

Substantial difficulties in this approach, though long recognized, were apparently underestimated by the Federal Reserve authorities. In the first place, the idea that a large volume of discounts is "restrictive" is by no means self-evident and can be justified only by a rather complex argument which depends particularly on the assumption that banks are reluctant to borrow from the Federal Reserve. The fact is, as many critics pointed out, that discounting supplies additional reserve funds to the banking system and in itself this is expansive, not restrictive. But this initial expansive effect, the Federal Reserve argued, is counterbalanced to an important degree by the fact that banks are reluctant to borrow, know that discounts "have a string on them" and must be repaid within a short time, and fear criticism by the Reserve authorities for borrowing too much or too frequently. Accordingly, Reserve officials maintained, almost as soon as discounts have been secured, banks make preparations to repay, and it is these preparations and the accompanying sense of unease among the banks which create the restrictive atmosphere.

In essence, the Federal Reserve authorities were really contending that reserves released through discounting are less expansive than reserves released through open market purchases which carry no obligation to repay. But this obviously did not support the Federal Reserve's oft expressed implication that a large volume of discounts in itself is restrictive.

Moreover, the argument puts a very heavy burden on the assumption that member banks are reluctant to borrow. For if they are not, the basis for the creation of a feeling of unease and acceleration of efforts of banks to get out of debt has been undermined. Dispute about the strength of the so-called reluctance to borrow among American banks goes back to the 1920s where it found ex-

[7] Roosa, "Monetary Policy Again," *Bulletin of the Oxford University Institute of Statistics*, XIV (August, 1952), 258.
[8] Simmons, "A Note on the Revival of Federal Reserve Discount Policy," *The Journal of Finance*, XI (December, 1956), 414.

pression in the controversy as to whether banks borrow only when they need funds, or borrow when they see an opportunity to profit from differentials between the cost of borrowing and the return from employment of the borrowed funds.[9] It is generally accepted today that banks do show some reluctance to borrow [10] but that this reluctance is not absolute; if profit opportunities are attractive enough, banks will borrow more reserve funds than would be appropriate for the central bank to release from a credit-policy standpoint. Thus, unless the Federal Reserve could curb borrowing by raising the discount rate or by rationing discounts, it could find that in periods of credit restraint the volume of borrowing would rise to undesirably high levels.

As things worked out, these potential difficulties did develop in late 1952 and early 1953, when the volume of bank borrowings from the Federal Reserve rose as high as $2.2 billion on one day in December, 1952, averaged $1.6 billion during the month, and were still as high as $1.2 billion in April, 1953. In May, Federal Reserve Board Chairman Martin found it necessary to re-emphasize in a speech that borrowing from the Federal Reserve is a privilege and not a right, that banks were expected to try to keep borrowings at a minimum both in amount and duration except in unusual circumstances, and that it was a misuse of the borrowing privilege to employ it for the "purpose of enlarging a bank's capital base, or earning a rate differential, or facilitating speculation of any kind." [11] The Federal Reserve described the difficulties which arose in this period in its reply to the 1954 Flanders Subcommittee:

Under the excess profits tax law then in effect, it was profitable for member banks in excess profits tax brackets to borrow to increase their tax base, and in order to improve their tax situations a few of these banks began to rely on borrowing at the Reserve Bank, rather than on adjustments in asset positions, in maintaining their reserve positions. Some

[9] Harris, *Twenty Years of Federal Reserve Policy*, I, particularly pp. 256–65; also Currie, *The Supply and Control of Money in the United States*, pp. 91–99; Turner, *Member Bank Borrowing*, pp. 67–90; Simmons, "Federal Reserve Discount Rate Policy and Member-Bank Borrowing, 1944–50," *Journal of Business of the University of Chicago*, XXV (January, 1952), 18–29.

[10] Otherwise bank borrowings would have risen much further in periods of credit restraint when borrowing for profit was possible. Whittlesey, "Credit Policy at the Discount Window," *Quarterly Journal of Economics*, LXXIII (May, 1959), 215.

[11] Martin, "Federal Reserve Bank Responsibilities," *Federal Reserve Bulletin*, XXXIX (May, 1953), 453–54.

other banks seemed willing to remain indebted at the Reserve Banks for extended periods in order to profit from differentials between market rates of interest and the discount rate. As these developments became apparent they were dealt with administratively by the Reserve Banks on a case-by-case basis.[12]

Administrative treatment of excessive or prolonged borrowing evidently consisted of telephone calls to or conferences with offending bankers.[13] While effective in bringing down borrowings moderately (from a $1.6 billion average in December, 1952, to $1.2 billion in April, 1953), this approach had extremely unfortunate effects on the money and bond markets. It created fears that the Federal Reserve authorities were "closing the discount window" and refusing to make credit available and thus contributed materially to the money panic psychology which in the spring of 1953 embarrassed Treasury financing and required Federal Reserve support to calm the bond market.[14]

Evidently upset by the experience, the Federal Reserve Board "initiated in 1953 a comprehensive re-examination of its discount function. . . ."[15] While the results of this study have never been made public, they doubtless were reflected in the February, 1955 revision of Federal Reserve Regulation A which governs discounting. The most important change was in the Foreword, or General Principles, of the regulation and was apparently intended to spell out what the Reserve authorities viewed as appropriate and inappropriate grounds for member bank borrowing. After the customary re-

[12] Flanders Committee, *1954 Hearings*, p. 12.

[13] *Business Week,* November 26, 1955, p. 26; Bopp, "Borrowing from the Federal Reserve Bank—Some Basic Principles," Federal Reserve Bank of Philadelphia, *Business Review,* June, 1958, pp. 3–9; and Whittlesey, *Quarterly Journal of Economics,* LXXIII, 210–12.

[14] The First National City Bank of New York, *Monthly Letter,* June, 1953, p. 60, ascribed Treasury financing difficulties to "the Federal Reserve's policy of complaining to banks that borrow too much or too regularly. These criticisms, however well justified they may have been in any particular case, created apprehensions that the Federal Reserve, after policing discounts down, might follow a narrowly restrictive policy this autumn when seasonally-expanding credit requirements have to be met." In retrospect the Bank's *Monthly Letter* for September, 1955, p. 101, said: "Much of the tension built up in the money market in the spring of 1953 was attributable to fears, induced by criticisms of borrowings, that the discount window was being shut down."

[15] Board of Governors of the Federal Reserve System, *Annual Report, 1953,* p. 8.

marks about discounting being a privilege and appropriate only to meet short-term, unexpected needs for funds or unusual situations, the Foreword went on to say:

In considering a request for credit accommodation, each Federal Reserve Bank gives due regard to the purpose of the credit and to its probable effects upon the maintenance of sound credit conditions, both as to the individual institution and the economy generally. It keeps informed of and takes into account the general character and amount of the loans and investments of the member bank. It considers whether the bank is borrowing principally for the purpose of obtaining a tax advantage or profiting from rate differentials and whether the bank is extending an undue amount of credit for the speculative carrying of or trading in securities, real estate, or commodities, or otherwise.[16]

It seems apparent, if the language of this paragraph is compared with Martin's May, 1953, remarks and the Reserve Board's December, 1954 reply to the Flanders Subcommittee, that the main purpose of the 1955 revision of Regulation A was to warn the banks clearly that a repetition of the 1952–1953 borrowing spree would be sternly resisted by the Federal Reserve authorities. But in addition to this warning that nonprice rationing of discounts would be carried out more stringently in the future, the authorities evidently also decided that their task of administering the discount mechanism would be easier if they made more use of the discount rate as an aid to screening requests for accommodation at the discount window. The market's first intimation that the discount rate would become a more active tool of credit policy came in a speech by Sproul:

changes in the discount rates of the Federal Reserve Banks might be made more frequently in such a period [of credit restraint], as the discount window of the Banks again became busy and as interest rates became more sensitive indicators of market pressures. In such circumstances, the discount rate could assume the role of an anchor for the whole structure of interest rates. And eventually it might lose some of its ponderous significance as a symbol while it gained in power as a ready weapon of monetary policy.[17]

Discount-rate changes took place with considerably greater fre-

[16] *Federal Reserve Bulletin,* XLI (January, 1955), 9. The entire text of "Regulation A, Advances and Discounts by Federal Reserve Banks," appears in this issue of the *Bulletin,* pp. 8–14.

[17] "Monetary Policy in Periods of Transition." Remarks at the Sixteenth Annual Pacific Northwest Conference on Banking, Pullman, Washington, April 7, 1955.

quency in 1955 and the following years, and the volume of borrowings never again reached the heights which had been briefly touched in 1952 and 1953 (see Table 5).

Federal Reserve discussions of the power and place of the discount mechanism among the other instruments of monetary policy have been somewhat more restrained since the 1952–1953 excessive borrowing experience. The discount mechanism is now looked upon more as an aid to assuring smooth functioning of the money market than as an aggressive instrument of policy. Thus, a 1957 article by Walker,[18] then economic adviser to the president of the Federal Reserve Bank of Dallas, listed the following five advantages offered by the discount mechanism: (1) It serves best to supply temporary seasonal demands for funds for it insures quick repayment, the amounts released are assessed by those in the best position to estimate requirements—the borrowing banks—and the needed funds go directly to the point of pressure; (2) When the authorities are uncertain of the strength of a revival they can permit discounts to supply needed funds, the build-up of borrowings serving to indicate, at the same time that it only partially satisfies, a growing strength of credit demands; (3) Discounting serves as a safety valve against excessively sharp restraint and thus permits monetary policy to be more restrictive than it might otherwise dare to be; (4) In advancing discount rates, the authorities can probe market reactions by allowing the rate to go up somewhat more in one or two districts; (5) Discount rate changes are an easily understood technique of informing the market of the monetary authorities' views of the economy and the credit situation.[19]

These points are not cited because they are all valid,[20] but because they indicate a more modest and at the same time more realistic view of the potentialities of discounting than was taken initially by the

[18] Walker, "Discount Policy in the Light of Recent Experience," *Journal of Finance,* XII (May, 1957), 223–37.

[19] *Ibid.,* pp. 226–30.

[20] It may be worthwhile to briefly note in passing some of the questionable points in Walker's list of advantages of the discount mechanism. The weakest points he makes are those relating to discounting or discount rate as an aggressive weapon of policy. Thus, the idea that discounting is useful because it serves as an indicator of growing strength of credit demands in a period of un-

TABLE 5

BORROWINGS BY MEMBER BANKS AND CHANGES IN THE
FEDERAL RESERVE DISCOUNT RATE, 1951–1959 [a]

Date	Borrowings ($ million)	Discount Rate [b] (percent)	Date	Borrowings ($ million)	Discount Rate [b] (percent)
1951			**1954**		
Jan.	212	1¾	Jan.	101	
Feb.	330		Feb. (5)	293	1¾
March	242		March	189	
April	161		April (16)	139	1½
May	438		May	155	
June	170		June	146	
July	194		July	66	
Aug.	292		Aug.	115	
Sept.	338		Sept.	67	
Oct.	95		Oct.	82	
Nov.	340		Nov.	164	
Dec.	657		Dec.	246	
1952			**1955**		
Jan.	210		Jan.	313	
Feb.	365		Feb.	354	
March	307		March	464	
April	367		April (15)	495	1¼
May	563		May	368	
June	579		June	401	
July	1,077		July	527	
Aug.	1,032		Aug. (5)	765	
Sept.	683		Sept. (9)	849	2¼
Oct.	1,048		Oct.	884	
Nov.	1,532		Nov. (18)	1,016	2½
Dec.	1,593		Dec.	839	
1953			**1956**		
Jan. (16)	1,347	2	Jan.	807	
Feb.	1,310		Feb.	799	
March	1,202		March	993	
April	1,166		April (13)	1,060	2¾
May	944		May	971	
June	423		June	769	
July	418		July	738	
Aug.	650		Aug. (24)	898	3
Sept.	468		Sept.	792	
Oct.	363		Oct.	715	
Nov.	487		Nov.	744	
Dec.	441		Dec.	688	

TABLE 5 (continued)

Date	Borrowings ($ million)	Discount Rate [b] (percent)	Date	Borrowings ($ million)	Discount Rate [b] (percent)
1957			**1959**		
Jan.	407		Jan.	557	
Feb.	640		Feb.	508	
March	834		March (6)	601	3
April	1,011		April	676	
May	909		May (29)	767	3½
June	1,005		June	921	
July	917		July	957	
Aug. (23)	1,005	3½	Aug.	1,007	
Sept.	988		Sept. (11)	903	4
Oct.	811		Oct.	905	
Nov. (15)	804	3	Nov.	878	
Dec.	710		Dec.	906	
1958					
Jan. (24)	451	2¾			
Feb.	242				
March (7)	138	2¼			
April (18)	130	1¾			
May	119				
June	142				
July	109				
Aug.	252				
Sept. (12)	476	2			
Oct.	425				
Nov. (7)	486	2½			
Dec.	557				

[a] Federal Reserve Bank of New York discount rate.

[b] Rates shown are new rates established, except for first rate (1¾%) which had been in effect since August, 1950.

Figures in parentheses are dates rates were effective.

---

certainty seems weak; without discounting market rates of interest would rise and serve the same function. The use of discount rate to probe market reactions to increases by setting discount rate higher in one or two districts also seems a trivial advantage; probing could be done by successive, smaller increases in a uniform discount rate or by finely tuned open market operations, with the market's reaction to changes in market rates of interest the indicator. Finally, the idea that discount rate changes represent signals which are "easily understood" and "can hardly be susceptible to misinterpretation" cannot be accepted after the August, 1957, discount rate increase which evidently (in view of the later statements of Reserve authorities) was widely misunderstood.

Federal Reserve authorities. A similarly more modest view was expressed by Roosa in 1959:

So long as there are frictions in redistributing reserves, with some banks always ending their reserve-computation periods in a deficient position, and unable to tap promptly all of the excesses lodged in other banks elsewhere, there will be need for borrowing at the Federal Reserve. And because this is, within reasonable limits, merely a mechanical facility, aiding the smooth functioning of the deposit-money process, no purpose would be served by trying to fend off borrowing by using a stiff "penalty rate" concept of the discount rate in this country. On the contrary, banks faced with unexpected withdrawals might, if the discount rate were set well above going money market rates, be induced to make abrupt curtailments of other loans or investments, in an effort to meet their reserve requirements, with upsetting, or at least capriciously disturbing, effects in their local communities.[21]

Thus, the Federal Reserve learned from experience that the discount mechanism and rate are not aggressive instruments of monetary control, but can be useful in a more limited role.

ECONOMISTS' VIEWS OF THE DISCOUNT MECHANISM

Most economists apparently approved of the way the discount mechanism was administered after 1955,[22] but there were some who wanted drastic changes. It seems appropriate to consider these views before any conclusion is drawn with respect to the lessons which experience has taught about the appropriate role of the discount mechanism.[23] It is not possible to test these views by reference to experience, as the Federal Reserve's ambitious conception of the discount mechanism was tested in 1952–1953, but this makes it all the more important to subject them to careful logical and theoretical analysis.

[21] Roosa, "Credit Policy at the Discount Window, A Comment," *Quarterly Journal of Economics,* LXXIII (May, 1959), 335.

[22] Joint Committee, *1958 Questionnaire,* pp. 6–7.

[23] See, for example, Friedman, *A Program for Monetary Stability,* pp. 35–45; Earl Rolph, "Discussion," *American Economic Review,* XLV (May, 1955), 413–14; Smith, "The Discount Rate as a Credit Control Weapon," *Journal of Political Economy,* LXVI (April, 1958), 171–77; Kareken, "Federal Reserve System Discount Policy: an Appraisal," *Banca Nazionale Del Lavoro, Quarterly Review,* XII (March, 1959), 103–25; Simmons, *Journal of Business of the University of Chicago,* XXV, 18–29 and *Journal of Finance,* XI, 413–21; the contributions of Charles F. Haywood, J. M. Culbertson, Donald C. Miller and Elmer Wood in "Lessons of Monetary Experience Since the Treasury-Federal Reserve Accord," *Journal of Finance,* XIV (May, 1959), 135–60, 177–81; and Samuelson, "Recent American Monetary Controversy," *Three Banks Review,* March, 1956, pp. 10–11.

MAKING THE DISCOUNT MECHANISM MORE POWERFUL. James Tobin recently proposed that the discount mechanism could be made into "the most powerful tool in the central banker's kit" [24] if the Federal Reserve Banks were to pay interest on excess reserve balances at the same rate they charge on member bank borrowings and if the member banks at the same time were released from prohibitions and limitations on the payment of interest on demand and time deposits. [25]

The purpose of paying interest on excess reserves would be to affect the banks' willingness to lend by changing the opportunity cost of loan funds. If banks can earn a return on surplus reserves, the cost of lending these funds is correspondingly increased and the net gain from lending correspondingly reduced. [26] An increase in discount rate would discourage lending and investing in two ways: (1) borrowing from the Federal Reserve Bank would become more expensive, and (2) holding funds idle as excess reserves would become more profitable. The apparent enlargement of bank earnings would be offset by the other features of Tobin's plan: the bank's competitive necessity to pay interest on demand deposits and higher rates on time deposits. [27] The interest paid on time and savings deposits and demand deposits would in turn increase the opportunity cost to depositors of investing current bank balances (e.g., in Treasury bills) or of shifting them to nonbank financial intermediaries (e.g., to a savings and loan association). This latter feature would give the Fed-

---

[24] Tobin, "Towards Improving the Efficiency of the Monetary Mechanism," *Review of Economics and Statistics,* XLII (August, 1960), 279.

[25] *Ibid.,* pp. 277–78.

[26] Banks already have alternative employments and returns on surplus funds, particularly in terms of the return they can earn by investing in Treasury securities and lending federal funds, or save by reducing indebtedness at the Federal Reserve. But these opportunity costs may vary considerably in their relation to monetary policy. Tobin's plan would have the Federal Reserve set the opportunity cost directly.

[27] Bank earnings conceivably could be depressed by the proposal, perhaps seriously. Bank expenses would be enlarged by the total of their demand deposits multiplied by the new discount rate (approximately) and by higher rates on their time and savings deposits, presumably almost immediately. Their earnings however presumably would go up more slowly; their holdings of outstanding intermediate and long-term Treasury securities would provide an unchanged income; loans and short-term securities could be marked up in yield but only as they came due and were refinanced.

eral Reserve some influence over the growth of nonbank financial intermediaries.[28]

The question is whether this proposal, even if it did achieve closer control over bank lending, would bring benefits enough to outweigh the costs in the form of disruption of the economy in general and the financial markets in particular. One problem is that if commercial banks, as a result of this proposal, held higher average reserves, as Tobin seems to expect,[29] the effect would be to reduce their average loan and investment accounts, and hence correspondingly reduce their contribution to "real" investment and economic growth. In a sense the result would be to effect an increase in "financial" investment, other things equal, at the expense of "real" investment.[30]

Another problem is that Tobin's new type of discount mechanism apparently would make reserve funds available without question and without limit to any bank desirous of borrowing.[31] The problems of overborrowing, experienced in 1952–1953, would be dwarfed; the potential for inflationary enlargement of the reserve base would be enormous. As a defense, there would be only the power to raise the discount rate and as Tobin says, the authorities "would have to be ready to change the rate promptly and drastically; counter-cyclical monetary control may well require much wider fluctuations in short-term interest rates than we have yet had the courage to try." [32] Moreover, it is worth noting that these wide swings in discount rates and connected short-term rates would take place at the initiative of borrowing banks insofar as they represented defensive measures against such borrowing.

It seems dubious that violent fluctuations in short-term rates, brought about more or less erratically as banks' desires to borrow rise and fall with profit opportunities, would be a suitable instrument

[28] Tobin assumes that the rate on deposits will be closely attuned to the discount rate and hence will be subject to Federal Reserve control.

[29] Tobin, *Review of Economics and Statistics,* XLII, 278–79.

[30] I am indebted to Professor James W. Angell for calling my attention to this point.

[31] This is implied by the statement that "the Federal Reserve itself would make a perfect Federal funds market at the discount rate" as well as by the general emphasis of Tobin's article on the discount rate and complete lack of any reference to administrative restraints on borrowing. For the quotation, see Tobin, *Review of Economics and Statistics,* XLII, 277.

[32] *Ibid.,* p. 279.

of monetary control for a central bank. In effect this would be to turn over the reins to the banks which it is the central bank's function to control. Moreover, wild swings in interest rates would upset Treasury financing and private borrowing without really serving any economic purpose, for the basic economic situation rarely changes so rapidly.[33] Indeed, more often than not such swings would be inappropriate to the general economic situation.

WEAKENING OR ABOLISHING THE DISCOUNT MECHANISM. In contrast to Tobin's view, most critics of current discounting procedures have concluded that discounting is already too important in our monetary arrangements; accordingly, they would weaken the Federal Reserve's authority over discount rate or abolish the discount mechanism entirely. A number of reasons have been given to support these proposals. First, discount rate changes are regarded as disruptive to the financial markets and the economy generally. In particular, these critics argue, changes in discount rate may have unpredictable consequences on market expectations. It is pointed out, for example, that while some changes in discount rate are meant to signal credit policy intentions, others merely represent an attempt to adjust discount rate to changes in the market structure of interest rates. The market has no trustworthy way of distinguishing between them. An example of how misleading a discount rate change could be was the increase from 3½ to 4 percent in August, 1957. At the time many observers viewed it as confirming the monetary authorities' determination to combat inflation with further credit restraint. But later statements by Federal Reserve officials emphasized that the adjustment was "technical" in nature, that is, dictated by the fact that Treasury bill yields had climbed well above the discount rate.[34]

Samuelson has pointed out that even when the market is perfectly clear about the import of a discount rate change, it is not at all obvious what the financial and business reaction will be. In the past, it was common to assume that a discount rate increase was a storm

[33] It may be, of course, that with such violent swings in short-term and perhaps long-term interest rates and in the availability of credit the level of real economic activity would be adversely affected and unstabilized. Then, there might be fairly rapid swings in economic activity.

[34] When one considers that both Reserve Board Chairman Martin and New York Reserve Bank President Hayes were making speeches into November, 1957, stressing the need for restraint, the market may have been right in interpreting the August discount rate advance as indicative of further restraint.

signal which counseled caution. But now, Samuelson has argued, things may be different.

Today, financial men know that the Federal Reserve "leans against the breeze," tightening money when it thinks the forces of expansion are strong and easing money when deflation seems a threat. Therefore it is rational for an investor to say, "Aha! the 'Fed' is raising interest rates; they must know that the current outlook is very bullish and if that is going to be so, I'd better expand my operations." Conclusion: announcement effects are often ambiguous.[35]

Other critics of discounting have concentrated on what they regard as an irremediable defect in the mechanism: the fact that reserves supplied through the discount window are expansionary and can be viewed as an undesirable escape from restrictive credit policies. In the words of Rolph: "Let us be clear that bank borrowing from the Federal Reserve Banks is inflationary; it is another way that banks obtain reserves." [36] Because discounting takes place at the initiative of member banks, Friedman has gone so far as to say "the Reserve System cannot itself determine the amount of money it creates through the discount window or, for that matter, by a combination of the discount window and the open market." [37] While few of the other critics would accept Friedman's view that open market operations are incapable of absorbing funds released through excessive borrowing, most do find it objectionable that "when credit is tightened and banks react by borrowing from the Federal Reserve, this reaction is a partial offset to the original tightening, since it increases aggregate member bank reserves and permits multiple credit expansion." [38]

One proposal for reform has been to eliminate the Federal Reserve's discretionary authority over discount rate. Warren Smith has suggested that discretionary changes in discount rate have been so unsettling to the markets that:

discount rate has been more of a hindrance than a help in implementing monetary policy, and . . . the technique of tying the discount rate rigidly to open market interest rates, which was adopted by Canada in 1956, has much to recommend it for the United States.[39]

Specifically, Smith would set the discount rate automatically 1 per-

[35] Samuelson, *Three Banks Review*, pp. 10–11.
[36] Rolph, *American Economic Review*, XLV, 413.
[37] Friedman, *Monetary Stability*, p. 3.
[38] Joint Committee, *1959 Staff Report*, p. 405.
[39] Warren Smith, *Journal of Political Economy*, LXVI, 171.

cent above the weekly rate on new 91-day Treasury bills sold at auction.[40] This, of course, would make changes in discount rate automatic reflections of the weekly bill rate and remove credit policy implications. In a sense, discount rate would also become a penalty rate,[41] since it would always be above the Treasury bill rate.

There is little doubt that such an arrangement would have some advantages. With more frequent changes, the discount rate would attract somewhat less attention. And a relatively high discount rate in relation to Treasury bill yields presumably would ease the task of discouraging excessive borrowing.

But it is doubtful that a floating discount rate on the Canadian model would bring as much improvement as its proponents hope. The expectational reactions to discount rate changes which concern Smith are really reactions to the whole course of monetary policy. It is, after all, the total effect of monetary policy and the aim of the monetary authorities which the business and financial community are concerned about. Discount rate is one indicator, but other indicators are watched too; for example, free reserves positions of banks and the Federal Reserve's open market operations. If discount rate is removed as an indicator, the private markets will watch whatever is left. With a floating discount rate the market would pay all the more attention to the Treasury bill rate and to the open market operations which influence it. It can hardly be doubted that monetary policy actions in these areas would be fully as upsetting to market expectations as discretionary changes in discount rate are now alleged to be.

It is perhaps worth recalling that successive rises in the weekly bill rate in Canada in 1959 and the accompanying increases in the discount rate proved so upsetting to the financial markets that the authorities had to intervene. The authorities did this by changing the size of the August 20, 1959, weekly bill offering (*after bids had been*

---

[40] *Ibid.,* p. 176.

[41] Smith is dubious about the possibilities of a penalty rate in a banking system with thousands of unit banks with varying asset portfolios. Thus, one bank might be borrowing on bills at 1 percent above the bill rate while another bank might hold certificates as its shortest maturity and borrow on these which presumably would yield more than bills. This could be met by setting discount rate at some margin over the *lowest yielding marketable* asset held by a bank but it must be recognized that this approach would give rise to complaints of discrimination by banks since not all would be paying the same discount rate.

accepted) in order to keep the average issue rate of interest from pushing discount rate above the 6.41 percent level set the preceding week.[42] The incident is cited only to indicate that tying the discount rate to the Treasury bill rate would merely shift the market's attention and the central bank's activity to another area; it would not eliminate problems. It should not be assumed, as Smith's discussion sometimes seems to do, that simply eliminating a discretionary discount rate would mask the central bank's presence in the market and eliminate any disturbing influence its actions might arouse. So long as a central bank is effective, it will, on occasion, have to be disturbing to the market.

Moreover, a floating discount rate would also involve some disadvantages. The central bank would lose something important if it gave up discretionary authority over discount rate. On the one hand, there might be occasions when the monetary authorities would want to shock the markets as the Bank of England did in 1957 and in 1961, when it raised Bank rate by 2 percentage points to 7 percent. On the other hand, discount rate has some independent significance as an anchor rate in the money-market rate structure and the authorities might want to use it to influence rates independently of what they were doing with open market operations. Thus discount rate could be held below the bill rate during recession to serve as, so to speak, a "down-drag" on open market rates; in prosperity its height above the bill rate could be varied depending on the extent of pressure the authorities wished to apply. These options would be lost with a floating discount rate automatically tied to Treasury bill rates.

A compromise proposal would give the monetary authorities some discretion by having the Federal Reserve periodically announce, not the discount rate, but the formula by which the discount rate thereafter would be calculated.[43] If the authorities wished to make money easy, they might announce that discount rate would thereafter be ⅛ percent or ½ percent below the weekly bill rate, and vice versa when they wished to tighten credit. Since these discretionary actions would all be credit policy changes, not technical adjustments, the scope for

[42] Saunders Cameron Ltd., "Market Letter" (Toronto, Canada), September, 1959, pp. 1–3.

[43] Federal Reserve Bank of St. Louis, "The Discount Mechanism and Monetary Policy," *Monthly Review*, XLII (September, 1960), 9.

market confusion as to their meaning would be considerably reduced. Doubtless there would still be uncertainty as to market reaction, but as we have noted the influence of any monetary policy action on expectations may be ambiguous. Also the occasions for discretionary action presumably would be considerably fewer than under present arrangements.

Other reformers would abolish the discount mechanism to close up what they consider an unwarranted escape hatch from restrictive credit policies.[44] This would seem to be a drastic solution to the escape problem, particularly in view of the fact that "there is no evidence that a unit change in open-market operations induces an opposing change in discounting large enough to reverse or substantially wipe out the original effect." [45] Moreover, when one considers the combination of discount rate, administrative rationing, offsetting open market operations, and the tradition against borrowing, it would seem that the Federal Reserve has more than enough powers to prevent member bank discounting from vitiating a policy of monetary restraint.[46]

At the same time, abolition of the discount mechanism could introduce a number of new difficulties for the central bank, for the banking system, for the Government securities market, and for the Treasury. Few of these difficulties have been adequately discussed or considered by the proponents of abolition so a brief discussion seems appropriate. We shall take up, in order, how the proposal for abolition would affect the Federal Reserve, the commercial banking system, the Government securities market, and the Treasury.

Samuelson has pointed out that the escape aspect of the discount mechanism can be regarded as a safety valve which may even strengthen the efficacy of monetary policy despite superficial appearances to the contrary. In Samuelson's words:

Without denying their offsetting tendency, I think a defense can be made for the use of rediscounts. They do provide an important safety valve, and without this safety valve the authorities might not dare to apply as

[44] Friedman, *Monetary Stability*, p. 44; Rolph, *American Economic Review*, XLV, 413–14; Smith, *Journal of Political Economy*, LXVI, 177; Kareken, *Quarterly Review*, XII, 112; Currie, *Supply of Money*, p. 182.

[45] Paul Samuelson, "Reflections on Monetary Policy," in "A Symposium," *Review of Economics and Statistics*, XLII, 266.

[46] Haywood, "The Adequacy of Federal Reserve Powers to Discharge Responsibilities," *Journal of Finance*, XIV (May, 1959), 139.

much contractionary or expansionary pressure. My old teacher, Joseph Schumpeter, was fond of pointing out that good brakes make cars go faster, an analogy which applies perfectly to the present point.[47]

In this connection it needs to be emphasized that Federal Reserve open market operations are carried out on the basis of forecasts of what bank reserve positions are expected to be. Should an incorrect forecast result in drastic tightening of bank reserve positions, the banks can borrow to cushion the shock. Without the discount facility, an incorrect forecast could bring on a banking crisis. It is more likely, as Samuelson suggested, that the absence of the discounting safety valve would make the Federal Reserve timid about acting on its forecasts.

The large number of banks in the United States, more than 13,000 at the close of 1959, means that any individual bank is constantly gaining or losing reserves and needs some mechanism by which it can be sure that it will be able to meet its legal reserve requirement. The discount mechanism fills this need. Roosa pointed out:

No individual bank can feel assured that it will get back from others each day or each week, a volume of deposits equal to those withdrawn. There may be an evening out over time, or through seasons, but the short swings for any single bank can be very wide indeed. So long as there are frictions in redistributing reserves, with some banks always ending their reserve computation periods in a deficient position, and unable to tap promptly all of the excesses lodged in other banks elsewhere, there will be need for borrowing at the Federal Reserve.[48]

Without the discount facility, individual banks would be forced into sales of Government securities or curtailments of loans to meet temporary reserve imbalances with consequent upsetting effects to security markets and local communities. Open market operations could not supply the needed reserve funds because of the forecasting problem, because the Reserve Banks could not possibly follow the reserve positions of the 7,000 member banks on a current basis, and because the problem is in good part one of the distribution of total reserves rather than the level.[49]

Friedman has suggested that banks might be permitted to run re-

---

[47] Samuelson, *Three Banks Review,* March, 1956, pp. 10–11.

[48] Roosa, "Credit Policy at the Discount Window: A Comment," *Quarterly Journal of Economics,* LXXIII (May, 1959), 335.

[49] That is open market purchases could not assure that the supplied reserve funds went to the individual bank in need. Walker, "Discount Policy in the Light of Recent Experience," *Journal of Finance,* XII (May, 1957), 223–37.

serve deficiencies but that they then would be charged a very high percentage penalty rate. This would be, in Friedman's words, "The equivalent of a truly 'penalty' discount rate . . . except that no collateral, or eligibility requirement, or the like would be involved." [50] Clearly, this would be resuscitating the essence of the discount mechanism with the important difference that the Federal Reserve could no longer discourage a bank from borrowing. In essence the discount mechanism would be replaced with the overdraft system. As in the case of Tobin's scheme, everything would depend on the height of the penalty rate. If market rates of interest moved up, the penalty rate might have to be adjusted upward to keep it a penalty. In other words the discount mechanism would have crept back under another name.

Abolition of the discount mechanism would mean that banks would make most adjustments in their reserve positions by selling Government securities. But while this would be an effective means, dollar for dollar, for an individual bank, the banking system as a whole could not secure large additional reserve funds in this way. The banking system would have to reduce loans and investments by a multiple (currently about 6 to 1) of its reserve deficiency in order to shrink its deposits to a point where the existing available reserves met the requirement. This would mean considerably greater swings in Government security prices and yields than we have heretofore experienced. After all, at certain periods of credit stringency in the past nine years member bank borrowings have risen to or beyond $1 billion. If these reserve funds had not been available, banks would have been able to hold $6 billion less loans and investments than they actually held. With the demand for money unchanged by the absence of the discount mechanism, it is obvious that loan rates and security yields would have risen much higher.[51]

[50] Friedman, *Monetary Stability*, pp. 44–45.

[51] John Kareken has argued (*Quarterly Review*, XII, 112) that lack of the discount facility would *not* affect the Government securities market. But his analysis is faulty. He said: "One can reasonably doubt that closing down the discount facilities would lead to sharper fluctuations in yields than those we have experienced since the Accord. Banks short of reserves would be forced to sell or run off their short-term holdings. Those in an opposite situation, however, would have a strong incentive—much stronger, it should be noted, than they have today—to retain the Treasury obligations already in their portfolios and perhaps to acquire more. With market fluctuations thus limited, the task left to official open market operations would be that much easier. Still, System

The main impact on the Treasury of an abolition of discounting would be the greater difficulty and expense of financing in the more unstable Government securities market which would result. But the Treasury might feel some additional adverse effects in its cash borrowing operations if lack of the discount facility made commercial banks less willing to underwrite the Treasury's new cash offerings.[52] It is often not realized how important the commercial banks have been in underwriting Treasury cash offerings.[53] The importance of

purchases could be used when necessary to relieve general selling pressure, thereby enabling individual banks to unload their securities quickly at no great loss."

The error is the assumption that when a reserve deficiency forces some banks to sell Government securities other banks would have a strong incentive to retain Governments or to buy more. This ignores the fact that broad swings in reserve positions affect almost all banks in the same way at about the same time. If bank reserve positions were tightening, banks still unaffected would be most likely to fear that they would be affected next and that the appropriate action was to husband excess reserves, not to buy Government securities. Indeed, under these circumstances, it would be rational for a bank to sell Governments in anticipation, before reserve positions tightened further and depressed security prices lower. In this assumed situation, the absence of the safety valve represented by the discount mechanism might even lead to disorderly conditions in the Government securities market. It will be recalled that the mere rumor that the discount window was being shut down created near panic conditions in the bond market in the spring of 1953. Kareken seems to admit considerable impact on the Government securities market in his final sentence where he says: "System purchases could be used when necessary to relieve general selling pressure." This is tantamount to providing a safety valve by means of open market operations rather than the discount mechanism. The escape from restraint would still be there; only the label would have changed.

[52] It is perhaps worth noting that the Federal Reserve Banks recognized forty years ago that banks' willingness and ability to assist Treasury financing was related to the terms at which the discount facility was available. Thus, when high "progressive" discount rates on bank borrowings beyond established credit lines at the individual Reserve Banks were instituted in 1920, the Federal Reserve Banks were careful to exempt borrowings for the purpose of carrying, and collateralized by, U.S. Government obligations. See the Board of Governors of the Federal Reserve System, *Annual Report,* 1920, pp. 58–59.

[53] Indeed, a number of observers in recent years have charged that adoption of the "bills only" policy by the Federal Reserve—and particularly the prohibition against Federal Reserve support of Treasury financing operations—had left the Treasury without any underwriting support. But it is obvious that the Treasury must have had an underwriter. The money market does not keep billions of dollars idle waiting for Treasury cash offerings. Someone must be willing to take them initially, carry them, and resell them to more permanent investors as they develop savings or other investible funds. The commercial banks have filled this role in recent years, taking almost always one-half of Treasury cash offerings and more often two-thirds. In the case of very short-term issues such as tax anticipation obligations the banks have taken substantially all of the offerings; on very long-term issues they have taken one-third or sometimes as little as one-tenth. This underwriting function is not as broad as

the discount mechanism to the underwriting banks is that it provides some assurance of emergency finance for a brief period if demands from permanent investors do not develop and unsettled market conditions make sale of the securities difficult without considerable loss. To be sure, the Reserve System may provide funds through open market purchases and repurchase agreements with Government securities dealers at times of major cash financing but this is regarded as less dependable than the discount mechanism.[54]

The availability of the discount facility for banks underwriting new Treasury security offerings is not provided for in Regulation A which governs discounting.[55] But banks may count on it as one of the informal arrangements which, though unwritten, constitute part of the essential fabric of the money market.[56] Abolition of the discount

---

that of underwriters of private security issues; the banks do not stabilize the price of the new issue but simply take it initially and bear the risk of price depreciation pending resale. See, *Treasury Bulletin,* August, 1960, pp. 40–42 and the *Treasury-Federal Reserve Study,* Pt. I, p. 43.

[54] For example, there is the experience of the underwriters of a cash offering of 1½ percent Treasury tax anticipation notes in August, 1958. After having committed themselves to buy on the assumption that a large amount of funds provided by open market operations would be available, the underwriting banks found that the expected reserve funds had been withdrawn before the new tax notes were delivered. The episode created bad feeling on the part of the institutions concerned on the grounds that they had been "sucked in" unfairly. A rather dry official account of the episode is provided in the *Treasury-Federal Study,* Pt. II, pp. 83–84.

[55] In fact, the Foreword to Regulation A warns against "profiting from rate differentials" or "extending an undue amount of credit for the speculative carrying of or trading in securities" and it might be possible to construe the underwriting of Treasury cash offerings as being prohibited as a reason for borrowing under these rules. However, in a recent article, "Borrowing from the Fed," in the Federal Reserve Bank of New York's *Monthly Review,* 41 (September, 1959), the Bank suggested that when "capital markets are congested, and interest rates are rising, when public bodies find they are unable to sell the bonds they have scheduled, at least at interest rates they are willing to pay" commercial banks which extend temporary financial assistance to such public bodies could expect that "the Federal Reserve Bank might extend temporary assistance" to the bank through the discount mechanism (p. 141). It does not seem far-fetched to assume that if the Reserve authorities are willing to allow the discount mechanism to be used for assistance to temporary extensions of credit to state and local public bodies, they would not deny emergency assistance to banks temporarily financing new issues of the United States Treasury.

[56] Such arrangements include among others the fact that two of the major New York banks feel an obligation to make funds available to Government security dealers at some rate at all times (see *Treasury-Federal Reserve Study,* Pt. I, p. 30), that dealers and banks bid for more Treasury bills than they really want (scaling the excess bids at rising yields) to minimize the possibility

mechanism accordingly might have some adverse effect on the willingness of banks to participate in Treasury cash financings.

When all these considerations are taken into account, it becomes doubtful that such a drastic step as abolition of the discount mechanism is advisable. There is too much risk that it would create problems of greater seriousness than any it would solve.

CONCLUSION ON ROLE OF DISCOUNTING

It seems clear that in the years of flexible monetary policy since 1951, there have been widely different conceptions of the role of the discount mechanism. The Federal Reserve in the initial years of the period, and Tobin more recently, regarded it as a leading if not the main instrument of monetary policy. On the other hand, a number of economists have regarded the discount mechanism as such a hindrance to monetary policy that it should be substantially weakened or even abolished. Experience apparently led the Federal Reserve to modify its original conception of how important the discount mechanism should be. While neither the views of Tobin nor of those economists who would abolish the discount mechanism entirely have been similarly tested, analysis suggests that experience would prove them untenable. Thus both extreme views—making the discount mechanism the leading instrument of monetary policy or abolishing it entirely—would seem to be mistaken.

What then is the appropriate role for discounting? It cannot be a weapon for unmitigated ease because the reluctance of banks to borrow induces some constraint into the money market when discounts are positive. Yet it cannot be a significant weapon of restraint because discounting releases funds, it does not withdraw them. Forcing repayment of discounts can be restrictive but restraint occurs only after discounts have made an easing contribution. Moreover, the restraint achieved by forcing the repayment of discounts is incapable of being applied in a sufficiently sensitive way to produce predictable results over short periods; on the contrary it may have unpredictable, explosively undesirable effects on the psychology of the money market.

that any of the weekly bill offerings might not be covered by sufficient bids, and that in the past when the reception of Treasury cash or refunding financings has been poor, major financial institutions have been encouraged by the Federal Reserve or Treasury authorities to subscribe and have done so as a public duty.

The answer must be that an appropriate role for discounting should reflect its essential nature. Discounting eases, but at the same time introduces some sense of constraint into the money market. Thus, the appropriate role for discounting would seem to be as a safety valve available to prevent sudden liquidity gaps in the market but only at a price and under administrative controls which prevent it from being an escape from credit restraint. From this point of view, discounting could also serve the market as a buffer against the other monetary weapons of the Federal Reserve without however being able to offset them completely or more than briefly. Samuelson has pointed out that this would permit the Federal Reserve to act aggressively and decisively without fear of demoralizing the market. In addition the discount rate, apart from its use to encourage or discourage borrowing, could be an independent influence on other short-term open market money rates. This conception of the discount mechanism seems to be what the Federal Reserve authorities have arrived at, after having given up the early pre-Accord hopes of a larger and more ambitious role.

The most promising avenue for improving the functioning of the discount mechanism would seem to lie in changing the method of setting the rate. Technical adjustments have sometimes been difficult for the market to distinguish from discount rate changes intended to signal changes in credit policy. Moreover, fear of disturbing the market may inhibit the Federal Reserve authorities from making needed technical adjustments in the rate under present arrangements.[57] But the idea of setting discount rate automatically at some fixed margin over the weekly Treasury bill rate would remove too much of the Federal Reserve's discretionary authority. A reasonable compromise might be to tie discount rate to the bill rate but permit the Federal Reserve to vary the relationship in accordance with monetary policy aims whenever it seemed appropriate. This would retain needed flexibility in the relation of the discount rate to other money market rates but also minimize the possibility of market misinterpretation of the meaning of discount rate changes.

[57] Federal Reserve Bank of St. Louis, *Monthly Review*, XLII (September, 1960), 8.

VIII

CHANGES IN CASH RESERVE REQUIREMENTS
AS A CREDIT CONTROL INSTRUMENT

THE FEDERAL RESERVE'S ATTEMPTS to make the discount mechanism a leading weapon of the post-Accord monetary policy contrasted sharply with its reluctance to employ changes in member bank cash reserve requirements as an active instrument of a flexible credit policy.[1] Reserve requirements stipulate what percentage of its demand and time deposits a member bank must keep uninvested and unlent in the form of cash in its vaults or as a deposit at its Federal Reserve Bank.[2] Table 6 shows the legal limits within which the Federal Reserve Board can change member bank reserve requirements, the level in force in December, 1960, and the amount of reserve required by each class of banks to meet the stipulated percentages.

A change of one percentage point in the reserve requirement against demand deposits would release or impound some $250 million for the Central Reserve City banks, about $400 million for Reserve City banks, and some $380 million for the Country banks, or a total beyond $1 billion. Clearly, changing these percentage reserve requirements is a most direct and powerful way for the Federal Reserve to affect the volume of bank reserves available for lending and investing. Moreover, this approach would reduce the Federal Reserve's intervention in the money market to the absolute minimum,

[1] The contrast is also marked when foreign experience is considered. According to the Federal Reserve Bank of New York: "In October 1957, variable cash reserve requirements were in force in thirty foreign countries, either by statute or by formal agreement between the monetary authorities and the commercial banks. . . . Variations in cash reserve ratios have become more frequent in recent years, as many countries have increasingly turned to this instrument as a part of flexible credit policies." See, Fousek, *Foreign Central Banking: The Instruments of Monetary Policy,* Ch. IV, particularly pp. 46, 50.

[2] On December 1, 1960, member banks' legally required reserves amounted to some $18 billion, of which all except about $2 billion of vault cash was required to be kept at the Federal Reserve Banks.

TABLE 6

MEMBER BANK RESERVE REQUIREMENTS,
DECEMBER, 1960

	LEGAL LIMIT (*percent of deposit*)			AMOUNT REQUIRED (*$ million*)	
	Maxi-mum	Mini-mum	In Force [b]	Average [c]	Per Point
Net Demand Deposits [a]					
Central Reserve City banks	22	10	16½	4,136	251
Reserve City banks	22	10	16½	6,612	401
Country banks	14	7	12	4,583	382
Time Deposits					
All classes of banks	6	3	5	2,889	578

[a] Net demand deposits are defined as total demand deposits less cash items in process of collection and less demand deposits due from domestic banks.

[b] As of December 1, 1960.

[c] For first fourteen days of December, 1960.

Source: Board of Governors of the Federal Reserve System, *Federal Reserve Bulletin*, XLVII (March, 1961), 313, and Release J.1 "Deposits, Reserves, and Borrowings of Member Banks," for the biweekly period ended December 14, 1960.

even beyond the minimum intervention achieved by confining open market operations to dealings in bills only. This is because changes in reserve requirements, releasing or impounding reserve funds, would be dealings in cash itself, rather than the nearest thing to cash, as Sproul pointed out in 1954. Attempting to show the absurdity of the bills only policy, Sproul said:

why not take the next step and, instead of dealing in the "nearest thing to money," deal in money itself? Instead of shying away merely from influencing longer-term markets directly, why not shy away from influencing the short-term market directly? Our operations in Treasury bills can and have caused distortion in the short-term market and between short and long markets. In other words, we might merely increase or decrease reserve requirements of particular banks or groups of banks in order to affect reserves directly, without the intervention of even Treasury bills. I introduce the idea, only as a sort of *reductio ad absurdum;* I wouldn't suggest it.[3]

Sproul's closing disclaimer of any intent actually to suggest such a procedure is in line with the cautious attitude taken toward reserve requirement changes by the Federal Reserve authorities in recent years. Table 7 shows that since 1951 there have been eight changes

[3] Sproul, "Central Banks and Money Markets," p. 7.

TABLE 7
CHANGES IN MEMBER BANK RESERVE REQUIREMENTS, 1917–1960
(*percent of deposits*)

Effective Date of Change		NET DEMAND DEPOSITS [a] Central Reserve City Banks	Reserve City Banks	Country Banks	TIME DEPOSITS Central Reserve and Reserve City Banks	Country Banks
1917 June	21	13	10	7	3	3
1936 Aug.	16	19½	15	10½	4½	4½
1937 March	1	22¾	17½	12¼	5¼	5¼
May	1	26	20	14	6	6
1938 April	16	22¾	17½	12	5	5
1941 Nov.	1	26	20	14	6	6
1942 Aug.	20	24				
Sept.	14	22				
Oct.	3	20				
1948 Feb.	27	22				
June	11	24				
Sept.	16, 24 [b]	26	22	16	7½	7½
1949 May	1, 5 [b]	24	21	15	7	7
June	30, July 1 [b]		20	14	6	6
Aug.	1, 11 [b]	23½	19½	13	5	
Aug.	16, 18 [b]	23	19	12		5
Aug.	25	22½	18½			
Sept.	1	22	18			
1951 Jan.	11, 16 [b]	23	19	13	6	6
Jan.	25, Feb. 1 [b]	24	20	14		
1953 July	1, 9 [b]	22	19	13		
1954 June	16, 24 [b]	21			5	5
July	29, Aug. 1 [b]	20	18	12		
1958 Feb.	27, March 1 [b]	19½	17½	11½		
March	20, April 1 [b]	19	17	11		
April	17	18½				
April	24	18	16½			
1960 Sept.	1	17½				
Nov.	24			12		
Dec.	1	16½				

[a] Demand deposits subject to reserve requirements which beginning August 23, 1935, have been total demand deposits minus cash items in process of collection and demand balances due from domestic banks (also minus war loan and Series E bond accounts during the period April 13, 1943, to June 30, 1947).

[b] First-of-month or midmonth dates record changes at Country banks and other dates (usually Thursday) record changes at Central Reserve or Reserve City banks.

in member bank reserve requirements. All of these were reductions,[4] releasing substantial amounts of funds in periods of economic recession or slowdown when the authorities wanted to stimulate increased lending and spending. In contrast, there were seven changes in only three years from 1948 to 1951. Four of these were increases, while three were reductions.[5] The failure to raise reserve requirements in the past ten years has not been unintentional: the Reserve authorities have made it quite clear that they do not view increases in bank reserve requirements as an appropriate tool of restrictive credit policy.

The question is whether this aloof attitude toward changes in reserve requirements impaired the effectiveness of monetary policy or whether it merely recognized the limitations of an occasionally useful but imperfect instrument. A brief discussion of the development of legal reserve requirements in the United States will serve as a useful background for the evaluation of the Federal Reserve's reasons for not using changes in reserve requirements more often as an instrument of monetary control.

BACKGROUND OF RESERVE REQUIREMENTS

One significant fact is that changes in bank reserve requirements lack traditional standing as an instrument of credit control. Reserve requirements originally were intended to enforce higher standards of prudence on banks and thus to serve as a protection to their solvency, the redeemability of their notes, and the safety of their depositors' funds.[6] The Federal Reserve Act in 1913 accepted this conception of a legal reserve requirement and, while adapting those in force under

[4] The one percentage point increase for Country banks on November 24, 1960, was designed to partially offset the new eligibility of vault cash as legal reserves. The net affect of the two moves was a release of reserve funds, in short an easing action.

[5] *Federal Reserve Bulletin,* XLVI (April, 1960), 381. The willingness to increase reserve requirements in 1948 reflected an attempt to impound the reserve funds which were necessarily released under the policy of supporting Treasury bond prices. This is to be noted because of the post-Accord fears of the Federal Reserve that increased reserve requirements could produce a disorderly bond market. In 1948, however, with the support program in force the Federal Reserve simply bought all the bonds offered for sale by banks to raise funds to meet the higher reserve requirement. No crisis was possible under these conditions, but an effective monetary policy was also denied by the support program.

[6] For the development of reserve requirements in the United States, see, the *Federal Reserve Bulletin,* XX (November, 1938), 953–72; and Rodkey, *Legal Reserves in American Banking.*

the National Banking Act, made no provision for changes in reserve requirements.

While a fixed legal reserve requirement was aimed at insuring banks' liquidity and solvency, in practice it also served as an aid to credit control since it represented a fulcrum on which central bank actions to release or absorb reserve funds could exert leverage. With a legal reserve requirement, member banks had to react if a restrictive credit policy reduced their reserves below the minimum legal level. Without a legal minimum they might have simply decided to get along with less reserves for awhile and their attitude toward making loans and investments could thus have been unaffected.

In the course of time it was recognized that reserve requirements could be a powerful lever of credit control as well as a fulcrum. Changes in the requirements which affected the proportion of total reserves that had to be held idle could have just as powerful an effect on banks' ability to lend and invest as open market operations which affected the total of reserve funds. For while a change in percentage requirements in itself neither adds to or subtracts from the total of member bank reserve funds, it does increase or decrease the amount of the total that banks can use and thus increases or diminishes the size of the credit structure and deposit structure that they can erect or maintain on the reserves they hold.[7]

The possibility of varying reserve requirements to affect the ability of banks to extend credit, in order to deal with an inflationary or deflationary situation, seems to have occurred first to the Federal Reserve Board in 1916. In its *Annual Report* for that year, the Board urged that it be given the power to raise bank reserve requirements in case of emergency and argued that this could be expected to "enable the Federal Reserve Board in prolonged periods of extreme ease in the money market to check any tendency toward . . . undue extension of credit." [8] Congress was cool to the idea. However, Keynes recognized the potential value of variations in cash reserve requirements and urged that the Bank of England be given "the power on thirty days' notice to vary the prescribed reserve proportions to a fig-

[7] For a description of the impact of changes in available reserves in a fractional reserve banking system, see Board of Governors of the Federal Reserve System, *Purposes and Functions*, pp. 14–30 and 50–52.

[8] Board of Governors of the Federal Reserve System, *Annual Report*, 1916, p. 28.

ure between 10 and 20 percent in the case of Demand Deposits and to a figure between 0 and 6 percent in the case of Time Deposits." [9] The British Macmillan Committee, reporting in 1931, recommended that the Bank of England be empowered to vary bank reserve ratios "within certain narrow limits," and added that the variation "probably should be quite small on any one occasion." [10] The idea did not take hold in England, but by 1933 the United States had passed legislation authorizing variable bank reserve requirements.

The adoption of variable reserve requirements in the United States reflected fear that some of the measures taken to ensure recovery from the depression might go too far and cause inflation. To protect against this possibility the Federal Reserve was given discretionary authority to change member banks' percentage reserve requirements without limit in a section of the Act of May 12, 1933, known as the Thomas Amendment, but use of the authority was made subject to the proclamation of an emergency by the President of the United States. In the Banking Act of 1935, discretionary power was given to the Federal Reserve Board without reference to the President within limits set by the 1917 legislation and twice the 1917 percentages, that is, between 13 and 26 percent for Central Reserve City banks.

The Federal Reserve Board's first use of its new power came in 1936 and 1937 when in a series of steps reserve requirements were doubled to the maximum level in an effort to absorb some of the billions of dollars of excess reserves which had resulted from the massive gold inflow during the 1930s. In succeeding years, changes in reserve requirements were generally made only when large changes in economic conditions or the reserve positions of the banks had taken place. Thus, requirements were reduced during World War II to enable the banks to absorb Treasury issues to finance the war, raised in 1948 and 1951 to absorb bank reserves at a time when the commitment to support Treasury bond prices made open market sales impracticable, and reduced in 1949, 1953, 1954, 1958, and 1960 to combat recessionary tendencies in the economy.

From time to time economists have suggested that more use might profitably be made of reserve requirement changes in implementing

[9] Keynes, *Treatise on Money*, Vol. II, p. 77; see also, pp. 260–61.
[10] Macmillan Committee, *Report*, p. 159.

monetary policy.[11] However, the Federal Reserve has been reluctant to do so, basing its reluctance on a number of arguments to which we now turn.

OBJECTIONS TO CHANGES IN RESERVE REQUIREMENTS

The major objection to the use of changes in reserve requirements as a weapon of monetary control is that reserve requirements would be too powerful and too blunt in their effects to be a suitable part of a program of credit restraint. Advocates of this point of view argue that reserve requirement increases would disrupt the banking system and demoralize the Government securities market. Hardly less significant is that changes in reserve requirements directly affect the profitability of banking and the ability of banks to build capital and grow. These obviously involve difficult questions of Government-business relations which are not easy to resolve, and which have stimulated strong reactions from all concerned.

TOO POWERFUL IMPACT OF CHANGES IN RESERVE REQUIREMENTS. The Federal Reserve has argued that it is just because changes in reserve requirements are so powerful and far reaching that they must be used sparingly or, as Goldenweiser has put it, "with caution." [12] As noted earlier, changes of only one percentage point in requirements would involve release or withdrawal of more than $1 billion in bank reserve funds. Moreover, these massive impacts are felt by all member banks immediately without regard to their individual money positions or lending and investing behavior.

To be sure, the Federal Reserve has expressed no objection to such powerful and widely diffused effects when it is reducing reserve requirements in order to combat economic recession. The idea is that in recessions the more quickly, more powerfully, and more widely dis-

---

[11] See, for example, Charles R. Whittlesey, "Reserve Requirements and the Integration of Credit Policies," *Quarterly Journal of Economics,* LVIII (August, 1944), 553–70 and Scott, "Regional Impact of Monetary Policy," *Quarterly Journal of Economics,* LXIX (May, 1955), 283. For a view opposing more use of changes in reserve requirements see Joseph Aschheim, "Open Market Operations *Versus* Reserve Requirement Variation," *Economic Journal,* LXIX (December, 1959), 696–704. Critical comments on Aschheim's views as well as his defense are to be found in the *Economic Journal,* LXX (December, 1960), by John Gurley and Richard Goode, pp. 616–18; by Richard Porter, pp. 618–20; Aschheim's defense, pp. 620–22.

[12] Goldenweiser, *American Monetary Policy,* p. 92.

tributed the effects of new reserve funds are felt, the better. Chairman Martin has pointed out that reserve requirement reductions can stimulate bank credit expansion more effectively than an equivalent addition to bank reserves through open market operations because:

It seems to be expected generally that an increase in reserve availability brought about by a change in reserve requirements is likely to be more permanent and that the added lending power will not be quickly withdrawn. Member banks, consequently, are likely to react more positively to a reduction in reserve requirements by moving promptly to expand and also to incorporate additional permanently desirable assets in their asset structures. They will be more likely to expand their long-term assets by purchasing mortgages and also to make customer commitments extending longer into the future, commitments for new term loans, for new lines of credit, and for future mortgage financing.[13]

However, such powerful and widespread effects could be disastrous in a period of credit restraint when the banks, the money market, and the capital market are already short of funds and extremely sensitive. Banks which had little or no excess reserves before the change [14] would find that their reserves would then be short of the new requirements and that they would have to take corrective action to restore their reserve positions. In our fractional reserve banking system with the average reserve requirement against demand deposits about 15 percent, an increase of $1 billion in the amount required (or less than 1 point in the percentage requirements) might well require liquidation of more than $6 billion of loans and investments. There is no question that this could have drastic effects on the security markets and the economy. Chairman Martin presented the disturbing possibilities to the Joint Economic Committee in 1959 in the following words:

If an increase in reserve requirements is imposed at a time when member banks' holdings of excess reserves are low, or completely offset by borrowing at the discount window, there are only three options open to the banking system to achieve compliance: (1) by wholesale liquidation

[13] Joint Committee, *1959 Employment Hearings*, Pt. 6A, p. 1465.

[14] Most banks would find themselves with little or no excess reserves in a period of credit restraint when reserve requirements are most likely to be increased. The apparent paradox of some $500 million excess reserves for all member banks throughout periods of credit restraint is explained by the fact that there are some 5,900 Country member banks, each with a small amount of excess reserves too trivial for investment or lending in the Federal funds market.

of loans in an amount several times the increase in reserves required (about six times at present), or (2) by sales of U.S. Government securities in comparable value (i.e., about six times at present) to nonbank investors, or (3) by borrowing at the discount window a sum equal to the amount involved in an increase in reserve requirements.

In the case of any combination of these, lower prices for U.S. Government securities could be expected. From the moment of the announcement, there would be a strong tendency for potential buyers of U.S. Government securities to defer their bids, thus tending to provoke a disorderly market that would force intervention by the system open market account. Such intervention to restore orderly conditions might require purchases in greater amounts [adding to the supply of new reserve funds] than were involved in the original increase in reserve requirements. As a result, the effort to combat overexpansion in a boom by reducing bank liquidity might induce disorder in the market for Treasury issues and, subsequently, a situation of even greater bank liquidity than had prevailed before the restraining action was initiated. These same problems do not arise when reserve requirements are reduced.[15]

The Federal Reserve has had some practical experience to justify its fears. The first use of the power to raise reserve requirements, doubling them in 1936–1937 in a series of steps, touched off anticipatory selling of some $700 million of Government bonds in the spring of 1937 after the second increase had been announced. At the time this volume of selling represented some 7 percent of the weekly reporting member banks' total holdings of direct Treasury obligations; sale of a comparable percentage toward the close of 1960 would have amounted to $2 billion in dollar volume. Moreover, this large volume of selling took place even though excess reserve balances were much greater than the increase in requirements and still totaled about $900 million even after the higher requirements were in effect. The bank selling disorganized the bond market and the Federal Open Market Committee felt impelled to enter the market to stabilize it with support purchases of $200 million Treasury bonds in March and April, 1937.[16]

Reserve requirement increases in 1948 and early 1951 also precipitated massive selling of Government securities as the banks tried to raise cash to meet the higher requirements, but in these cases the Treasury market was being supported by the Federal Reserve and hence no disorder resulted. However, this meant provision of reserve

---

[15] Joint Committee, *1959 Employment Hearings*, Pt. 6A, pp. 1463–64.
[16] Board of Governors of the Federal Reserve System, *Banking and Monetary Statistics* (Washington D.C., 1943) p. 154; and *Annual Report, 1937*, p. 6.

funds in some degree,[17] and to that extent offset the restrictive effect of the increases in reserve requirements.

These episodes made a deep impression on responsible Federal Reserve officials. Their testimony before Congress and other expressions of opinion on reserve requirements increases have been studded with references to how such increases have "collapsed the Government securities market on us," [18] "destroyed our market for Government bonds," [19] or "knocked the spots off the bond market." [20] In less colorful language, Riefler's testimony in 1958 before the British Radcliffe Committee painted much the same picture. Riefler said

it would only be in peculiar circumstances that we could raise reserve requirements. Under the free market technique, any announcement of a rise in reserve requirements would mean that buying in the Government securities market would dry up, and we would have to go in and support the market, which we would not want to do, so it is very difficult.[21]

Moreover, the Federal Reserve argued, it is unnecessary to subject the economy to the drastic effects of reserve requirement increases because the problem of the monetary authorities in a boom is not one of contracting the size of the reserve base but simply of slowing its rise.

Hence, unless redundant excess reserves remain from the preceding period of ease or there is a substantial inflow of reserves from other sources, a restrictive policy does not require that bank reserves be absorbed but simply that they be held stable or allowed to increase at a slower rate.[22]

This policy can be well served by conducting open market operations to provide fewer reserves than normal for seasonal and growth needs. The result is a gradually mounting pressure on the banking system which is "felt individually and gradually by the member banks through the operation of market forces. For example, sales of securities in the open market may be reflected in withdrawals of deposits at some banks by customers." [23] As Goldenweiser put it:

This sort of transaction is familiar to the bank; some withdrawals of deposits occur all the time and other deposits are made; if the net is a loss

[17] The Open Market Committee offset purchases of long-terms with sales of short-term Government securities to the maximum extent possible whenever it had to make support purchases.
[18] Joint Committee, *1959 Employment Hearings*, Pt. 6A, p. 1462.
[19] *Ibid.*, p. 1286.
[20] *Ibid.*, p. 1482.
[21] Radcliffe Committee, *Minutes of Evidence*, Question No. 9493.
[22] Joint Committee, *1959 Employment Hearings*, Pt. 6A, p. 1497.
[23] *Ibid.*, p. 1463.

of deposits the bank has its accustomed way of meeting the situation. If the shortage of reserves is the result of an operation by the Federal Reserve, the bank may even not be aware of the fact.[24]

While it is clear that reserve requirement changes involving increases or decreases of $1–$3 billion would have massive and undesirable effects on the economy and the securities markets, it is by no means obvious that reserve requirement changes would have to involve such large amounts. As Shaw said:

The large and infrequent changes in reserve ratios, which the Federal Reserve takes to be the result of defects in the instrument, may instead be responsible for those defects. Open market operations of comparable magnitude can also be a shock to the markets.[25]

Thus, if a 1 point change in requirements is regarded as too powerful because it would impound or release more than $1 billion, then a ¼ point or even 1/10 point change which would release $250 million or $100 million, respectively, would presumably be less objectionable.

The Federal Reserve's comment on this suggestion is that:

very small fractional changes at relatively frequent intervals, however, would create very difficult problems of adjustment for member banks and would almost certainly be disruptive to the smooth flow of credit in the market.[26]

It may be granted that banks would find more frequent changes in reserve requirements upsetting in a policy-making sense [27] and also more costly in terms of their bookkeeping arrangements. But so far as "problems of adjustment" to the impact on reserve positions are concerned, it is difficult to see why these should be appreciably more difficult than losses of reserves due to open market operations or to the Treasury's frequent (for large banks, two or more times a week) withdrawals from its Tax and Loan deposit accounts with some 11,000 commercial banks.[28]

Taking all these considerations into account, it would seem that small changes in reserve requirements would involve a great deal less

[24] Goldenweiser, *American Monetary Policy*, p. 92.

[25] Flanders Committee, *1954 Hearings*, p. 74.

[26] Joint Committee, *1959 Employment Hearings*, Pt. 6A, p. 1463.

[27] Bankers could no longer count on the proportion of their resources that had to be tied up in reserves as being relatively fixed. But if changes were small, this would not seem to be a serious problem.

[28] For a description of the Tax and Loan Account depositary system, see the Treasury's reply to questions by Congressman Patman in Joint Committee, *1959 Employment Hearings*, Pt. 6A, pp. 1191–1205.

risk of unsettling the economy and the markets than the large changes
the Federal Reserve System has customarily made. While the impact on
the Government bond market might not be proportional to the size of
the change in reserve requirements because of possible effects on expectations, it would seem unlikely that a panic could develop out of a
¼ or ½ point increase.[29] If moderate increases in reserve requirements stimulated some modest selling of long-term Governments by
banks, this theoretically might be a way for the Federal Reserve to
exert direct pressure on the long-term markets without the necessity
of selecting particular issues to deal in,[30] a problem sometimes cited
in discussions of "bills only." And as we shall see, after a discussion
of the problems created by the special impact of reserve requirement
changes on the commercial banks, there are occasions in periods of
credit restraint when small changes in reserve requirements would
have distinct advantages over open market operations involving the
same amount of reserve funds.

RESERVE REQUIREMENTS AND THE BANKS: A POLITICAL PROBLEM.
Changes in reserve requirements involve difficult problems of equity
and Government-business relations, which the other instruments of
monetary policy so far considered, do not involve.[31] For while, in one
sense, changes in reserve requirements are the most impersonal of
the instruments—involving only bank reserve balances and permitting
the Federal Reserve to abstain from intervention in the Government
securities market—in another sense, they are the most personal and
discriminatory—involving, as they do, substantial and specific impacts on the commercial banks to which they apply. As a result very
little discussion of reserve requirements has been possible in recent
years without intrusion of questions involving the banks' interests,

[29] The likelihood of a panic in the bond market would be decreased if the
authorities informed the market that small-scale reserve requirement changes
were chosen so as to avoid unsettling the market. Prospective sellers would
then face the possibility that their sales would be made at the low of the market, since the authorities clearly did not wish a sharp break and might take
action to support the market.

[30] While this course might appeal to advocates of minimum intervention,
the uncertainty of response probably makes it less effective than direct dealings
in the long-term market.

[31] However, the use of selective credit controls which interfere with the
operations of specific business sectors does involve the same sorts of Government-business relations and questions of equity and this is one of the reasons
why the Federal Reserve has been reluctant to use selective controls.

discrimination against banks, subsidies to banks, whether the power of the banking system to create deposits involves usurpation of the Congressional power to coin money, and the like.

Some of the issues raised appear to be unimportant or specious. For instance, the assertion that changes in reserve requirements are somehow more arbitrary than open market operations and more likely to penalize a bank which has been acting in conformity with the aims of monetary policy seems questionable. When the Federal Reserve sells securities in the open market, no one can predict which bank will hold the account of the buyer of the securities and therefore which bank will unexpectedly lose reserves. It may be a bank which is in a particularly difficult reserve position through no fault of its own, and this bank will then be considerably embarrassed by the loss of reserves, just as it would be if its reserve requirements had been increased. On the other hand, soon after open market operations take place and are transmitted through the banking system, they become anonymous, and after the initial transactions, no bank could be aware that its difficulties had stemmed from a specific Federal Reserve action. Thus, open market sales are likely to arouse less opposition than reserve requirement changes simply because they are less visible.

Nevertheless it cannot be denied that real questions of advantage and disadvantage and discrimination are involved in changing reserve requirements. For one thing, the legal requirements imposed by the Federal Reserve apply only to member banks, which number some 6,200. More than 7,000 nonmember commercial banks are unaffected directly, although their state banking authorities may, and often do, impose the same reserve requirements. Thus the competitive position of member banks vis a vis nonmember banks could be impaired by reserve requirement increases. Moreover higher bank reserve requirements would also widen the competitive advantages of nonbank lenders, most of which are subject to much lower or no legal reserve requirements. Member banks are unable to lend as much as nonmember banks or nonbank lenders out of a given deposit because more is required of them as a cash reserve. This in turn means that a correspondingly larger proportion of member banks' total resources must be held in nonearning cash, reducing their ability to attract time deposits by paying competitive rates of interest [32] and also their ability to earn profits and thus grow.

The Federal Reserve has explained its policy of making only reductions in bank reserve requirements in recent years on the grounds that they had been raised too high [33] and that tying up too much of the banks' assets in cash has adverse implications for the future stability and growth of the economy. The Federal Reserve set out its position in a 1959 statement to the Joint Economic Committee in the following language:

Long-term growth in the demand-deposit component of the money supply requires not only an adequate supply of reserves to the banking system but also provision for an adequate capital structure. If deposits and risk assets grow more rapidly than the capital accounts, this gradually undermines the protection against loss that these capital accounts provide, first to the depositors, and second to the Government, the insurer of deposits through the FDIC. The ratio of capital to liabilities and risk assets in the banking system will not be affected much, one way or the other, by monetary policy actions in the short run. In the longer run, however, the level of reserve requirements, along with many other factors, will play a part in determining the rate at which banks are able to add to their capital, either by retained earnings or the attraction of new investment.[34]

However, a number of congressmen and economists have appeared to take the view that whatever problems the banks may have, they should solve these themselves. From this standpoint, reserve requirement reductions represent a gift to the banks since they permit the replacement of nonearning cash with profitable loans and investments. Hansen made an outspoken statement of this point of view in a recent comment on an American Bankers Association proposal for reducing bank reserve requirements:

The bankers are, in effect, asking Congress to hand them on a silver platter $9.8 billion of earning assets in place of an equivalent amount of unearning cash assets which they are now required to hold as reserves.[35]

An associated criticism which found strong support in Congress was that lowering reserve requirements not only fattened bank earnings but also resulted in lower Federal Reserve earnings. If needed

[32] Another factor is Federal Reserve Regulation Q which until 1962 prohibited rates of more than 3 percent on commercial bank time deposits.
[33] Joint Committee, *1959 Employment Hearings*, Pt. 6A, p. 1458.
[34] *Ibid.,* p. 1499.
[35] Hansen, "Bankers and Subsidies," *Review of Economics and Statistics,* XL (February, 1958), 50.

reserve funds had been supplied by open market purchases, the Federal Reserve could have earned interest on the securities purchased, and this would have benefited the Treasury and taxpayers since the Reserve System turns over its net earnings to the Treasury.[36] This sentiment in Congress found expression in a written qualification to a 1959 bill authorizing the inclusion of vault cash as legal bank reserves to the effect that "it is not the intent of this legislation to encourage or cause the Federal Open Market Committee to reduce the Federal Reserve System's holdings of Government securities." [37] It cropped up also in the refusal of Congress to authorize elimination of the 4¼ percent interest rate limit on new Treasury bond issues unless the Federal Reserve agreed to accept an amendment to the legislation, expressing the sense of Congress that needed reserve funds should be supplied to the market by open market purchases of Government securities and particularly bonds rather than by lowering reserve requirements.[38]

If some economists and congressmen were concerned about the trend to lower reserve requirements, bankers had been equally upset some years earlier when reserve requirements were being raised to record levels. In 1950 one observer who appeared to be speaking for the banking community said:

At times the [Federal Reserve] Board has given the impression that it is more ready to raise requirements than to lower them. When requirements were doubled in 1936–37, the stated purpose was to reduce the large volume of excess reserves. During World War II, however, when requirements could easily have been lowered to their original levels, they were reduced only slightly. Some bankers fear, therefore, that if the Board's authority over reserve requirements were to be increased, the tendency over a long period of years might be in the direction of ever higher requirements.[39]

And a major bank commented on the 1948 increases in reserve requirements as follows:

The stated reason for authorizing increases in the reserve requirements at this time was "to enable the Federal Reserve System to acquire more—if necessary many more—long-term government securities to

[36] For a congressional staff analysis of this point, see Joint Committee, *1959 Employment Hearings*, Pt. 6A, pp. 1254–55.

[37] U.S. Congress, Senate-House Conference Report, *Member Bank Reserve Requirements*, House Report No. 651, 86th Cong., 1st Sess., 1959, p. 5.

[38] See, for example, Joint Committee, *1959 Employment Hearings*, Pt. 6A and particularly pp. 1241–45 which gives the amendment.

[39] Adams, *Monetary Management*, p. 80.

maintain the long-term yield level." In this way, Chairman McCabe of the Federal Reserve Board stated, "new reserves created by such System purchases could be absorbed through increases in reserve requirements and thus be unavailable for multiple credit expansion."

By this "solution" the Federal Reserve presumably would continue to inflate their government bond holdings without predetermined limit, and in so doing facilitate increased lending by nonbank lenders. The reaction of the practical banker—if one had been called upon to testify—might well have been: "Why crack down on us so that our competitors can take the business?" . . . It makes little practical difference, from the standpoint of inflationary credit expansion, whether a given loan is granted by a commercial bank or by some other type of lending agency.[40]

It seems clear that the Federal Reserve will be criticized whatever actions it takes on reserve requirements. But no action at all is also likely to draw criticism. Bankers will claim current requirements are too high. Critics of banks and advocates of Federal Reserve support for Treasury security prices, on the other hand, might well call for higher reserve requirements to hold down bank earnings and to absorb reserves released by support operations.

In this environment, the one encouraging aspect is that bankers' criticism of reserve requirements changes was stimulated by the fear that the changes were on a one-way street leading up while Congressional criticism reflected concern that reserve requirement changes were on a one-way street going down. Presumably, both sides would be less concerned about reserve requirement changes if, over the period of the cycle, there were both upward and downward changes. This suggests that a modest program of flexibility in reserve requirements need not be ruled out by the political sensitivity of the instrument.

THE CASE FOR MORE USE OF RESERVE REQUIREMENT CHANGES

The case for using changes in reserve requirements more frequently is that the effectiveness of monetary policy could be appreciably improved if its impact was felt more quickly and more pervasively throughout the economy. Even small-scale reserve requirement changes affect all member banks immediately. This is important in an economy with almost 14,000 commercial banks spread across a continent. In this kind of an environment, the gradual impact of

[40] First National City Bank of New York, *Monthly Letter*, September, 1948, p. 101.

open market operations on bank reserve positions can be a defect as well as the advantage that Federal Reserve spokesmen have been inclined to emphasize.

Open market operations initially affect bank reserve positions and deposits in major money centers and have only a lagged and gradual impact on the deposits, loans, and investments of smaller banks throughout the nation.[41] This is a significant drawback, particularly at turning points in monetary policy. Much recent criticism has charged that the effectiveness of monetary policy has been impaired by the relatively long time-lags which ensue before it takes hold.[42]

One such criticism, which will be examined in some detail in Chapter X, is that the money supply has not responded promptly to shifts in the monetary policy and accordingly has often continued to rise for many months after monetary policy has shifted to credit restraint. Such perverse behavior has sometimes been paralleled during recession when the money supply occasionally has declined for months after the Federal Reserve had shifted to a policy of monetary ease. But the lag in the response of the money supply to changes in monetary policy has been much less marked in recessions when reserve requirement reductions have been used as a part of credit-easing policies. This presumably is because the reserve requirement reductions have affected the deposits of small- and medium-sized banks throughout the country promptly and accordingly have been reflected in the behavior of the money supply fairly quickly. It is difficult to escape the conclusion that reserve requirement increases in periods of credit restraint could have a similar effect in quickening the response of the money supply to restrictive monetary policies as well as in exercising a more prompt influence on small- and medium-sized banks' loan and investment operations.

It would not be necessary for reserve requirement increases to be frequent or very large in order for them to quicken the response to restrictive monetary policies. They would be most effective at turning points in monetary policy; thereafter open market operations could

---

[41] Scott, *Quarterly Journal of Economics*, LXIX, 269–84.

[42] Thomas Mayer, "The Inflexibility of Monetary Policy," *Review of Economics and Statistics*, XL (November, 1958), 358–74. Milton Friedman, Edward Shaw, and James Angell have also called attention to the lag with which discretionary monetary policy affects the money supply but this will be taken up in detail in Chapter X and therefore references are not cited here.

be used except where deepening recession or substantial inflationary excesses called for more powerful impacts. Indeed they should be handled to minimize adverse impacts on banks, so far as is consistent with achieving monetary objectives. The best solution might be relatively small increases—perhaps on the order of ¼ or ½ percentage point to involve $250 to $500 million—early in an economic expansion. Such prompt use might reduce the over-all intensity of restraint that might otherwise have to be imposed over a longer period. The goal would be quicker diffusion of credit restraint, not necessarily a more massive impact than open market sales of Government securities could provide.

CONCLUSIONS ON RESERVE REQUIREMENTS

The Federal Reserve's reluctance to use reserve requirement increases as a weapon of credit restraint has probably impaired the effectiveness of monetary policy in recent years. Reserve requirement increases would have probably affected the lending and investing of small- and medium-sized banks more promptly than have the open market sales of Government securities which the Federal Reserve has relied upon as its only weapon of credit restraint. Accordingly, the money supply would probably have responded more quickly to changes in monetary policy and hence would have behaved perversely to a considerably smaller extent.

The political problems raised by increasing reserve requirements are real ones. But bankers' objections to reserve requirement increases might be lessened if experience showed that they were relatively moderate and were on balance, as seems likely to be consistent with the aims of long-run credit policy, outweighed by decreases. In any case, the Reserve authorities are open to particular criticism for not experimenting with small reserve requirement increases, since their major objection was the bluntness of the instrument.[43]

To sum up: The desirability of restraining the money supply more promptly, as well as banks' lending and investing, when credit policy is tightened argues for some use of increases in reserve requirements

---

[43] This failure is all the more puzzling in view of admissions, dating back at least ten years, of Federal Reserve spokesmen. "It would be possible to work out techniques of small, gradual changes in reserve requirements, with adequate advance notice, that could be used as effective instruments of current regulation of credit." See, Goldenweiser, *American Monetary Policy*, p. 93.

in periods of credit restraint. Prompt application might reduce the intensity of general restraint that might otherwise have to be applied over a longer period.[44] Large increases in reserve requirements are not likely to be appropriate except in the eventuality of a major inflationary surge in which the economy needed a drastic shock.

[44] Reserve requirement changes might also be useful in such routine tasks as supplying or mopping up funds in connection with the seasonal rise and fall of currency circulation, if they were moderate in size. For example, the post-Christmas return flow of currency to the banks each year supplies $1 to $1.5 billion of redundant reserves, which the Federal Reserve now absorbs by means of sales of Treasury bills. But this is an operating decision best left to the judgment of informed officials, once they have seriously considered the alternative of moderate reserve requirement changes.

IX

THE FAILURE TO USE

SELECTIVE CREDIT CONTROLS

THE FEDERAL RESERVE conspicuously failed to make any use of selective credit controls after 1952, apart from margin requirements on loans for the purchasing or carrying of listed stocks. This requires some discussion since a number of economists have suggested that selective controls might be useful supplements to general credit policy.[1] In its 1945 *Annual Report,* the Federal Reserve's Board of Governors advocated permanent status for the selective regulation of consumer credit "as an integral part of the System's function of maintaining sound credit conditions." [2] In 1951 Reserve Board Chairman Martin told Congress "selective measures of credit restraint are an effective and necessary supplement to general credit measures." [3] In 1956 the President of the United States, when he transmitted his annual economic report, suggested, "Although present conditions do not call for the use of any authority to regulate the terms of instalment credit, this is a good time for the Congress and the Executive Branch to study the problem." [4] The Federal Reserve's Board of Governors accordingly undertook a major study of consumer credit in 1956 to "appraise the arguments for and against standby authority to set limits on downpayments and maturities of instalment credit." [5] Thus selective credit controls were by no means a dead

[1] See, for example, the replies of economists in Douglas Committee, *Compendium,* pp. 342–45; Byrd Committee, *1958 Compendium,* pp. 513–758; and Joint Committee, *1958 Questionnaire,* p. 4.

[2] Board of Governors of Federal Reserve System, *Annual Report,* 1945, p. 24.

[3] U.S. Senate, Committee on Banking and Currency, *Defense Production Act Amendments of 1951, Hearings,* 82d Cong., 1st Sess., 1951, p. 312.

[4] *Ibid.,* p. vi.

[5] Board of Governors of the Federal Reserve System, *Consumer Instalment Credit,* Pt. II, Vol. I, p. xiii.

issue during 1951 to 1959; nor were they obviously discredited. The balance of this chapter describes the nature of selective credit controls used in the United States, the attitude of the Federal Reserve toward such controls, and the case for and against selective controls.

NATURE OF SELECTIVE CREDIT CONTROLS

Selective credit controls are administrative regulations designed to control the use of credit for specific purposes or in specific areas in contrast with general credit controls which affect the cost and availability of all credit. Selective controls bypass the reserve base and money supply and directly influence the availability of credit administratively. They do not change the lending or investing powers of the individual bank, banking system, or nonbank lender since they do not affect the reserve base or the money supply, but they do affect a lender's ability to lend by reducing the number of eligible borrowers for particular types of credit.

In the United States, selective credit controls have mainly been used to restrict credit, though there have been proposals for controls that would encourage selective lending, and there has been experience with such measures abroad.[6] Here, the focus has been on consumer credit (under Federal Reserve Regulation W during World War II, from September, 1948, to June, 1949, and from September, 1950, to May, 1952), real estate credit (under Federal Reserve Regulation X from October 12, 1950, to September 16, 1952), and stock market credit (controlled since 1934 under Federal Reserve Regulations T and U which stipulate minimum margin requirements on loans for the purchasing or carrying of stocks listed on national securities exchanges).[7]

---

[6] See the proposal by Leo Fishman in *The Commercial and Financial Chronicle*, March 7, 1957, p. 15. For foreign experience, see Fousek, *Foreign Central Banking*, Chapter VI; and Patman Committee, *Compendium*, Pt. I, pp. 503–19. Secondary reserve requirements against deposits, or reserve requirements against loans and other assets, are sometimes considered to be selective controls, presumably because they would require or encourage the investment of funds in Government securities. But these schemes have stimulated much less discussion since flexibility was restored to general credit controls. For discussion of them, see Patman Committee, *Compendium*, Pt. 1, pp. 121–29, 477–93; and Hart, *Defense and the Dollar*, Ch. IV and pp. 86–89.

[7] The most recent form of Regulation W, applied in 1950, can be found in the *Federal Reserve Bulletin*. The initial regulation is in the issue of September, 1950, pp. 1177–85; while the October, 1950 stiffening amendment is in Oc-

These types of selective credit control have seemed most feasible in terms of criteria developed by the Federal Reserve.

To be effective, selective regulation of credit must relate to an area which is reasonably definable in terms of such things as the purpose of the credit, the collateral for it, or the nature of the credit contract. Trade practices should be specialized and sufficiently standardized so that the regulation can be applied in terms of a continuation or extension of those procedures rather than a drastic disruption of them.

Furthermore, the credit area subject to regulation must be important enough in terms of size and volatility so that its regulation can help to reinforce general credit measures; and the flow of credit should be responsive to practicable adjustments in the borrower's equity or loan maturity. The selective credit regulation must not unduly impede permitted credit transactions and there must be a minimum possibility of successful evasion in the case of other transactions. Lastly, the constructive results of regulation must be great enough to outweigh the burdens associated with it—both on those subject to it and on those administering it.[8]

It is generally agreed that selective control of stock market credit, the control with which the Federal Reserve has had most experience, has successfully met these requirements despite occasional regulatory problems.[9] However, selective control of consumer and real estate credit has occasioned considerable controversy.

Both Regulation W, governing consumer credit, and Regulation X, governing real estate credit, have relied on administrative control

tober, 1950, pp. 1282–83. Regulation X is in *Federal Reserve Bulletin*, XXXVI (October, 1950), 1314–21; an accompanying press statement is on pp. 1284–86. The regulations governing stock margin requirements are available from Federal Reserve Banks as pamphlets: *Regulation U, Loans by Banks for the Purpose of Purchasing or Carrying Stocks Registered on a National Securities Exchanges, as amended to July 28, 1960;* and *Regulation T, Credit by Brokers, Dealers, and Members of National Securities Exchanges, as amended to July 28, 1960.*

[8] Patman Committee, *Compendium*, Pt. 1, p. 403. Proposals for many other selective controls—on business inventory investment, plant and equipment investment, various types of bank loans (see Joint Committee, *1959 Staff Report*, pp. 394–401)—have been criticized as not meeting these requirements in one or another respect (see Patman Committee, *Compendium*, Pt. 1, pp. 402–4).

[9] Patman Committee, *Compendium*, Pt. 1, pp. 402–4; also see Marcus Nadler's comments, in Board of Governors, *Consumer Instalment Credit*, Pt. II, Vol. II, pp. 19–20. This is not to say there has not been opposition to stock margin requirements. The New York Stock Exchange, for example, has often criticized specific changes in margin requirements. But even Stock Exchange spokesmen have recognized that the Federal Reserve's view of need for change in margin requirements may be more authoritative than their own as was indicated by G. Keith Funston, president of the New York Stock Exchange, in 1955 before the Senate Banking and Currency Committee. See *Stock Market Study, Hearings,* 84th Cong., 1st Sess., 1955, pp. 33–34.

over maximum loan values (or minimum down payments) and maximum maturities (or minimum monthly repayments). Eastburn has described the rationale of this approach:

> The first is, in a sense, a *liquidity* requirement, for it specifies that a borrower must use a certain portion of cash in the purchase of regulated goods such as consumers' durables, real estate, or shares of stock. The second, the result of maturity and amortization requirements, is essentially an income requirement because in most cases it means that current incomes must be large enough to support the periodic (usually monthly) payments on the loan.[10]

The down payment or maximum loan value requirement determines the total amount of mortgage or consumer credit which can be supported by a given amount of cash. The higher the down payment, the smaller the amount of credit involved in any given transaction. But changes in down-payment requirements also have another effect. They can influence the volume of sales of homes or durable goods since a higher requirement may force some would-be purchasers to stay out of the market until they accumulate enough cash to cover the down payment.[11]

The maximum maturity requirement determines how fast a given loan must be repaid and, accordingly, how big the monthly repayments must be. Here also there is an additional effect. Bigger monthly repayments may decrease the volume of sales of homes or durable goods if some people find the larger repayments too big in relation to income to be carried comfortably.[12]

FEDERAL RESERVE'S VIEW OF SELECTIVE CREDIT CONTROLS

Selective credit control devices might be expected to be frowned upon by the Federal Reserve authorities for a number of reasons. They are not traditional credit control measures and, indeed, the types of credit they regulate were largely unknown when the Federal

[10] Eastburn, "The Philosophy of Selective Credit Regulation," in *Readings in Money and Banking,* ed. by Whittlesey, p. 112.

[11] It may be noted that an increase in down-payment requirements has a once-and-for-all effect; as people build up cash balances by saving, they are put in a position to restore their previous level of purchases of durable goods. Also, down-payment requirements have the largest impact when consumer liquidity is low. This underscores the importance of general credit controls as a backstop.

[12] For some empirical evidence of the importance of the maturity requirement in broadening and narrowing the demand for instalment credit, see Board of Governors, *Consumer Instalment Credit,* Pt. I, Vol. 1, pp. 132–35.

Reserve Act was passed. By their very nature they intrude in particular markets and thus interfere with the market mechanism's allocation of credit and goods. Moreover, they bring the central bank as an imposer of restraint into direct contact with the public and thus increase the likelihood of resistance to its actions.

Nevertheless, Federal Reserve spokesmen occasionally have suggested that selective controls on consumer and real estate credit might be useful and effective tools of a central bank policy. While the most positive expressions of this point of view have come from officials of the Federal Reserve Bank of New York,[13] spokesmen for the Federal Reserve board have also expressed approval. Thus, Reserve Board Chairman Martin commented in 1957 on the 1952 suspension of Regulation W in the following words:

My own judgment was, and I expressed it at the time to the Congress, we would have been a little wiser, much as I disliked Regulation W, if we had not released Regulation W and Regulation X quite as quickly as we did in 1952. . . . It is very easy to make statements about things that might have been done differently, but we did have an enormous buildup and increase in consumer instalment credit as soon as those regulations were taken off.[14]

Asked on another occasion whether the Federal Reserve authorities "have all the weapons or tools that you need to do an effective job," Martin replied: "I think there are selective credit controls, such as housing credit and consumer instalment credit, which we had at one time which could be used as supplements, but certainly not as alternatives to general controls." [15]

---

[13] Thus, Allan Sproul, then president of the New York Federal Reserve Bank, said in 1955: "we would not jeopardize our general freedom from direct controls by giving the Federal Reserve System permanent authority to regulate consumer credit. . . . The same or something similar might be said of mortgage financing. . . . Our experience, thus far, suggests to me that general credit controls can exert an effective influence on these particular types of credit only with a considerable lag, and that we cannot rely upon countervailing forces in the economy to maintain overall stability." "Reflections of a Central Banker," pp. 8–9.

Also, his successor as president of the New York Federal Reserve Bank, Alfred Hayes, in 1958 said: "Conceivably, monetary policy might have done better to supplement its general credit controls with some more selective controls, especially in the area of consumer credit, designed to check particular distortions before they had gone too far." "Monetary Policy in a Recession," p. 3. See also, Mr. Hayes' remarks in Byrd Committee, *1958 Compendium*, pp. 73–74.

[14] Byrd Committee, *1957 Hearings*, p. 130.

[15] Joint Committee, *1956 Monetary Policy Hearings*, p. 76. See also the

How then explain the Federal Reserve's failure to make more use of selective credit control measures? Superficially, the answer might appear to be that the Federal Reserve can regulate only where it is authorized to do so and, as Chairman Martin's comment above indicates, Congress withdrew authority to selectively regulate credit in 1952. But this explanation ignores the fact that public concern over the 1955 boom in consumer credit, reflected in the President's request in 1956 for study of the regulation of consumer credit, provided a favorable opportunity for the Reserve System to request authority for selective controls if it really wanted them. Instead the Reserve Board, after completing the requested study, said:

special peacetime authority to regulate consumer credit is not now advisable. The Board feels that the broad public interest is better served if potentially unstabilizing credit developments are restrained by the use of general monetary measures and the application of sound public and private fiscal policies.[16]

This citation suggests that part of the Board's reluctance to use selective controls stems from a belief that selective controls and general monetary measures are alternative rather than complementary tools; if general credit measures are available, selective controls are not needed. Chairman Martin provided some confirmation for this interpretation in 1958 when he explained the Board's 1957 decision on consumer credit controls as follows:

we came to the conclusion that at this particular time . . . we would not be able to achieve anything with consumer credit regulation now. If you are talking about it in an atmosphere of freer markets, which we didn't really have in this country up until the middle of 1951–52 then you have to make a great shift in your thinking.[17]

But proponents of selective credit controls have long argued that their main contribution to monetary policy would be as *supplements,* not substitutes, for general credit controls.[18] And of course Chair-

---

comment of Winfield Riefler, assistant to the chairman of the Federal Reserve Board, before the British Radcliffe Committee to the effect that: "I personally think that there is a case for them [selective controls]." *Minutes of Evidence,* Question 9823.

[16] *Federal Reserve Bulletin,* XLIII (June, 1957), 648.

[17] U.S. Congress, Joint Economic Committee, *1958 Hearings on the President's Economic Report,* 85th Cong., 2nd Sess., 1958, p. 400.

[18] Saulnier, "An Appraisal of Selective Credit Controls," *American Economic Review,* XLII (May, 1952), 248–50; Shay, "Regulation W: Experiment in Credit Control," *University of Maine Bulletin,* LV (April, 1953), 50, 168; and Shay, Consumer Credit Control as an Instrument of Monetary Policy for

man Martin himself in 1956 had taken this stand. In light of this apparent contradiction, it is necessary to look elsewhere for an explanation of the Board's coolness to consumer credit controls and selective controls in general.

There is reason to believe that the Board's reluctance to use selective controls really reflected concern about possible business resentment of selective controls and accompanying problems of administration and enforcement. As the Board put it in the eighth and final finding of the 1956 consumer credit study:

Under peacetime conditions, special regulation of consumer instalment credit would inevitably present problems of compliance to the financing and business concerns subject to it, and of administration and enforcement to the agency of Government responsible for the regulation.[19]

This concern with the problem of administration of selective credit controls has been serious, continuing, and long-lived.[20] Indeed such concern may well have been the reason why selective regulation of real estate credit did not accompany Regulation W when it was first adopted in 1941.[21] In 1947 Reserve Board Chairman Eccles, commented on the failure to adopt real estate credit controls.

There was a good deal of consideration given by the War Stabilization Board . . . to getting an Executive Order that would give to the Federal Reserve Board authority to regulate and control real-estate credit of all kinds. We were opposed to that. We studied it very extensively, and we were opposed to it because we simply could not figure out how on earth we could administer it.[22]

Twelve years later, in a statement to the Congressional Joint Economic Committee, the Federal Reserve made it clear that its reservations about selective credit controls still concerned, not their effectiveness, but "equity and administrative feasibility" and the fact that "such regulation has been vigorously opposed by interested groups whenever it has been proposed." [23]

Economic Stability," in Board of Governors, *Consumer Instalment Credit,* Pt. II, Vol. II, pp. 45–47.

[19] *Federal Reserve Bulletin,* XLIII (June, 1957), 648.

[20] Good background material, drawing on unpublished material in the files of the Federal Reserve System as well as on published statements and documents, is presented in Shay, *University of Maine Bulletin,* LV, Chapter IV; and Eastburn, "Real Estate Credit Controls as a Selective Instrument of Federal Reserve Policy," pp. 52–64. Cited hereafter as *Real Estate Credit Controls.*

[21] *Ibid.,* pp. 62–63.

[22] U.S. House, Committee on Banking and Currency, *Government Credit, Hearings,* 80th Cong., 1st Sess., 1947, Pt. II, pp. 248 ff.

[23] Joint Committee, *1959 Employment Hearings,* Pt. 6A, pp. 1490–91.

With respect to effectiveness, the statement said:

there is little question but that restrictive regulation of the terms offered to instalment and mortgage borrowers would effectively reduce the total demand for credit and thus relax somewhat the upward pressure on interest rates. Conversely, it is also certainly true that the liberalization of terms, both as to downpayments and maturities, which has taken place since 1952 has contributed to the demand for credit and the upward pressure on rates in the recent period.[24]

But when it took up the question of whether regulation was desirable, the Board backed away from the responsibility of a decision and said:

After weighing the many conflicting arguments enumerated in the study submitted by the Board in 1957 (see Part I, vol. I, ch. 16) the Congress may determine that the balance favors establishment of permanent authority to regulate consumer credit. To be fully effective, such authority would have to cover long- as well as short- and intermediate-term credit and should be permanent, broad, and flexible in character. Application of the regulations should be limited to periods when the need is sufficient to justify the considerable burden such regulation imposes on the businesses directly affected and toleration of the discriminatory aspects which are unavoidable.

The Board does not feel justified, at this time, in taking the initiative in a recommendation to Congress in this matter. The effectiveness and workability of this kind of selective regulation depends heavily on broadly based acceptance and support. Whether such support exists can best be determined in the forums of the Congress itself.[25]

It may be questioned whether this kind of position is an appropriate one for the central bank to take when asked to appraise a new type of credit control. Congress needs more of a guide from the expert judgment of the central bank if it is to accurately appraise and weigh the gains against the drawbacks of selective regulation. But leaving this to one side, the Federal Reserve's position raises two questions: (1) Would the constructive results of selective credit control outweigh the burden of the administrative and enforcement problems they bring with them? and (2) Are administrative and political problems of selective control as serious as the Board has suggested?

THE CASE FOR SELECTIVE CREDIT CONTROLS

Proponents of selective credit controls argue that there are strategic credit areas which are volatile and at the same time relatively insensitive to general credit controls. Hence selective control of such

[24] *Ibid.,* p. 1490.
[25] *Ibid.,* pp. 1490–91.

types of credit is needed to supplement general credit controls and insure that monetary policy is effective in all areas of the economy. Without the power to control credit selectively, the Federal Reserve at times may be faced with a dilemma in which the restraint of over-rapid expansion of credit and production in an insensitive area of the economy might require more severe general credit restriction than would be appropriate for the economy as a whole.[26]

The classic example of this type of problem occurred in the late 1920s when excessive credit-use and speculation in the stock market became extremely worrisome to Federal Reserve authorities. Yet the degree of general credit restraint required to curb stock speculation seemed far too severe to many Federal Reserve officials for the health of the rest of the economy. The dilemma led to vacillation and a monetary policy which was suited to neither the stock market situation nor to general economic conditions. As Harris put it: "A dear money policy not firmly and consistently applied was responsible for dear money for industry and the continuance of large demands by speculators." [27] It was as a result of this experience and of the ensuing 1929 stock market crash that legislation authorizing selective control of stock market credit was adopted in 1934.

While no parallel to the 1929 stock market situation has developed, proponents of selective controls found cause for concern in the extremely rapid expansion of consumer and mortgage credit in 1955 despite a policy of general credit restraint. Consumer installment credit rose $5.6 billion or 16.6 percent in 1955, compared with a gain of only $0.6 billion or 2.5 percent in 1954 when monetary policy was trying to encourage credit expansion. Home mortgage credit rose $12.5 billion or 16.5 percent in 1955, compared with an increase of $9.6 billion in 1954. The surge in credit use, it has been said, encouraged and facilitated unsustainable levels of activity, par-

[26] See the following contributions in Board of Governors, *Consumer Instalment Credit*, Pt. II, Vol. II: Nadler, pp. 3–29; Shay, pp. 37–68; Smithies, pp. 71–72; Turner, pp. 103–11; Hart, pp. 144–46; Mack, pp. 149–51. Also see Miller, "Monetary Policy in a Changing World," *Quarterly Journal of Economics,* LXX (February, 1956), 23–43; *United States Monetary Policy,* pp. 73–89; James W. Angell, "Appropriate Monetary Policies and Operations in the United States Today," *Review of Economics and Statistics,* XLII, 251.

[27] Harris, *Twenty Years of Federal Reserve Policy,* Vol. II, p. 507 but see also pp. 473–611. Also see, Hardy, *Credit Policies of the Federal Reserve System,* Ch. VII, particularly pp. 128–35; and Goldenweiser, *American Monetary Policy,* pp. 152–56.

ticularly in the automobile industry, gave rise to a boom atmosphere in the economy at large, and helped stimulate overexpansion in business capital investment in 1956.[28] Had selective controls on consumer and mortgage credit been in force, it has been argued, they could have held the pace of credit expansion in these areas to more sustainable levels, reduced the secondary stimulation to overexpansion elsewhere in the economy, and helped check not only inflation but also the ensuing economic reaction.[29]

While discussions of the desirability of selective credit controls often link consumer and mortgage credit, it has become increasingly recognized that the two types of credit need separate consideration. Consumer credit, it is felt, is in greater need of special selective control.[30] Mortgage credit, on the other hand, has been quite responsive to general credit controls in recent years because of special circumstances growing out of Government efforts to aid the mortgage market. But the desirability of selective control of mortgage down payments and maturities is still a live issue because the special circumstances making the mortgage market sensitive to general monetary policy could be changed, particularly since there is considerable objection to the arbitrary way in which the present arrangements operate.

UNSTABILIZING INFLUENCE OF CONSUMER CREDIT AND MORTGAGE CREDIT. Perhaps the most striking aspect of consumer installment credit and mortgage credit in the postwar years has been their vast secular (or structural) expansion. Consumer installment credit rose almost sixteen-fold from 1945 to 1959, from $2.5 billion to $39.9 billion. Mortgage credit outstanding on one-to-four-family homes increased more than seven-fold in the same period, from $18.6 billion to $130.8 billion. In popular discussion, this massive debt expansion has been the main focus of interest, stimulating expressions of concern about moral deterioration or about individuals' ability to bear the burden of so much debt. But by and large economists have tended to concentrate their attention on the cyclical pattern of this

[28] Board of Governors, *Consumer Instalment Credit,* Pt. II, Vol. II, p. 147. Also U.S. Department of Commerce, *Survey of Current Business,* September, 1955, p. 24.

[29] Arthur Smithies, "Uses of Selective Credit Controls," in *United States Monetary Policy,* pp. 83–84.

[30] See Nadler's view in Board of Governors, *Consumer Instalment Credit,* Pt. II, Vol. II, p. 21.

debt expansion.[31] They have been concerned about whether it was helpful or harmful to economic stability.

Theoretically, it can be shown that from a cyclical stabilization standpoint consumer debt is more important than mortgage debt even though mortgage debt was more than three times as large as consumer instalment debt at the close of 1959. This is because consumer debt is largely short-term, and the monthly repayment burden of short-term debt is much larger than the monthly repayment burden of the same amount of long-term debt. For example, a $2,400 automobile loan of 24 months maturity would involve a repayment burden of $100 monthly. To get the same repayment burden on a 20-year 5 percent mortgage one would have to incur $15,000 debt. In this example, the repayment burden of consumer debt would be more than six times the repayment burden of mortgage debt.[32]

In fact, there seems to be considerable agreement that consumer installment credit has generally been an unstabilizing influence on the economy in recent years.[33] It has tended to add considerably to inflationary pressures at times of high demand for goods and to add little to or even subtract from demand at periods when there is a general deficiency of demand. For example, consumer installment debt showed increases of from $2.3 to $5.6 billion in prosperous years since 1952 (when selective regulation was suspended) but grew only $0.6 billion in the recession year of 1954 and actually declined $0.1 billion in 1958, also a recession year.

Moreover, consumer installment credit is closely associated with purchases of durable goods which themselves are volatile. Thus it has probably further unstabilized an already unstable component of

---

[31] This does not mean that there has not been concern that consumer and mortgage credit have risen too fast over the postwar years as a whole with adverse effects on construction costs (which have risen faster than consumer prices or wholesale prices), the availability of resources for other investment programs, and perhaps on the economy's over-all growth. See, U.S. Senate, Committee on Banking and Currency, Subcommittee on Housing, *Study of Mortgage Credit, Hearings,* 86th Cong., 1st Sess., 1959, p. 176, and Appendix, pp. 152–53, 302, 307. Cited hereafter as Sparkman Committee, *Mortgage Hearings.* See also, Smithies, "Uses of Selective Credit Controls" in *United States Monetary Policy,* pp. 85–86; Board of Governors, *Consumer Instalment Credit,* Pt. II, Vol. I, pp. 236–45.

[32] Board of Governors, *Consumer Instalment Credit,* Pt. II, Vol. I, pp. 6–8.

[33] *Ibid.,* Pt. II, Vol. I, pp. 3–42, 64–69, 245–46, 422–23; and Pt. II, Vol. II, pp. 5, 22, 29, 41–42, 146–51, 159–60.

demand and production.[34] Some economists have even suggested that in recent years at least, consumer credit may have played a role in *initiating* recession and recovery, but this is a minority view.[35]

The destabilizing cyclical behavior of consumer installment credit seems to stem from both the demand and supply side. On the one hand, borrowers are more optimistic and hence more willing to incur debt in periods of prosperity. On the other hand, lenders find more good credit risks among prospective borrowers in periods of high income and employment than they do when people are unemployed. In addition, lenders too may be affected by currents of optimism in prosperity so that they ease their standards of creditworthiness and terms of lending.[36] In recession all of these considerations operate in reverse.

Home mortgage debt has not seemed to act as an unstabilizing influence in recent years, at least when viewed from a cyclical standpoint. In recent years the smallest increases in home mortgage debt have come in the final years of cyclical expansion, such as 1953 and 1957, rather than in recession years. Recession years have shown very large increases in mortgage debt, exceeded only by the increases in the first year of recovery such as 1955 and 1959. In general the pattern has been for the big increases in mortgage credit extension to take place in recession and early recovery when the economy has needed the stimulation of credit creation.[37] This picture of countercyclical behavior of home mortgage credit is reinforced when housing construction activity is examined, for housing starts precede by several months the creation of the mortgages which permanently finance starts (start-construction is financed in the interim by builders' working capital and short-term construction loans).[38] Many economists have concluded that in recent years at least "residential con-

[34] *Ibid.,* Pt. I, Vol. I, pp. 143–47, 218–34; and Pt. II, Vol. I, pp. 6–18, 149–50.

[35] *Ibid.,* Pt. II, Vol. II, p. 149; and Pt. I, Vol. I, p. 215.

[36] *Ibid.,* Pt. I, Vol. I, pp. 119–39, 223–28.

[37] For a discussion of the countercyclical behavior of mortgage credit and residential construction, see, Guttentag, "Some Studies of the Post-World War II Residential Construction and Mortgage Markets," pp. 1–33. Cited hereafter as *Some Studies.*

[38] O'Leary, "The Effects of Monetary Policies on the Mortgage Market," *Journal of Finance,* XIII (May, 1958), 177–78.

struction has behaved in a countercyclical fashion and, in the aggregate at least, has contributed to economic stability." [39]

This divergence in the behavior of consumer credit and home mortgage credit has reflected special influences on the supply side of the mortgage credit market. The demand for mortgage credit is presumably affected by waves of borrower optimism and pessimism related to general economic conditions just as is consumer credit demand. But mortgage lenders' willingness to lend is much less affected by prosperity or recession because Government guarantees or insurance of private mortgage loans have substantially decreased risks of loss to lenders because of borrowers' failures to repay.[40] Moreover, the Government guarantee and insurance of mortgages have involved certain accompaniments, such as the setting of fixed maximum interest rates on eligible mortgages, which have tended to increase and decrease lenders' willingness to lend on such mortgages in a countercyclical fashion.

Thus, consumer installment credit has rather clearly been an unstabilizing influence in the economy at large. Mortgage credit has on balance been a force for stability but, only because of special circumstances which may not continue indefinitely.

INSENSITIVITY TO GENERAL CREDIT CONTROLS. A major part of the case for selective controls is the allegation that consumer credit is relatively insensitive to the influence of general credit controls. For one thing, most borrowers of consumer or home mortgage credit pay primary attention to down-payment requirements and the amount of monthly repayments and relatively little to interest rates charged.[41] And the size of monthly repayments is relatively little affected by changes in interest rates, even in the case of mortgage borrowing where interest makes up a large part of total cost. For example, an increase in rates from 5 to 6 percent on a 20-year mortgage loan of $10,000 would increase the required monthly payment from $66.00 to $71.64 or by about 8 percent.[42] In any short period, mortgage interest rate changes are likely to be smaller than this with correspondingly smaller impact on monthly payments. Because of the

[39] Joint Committee, *1959 Staff Report*, p. 400.

[40] Sparkman Committee, *Mortgage Hearings*, Appendix, pp. 290–93.

[41] Board of Governors, *Consumer Instalment Credit*, Pt. II, Vol. I, p. 243; and Pt. II, Vol. II, pp. 21–22.

[42] Eastburn, "Real Estate Credit Controls," p. 12.

shorter term involved, consumer installment debt monthly repayments are much less sensitive to interest rate changes. Moreover, any lengthening of repayment periods or reduction of down payments which accompanied an interest rate increase could wipe out the deterrent effect of the interest rate increase.

Second, there is reason to believe that both the cost and availability of consumer credit are insensitive to general credit conditions. One evidence is the infrequency of changes in the interest rate charged on consumer loans. One of the major commercial bank lenders of consumer credit kept its consumer loan rate unchanged from 1937 to 1955 and has made only two changes since then, despite the vast changes in general credit conditions which had occurred over this period.[43] In contrast, the commercial bank prime loan rate to business borrowers was changed nineteen times during the same period.[44]

Third, there is some evidence that both bank and nonbank lenders to consumers have occasionally changed down-payment requirements and repayment periods perversely with respect to general credit conditions, that is, down payments have been reduced and repayment periods lengthened at times when general credit policy was tightening.[45] One reason for this appears to be that volume is extremely important for profitable consumer lending; hence, an increased cost of funds to the lender may be offset by encouraging a larger volume and reducing overhead costs per dollar loaned.[46] Another reason for lenders' reluctance to cut back on consumer credit has been that the return on consumer loans is high compared with returns on other types of loans.[47] In addition, consumer credit extended by sales finance companies connected with manufacturers of durable goods apparently has been used as a sales aid, and hence has been less sensitive to the impact of general credit controls on the profitability of financing operations.[48]

[43] Records of the First National City Bank of New York. For a discussion of finance company charges to borrowers see Board of Governors, *Consumer Instalment Credit*, Pt. I, Vol. II, p. 127.

[44] Records of the First National City Bank of New York.

[45] Board of Governors, *Consumer Instalment Credit*, Pt. I, Vol. I, pp. 119–39, 211, 215, 223, 259–80; Pt. I, Vol. II, pp. 66–163; and Pt. II, Vol. II, pp. 149–51, 159–60.

[46] *Ibid.*, Pt. I, Vol. I, pp. 67–68; and Pt. II, Vol. II, pp. 57–58.

[47] *Ibid.*, Pt. II, Vol. I, pp. xxiv; and Pt. II, Vol. II, pp. 3, 14, 150.

[48] *Ibid.*, Pt. I, Vol. I, pp. 135, 350–51; and Pt. I, Vol. II, pp. 159–63.

Fourth, the ability of the Federal Reserve to bring general credit controls to bear on consumer and mortgage credit has been handicapped by the fact that nonbank lenders outside the sphere of direct Federal Reserve influence are particularly important in these types of lending. In 1959 commercial banks accounted for no more than 34.3 percent of the increase in consumer installment credit and only about 12 percent of the increase in mortgage credit on one-to-four-family homes.[49] Nonbank lenders may of course be affected by general credit controls, but the effects would appear only gradually and indirectly through the impact of general credit controls on the ease of raising funds in the open market, on the availability and cost of bank credit if they rely on bank financing, and on the liquidity of their investment portfolios. The problem of reaching the nonbank lenders through general credit controls is likely to be particularly difficult if the Federal Reserve relies on "bills only" open market operations. Donald Jacobs has argued that this would hold true even for sales finance companies which, of all the nonbank lenders, rely most heavily on bank credit and short-term borrowing in the open market and hence are most likely to be subject to the influence of Federal Reserve policy actions in the short-term market.[50]

Despite all these considerations and the independent behavior of total consumer credit, there is some support for the view that general credit policy influences consumer credit. Paul Smith's study of the period from mid-1955 to the end of 1956, when general credit policy was restrictive, compared consumer lending by banks which gained deposits over the period with consumer lending by banks which lost deposits. He found that declining-deposit banks increased consumer lending much less than increasing-deposit banks. And declining deposits, of course, reflect a greater impact of general credit policy. In general, declining-deposit banks showed smaller loan increases in almost all loan categories than increasing-deposit banks, and consumer loans were held back as much or more than other loan categories.[51]

---

[49] *Federal Reserve Bulletin,* XLVI (April and December, 1960), pp. 415, 409, 1387; and Federal Home Loan Bank Board, release on "Estimated Home Mortgage Debt," September, 1960.

[50] Board of Governors, *Consumer Instalment Credit,* Pt. II, Vol. I, p. 408.

[51] Paul Smith, "Response of Consumer Loans to General Credit Conditions," *American Economic Review,* XLVIII (September, 1958), 649–55.

However, Smith's study also indicated that medium-sized banks did not impose restraint on consumer loans as quickly as they held back other types of lending.[52] This suggests that even where general credit policy has effect in cutting back bank deposit volumes, the impact on consumer lending might sometimes be delayed. Moreover, Smith's study did not determine whether, in fact, general credit policy does promptly and appreciably affect the deposit positions of the banks which extend the bulk of consumer credit, that is, small to medium-sized banks.[53] It is significant in this connection that net deposits of Country member banks (which held 46 percent of "other loans to individuals," largely consumer credit, on June 30, 1955) rose $6 billion during the period Smith studies, accounting for approximately two thirds of the $9.4 billion gain in all member bank deposits.[54] If general credit policy affects only slightly or belatedly the deposits of the banks which do the bulk of bank consumer lending, it may still be true that consumer credit is relatively insensitive to general credit policy.

There is, however, little doubt that in recent years mortgage credit has been quite sensitive to general credit controls, providing a sharp contrast to consumer credit. As a matter of fact, its sensitivity has been so marked as to arouse protests that general credit controls have had a discriminatorily severe impact on building.

But this special sensitivity has been mainly an accidental by-product of the rigidity of contract rates of interest set by administrative decision or by law on mortgages eligible for guarantee by the Veterans Administration or for insurance by the Federal Housing Administration. In periods of prosperity, when monetary policy is restrictive, interest rates generally rise, increasing the return on investments such as corporate bonds which are competitive with VA and FHA mortgages as outlets for investible funds. Since the rates available on VA and FHA mortgages do not rise at all, or are adjusted upward only with considerable lag, their attractiveness to institutional investors is reduced and the flow of funds into such mortgages is correspondingly lessened. In recessions, when monetary

---

[52] *Ibid.,* p. 654.

[53] See, Nadler's discussion of this point in Board of Governors, *Consumer Instalment Credit,* Pt. II, Vol. II, pp. 14–16.

[54] Calculated from tables presented in *Federal Reserve Bulletin,* XLII (February, 1956), 141, and XLIV (August, 1958), 948–49.

policy is easy, the process works in reverse. Competitively determined interest rates decline while contract rates on VA and FHA mortgages remain relatively unchanged, attracting a greater flow of funds into such mortgages.[55] The result is, as Warren Smith pointed out,

Changes in differentials between the rather rigid interest rates on FHA-insured and VA-guaranteed mortgages and yields on corporate bonds have had a strong effect on housing starts under the FHA and VA programs. When these differentials widen, as in 1953–54, residential construction is stimulated by an ample flow of mortgage funds; when they become narrower, as in 1955–57, the supply of funds is drained away into competitive uses with a restrictive effect on homebuilding.[56]

However, if contract interest rates on VA and FHA underwritten mortgages were permitted to fluctuate with market conditions, as many economists have recommended,[57] it is likely that much of the influence of general credit controls over mortgage credit and housing construction would disappear.[58] In that case there might well be need for selective control of home mortgage down payments and maturities to supplement the impact of general controls. It is not easy to assess the likelihood of VA and FHA mortgage interest rates being permitted, in the future, to fluctuate more freely. Many congressmen favor setting mortgage interest rates below market levels since they regard this as a benefit to deserving and needy borrowers. On the other hand, there is widening appreciation of the view expressed by most economists and many housing industry spokesmen that mortgage interest rates fixed at artificially low levels benefit the few who manage to secure funds but disadvantage many more people who cannot borrow because lenders refuse to lend at the unattractive rates.[59]

In summary, then, general credit controls affect consumer credit insufficiently and tardily. While general controls have influenced home

---

[55] Sparkman Committee, *Mortgage Hearings,* Appendix, pp. 197–98, 243, 296. The effective rate of return to a lender could be increased by buying VA or FHA mortgages at a discount from par and to some extent this happens. But there is considerable reluctance among some lenders, particularly insurance companies, to buy at discounts and discounts on VA mortgages are particularly avoided. See remarks of Saul Klaman, Sparkman Committee, *Mortgage Hearings,* p. 183.

[56] *Ibid.,* pp. 159–60.

[57] *Ibid.,* pp. 202, 238, 280–83, 357; and Joint Committee, *1959 Staff Report,* p. 401.

[58] Joint Committee, *1959 Staff Report,* p. 400.

[59] *Ibid.,* p. 401; and Sparkman Committee, *Mortgage Hearings,* pp. 160, 182.

mortgage credit appreciably, this may not hold true in the future if interest rates on Government underwritten mortgages are freed from their current rigidity.

EFFECTIVENESS OF SELECTIVE CONTROL. The effectiveness of selective control over consumer credit is considered a proven fact by proponents of selective credit measures and, more significantly, is conceded by many, if not all, opponents of selective controls.[60] But there is no such substantial agreement on the efficacy of selective control of home mortgage credit. Accordingly, this section deals separately with Regulation W's effectiveness in regulating consumer credit and Regulation X's efficacy in controlling home mortgage credit.

Selective control of consumer credit can be judged by a number of criteria, but two appear to be of major importance. First, it may be asked whether changes in down-payment requirements and maximum maturities have significantly affected the use of consumer credit. Second, it may be asked whether such controls have been effective in narrowing or broadening the market for consumer credit and the volume of sales of consumer durable goods.

There seems to be fairly general agreement that Regulation W has proved effective in bringing about desired changes in the terms of actual consumer credit transactions and in influencing the volume of such credit outstanding. It should be noted that because of the strong trend in consumer credit figures, the result of restrictive selective regulation has been a flattening out in the increase of outstandings rather than an absolute decline. When such restrictions have been lifted, the volume of credit has surged upward. Whittlesey said, "the correlation between changes in the volume of consumer credit and changes in the terms of Regulation W is dramatically apparent." [61]

This reflects in good part the fact that changes in down-payment requirements and maximum maturities automatically influence the volume of credit outstanding; higher down payments reduce the amount of credit involved in a given transaction and shorter maturities mean faster repayment of a given amount of debt, both these effects reducing the average volume of debt outstanding. Using this kind of relationship Young and Fauver calculated that the more re-

---

[60] See Lester Chandler's remarks, Board of Governors, *Consumer Instalment Credit*, Pt. II, Vol. II, p. 32; also Milton Friedman's assumptions, *Ibid.*, p. 75.
[61] Whittlesey, "Old and New Ideas on Reserve Requirements," *Journal of Finance*, VIII (May, 1953), 194.

strictive consumer credit terms in effect from October, 1950, to September, 1951, reduced the volume of installment credit outstanding by $2.1 billion, compared with what it would have been on the basis of preregulation terms and the same volume of sales as under the restrictive regulation.[62] Simply reducing the amount of use of consumer credit is a worthwhile achievement even if consumer buying is not reduced, for new credit creation adds to the money supply and also frees consumers' liquid assets for other expenditures. But if consumer credit regulation did no more than this it would be open to the charge that it did not affect the flow of spending; it could be argued that consumers might continue to exert inflationary pressure by financing purchases out of liquid asset accumulations.

There is, however, reason to believe that consumer credit controls have also affected the volume of sales of consumer durables. Saulnier said that the September, 1948, imposition of restrictive Regulation W terms "was beginning, by early 1949, to have a very dampening effect on consumer durable goods purchases" and that the subsequent easing of terms, beginning in March and April, 1949, was responsible "in no small part" for increases in sales of consumer durable goods which took place in the last half of 1949.[63] Saulnier also concluded that the 1950 reimposition of Regulation W "suggests a fairly sensitive reaction of consumer instalment sales credit to changes in terms" and that "the control authorities . . . can produce very substantial decreases in consumer spending on selected durable goods." [64]

Additional support for belief in the efficacy of Regulation W was provided by the Federal Reserve's 1956 study of consumer credit.[65] Higher down-payment requirements were found to exclude some potential borrowers and buyers from the market; [66] lower down payments, to enlarge the number of potential buyers able to make credit-financed purchases.[67] Shortening the maximum repayment period

[62] Ralph Young and Clarke Fauver, "Measuring the Impact of Consumer Credit Controls on Spending," *Journal of Finance,* VII (May, 1952), 400–401.
[63] Saulnier, *American Economic Review,* XLII, 260.
[64] *Ibid.,* pp. 260–61.
[65] Board of Governors, *Consumer Instalment Credit,* Pt. I, Vol. I, Ch. 7 and pp. 92, 223; and Pt. II, Vol. I, pp. 125–34.
[66] *Ibid.,* Pt. I, Vol. I, p. 138; and Pt. II, Vol. I, p. 128.
[67] *Ibid.,* Pt. I, Vol. I, 138–39; and Pt. II, Vol. I, pp. 128–33.

(and thus increasing the size of the monthly repayments required) was found to contract the demand for automobile credit,[68] while lengthening maximum repayment periods "brought some instalment buyers into the market who might not otherwise have bought." [69] Similar effects of changing repayment periods were observed in studies of consumer durables other than automobiles.[70] Thus, Regulation W would seem to have been effective in changing the amount of credit required to finance a given volume of transactions and in influencing the volume of transactions.

The effectiveness of Regulation X in controlling home mortgage credit and residential construction is a good deal more controversial than the effectiveness of Regulation W. A number of economists have had no hesitation in expressing the opinion that Regulation X was ineffective. O'Leary said:

It is difficult to escape the conclusion that Regulation X had little value as a means for promptly bringing under control the sharp increase in expenditures for residential construction the critical year following its enactment.[71]

Saulnier asserted that Regulation X was intended to reduce housing starts from an annual rate of almost 1,400,000 to 850,000 or by about 40 percent and he added:

As matters turned out, the reduction was considerably less than the original goal. . . . Even with a somewhat greater shortage of strategic materials than had originally been expected and with a distinct tightening of the money market in early 1951 as a result of the Treasury-Federal Reserve Accord, the reduction seems to have been only about 25 per cent for 1951 as a whole.[72]

And Smith emphasized that the main problem was:

the regulations were anticipated and financing arrangements which were exempt from regulation were entered into prior to the application of the controls. Thus, there was a very large backlog of liberal financing arrangements to be worked through before the controls could exert their effects.[73]

---

[68] *Ibid.,* Pt. I, Vol. I, p. 132; and Pt. II, Vol. I, p. 128.
[69] *Ibid.,* Pt. I, Vol. I, p. 134; but also see pp. 132–35.
[70] *Ibid.*
[71] O'Leary, *The Journal of Finance,* XIII, 180.
[72] Saulnier, *American Economic Review,* XLII, 261–62.
[73] Sparkman Committee, *Mortgage Hearings,* Appendix, p. 251.

O'Leary concluded:

The experience with Regulation X showed that direct controls are an inherently unsatisfactory device for controlling residential mortgage credit.
Because of the need for advance consultation with industry advisory
groups and the tendency for a buildup of forward commitments to take
place, it is questionable whether this type of control could ever be made
effective.[74]

The case against Regulation X rests, then, on three foundations:
(1) The regulation took hold only slowly; (2) The regulation did not
achieve as large a reduction in housing starts as had been originally
planned; and (3) The lagged and inadequate effect of Regulation X
was inevitable because of the backlog of pre-Regulation X commitments which had been built up earlier. It can be argued however that
these contentions overstate the case against Regulation X-type controls and that there is reason to believe that Regulation X *was*
effective.[75]

First, the evidence of monthly data on housing starts does not
square with O'Leary's statement that "because of the commitment
backlog, Regulation X was barely starting to be effective with regard
to construction at the time that it was decided, in the spring of 1952,
that the regulation was no longer needed." [76] Seasonally adjusted
privately-owned nonfarm housing starts declined from a peak of
1,486,000 (annual rate) in August, 1950, to an annual rate of 1,107,-
000 in November, 1950. After a brief resurgence in December, January, and February, housing starts turned down again and reached a
low of 918,000 (annual rate) in July, 1951,[77] when Congress liberal-
ized Regulation X and accompanying restrictions on VA and FHA

[74] O'Leary, *Journal of Finance*, XIII, 186. For a description of the institutional arrangements of the mortgage market, and particularly the forward or
advance commitment process, see Mortimer Kaplan, "Recent Institutional Arrangements in Mortgage Lending," *Journal of Finance*, XIII (May, 1958),
188–200.

[75] Strictly speaking, Regulation X applied only to terms on conventional
mortgages. Government-underwritten mortgages, such as VA and FHA mortgages, were regulated by administrative order of the Housing and Home Finance Administrator after consultation with the Administrator of Veterans
Affairs and the Federal Reserve Board. However, all these regulations were intended as a package and it is convenient often to speak as though Regulation
X covered all mortgages.

[76] O'Leary, *Journal of Finance*, XIII, 179.

[77] Housing and Home Finance Agency, *Housing Statistics, Historical Supplement,* December, 1958, p. 6.

mortgages, effective September 1, 1951,[78] and housing starts turned up again. These declines reflected the combined impact of Regulation X itself, effective October 12, 1950, and some earlier tightening of terms on VA and FHA mortgages on July 19, 1950, which were similar in nature and effect to Regulation X.

Second, the reduction of housing starts after adoption of Regulation X did not fall as far short of the goal as Saulnier's comment would, suggest. The point is that the goal was actually a one-third reduction from the current level of housing starts, not a 40 percent decline as Saulnier implied.[79] It was believed in September, 1950, when Regulation X was formulated, that 1950 housing starts would total about 1,250,000,[80] so that a one-third reduction from this level implied 800,000 to 850,000 starts for 1951 as a goal. Saulnier derived 40 percent as the planned reduction by comparing 850,000 with 1,352,000 starts in 1950, but this latter total was the number of houses actually started, a figure not known until well after 1950 had closed and therefore obviously not available to the formulators of Regulation X in setting their goal. The 25 percent reduction in starts actually achieved in 1951 was less than the 33 1/3 percent goal, to be sure, but it was much closer to the target than Saulnier's discussion would indicate. Furthermore, the 1951 starts total might have been somewhat lower if it had not been for the Congressional liberalization of housing terms effective September 1. In August, 1951, the annual rate of housing starts was running 35 percent below the August, 1950, figure.[81]

Of course, it can be argued, as did Saulnier in the passage cited, that some of the decline in starts reflected shortages of materials and the impact of rising interest rates or even, as Smith suggested, a weakening of "real" demand for housing.[82] Shortages probably were responsible for some decline in starts but in assessing their impor-

---

[78] Eastburn, "Real Estate Credit Controls," pp. 152–60.

[79] See, for example, the press statement issued in connection with the imposition of Regulation X: "housing production in 1951 shculd be reduced about one third below the current record level of home building, or not more than 800,000 units." *Federal Reserve Bulletin*, XXXVI (October, 1950), 1284.

[80] Eastburn, "Real Estate Credit Controls," p. 130, footnote 1.

[81] Housing and Home Finance Agency, *Housing Statistics, Historical Supplement*, p. 6.

[82] Sparkman Committee, *Mortgage Hearings*, Appendix, p. 251.

tance in the over-all picture, it should be remembered that materials availability improved rather quickly and by mid-1951 had become a major part of the case for relaxation of Regulation X.[83] The impact of rising interest rates after the March, 1951, unpegging of the bond market doubtless had considerable effect on the willingness of lenders to make forward commitments, but it is questionable whether it could have had appreciable effect on starts before July.

So far as the real demand for housing is concerned, some factors did show sizable declines, notably new household formations and the backlog of couples without their own households. However, the declines in these variables were less than the decline in housing starts. Moreover, even after the decline, both new household formations and the backlog of couples without their own households remained well above the rate of housing-starts.[84] Finally, in appraising this explanation, it deserves emphasis that the decline in housing starts began around the middle of 1950 when these real demand factors were still at or near record levels. The temptation is great to accept Miles Colean's conclusion that the 1950–1951 decline in housing-starts was due to

the shutoff of the authority of the Federal National Mortgage Association to make advance commitments at par and to the imposition of restrictions on loan-to-value ratios and maturities of FHA and VA loans and the other controls attendant on the Korean War. The fundamental sources and characteristics of demand could not have changed with the abruptness with which the number of new housing starts dropped.[85]

Third, the large backlog of pre-Regulation X financing commitments did not have as much influence in maintaining the volume of housing starts as is generally believed.[86] The main reason for this is

[83] Eastburn, "Real Estate Credit Controls," pp. 152–60.

[84] New household formations declined from 1,592,000 in 1950 to 1,308,000 in 1951, or by 18 percent; the number of married couples without own households declined from 2,016,000 in 1950 to 1,758,000 in 1951, or by 13 percent. New privately-owned nonfarm starts declined from 1,352,000 in 1950 to 1,020,000 in 1951, or by 25 percent. Sparkman Committe, *Mortgage Hearings,* Appendix, pp. 245–46.

[85] Sparkman Committee, *Mortgage Hearings,* Appendix, p. 294. Guttentag also thought that Regulation X, aided by other governmental actions, was responsible for the downturn in housing. See Guttentag *Some Studies,* pp. 223–25.

[86] This is not to say that the backlog had no effect. It almost certainly did have, and its relative lack of effect in 1950–1951 was due in good part to special circumstances concerning the pre-Regulation X tightening of terms on VA and FHA mortgages.

that the commitments entered into just before the imposition of Regulation X did not represent an escape from restriction because the July 19, 1950, tightening of terms on VA and FHA mortgages had already imposed restrictions about as severe as those required in connection with Regulation X itself.[87] The July tightening eliminated the no-down-payment VA loans which had sparked housing demand in 1949–1950,[88] doubled down-payments on FHA-financed homes costing $5,000 or less from 5 to 10 percent, and also required buyers to add to their down payments any increase in building costs and prices which took place after July 1, 1950.[89] Thus most of the VA and FHA pre-Regulation X backlog involved financing terms which were about as restrictive as those under Regulation X,[90] and presumably had about the same effect on demand.

In addition, economic organization of the construction industry is such that builders have incentive to reduce the scale of their current operations long before their backlog of work is exhausted if they foresee any sharp reduction in the flow of incoming business. This is done to ensure that there will be enough future work to keep a nucleus of experienced work-crews going until business picks up again, and operations and employment can be enlarged once more. Thus

[87] Eastburn, "Real Estate Credit Controls," p. 109, footnote 1.

[88] More than 40 percent of VA-guaranteed first mortgage loans in the year ending June 30, 1950, were made without a down payment. U.S. Administrator of Veterans Affairs, *Annual Report,* 1951, p. 95.

[89] Housing and Home Finance Agency, *Annual Report,* 1951, p. 216; *Federal Reserve Bulletin,* XXXVI (October, 1950), 1285; and XXXVII (July, 1951), 785; Eastburn, *Real Estate Credit Controls,* Chapter VIII and p. 203. According to Eastburn the July 19, 1950, cost freeze on FHA and VA lending procedures meant that "the difference between the valuation made by the FHA or VA and the purchase price had to be included in the downpayment. The amount by which price increases raised down payments on FHA loans varied on houses in different price ranges, but it was regarded as a fair, but rough, estimate to add six percentage points to the indicated average down payments actually being made to get the effect of the cost freeze" (p. 139).

[90] As an illustration, based on schedules given in sources cited in the preceding note, Regulation X and the accompanying restrictions called for a 10 percent down payment on a $5,000 FHA-financed home and a 23 percent down payment on a $10,000 FHA-financed home. The July 19 restrictions called for a 10 percent down payment on $5,000 homes and 17.5 percent on $10,000 FHA-financed homes, but in addition the buyer had to pay the difference between the actual price and what the FHA valued the house at on the basis of July 1 costs or about 6 percent additional on the average. Thus, both the July 19 and October 12 restrictions involved a down payment of about 23 percent on a $10,000 FHA-insured home. The October 12 restrictions did call for a 5-year shorter loan maturity, however.

if a firm has a backlog of work sufficient to keep a hundred men busy for three months but has reason to expect a sharp drop in the amount of work to be done after that, it will not produce at full speed until the three months of work are completed. Rather it is likely to lay off newly acquired or temporary employees, and thus cut down the scale of production immediately in order to make sure that its key employees will have work for six or nine months.[91] Hence even a large backlog of forward commitments will not prevent credit restraint or selective controls from having some impact fairly quickly.

The fact that Regulation X had more effect than is commonly believed was due in good part to the special circumstance that much of the backlog of pre-Regulation X mortgage commitments carried terms as restrictive as those imposed under Regulation X. Thus, contrary to general belief, the backlog of exempt commitments did not represent an escape from regulation. But this was a special circumstance and unlikely to support the efficacy of a selective control like Regulation X in the future. It is true that the economic organization of the building industry would probably bring about some response to selective regulation even if there were a backlog of truly exempt mortgage commitments. But there is little doubt that a Regulation-X type of control would be more effective if it were possible to hold down the number of exempt commitments. Discussion of methods of avoiding any build-up in exempt commitments is deferred to the section on administrative problems of selective controls.

SELECTIVE CREDIT CONTROLS, INTEREST RATES, AND ECONOMIC GROWTH. A number of economists have pointed out that the use of selective credit controls could permit a central bank to impose a given degree of credit restraint without as much of a rise in interest rates as would occur if only general credit controls were used.[92] This is because selective credit controls of the type of Regulation X and Regulation W operate initially on the *demand* for credit and exclude some potential borrowers through the down payment and maturity requirement. To the extent that the excluded borrowers do not succeed in

---

[91] Maisel, *Housebuilding in Transition*, p. 83.

[92] Patman Committee, *Compendium*, Pt. II, pp. 414–15, 425–26; testimony of William McChesney Martin before Senate Banking and Currency Committee, U.S. Senate, Committee on Banking and Currency, *Defense Production Act Amendments of 1951, Hearings*, p. 312; Miller, *Quarterly Journal of Economics*, LXX, 34–36; Eastburn, in *Readings in Money and Banking*, pp. 110–11.

getting other types of credit, the total effective demand for credit is reduced without affecting the supply of credit. With the supply of credit unaffected and the demand somewhat lower, interest rates generally should be somewhat lower than they would be if selective controls had not been used. General credit controls, in contrast, operate initially by reducing the *supply* of credit so that fewer demands can be satisfied; ordinarily, borrowers' competition for a smaller supply of funds then produces somewhat higher interest rates.

Some observers have noted that this characteristic of selective credit controls could be an important advantage in periods when heavy credit demands and restrictive general credit policies had pushed interest rates up beyond tolerable limits. Thus, when public protests or difficulties of Treasury financing were blocking any further tightening of general credit controls, the authorities could increase over-all restraint by tightening selective credit controls. In some circumstances, conceivably, they could tighten selective controls—e.g., on real estate credit—while at the same time easing back a bit on general credit tightening measures.[93]

This use of selective credit controls, however, raises some problems. It would hardly be appropriate, for example, to tighten consumer credit controls or mortgage credit controls in order to permit some relaxation of general credit restraints if the automobile industry and residential construction were having a bad year. Apart from the question of appropriateness, the industries affected would vigorously resist such imposition of selective controls. Thus opportunities to use selective controls to avoid undue increases in interest rates at periods of special pressure in the money market might be less frequent than would be thought at first glance. Nevertheless, selective controls, judiciously used, doubtless could provide valuable assistance to monetary policy at strategic moments by helping to avoid an overload of pressure on the Government securities market. At the same time, temptations to abuse this approach, likely because of the attraction of insuring acceptable financing terms to the Treasury, would be offset by the protests of industries affected.

It may be noted that whenever it has been appropriate to use them to lessen the amplitude of interest rate increases, selective credit con-

---

[93] Patman Committee, *Compendium*, Pt. II, p. 415; Miller, *Quarterly Journal of Economics*, LXX, 35–36.

trols would have had side benefits for the economy as well as for the Treasury. A somewhat lower level of interest rates would have drawn less idle money into active circulation. Thus increases in velocity, which on occasion have offset some of the impact of restriction of the money supply, would have been smaller. Moreover, a little lower level of interest rates would have been less restrictive of capital investment programs, a particularly important consideration in recent years because of the emphasis on economic growth.

Some economists would use selective controls to encourage growth directly by limiting the credit and resources devoted to consumer durable goods and even housing, and thus encouraging, a greater flow into more "productive" business investment programs.[94] While this would seem to have appeal, on closer examination a number of difficulties arise.

First, using a selective control to check the flow of resources into residential housing would run head-on into well established Government policies of encouraging a greater flow of capital into housing construction. The typical Congressional attitude is that housing has been getting too little of the capital supply, not that it has been getting too much.[95] If the national policy is to encourage growth by reducing the amount of capital devoted to residential construction, the simplest way of going about it would be for the Federal Government to reduce the encouragements it has given to housing in the form of mortgage guarantees and insurance programs, direct purchases of mortgages. and long-term loans at preferential rates.

Second, a decision to encourage economic growth by holding back consumption and housing expenditures through selective controls would mean a great deal more interference in private markets than a decision to use selective controls occasionally when particular markets seem to be destabilizing the economy or when general credit controls need some temporary assistance. Enlarging the proportion of resources devoted to capital investment presumably would mean a continuing selective restraint on consumers' desires to purchase durable goods and homes and a steady restriction of the ability of these

[94] Board of Governors, *Consumer Instalment Credit*, Pt. II, Vol. II, pp. 68–72.

[95] See, for example, Joint Economic Committee, *Report on the January 1959 Economic Report of the President*, 85th Cong., 2d Sess., 1959, p. 15; Sparkman Committee, *Mortgage Hearings*, pp. 175–78, 189–99.

industries to produce goods and profits. There is little doubt that this type of selective credit regulation would run into a great deal more opposition than a cyclically-stabilizing selective credit control program, which would be restrictive only when there was some immediate and obvious reason.

Third, and perhaps most important, there is not only uncertainty as what encourages economic growth but also disagreement as what is meant by it.[96] This diversity of opinion has in turn led to sharply varying views about the relation of consumption and economic growth and accordingly disagreement as to the role of selective controls in influencing the growth process. Ervin Miller has argued that consumer credit and the increased consumption of durable consumer goods have "contributed to economic growth" [97] at least in the "broad, quantitative sense." [98] Miller would classify purchases of consumers' durables as investment, though he concedes that many authorities would classify them as consumption.[99] Other economists stress that consumer credit and mortgage credit divert resources from business investment which is regarded as more productive than "investment" in consumer durables, which they regard as really consumption, in any case.[100] Friedrich Lutz argued that "the generalization seems justified that consumer credit on the whole slows down economic growth." [101] It is noteworthy that each of the participants in this controversy carefully points out the difficulties of reaching firm conclusions. In view of the lack of conviction on all sides, it would seem most reasonable to accept Moses Abramovitz's conclusion that "a decision to impose consumer finance controls ought to be made on the basis of considerations other than those concerned with economic growth." [102]

Thus the case for the use of selective credit controls to ease the burden on general credit controls and limit the upward movement of interest rates at times of special pressure in the money market has some plausibility. But this probably ought to be an infrequent goal

[96] See, for example, Board of Governors, *Consumer Instalment Credit*, Pt. II, Vol. I, pp. 169–254.

[97] *Ibid.*, p. 201.   [98] *Ibid.*, p. 203.

[99] *Ibid.*, pp. 194–96.

[100] *Ibid.*, pp. 234–45; Pt. II, Vol. II, pp. 70–71; and *United States Monetary Policy*, pp. 73–81.

[101] Board of Governors, *Consumer Instalment Credit*, Pt. II, Vol. I, p. 241.

[102] *Ibid.*, p. 253.

for the administrator of selective controls, because overuse might create such resentment as to destroy their usefulness in their main task of controlling occasional distortions in the pattern of consumption and credit use. The use of selective controls to encourage economic growth by limiting the proportion of income and resources devoted to consumption is a good deal more controversial and probably should be avoided until more knowledge is at hand on the nature of the growth process.

OBJECTIONS TO SELECTIVE CREDIT CONTROLS

There are a number of objections to selective control of the use of credit in particular areas. Some observers deny the effectiveness of selective controls, but this is not a common view. However, other objections do carry considerable weight with most observers. The most seriously regarded objections have to do with the way in which consumer and real-estate credit controls would interfere with the operation of the market mechanism, with the administrative problems involved in such selective controls, and with the probability of large scale and widespread resentment of the discriminatory aspects of selective controls.

INTERFERENCE WITH THE FREE MARKET. A fundamental objection to selective controls on the part of many economists, as well as representatives of affected industry groups, is that selective controls by their nature represent interference with the allocation function of the market and represent therefore "a long step in the direction of Government planning." [103] Thus Donald B. Woodward, then economist for the Mutual Life Insurance Company of New York, told the 1951 Patman Subcommittee "selective credit controls . . . impair the free working of the forces of demand and supply by authoritarian exclusion or limitation of one or more segments of the economy from the market." [104] And Ray B. Westerfield told the same Congressional subcommittee:

Selective credit controls . . . are not compatible with the free enterprise economy. . . . Under the free enterprise system free markets and pricing will afford what control is needed within the "general tightening of

[103] The New York Clearing House Association, *The Federal Reserve Re-Examined,* p. 123.
[104] Patman Committee, *Compendium,* Pt. II, p. 1080.

credit" which deals with the whole economy and does not try to allocate, foster, or depress, or otherwise exercise discriminatory pressure within the economy.[105]

These views found expression in the Patman Subcommittee *Report* in the following words: "Selective credit controls have the *a priori* disadvantage that they tend to transfer the use of credit from more-wanted to less-wanted channels as measured by the normal criteria of the price system." [106]

A similar case was made by a number of opponents of selective control during the Federal Reserve's 1956 study of consumer credit regulation. Milton Friedman argued that "consumer credit control forbids individuals from making contracts among themselves that they regard as mutually beneficial and that do not harm others" [107] and went on to assert that so far as monetary policy is concerned:

The relevant total from the point of view of aggregate demand, is credit of all kinds. Given the general credit situation, expansions and contractions in consumer credit are in large part bound to be at the expense of other types of credit . . . general monetary control comes close to operating on the relevant base that is, credit of all kinds, so it is hard to see any argument for operating specifically on consumer credit.[108]

[105] *Ibid.*, p. 1079.

[106] U.S. Congress, Joint Committee on the Economic Report, Subcommittee on General Credit Control and Debt Management, *Monetary Policy and the Management of the Public Debt, Report*, 82d Cong., 2d Sess., 1952, p. 37.

[107] Board of Governors, *Consumer Instalment Credit*, Pt. II, Vol. II, p. 103.

[108] *Ibid.*, p. 85. E. C. Simmons' contribution to the same study (pp. 112–37) took this kind of argument one step further, as had Friedman in other forums, by arguing that the central bank should not even be concerned with "credit of all kinds"—as Friedman put it in the passage cited—but should confine itself to "provision of the correct volume of money" (p. 116). This view lays itself open to the rejoinder that in the American economy, and in most modern economies, the volume of money is affected *through* the *credit-creating* activities of commercial banks. Herbert Stein in commenting on Simmons' paper said: "The central bank does not control the money supply by hiding money under rose bushes. It does it by operating on certain institutions—banks—that are in the business of extending credit" (p. 140). Simmons admitted this but argued that such incidental credit control by the central bank is only a means to the end of controlling the money supply. To try to make credit control an important purpose of the central bank, Simmons argued, runs into the insuperable obstacle that "no criteria exist for determining either the total volume of funds that should be made available to borrowers or the kinds of loans that should be made" (p. 112). While this sounds like an imposing objection, the fact is that practically all central banking decisions—including those involved in determining the total volume of money that should be made available—are cut and try affairs in which judgment and the response of a number of market criteria are important elements. And there is no reason why the criteria used in deciding on the correct volume of money—the behavior of employment, prices, production,

These views deserve consideration, if only because they are so widely held. We have already argued that the very existence of a central bank means that exclusive reliance on the decisions of a free market has been rejected. To be sure, it must be admitted that selective credit controls involve a greater degree of interference with private market decisions than do, for example, open market purchases or sales of Treasury securities. But once a completely free market system has been given up, the question is whether any particular interference is justified by the ends to be achieved, including a considerable degree of freedom in the economy as a desirable end, not whether it would infringe on some ideal conception of a free-market enterprise economy which does not in any case exist.

Without disparaging the advantages of free markets and the price system, the Patman Subcommittee's observation that selective controls transfer the use of credit from more-wanted to less-wanted channels is open to question. The observation is presumably based on the idea that the consumer will pay more for accommodation than will a business firm, and hence should get the credit. But suppose the consumer does not realize how high an interest rate he is paying? Suppose he has been high-pressured into an automobile "deal" without real knowledge of the costs or consequences involved? Does this demand from him still represent more of a "want" than the presumably more closely calculated loan demand of a businessman? Robert C. Turner commented that this sort of argument

is based upon an implicit assumption of an economy of scarcity, populated by consumers who have unlimited wants which are very real, very urgent, and fully understood and calculated. The fact is that, in the American economy, a substantial portion of total demand is demand which is in part created by sellers, which can be and is manipulated by advertising, model changes, and easy credit terms. The assumption of a consumer who is a rational, calculating measurer of pain and pleasure does not fit very well into the contemporary environment.[109]

Moreover, Friedman's rejection of interference with individual contracts which are regarded as mutually beneficial cannot be regarded as justification for the rejection of selective credit control. It

---

etc.—could not be used by the central bank to help determine whether over-all credit use should be encouraged or discouraged. Indeed, this, in practice, is done, for as Simmons admitted the Federal Reserve does give some place to credit control in its objectives.

[109] *Ibid.,* p. 107.

it too sweeping. A moment's reflection is enough to show that this sort of argument would reject interference with a "pusher's" sale of narcotics to an addict; both presumably would be satisfied by the transaction, others would not be harmed, and hence there would be no grounds, in Friedman's view, for interference by society. The point is, however, that society does reserve the right to interfere in order to protect individuals from their own ignorance or weakness. And it naturally wields this power more aggressively where third parties are endangered.

The case for controlling consumer and mortgage credit is that they may contribute to economic instability for everybody, that consumer credit is now insensitive to general credit controls and mortgage credit could be, and that both these types of credit can be controlled by selective measures. To be sure, some selective credit measures might diminish freedom and viability of the economy more than they would improve stability or encourage growth. But this is something to be evaluated separately in each case, not something to be arbitrarily assumed in advance.

STABILIZING PARTICULAR MARKETS—AN UNDESIRABLE GOAL OF ECONOMIC POLICY. Much of the objection to selective control stems from the belief that its advocates want to stabilize the entire economy by imposing stability on each major segment of the economy. The fallacy of trying to stabilize every sector, opponents of selective controls point out, is that flux and change are necessary in a dynamic, growing economy which must constantly adjust to changing tastes, costs, technology, and competitive conditions at home and abroad.[110] Stabilizing each sector of the economy would prevent needed adjustments, regiment the economy, lead to economic stagnation and eventually destroy the nation's competitive power in world markets.

There is no doubt that flexibility in the economy is important. But proponents of selective controls do not necessarily desire absolute stability in any or all particular sectors. Most often the aim is not to stabilize rigidly but simply to dampen fluctuations in particular sectors which seem to be going to excess and creating problems for the future. And while "going to excess" is admittedly not easy to define, advocates of selective control apparently think in terms of the difficulties caused for economic balance by very rapidly growing sectors,

[110] *Ibid.*, p. 78.

of "borrowing demand from the future" by excessively easy credit terms in any particular year, of overuse of resources which leads to inflationary price increases beyond those useful in attracting resources from other areas of the economy, and of the creation of a "boom" atmosphere which leads to unsustainable expectations and expansion [111] in other sectors of the economy. As noted previously, the explosive surge of automobile sales in 1955, facilitated by radical easing of installment credit terms, was an example of what proponents of selective controls would wish to modify by their use.[112]

Some objectors to selective controls contend that fluctuations in particular sectors, for example, in consumer durable goods, would be poor guides for monetary policy and might result in inequities. Consumer credit controls might restrict the specific industries they affect more than would be warranted by general economic conditions. Friedman's argument, for example, is that rising demand for automobiles might be offset by a falling demand for other consumer goods, or a decline in demand for producer goods.[113] And, it is argued, even though these offsetting declines in demand may not be as visible as a spectacular rise in automobile production, they are important from the point of view of general economic stability. The error in this objection is that it ignores the fact that a shift of demand to automobiles which involves increased consumer credit may well mean an increase in total consumer demand at least equivalent to the net increase in credit. So far as the possibility of offsetting shifts in demand for producer goods goes, major increases in demand for consumer durables are equally likely to give rise to increases in demand

[111] *Ibid.*, pp. 146–7.

[112] *Ibid.*, pp. 3, 20–22, 146.

[113] *Ibid.*, pp. 78–79. Friedman also argues that in some cases increases in demand for consumer durables and consumer credit may reflect general increases in demand as a result of increases in the supply of money or expectations of price increases and concludes that in these cases control on consumer credit would merely divert the demand for credit into other channels. But this ignores the fact that the unavailability of consumer credit in the desired amount would reduce the buying power of consumers, whose ability to borrow in other areas is relatively limited, and hence might achieve an over-all reduction in demand. Moreover business demand for producer goods might well be reduced if consumer credit controls kept activity in consumer durable goods industries below boom levels and thus prevented any shortages of producer capacity from developing. Finally, it must be remembered that most advocates of selective controls want them to be supplements to general controls; hence it is unlikely that any large build-up of repressed demand would take place.

for producer durables, partly because of the impact on business expectations of big increases in consumer buying and partly because of the technical implications of the acceleration principle.

Still another objection is that consumer credit controls reach only a small segment of durable goods production and hence are not likely to be the best method or even superior to general credit controls in controlling fluctuations in durable goods or in countering the secondary repercussions of such fluctuations. As Friedman puts it:

There is nothing special . . . about goods purchased through the use of consumer credit. They are only a part, and indeed a small part, of the relevant total. What is called for is a measure that will affect this total, rather than one that operates on a small part of it.[114]

The answer of advocates of selective controls to this objection has been that consumer credit regulation or mortgage credit regulation is not conceived of as the best method.[115] Rather it is thought to be a feasible way of supplementing general credit controls in an area which has become important and which general controls may not reach quickly enough or powerfully enough at strategic points in time. However, some students have suggested that the rise in importance of consumer credit represents a basic shift in the nature of the economy's response to general credit controls and therefore this justifies new approaches to central banking techniques.[116] In any case, the significance of Friedman's point that goods purchased through the use of consumer credit are only a small part of the total of durable goods production seems dubious. From the point of view of economic stability, it is not the totals of consumer credit and durable goods production which are significant but the changes in the totals. Fluctuations in consumer credit are of major significance in comparison to fluctuations in production of consumer durable goods and these in turn can outweigh fluctuations in production of producers' durable goods. In 1955 consumer installment credit outstanding rose $5.4 billion while production of consumers' durables rose $7.2 billion. The $7.2 billion rise in production of consumer durables in turn compared with a rise of $2.3 billion in producers' durable goods.[117]

[114] *Ibid.*, p. 83.
[115] *Ibid.*, Pt. II, Vol. I, p. 245; and Pt. II, Vol. II, pp. 106, 108.
[116] Sayers, *Central Banking After Bagehot*, pp. 30–34.
[117] *Federal Reserve Bulletin*, XLVI (April, 1960), 414, 430.

Thus, if it is accepted that the purpose of selective controls is not to prevent fluctuations in particular sectors of the economy but merely to modify them in the interests of general economic stability, most of the economic case against selective controls is weakened. Consumer credit and mortgage credit have become large parts of the credit structure in recent years, and whether or not one accepts the view that they are especially strategic elements, their very size would seem to justify attempts to insure that they are promptly influenced by monetary policy.

DIFFICULTIES OF TIMING. Another objection to selective credit controls is that the central bank would have special difficulty in deciding when to put them in force, or when to change terms if they were in force.[118] Friedman has pointed out that a central bank has difficulty enough in applying general credit controls where the judgment required is merely whether aggregate demand is tending to decrease or increase at too rapid a rate. Any selective credit controls, he asserts, would require a double judgment: (1) Whether a particular sector is expanding or contracting too rapidly; and (2) Whether such rapid expansion or contraction is likely to be destabilizing, or whether it is being offset by changes in the other direction elsewhere.[119]

One may grant the difficulties of exercising discretionary controls over the economy. But it does not follow that selective controls would increase these difficulties appreciably. In the first place, the central bank might well find it easier to identify what is happening in a particular sector of the economy than to determine whether the economy as a whole is moving up or down too fast, if only because the general economy is almost always full of confusing cross currents. In the second place, the difficulties of judging whether rapid changes in specific sectors of the economy are being offset by shifts elsewhere are real ones. But this is not a problem peculiar to the application of selective controls. Determination of appropriate general credit policy also rests heavily on judgment. The steel industry, for example, could experience a decline in demand and production while strength in other industries nevertheless resulted in over-all increases

[118] Board of Governors, *Consumer Instalment Credit*, Pt. II, Vol. II, pp. 84, 141.
[119] *Ibid.*, p. 84.

in production and some upward pressure on prices. Which is the important trend for the future direction of the economy and for the proper general credit policy? It seems clear that the monetary authorities cannot avoid the need for judgments by eschewing the use of selective credit controls. Moreover, selective controls would seem to pose no greater difficulties of recognition of the need for action than do general controls.[120] It is worth noting that this was the conclusion reached by the Federal Reserve in its staff study of consumer credit controls which said:

timing of actions with respect to instalment credit terms does not present unique problems that are not encountered in the timing of other actions in the field of monetary policy. Whether or not instalment credit is subject to regulation, both it and the closely related durable goods industries are bound to be of great importance in any assessment of the economic situation, and developments in these areas must be followed closely.

The major problems of timing in the past related to the absence of specific legislative authority to act or to uncertainty arising from pending changes in such authority. If continuing specific authority to regulate consumer credit existed, there is no reason to suppose that timing per se would be any more or less of a problem than it is in, for example, the regulation of stock market credit under the Securities Exchange Act of 1934.[121]

ADMINISTRATIVE PROBLEMS

Some economists who otherwise might favor selective control of consumer installment and/or mortgage credit have been deterred by what they regard as insuperable difficulties of administering and insuring compliance with the regulations. Much of the Federal Reserve's reluctance to seek authority for selective controls has stemmed from concern that the administration of such controls would be extremely difficult. Appreciable noncompliance with regulations, it is feared, would not only reduce the effectiveness of the selective con-

[120] While the point involved is not recognition, it could be argued that the central bank might act more quickly if it had selective controls at hand. If the authorities were concerned about the widespread impact of further tightening of general controls, or of creating difficulties of finance for the Treasury, they might well be slower to use general controls than they would be to use an appropriate selective control. On the other hand, the authorities might also go slow with selective controls if the contemplated tightening of terms were serious enough to affect the controlled sector appreciably, simply because all of the impact would fall on a relatively narrow sector.

[121] Board of Governors, *Consumer Instalment Credit,* Pt. I, Vol. I, p. 309.

trols themselves but might also lead to a general decline in public respect for the Federal Reserve in all areas of its operations. Chandler has expressed this viewpoint:

I do not deny that these controls can be "effective" in the sense of exerting a significant influence on the total volume of consumer credit. But I fear that this type of "effectiveness" would be accompanied by avoidances and evasions so widespread and numerous as to discredit the regulations, to subject the regulatory authority to ridicule and even to charges of corruption, and to tend to shift business from the more reputable to those with more elastic consciences.[122]

The problem of dealing with evasion of regulations is increased by the large number of vendors and lenders subject to selective credit controls. Thus while there are about 6,200 member banks in the Federal Reserve System,[123] the number of individuals and firms subject to Regulation W amounted to about 195,000,[124] and there were more than 50,000 [125] subjected to Regulation X. The number of transactions subject to the regulations would run into the millions. To be sure, as Nadler has pointed out, a very substantial portion of consumer credit is extended by banks or major finance companies, and these lenders, it is generally agreed, would comply with selective credit regulations. A similar argument can be made in the case of mortgage credit. Nevertheless, it can still be objected that "fringe" lenders would present a considerable problem, and even responsible complying lenders might inadvertently engage in illegal transactions if they were misled by borrowers or were ignorant of actual terms on consumer credit instruments or mortgages purchased from vendors or dealers and mortgage originators. Before examining the actual experience with evasion and noncompliance during the periods when selective controls of consumer and real estate credit were in effect, a brief description of the major forms which evasion or avoidance might take is appropriate.

DOWN-PAYMENT REQUIREMENTS. As noted earlier, selective credit controls as used in the United States have relied heavily on the imposition of minimum down-payment requirements. The down-payment requirement, however, has proved particularly subject to evasion. In

[122] *Ibid.*, Pt. II, Vol. II, p. 32.
[123] *Federal Reserve Bulletin*, XLVI (April, 1960), 387.
[124] U.S. Congress, Joint Committee on Defense Production, *Second Annual Report*, 82d Cong., 2d Sess., 1952, p. 257.
[125] *Ibid.*, p. 258.

the automobile industry where the practice of paying for a new car by trading in a used car is common, dealer overallowances on the value of used-car trade-ins have been used to eliminate the need for the buyer to pay cash to cover the down-payment requirement. The dealer compensates for a used-car overallowance by marking-up the over-all price of the new car.[126]

This sort of evasion can be met by shifting from a down-payment requirement related to reported selling price to a maximum loan value requirement related to dealer cost. This takes the variables governing the real down payment out of the hands of the dealer. As a matter of fact, lenders themselevs began to shift to this sort of requirement in late 1955 (when consumer credit regulation was *not* in effect) because evasion of down-payment requirements was eliminating the borrower's equity in purchased automobiles and correspondingly increasing the risks of repossession and loss.[127] Thus a shift to this form of consumer credit regulation would be following a procedure already adopted by the market and hence more acceptable. Of course, there would still be a problem of ensuring that loan values did not exceed permitted maximums if these were much below what lenders would grant in their own interest. But here compliance would be helped by the fact that banks and major finance companies, directly or indirectly, account for so much of the consumer credit extended.

MAXIMUM MATURITIES. There seems to be agreement, even from critics of consumer credit controls, that evasion of maximum maturity limitations on installment loans has been much less of a problem than evasion of down-payment requirements.[128] Determined and ingenious borrowers can find avenues of escape from maturity limitations, as Chandler has pointed out,[129] but these do not seem to involve major loopholes. To be sure, if only installment credit is regulated, as many proponents of consumer credit regulation propose, a borrower could avoid the controls on maturity of loan by shifting to an unregulated single payment loan. But this would seem impractical for the great

[126] Board of Governors, *Consumer Instalment Credit*, Pt. II, Vol. I, pp. 428–31.

[127] *Ibid.*, Pt. I, Vol. II, p. 71; and Pt. II, Vol. I, pp. 428–30. It is also noteworthy that the Federal Reserve Board which had been collecting statistics on down payments as a percent of cash selling price shifted over to a ratio of loan to dealer cost. *Ibid.*, Pt. II, Vol. I, p. 155.

[128] *Ibid.*, Pt. II, Vol. II, pp. 34–35. [129] *Ibid.*

majority of prospective consumer borrowers who were seeking to buy automobiles or other expensive consumer durable goods.

Another way for a borrower to evade a limit on maximum maturity would be to borrow initially for the permitted period but to plead for an extension of the loan on grounds of hardship before full repayment had been made. A variant of this approach would be for the borrower to secure a second loan to help repay an initial loan. While these are feasible escapes, they depend in good part on lender cooperation. It may be questioned whether any considerable number of lenders would be willing to risk punishment for evading selective credit controls when general credit controls, by keeping credit generally tight, were insuring a sizeable unsatisfied demand for credit from "legitimate" borrowers.

EXEMPTION OF PRIOR COMMITMENTS. While not an evasion in the sense of an illegal avoidance of regulation, the practice of exempting from regulation transactions entered into before the effective date of regulation is generally regarded as a serious loophole in selective credit regulation. The aim of such exemption is a creditable one: to avoid retroactive impact of regulations. But the practical effect is undesirable. When consumers become aware that controls are coming, they naturally attempt to anticipate them by speeding-up their borrowing and purchasing of soon-to-be-controlled items. The major problem of this type arose, as noted earlier, in the administration of mortgage credit controls because of the great importance of the forward commitment in the mortgage market and building industry. It is incorrect to assume that mortgage credit controls under Regulation X were made ineffective by a backlog of forward commitments exempt from the controls. But there is little doubt that Regulation X would have been more effective if the backlog of exempt transactions had been smaller.

There are several reasons for believing that in the future it would be possible to hold the build-up of exempt commitments below the levels reached in 1950. First, lenders' willingness in 1950 to make extensive forward commitments of funds reflected confidence in their ability to sell Government securities, if necessary, at known-in-advance prices to raise the promised funds when the commitments came due, and this in turn rested on the fact that the Federal Reserve Banks were supporting the Government securities market.[130]

---

[130] O'Leary, *Journal of Finance*, XIII, 180.

In an unsupported market lenders would have to relate commitments more closely to their inflow of savings. Moreover, in an unsupported market in which interest rates were rising, lenders would have incentive to slow up on forward commitments because future lending terms presumably would be more remunerative.

Second, it would be possible to limit the build-up in forward commitments by curtailing the time period between discussion of selective credit regulation, announcement of the decision to impose such controls, and the date on which they would be effective. One approach might be to make the controls effective upon announcement. In 1950 the one day of grace allowed between the October 11 announcement of Regulation X and the October 12 effective date evidently permitted something like 65,000 extra commitments to be entered into on pre-Regulation X terms, about one sixth of the total estimated backlog of 400,000 exempt commitments.[131] Incentive to build up commitment backlogs was also provided by the lengthy discussions with housing industry spokesmen which preceded the initial imposition of Regulation X and put the entire market on notice that more restrictive terms were in the offing. Such extended discussions presumably would not be necessary if controls were already authorized on a standby basis.

It is worth noting, as a matter of fact, that most of the preliminary discussions about Regulation X concerned control of terms on conventional mortgages, and yet when the regulation was imposed, it called for conventional mortgage terms that were very little different from what the industry had been using.[132] In other words, much advance notice of restriction was given, stimulating the build-up of exempt commitments of FHA and VA mortgages, but so far as the conventional area was concerned little restriction was imposed. This experience raises the question whether in the future selective controls should be imposed only on mortgages guaranteed and insured by the Veterans Administration and the Federal Housing Administration

---

[131] Eastburn, *Real Estate Credit Controls*, p. 153. I have assumed that only VA and FHA mortgage commitments were entered into on this final day before Regulation X went into effect because of the greater difficulty of obtaining a conventional commitment. Moreover, I have assumed that the bulge in FHA applications in the week ending October 13, 1950, over the weekly average of the preceding months was attributable to applications filed on October 11 and have accordingly allocated 15,000 of the 23,000 applications received during the week to October 11. Both these assumptions are almost surely incorrect in some degree but are not believed to be seriously in error.

[132] Eastburn, *Real Estate Credit Controls*, pp. 203–4.

since these agencies can make changes practically overnight in the terms of mortgages eligible for their guarantee or insurance.

Such apparently discriminatory regulation could be justified in several ways. First, conventional mortgage terms have been consistently and considerably more restrictive than FHA or VA mortgage terms.[133] Accordingly it has been relaxation or stiffening of FHA and VA mortgage terms which has broadened or narrowed the demand for mortgages and homes by including or excluding marginal borrowers.[134] Second, it can be argued that changing terms on VA and FHA mortgages would mainly alter the amount of Government subsidy provided private borrowers rather than impose a net new burden of Government interference as would happen in the case of consumer credit regulation or regulation of conventional mortgages.

RECORDS OF VIOLATIONS. In view of the widespread fear that evasions and violations of selective credit controls might make them a mockery, one would think that the experience with Regulation W and Regulation X was riddled with wholesale violations. Yet, so far as the published record goes, this is very far from the truth. The picture revealed by the official records of enforcement is one of rather good compliance with the regulations.

In the September 18, 1950, to May 7, 1952, period of experience with Regulation W, the Federal Reserve investigators found 1,563 willful violations,[135] but there were only 150 deemed serious enough to be referred to the Federal Reserve Board for further disciplinary action.[136] Since there were approximately 195,000 individuals and firms registered as doing an installment credit business,[137] this is about 8 willful violations per 1,000 registrants and less than one serious violation per 1,000 registrants. If the violations were measured in terms of the much larger number of transactions, the violations percentage would, of course, be smaller.

---

[133] This follows from the fact that the VA and FHA guarantee and insurance programs are in the nature of a subsidy to the borrower, the Government's backing permitting him easier borrowing terms than he would get in a completely private—that is, conventional—transaction.

[134] This is one reason why most of the fluctuation in mortgage recordings and housing starts has been in VA and FHA mortgages and starts. The major reason, of course, is that the inflexibility of contract interest rates on VA and FHA mortgages has reduced lenders' desire for them in periods of rising interest rates and thus shut off the supply of financing for them.

[135] Board of Governors, *Consumer Instalment Credit*, Pt. I, Vol. I, p. 303.

[136] Joint Committee on Defense Production, *Second Annual Report*, p. 257.

[137] *Ibid.*

This record would seem to justify the conclusion in the Federal Reserve's staff study of consumer credit that:

By and large the standards of compliance were very high. Many of the institutions subject to the regulation were accustomed to some degree of regulation, by State or Federal authorities, and their operating methods and procedures required little modification. In many other cases, the pre-existing relationship between the vendor or originator and his source of financing involved the application of standards similar to those specified by the regulation, although perhaps less restrictive.[138]

This does not mean that there were no problems, particularly with practices on the fringe of installment credit selling. The same Federal Reserve staff study observed that when Regulation W was suspended in May, 1952, "those who were directly engaged in the work of enforcement were beginning to feel that compliance was deteriorating." [139] But, on balance, the Federal Reserve staff went on to conclude "while the problems of administration, compliance, and enforcement loomed large to those immediately responsible, there is no evidence that they actually threatened the over-all effectiveness of regulation at any time." [140]

An examination of the experience with Regulation X from October 12, 1950, to September 18, 1952, discloses a similarly small number of violations. With some 50,000 registrants subject to Regulation X, the Federal Reserve and other supervisory agencies discovered only 49 apparently willful violations, and of these, only 7 were referred to the Federal Reserve Board for action.[141] This amounted to about one serious violation per 1,000 registrants, approximately the same ratio as had prevailed with Regulation W.[142]

[138] Board of Governors, *Consumer Instalment Credit*, Pt. I, Vol. I, p. 310.
[139] *Ibid.*, p. 314.
[140] *Ibid.*, p. 315.
[141] Eastburn, *Real Estate Credit Controls*, pp. 120–22. Eastburn reports a larger number of total violations but these are described as inadvertent, owing to unfamiliarity with the regulation and no penalty was deemed appropriate.
[142] Of course there were doubtless many violations that were not discovered, particularly among fringe vendors and lenders who were either ignorant of details of the regulations or who assumed they could violate with impunity because of their relatively small size. But for purposes of effective control such small violations need not be weighted heavily in assessing the possibilities of selective controls. As Lutz said: "In questions of economic policy we cannot be perfectionists. The fact that we cannot control all consumer credit is no reason for not controlling instalment credit. The Government does not cease to levy taxes because some people succeed in evading them, or to impose duties on imports because a good deal of smuggling is done, or revoke the antitrust laws because a good deal of smuggling is done, or revoke the antitrust laws

The Federal Reserve's 1952 report to the Congressional Joint Committee on Defense Production concluded, "The record indicates a high degree of cooperation on the part of registered lenders in complying with the provisions of the regulations." [143]

Looking to the future, Eastburn concluded on the basis of his study of real-estate credit regulation:

If real-estate credit controls are ever reimposed, the Federal Reserve should encounter fewer conflicts among the principles of effectiveness, equity, and simplicity of administration. Experience with Regulation X should make solution of some of the administrative problems easier and make possible a more effective, more equitable, and more workable regulation. [144]

POLITICAL PROBLEMS OF SELECTIVE CREDIT CONTROL. One aspect of selective credit control on which both opponents and proponents agree is that they generate substantial opposition from the industries and groups they regulate. As Raymond Saulnier said:

Unlike conventional credit control devices, selective credit regulations are direct, immediate, and personal in their effect on the individual and the business concern. The hand of the monetary authority is clearly evident in their workings, which is sharply in contrast with the indirect and impersonal operation of the traditional controls. Their actual effect in restraining credit extensions may be no more severe, but it is at least clear that there is a hand at work and little doubt as to its identity. Furthermore, the effect is felt, not by a relatively few financial institutions alone, but by a very large number of manufacturers, dealers, merchants, salesmen, by no means the least, consumers.

The primary significance of this fact for the strategy of inflation control is this: opposition to a selective credit control measure, however much the measure may be needed, can be rallied against the monetary authorities from a very broad base of the population. [145]

There is no doubt that the vast majority of business men affected by selective credit controls have consistently opposed them. In the Federal Reserve's 1956 study of consumer installment credit regulation for example, a survey of business opinion revealed that some 600 spokesmen of affected industries were against consumer credit controls, while only 133 favored them. [146]

---

because they are not completely effective in preventing monopolies." Board of Governors, *Consumer Instalment Credit*, Pt. II, Vol. I, p. 245.

[143] Joint Committee on Defense Production, *Second Annual Report*, p. 258.

[144] Eastburn, *Real Estate Credit Controls*, p. 126.

[145] Saulnier, *American Economic Review*, XLII, 253–54.

[146] Board of Governors, *Consumer Instalment Credit*, Pt. III.

Labor unions too have opposed selective credit controls,[147] in part as representatives of the industries in which their members earn a living and in part as spokesmen for the lower income groups which are said to be discriminated against by restrictions on access to consumer and mortgage credit. In a typical statement, United Automobile Workers' President Walter Reuther in 1950 said:

I have documents here from various organizations throughout the country indicating that the impact of regulation W has cut the sales of new cars from 40 to 50 percent, in various parts of the country, and the sales of used cars as high as 65 percent.

Now, as I said before, the little fellow is being priced out of the market. The fellow who buys a Cadillac has no trouble; he can get his Cadillac. It is the fellow who needs a car for transportation that is being priced out of the market. . . . Now, why penalize the fellow who is down there where they have an awful time making ends meet, when Regulation W leaves the fellow on top completely in the clear.[148]

Congress, in turn, has been responsive to business and labor opposition to selective controls. It has consistently opposed permanent power for the Federal Reserve to control consumer and real estate credit. Indeed in 1951, after having given such authority as an emergency grant, Congress intervened directly to liberalize terms on consumer and mortgage credit in the Defense Production Act Amendments of 1951 and 1952. In short, as Chandler said, "Congress has never indicated that it would really support effective controls of this type." [149]

However, the record of Congressional and public opposition to selective controls does not necessarily prove their unsuitability for use by the Federal Reserve. The key point is that the bulk of the opposition to selective controls came when they were the only effective restraining arm of the Federal Reserve. Thus it is possible, if not probable, that much of the opposition to selective restraint was opposition to restraint, not to the selective aspect of it. It must be re-

---

[147] The AFL-CIO and the United Mineworkers opposed consumer credit controls in their replies to the 1956 Federal Reserve survey. *Ibid.*, pp. 227–28.

[148] U.S. Congress, Joint Committee on Defense Production, *Defense Production Act, Regulation W-Automotive, Hearings,* 81st Cong., 2d Sess., 1950, pp. 52–53. Consumer groups, interestingly enough, have not opposed selective credit controls but neither have they favored them. They appear to be more interested in protecting consumers against excessive interest rates and high finance charges. Board of Governors, *Consumer Instalment Credit*, Pt. III, pp. 227–29.

[149] *Ibid.*, Pt. II, Vol. II, p. 36.

membered that general credit controls were either inoperative or only newly restored to use during the periods in which selective credit controls were effective. Hence all of the resentment against credit restriction tended to be focused on the selective measures.

There is support for this argument in the fact that public and Congressional opposition to monetary policy reached new peaks during 1955–1957 and 1958–1960, even though selective controls were no longer in operation. In particular it is worth noting that the automobile industry, which had been such a bitter opponent of selective consumer credit control in 1950–1952, was no less critical of general credit controls in 1956 when these were the mechanism of restraint. Thus Harlow Curtice, then president of General Motors Corporation, attacked general credit restraint as the cause of reduced automobile sales and on May 15, 1956, charged that the "policy is not warranted and should be reversed, and promptly." [150] Charges have also been heard that general credit policies discriminate against housing, school construction, essential state and local government projects, small business, etc.[151]

Under these circumstances, paradoxical as it may seem, the use of selective credit controls could reduce rather than increase opposition to restrictive credit policies. As matters now stand, with exclusive reliance on general credit measures, the Federal Reserve has no reply to critics who charge that credit restraints are too severe or bear too heavily on specific parts of the economy. But if selective credit measures were in use the authorities could point to their employment as evidence of desire to spread the burden of credit restraint and to reduce upward pressures on interest rates within the limits of the need for some type of credit restraint. Demands for lower interest rates could be met by pointing out that the necessary compensatory stiffening of selective credit terms would be excessive and probably unacceptable to the industries directly affected. Opponents of selective credit controls, in turn, would have to meet all the arguments against intensification of general controls, since the Federal Reserve could argue that intensified general-credit restraint would be necessary to compensate for relaxed selective controls.

In other words, the Reserve System might find that the addition of

[150] *The New York Times,* May 16, 1956, p. 49.
[151] There is a voluminous literature, but see Flanders Committee, *1954 Hearings;* Joint Committee, *1956 Monetary Policy Hearings;* Byrd Committee, *1957 Hearings;* Joint Committee, *1959 Employment Hearings.*

selective controls to its tool kit would enable it to play off one opponent of monetary restraint against another. In the most optimistic view, opponents of selective controls would become supporters of general controls; those disadvantaged by general controls would support selective controls. But even without assuming this, it seems plausible that increasing the number of types of restraint would decrease the opposition to any one. Thus, use of selective controls might divide, rather than multiply, the opposition to monetary policy.

CONCLUSIONS ON FAILURE TO USE SELECTIVE CONTROLS.

The question concerning possible use of selective credit controls is whether they could make enough of a contribution to the Federal Reserve's ability to influence economic activity to compensate for their drawbacks. This needs emphasis because some discussions assume that selective credit controls are damned if some drawbacks to their use can be shown, and blessed if demonstrated to do anything at all. Selective credit instruments, like all the other instruments of central bank policy, have advantages and disadvantages. The issue is not whether they are perfect instruments but whether their advantages outweigh their disadvantages.

The Federal Reserve's assessment of these considerations has granted the effectiveness of selective control, but has put greater emphasis on difficulties of administration and enforcement. This position needs to be judged with care. To be sure, the Federal Reserve, as the agency which has had practical experience with Regulation W and Regulation X, must be assumed to have special competence in assessing administrative feasibility if not political acceptability.[152] But there is reason to suspect that recent statements by Federal Reserve officials have exaggerated the problems of administration and enforcement.[153] The fact is that the Federal Reserve generally expressed satisfaction with the administrative feasibility and performance of selective controls *when they were in force*. And the pub-

---

[152] The point is that a technically expert agency may make its largest contribution by giving its honest economic opinions, not by trimming these to what it conceives the "political winds" to be. The political problems will not disappear, but those in the Congress who have to deal with them will be better armed by having expert, uncensored opinion. Eastburn, assessing the experience with Regulation X, concluded, "the Board is better off determining policy on economic grounds." *Real Estate Credit Controls*, pp. 186–87.

[153] This is not a new development as Eastburn has pointed out in his study of the experience with Regulation X. *Ibid.*, pp. 63–64.

lished record of violations of Regulations W and X suggests that this satisfaction was justified since evasion was not a serious problem.

The implication is that the Federal Reserve's recent misgivings about selective controls reflect a desire to keep itself free of the administrative problems associated with selective controls. Such an attitude is perhaps understandable, as is the more basic policy of insisting on minimum intervention in the money market. These policies seem to promise central bankers freedom from political attacks and public resistance to monetary policies. But it should be apparent by now, particularly in view of the drumfire of Congressional and public criticism of monetary policy, that even minimum intervention does not guarantee that the central bank will have immunity from public scrutiny and criticism. The nation has grown too sophisticated for even the complexities of general controls to go unnoticed. In this environment, the fact that selective controls might pose some problems of administration, or occasion some resistance from regulated industries, lessens in importance as an objection to their employment.

Thus, Regulation W and X type of controls, on the record of experience, could supplement general controls without posing major problems. To insure timely application, the Federal Reserve should have authority to impose selective controls. Indeed, controls might be kept continuously in effect, but at levels which would merely formalize terms set by major lenders themselves. In this way, the controls, while not restrictive in normal circumstances, would automatically prevent any radical easing of credit terms by lenders such as occurred in 1955. In addition, if sudden surges of demand caused excessive credit expansion under *existing* terms, selective controls, being already in force, could be tightened without a long delay.

It follows that the main function of selective controls would be to prevent surges of demand for consumer durables or housing from destabilizing the economy, and to check activity in these areas, if need be, in the early stages of business expansion when the economy's liquidity is still high and general credit controls have not had time to take hold. They might also have a role to play if general controls became so restrictive that further general tightening would have unduly harsh effects on the economy or on Treasury financing.

Part III
THE FEDERAL RESERVE'S CONTROL
OVER FINANCIAL VARIABLES

X

THE FEDERAL RESERVE'S CONTROL

OF THE MONEY SUPPLY

THE FEDERAL RESERVE Board's management of bank reserve positions and the money supply has been vigorously criticized. Moreover, the criticisms have come from economists who agree that control of the money supply is most important for monetary policy as well as from those who feel it has been overemphasized.

Accordingly, this chapter discusses and evaluates the Federal Reserve's emphasis on and efficiency in controlling the money supply with a view to drawing some conclusion as to whether a broader view of monetary policy would have been more effective. The first part of the chapter considers the criticisms which charge that the Federal Reserve has failed to influence the money supply appropriately and propose that it should be relieved of its power to exercise discretionary power over the volume of money. The balance of the chapter takes up a variety of criticisms which minimize or deny the importance of the money supply for a central bank policy and which instead assert that: (1) Interest rates, not the money supply, are what really matter; (2) The growth of near-money liquid assets makes the money supply less important; (3) The expansion of non-bank financial intermediaries makes the Federal Reserve's control over the banking system and bank deposits inadequate; and (4) General liquidity, not money, is what the central bank should try to control.

INAPPROPRIATE INFLUENCE OVER THE MONEY SUPPLY?

It would be hard to imagine a more fundamental challenge to the Federal Reserve's recent monetary policy than the allegation that under its control the money supply has acted in a destabilizing manner.

Yet highly respected economists have charged that since the Federal Reserve has been in existence, the money supply has displayed excessive and even perverse movements in relation to economic activity. In view of this record, the critics say, monetary policy could make a greater contribution to economic stability and growth if the Federal Reserve gave up its attempts to control the money supply countercyclically and simply aimed at increasing the money supply (actual or potential) each year by some constant percentage rate, for example, 4 percent, related to the long-term annual rate of growth in real production.[1]

This far-reaching recommendation would radically change, if not emasculate, central banking as we know it. Accordingly, close analysis of the evidence relevant to the criticism and suggested reform are indicated. The critics' argument runs as follows: (1) Fluctuations in the money stock since the establishment of the Federal Reserve System have been far greater and more destabilizing than they were prior to the adoption of discretionary central bank control over the money supply; (2) The cyclical behavior of the money supply under Federal Reserve control has been destabilizing, with the volume of money or its rate of growth declining in recessions and rising in prosperity; and (3) A steady rise in the money supply at about the rate of growth in real gross national product would be more appropriate to both the longer term and cyclical needs of the economy.

The analysis will focus first on the question of whether the money supply has behaved as erratically and perversely as the critics claim, both in long-run and cyclical terms, and then will consider whether a policy of increasing the money supply by some constant percentage rate each year would be a desirable and feasible improvement.

LONGER-RUN FLUCTUATIONS. Shaw has suggested that the sharp changes in longer period rates of growth of the money supply, shown in Table 8, are *prima-facie* evidence of inadequate performance by the monetary authorities.

Shaw has attributed these wide swings in the rate of growth in the

---

[1] See Milton Friedman's testimony in Joint Committee, *1959 Employment Hearings*, Pt. 4, pp. 605–48, and his statement in Joint Committee, *1958 Prices Compendium*, pp. 241–65; Edward S. Shaw, "Money Supply and Stable Economic Growth," in *United States Monetary Policy*, pp. 49–71; James W. Angell, "Appropriate Monetary Policies and Operations in the United States Today," *Review of Economics and Statistics*, XLII, 247–52.

TABLE 8

STOP AND GO IN MONETARY POLICY, 1896–1957

Period	Change in Nominal Money ($ billion)	Annual Rate of Change (percent)
1896–1914	7.5	6
1914–1919	11.4	15
1919–1933	– 3.5	– 1
1933–1941	27.7	14
1941–1945	55.5	21
1945–1951	22.2	3
1951–1957	13.2	2
1896–1957	134.0	6

Source: Edward S. Shaw, "Money Supply and Stable Economic Growth," in *United States Monetary Policy*, p. 53.

money supply to shifts in control over monetary policy between the Treasury and the Federal Reserve. The Treasury is held responsible for excessively rapid money creation in 1914–1919, 1933–1941, and 1941–1951. The Federal Reserve, on the other hand, is accused of being unduly restrictive, with responsibility for the decrease in money supply from 1919–1933 and inadequate growth from 1951–1957. Both authorities are viewed as responsible for the poor over-all performance of the money supply. Shaw concludes that discretionary control over the money supply

builds into the monetary system an enormous capacity for both inflation and deflation. In successive trips back to the Congressional fix-it shop, the system's elasticity has been increased. As it is now put together, the United States monetary system is a brilliant solution for short-period instability in some security markets. But it has financed long-period inflation on the commodity markets, interrupted by painful episodes of excessive deceleration in monetary growth and declines in price levels. In its first half-century, the system has not created the temperate monetary environment that is most congenial to stable growth in real terms.[2]

The facts Shaw objected to—the wide swings in the rate of money creation—are just about indisputable. But it can be questioned whether all the blame can be laid on discretionary monetary policy. For one thing, the most striking instances of excessive money creation occurred during World Wars I and II and during the Great Depression, all national emergencies. It seems disingenuous to suggest

[2] Shaw, *United States Monetary Policy*, p. 59.

that an automatic rule limiting money creation to 4 percent a year would have been permitted to hamper the Federal Government's ability to finance either of the world wars or to fight the Great Depression with massive dosages of new liquidity. Sovereign governments do not and cannot tolerate arbitrary limitations on their powers when their survival is at stake. These instances of excessive money creation were attributable to the exigencies of emergency situations. After all, there was excessive money creation during the Civil War when there was no discretionary monetary policy.

So far as the Federal Reserve's restriction on monetary growth is concerned, it can be argued that some slowing down in monetary growth after World Wars I and II was appropriate in view of the preceding massive money creation which Shaw deplores. At such times the economy can draw into active use idle and excess money balances previously accumulated.

CYCLICAL BEHAVIOR. The associated criticism that the cyclical behavior of the money supply has been inappropriate is more difficult to dismiss. In Friedman's words:

If one looks . . . at the behavior of the stock of money, not of interest rates, then you will find that the Federal Reserve System has been typically and traditionally easy during periods of boom and tight during periods of contraction, and consequently, it has tended, not intentionally, of course, to contribute to the instability in our system rather than the reverse.[3]

Friedman supports his assertion by pointing out that the *growth* of the money supply has slowed or even stopped in recessions, when more money is needed, but has accelerated in prosperity when extra money merely provides fuel for inflation.

It should be noted in passing that this behavior of the money supply does not mean that "the Federal Reserve System has been typically and traditionally easy during periods of boom and tight during periods of contraction." Apart from neglecting Federal Reserve influence on interest rates, this statement ignores the fact that the money supply would naturally tend to decline in recession and rise in prosperity even if there was no Federal Reserve System.[4] The ac-

[3] Joint Committee, *1959 Employment Hearings*, Pt. 4, p. 614.
[4] This is because the money supply, mainly stemming from the deposits created by bank leading and investing, is so importantly influenced by the demand for credit which itself fluctuates cyclically.

curate criticism is that the Federal Reserve has failed to offset or reverse the natural pro-cyclical behavior of the money supply.

But even when the criticism is put in these terms, it can be argued that the Federal Reserve's record in controlling the money supply is not as bad as Friedman and Shaw have suggested. The weak point in their criticism is that it has been based on the behavior of the *total* money supply.[5] It is well known that aggregate data can conceal significant movements in components. To evaluate the Federal Reserve's influence on the money supply adequately, one would have to examine the possibility that specific parts of the money supply are affected more quickly and more appropriately than is the total money supply. If some parts are affected more quickly than the total, and the parts promptly affected can be said to be *strategic* in the sense of being particularly significant in the over-all economic process, then lags in the Federal Reserve's influence over less important sectors of the money supply may not be crucial drawbacks to the effectiveness of monetary policy. It can be argued that this is indeed the case.

The money supply as traditionally defined is made up of private checking account deposits (demand deposits, adjusted) plus currency in circulation outside banks. Demand deposits provide the bulk of the money supply (accounting for $112 billion of a $140.2 billion money supply on December 31, 1959) and are also much more subject to Federal Reserve policy than currency in circulation. Accordingly, it is really the Federal Reserve's influence over the demand deposit total which has been called inadequate or even perverse by the critics. A breakdown of the deposit component is possible because several classes of Federal Reserve member banks report the total of demand deposits adjusted they hold in their weekly statements of condition. This is true for example of the weekly reporting member banks in New York City and elsewhere in the country. Subtracting both these weekly reporting member bank deposits from the

---

[5] We refer here, as the following pages suggest, to the fact that *components* of the money supply may be appropriately affected by Federal Reserve policy, even though the *total* is not. But in a broader sense it needs to be noted that many economists (as noted in the latter half of this chapter) would object to Friedman's and Shaw's equation of money supply behavior with monetary policy because this approach leaves out the behavior of interest rates, capital values, and monetary velocity. Thus a charge that monetary policy has acted perversely is surely exaggerated. But it is serious enough if behavior of the money supply is perverse, as Friedman alleges.

total demand deposit component of the money supply provides a third segment of the money supply: demand deposits in all other banks.

With this breakdown, it is then possible to compare the response of these three segments of the money supply as well as the total to Federal Reserve monetary policy. Monetary policy, in turn, can be represented by bank's net reserve positions since these are directly influenced by the Federal Reserve.[6] Business conditions, to which monetary policy responds, can be represented by the Federal Reserve's industrial production index.

Chart 1 presents all of these quantities so that movements in them can be compared with one another. Comparison of the movements in the banks' net reserve positions with movements in the industrial production index measures how rapidly monetary policy responded to changes in business conditions. Comparison of changes in the total money supply [7] with the industrial production index and net bank reserve positions measures how fast the total volume of money responded to business conditions and changes in monetary policy. And comparison of changes in business conditions and bank reserve positions with changes in the various segments of the money supply pro-

[6] Banks' net reserve positions in 1951–1959 could be regarded as a sensitive indicator of the direction of Federal Reserve policy. In particular, movements in bank reserve positions usually preceded explicit Federal Reserve announcements of changed policies—such as those represented by announcements of changes in discount rate—as they permitted the authorities to feel their way toward a changed policy. Using net reserve positions as a measure of policy changes tends to maximize the lags of money supply changes behind policy changes but does not affect their lag behind changes in business conditions. Bank reserve positions tend to be easy when free reserves exist, that is when excess reserves are higher than bank borrowings from the Federal Reserve, and tight when net borrowed reserves exist, that is, borrowings or discounts rise above excess reserves. For an official discussion of net reserve positions, see Federal Reserve Bank of New York, "The Significance and Limitations of Free Reserves," *Monthly Review*, XL (November, 1958), pp. 162–67.

[7] The money supply figures shown in Chart 1 are the data which have long been made available for the last Wednesday in each month. More recently—see the *Federal Reserve Bulletin*, XLVI (Octobr, 1960)—the Federal Reserve has made available new money supply figures which are semimonthly averages of daily figures and which are also slightly more inclusive. The semimonthly averages exhibit more stable behavior, as might be expected, but they are not well suited to comparison with deposit data for the weekly reporting member banks, which is available only on a Wednesday basis. Accordingly, to facilitate comparative analysis of components of the money supply, the older data are used. Comparison of the new with the old money supply series indicates that turning points are not affected by the shift from single date to semimonthly average data.

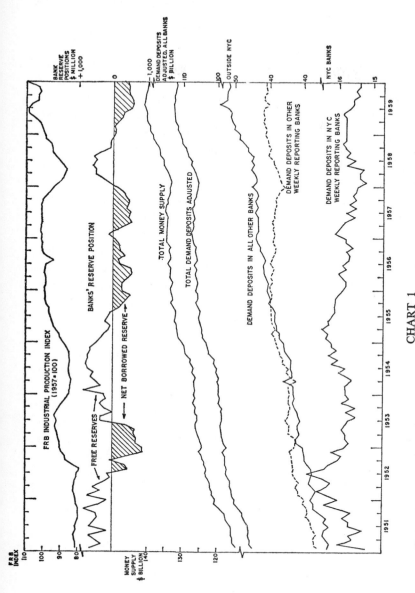

CHART 1

CHANGES IN INDUSTRIAL PRODUCTION INDEX, NET BANK RESERVE POSITIONS,
AND SELECTED SEGMENTS OF THE MONEY SUPPLY, 1951–1959

Note: Figures on demand deposits in "Other Weekly Reporting Banks" for 1951–1958 adjusted
upward by 7 percent to reflect July 9, 1959, broadening in the coverage of the series.

vides evidence as to the differential impact of monetary policy on the various parts of the money supply.

Chart 1 reveals a number of significant facts bearing on the Friedman-Shaw criticisms.

1. Monetary policy, as measured by the banks' net reserve positions, responded rather promptly to changes in industrial production. In 1954 the Federal Reserve was tightening bank reserve positions (that is, reducing free reserves and gradually moving the position to one of net borrowed reserves) by August, some three months before a pronounced uptrend in industrial production began. In 1957 bank reserve positions were being eased by October, only one month after industrial production had begun its decline. Even in 1953 and 1958, when unsettled conditions in the bond market interfered with the adjustment of bank reserve positions to the business situation, the record was not too bad. Indeed, in 1953 the efforts to counter unsteadiness in the bond market resulted in bank reserve positions being eased three months before business activity turned down. In 1958 a disorderly bond market delayed a tightening of bank reserve positions until August, three months after business had turned up. In general, bank reserve positions were easiest when industrial production was cyclically lowest, and tightest when industrial production was highest, clearly appropriate countercyclical behavior.

2. Although the chart confirms Friedman's assertion that the money supply as a whole behaved pro-cyclically in recent years, an examination of the behavior of the money supply by segments reveals that substantial and important parts of the money supply responded fairly quickly to changes in busines conditions and monetary policy actions, and thus behaved *countercyclically*. Note, for example, that while the total money supply increased throughout the 1955–1957 business expansion, the portion represented by demand deposits in New York banks was declining by April, 1955, within five months of the upturn in business, and continued to decline for the next two and one-half years in response to the Federal Reserve's restrictive credit policy. The segment of the money supply represented by demand deposits in weekly reporting member banks outside New York also responded fairly quickly to shifts in business conditions and monetary policy, though not always as quickly or decisively as deposits in the New York banks. For example, demand deposits in

weekly reporting banks outside New York City ceased expanding and leveled off by March, 1955, and were declining by February, 1956. Since a leveling off of growth in the money supply can be considered restrictive in an economy in which real production is growing some 3 percent a year, the first response of these deposits to changed money conditions came within four months.

With minor exceptions, the same pattern of fairly prompt response to changes in business conditions is shown by the chart at the other points of major change in the industrial production index.

3. The failure of the money supply as a whole to respond appropriately to changes in business conditions stemmed from the inability of the Federal Reserve to influence deposits promptly in the thousands of commercial banks which do not report weekly (shown on the chart as All Other Commercial Banks) and which are mainly small and medium-sized institutions. Thus demand deposits in these banks rose throughout 1955 and 1956 in defiance of the Federal Reserve's restrictive credit policy and did not level off before 1957, a full two years after business had turned up and credit restraint had been imposed.

4. However, even in the case of these banks, the Federal Reserve's inability to achieve prompt and appropriate influence over their deposits was a problem only in periods of business expansion and credit restraint. Table 9, based on the same data as Chart 1, shows that Federal Reserve monetary policies affected deposits of All Other Commercial Banks quite promptly in periods of recession when reserve requirement reductions were used as an important tool of easy monetary policies. Thus in 1953 the portion of the money supply in these banks began to rise in July, only two months after reserve positions were eased appreciably and one month before business turned down. In 1958, deposits in these banks turned up in February, almost immediately after a reduction in reserve requirements and only five months after industrial production turned down. Indeed it was only in credit restraint phases that deposits in these small and medium-sized banks showed lags of as much as 15 or 26 months behind changes in business.

5. The response of the total money supply to changes in business conditions and monetary policy has been considerably prompter in business recessions than in business expansions; that is, induced

TABLE 9

LEAD OR LAG IN THE RESPONSE OF BANK RESERVE POSITIONS AND MONEY SUPPLY TO CHANGES IN INDUSTRIAL PRODUCTION

	Date of Change	Number of Months of Lead (+) or Lag (−)	Date of Change	Number of Months of Lead (+) or Lag (−)
Downturn in Industrial Production Index	August, 1953		September, 1957	
Easing in Bank Reserve Position	May, 1953	+ 3	October, 1957	− 1
Upturn of Money Supply in:				
New York City banks	October, 1953	− 2	February, 1958	− 5
Other weekly reporting member banks	April, 1954	− 8	January, 1958	− 4
All other commercial banks	July, 1953	+ 1	February, 1958	− 5
Total money supply	May, 1954	− 9	February, 1958	− 5
Upturn in Industrial Production Index	November, 1954		May, 1958	
Tightening in Bank Reserve Position	August, 1954	+ 3	August, 1958	− 3
Downturn or End of Rise of Money Supply in:				
New York City banks	April, 1955	− 5	November, 1958	− 6
Other weekly reporting member banks	March, 1955	− 4	February, 1959	− 9
All other commercial banks	January, 1957	− 26	August, 1959	− 15
Total money supply	December, 1956	− 25	August, 1959	− 15

Source: Board of Governors of the Federal Reserve System for industrial production index and total money supply seasonally adjusted. Chase Manhattan Bank for seasonally adjusted demand deposits of weekly reporting member banks in New York City and weekly reporting member banks outside of New York City.

countercyclical upturns in the money supply have come relatively quickly in relation to the downturn in business and resultant shift to ease in Federal Reserve monetary policy. Moreover, Federal Reserve credit easing actions, to combat recessions, have usually affected the different sectors of the money supply at about the same time.

The prompter response of the money supply to policy actions in recession perhaps reflects to some extent the fact that the Federal Reserve authorities act quickly and decisively to combat recessions but tend to delay a bit in applying restrictive measures for fear of nipping an incipient recovery in the bud. But the more nearly simultaneous response of all sectors of the money supply to anti-recession credit policy suggests also that the policy of using reserve requirement changes to combat recession in business, but not expansion, may be partly responsible. Changes in reserve requirements affect the entire banking system immediately, while the open market operations used to apply monetary restraint in periods of business expansion impinge first on major money market banks and only later on the small banks throughout the nation.[8]

To summarize briefly, analysis reveals that substantial parts of the money supply responded to changes in the business situation and monetary policy much more promptly than did the total money supply in the 1951–1959 years. Deposits in New York City banks were affected first; deposits in other weekly reporting member banks responded a little less rapidly but still within eight months. Deposits in both these classes of banks accounted for more than half of total demand deposits, adjusted, and more than two fifths of the total

[8] Federal Reserve open market transactions in Government securities affect the New York banks first because it is there that the Federal Reserve's Open Market Account is conducted by the Federal Reserve Bank of New York and there that the main offices of most Government security dealers are located. If the Open Market Account sells securities, the checks which dealers use to pay for them are usually drawn on New York or Chicago banks whose reserve accounts are debited when the checks are collected. The associated impact on deposits follows quickly when the dealers, fulfilling their major function as merchants in securities, sell the Treasury bills to major business corporations whose national bank accounts are usually with banks in New York or other principal cities or when banks take action to restore reserve positions by selling securities. Open market operations would also have their initial impact on deposits in the money market centers when the Federal Reserve was buying Government securities in recession but, as noted in the text, the fact that the authorities also use reserve requirement reductions in recessions spreads the impact of easier reserve conditions widely throughout the country.

money supply. So the Federal Reserve rather consistently did exercise reasonably prompt influence on a substantial portion of the money supply. In addition, in recessions even the deposits in the remaining commercial banks of the American banking system were affected fairly quickly.

Moreover, the deposits in New York City and other leading banks which responded quickly to monetary policy could be regarded as *strategic,* representing as they do deposits in the major money centers of the nation. Banks in these centers are the principal lenders. The demand deposits they hold are owned by the major business corporations which account for a large portion of business activity, investment, and employment. Reflecting this institutional background, deposit conditions in the larger banks set the tone in the money markets of the nation to a much greater extent than do deposits in small and medium-sized banks. Although discussion of the velocity or turnover of the money supply must be deferred until Chapter XI, it may be noted here that there is some reason to believe that the sectors of the money supply which are most promptly affected by monetary policy also display the greatest velocity. This provides some additional support for the belief that the parts of the money supply most sensitive to monetary policy are also the most actively linked to business and financial transactions.

It is hard to escape the conclusion that monetary policy has been considerably more successful in influencing important parts of the money supply appropriately than the comments of Friedman and Shaw would suggest. This does not deny that it would have been better if the total money supply had responded more quickly to Federal Reserve policy or if the sensitive segments had been more quickly responsive. But, as suggested in Chapter VIII on the use of variable reserve requirements, a greater responsiveness of the money supply to monetary policy might well follow if somewhat more frequent use were made of modest reserve requirement changes to implement both restrictive and expansionary policy, since reserve requirement changes produce an immediate impact on the reserves and deposit-creating capabilities of small and medium-sized banks as well as on major money market banks. Even without this improvement in monetary management, however, it is doubtful that discretionary control over the money supply has been so poor as to justify replacing it with an automatic rule, particularly when the drawbacks of the proposal for an automatic 4 percent annual increase in the money supply are considered.

AUTOMATIC INCREASES IN MONEY SUPPLY. In the opinion of its advocates, an automatic annual increase in the money supply at approximately the long-term rate of increase in real production would provide more stable money conditions than have prevailed under discretionary policies in the past, would stabilize expectations by creating a climate of certainty as to what future money conditions would be, and would evade the problems posed for discretionary monetary policy by lags between the time monetary actions are taken and the time they have effect on the economy.[9] But such a plan would also involve a number of difficulties.

Question of Definition of Money Supply. One problem is to insure that the quantity which is to be increased every year is in fact what the economy is using as money. The crux of the difficulty is the artificiality of any legal definition. The moneyness of assets is a fluid and shifting quality, depending on business habits and institutions which themselves shift over time. At any point of time there is a question as to what should be included in a definition of the money supply, as a glance at any money and banking textbook will indicate.[10] It can reasonably be asked whether the money supply should also include commercial bank time deposits, savings bank deposits, savings and loan shares, and perhaps some or even all U.S. Government securi-

---

[9] The conception that steady growth in the money supply at the same rate of growth as that of real production would be the maximum contribution that monetary management could make to economic stability and growth is not a new one. In 1931 Lionel Edie said: "The most important legislative mandate would be a provision that one of the objectives of Federal Reserve policy shall be the maintenance of the annual rate of growth of volume of credit in the United States in balance with the long-term average annual rate of growth of production in the United States. . . . Central banks should aim at so regulating the reserves of the banking system that the outstanding credit built upon those reserves will expand at the same rate as the long-term growth of production." *The Banks and Prosperity* (New York: Harper & Bros., 1931), pp. 47, 117–18.

In 1936 Angell said, "If the ultimate objective of policy is to induce a greater degree of stability in national and individual money income . . . then the most effective procedure is to stabilize the quantity of money itself. This quantity would not be held absolutely constant, perhaps, but it would be allowed to change only gradually and evenly." *The Behavior of Money*, p. 163. And in 1940 Carl Snyder made the point again. *Capitalism the Creator* (New York, Macmillan, 1940), pp. 220–21.

[10] See, for example, E. S. Shaw, *Money, Income, and Public Policy* (Chicago, Richard D. Irwin, 1950), pp. 14–15.

ties. The major problem is that a fixed rule freezes the definition over time even though the economy may be gradually attributing greater moneyness to an asset not regulated. Thus, if a fixed rule had in the early 1800s fixed a regular percentage increase in the supply of bank-notes—the major component of the money supply at the time—the rule would have become largely irrelevant with the emergence of demand deposits as the major type of money. It is no answer to say that in the event of such institutional shifts the rule could be changed, for this merely admits discretion by the back door. It is the strength of a discretionary monetary policy that it can take account of the changing moneyness of financial assets and the development of new financial institutions and practices insofar as they affect the role of money.[11]

Difficulties of Ensuring Steady Money Growth Rate. There is also the troublesome fact that proposing a steady percentage growth in the money supply, however defined, does not achieve it. To be sure, Friedman has implied that the Federal Reserve has finger-tip control over the money supply: "There is no doubt that if it wanted to, it [the Federal Reserve] has both the formal power and the actual technical capacity to control the total stock of money with a time lag measured in weeks and to a degree of precision measured in tenths of 1 percent." [12] But this is mistaken, as is apparent from the lags between changes in bank reserve positions (which the Federal Reserve can influence immediately) and the total money supply. The difficulty is that the money supply hinges on the willingness of banks to lend or invest excess reserves, the willingness of business and individuals to borrow, the asset preferences of individuals and nonbank institutions—all of which are subject to only imperfect control by the Federal Reserve.[13]

Difficulties of control might be particularly acute in recession or

---

[11] This is not to say that discretionary policy has always taken due account of such changing circumstances. As the balance of this chapter indicates, there has been considerable criticism that the Federal Reserve has *not* sufficiently recognized the importance of liquid assets and nonbank financial intermediaries in affecting the demand for money. But the point is that discretion *permits* allowance for these factors, while an automatic rule would *prohibit* the most perceptive central banker from acting as his knowledge and experience counseled.

[12] Joint Committee, *1959 Employment Hearings,* Pt. 4, p. 609.

[13] Compare, for example, Shaw, *Money, Income and Public Policy,* pp. 1–224, but particularly pp. 141–42, 153, 183, 223.

depression. For one thing, it is entirely possible for the Federal Reserve to be supplying excess reserves to the banks and for the banks to be using the new reserves to create new deposits in payment for Government securities without achieving expansion in the money supply at the desired rate because business and individuals were repaying loans, and thus extinguishing their deposit balances. In a serious depression, as during the 1930s, the banks might not even be willing to invest the excess reserve balances supplied to them by the central bank so these could pile up without affecting the money supply.

In ordinary circumstances, the difficulties might be less dramatic but nevertheless could pose problems for a policy committed to a 4 percent annual increase in money supply. For example, suppose that the money supply began to rise more than 4 percent a year because of increased loan demands. Since there are constantly small jiggles in the money supply, the authorities would be likely to wait to see whether the trend was *really* moving away from 4 percent. By the time they acted, the money supply might be moving up considerably faster than 4 percent a year. Apart from the initial delay, their action would take effect with some lags, as we have seen. In fact, the restrictive impact on the money supply might take effect months later when conditions had changed and private repayments of loans were decreasing the money supply. Thus, perversity in the money supply could reappear, even under the 4 percent automatic increase rate.

Angell's reform proposal would avoid such problems since he simply advocated that the Federal Reserve increase the supply of *bank reserves* so that the maximum amount of deposits *creatable* would increase by 4 percent a year.[14] Presumably, whether or not deposits rose correspondingly, the central bank would continue to add 4 percent more to the reserve base and increase the potential of deposit creation. This approach escapes the problems posed by independent movements in the money supply but would appear to raise other troublesome questions. Suppose that deposits failed to increase in conformity with the increased availability of reserves over a protracted period, as happened in the Great Depression. Clearly, this would lay the basis for a potential deposit increase of considerably more than 4 percent a year at some point and if the private demand for bank

[14] Angell, *Review of Economics and Statistics*, XLII, 250.

credit or banks' willingness to invest improved appreciably, a sharp and perhaps destabilizing rise in the money supply conceivably could occur. If Angell's money managers held to his rule, they would ignore such a development and simply go on adding 4 percent a year to the reserve base, regardless of whether the money supply and use of bank credit currently was rising too fast. But it is more likely that they would recall that stable growth of the money supply was their real objective and would accordingly intervene and use open market policy to curb an excessive rise in the money supply. At this point, however, they would be exercising discretion. It might be added that they would also be joining Friedman and Shaw's money managers and running into the problems outlined in the preceding paragraph.

These, of course, are only hypothetical objections to the "automatic increase" rule and only actual experience with central bank operation under such a rule could give a definitive answer as to its practicability. This analysis, however, does suggest that the mere adoption of such a rule would not preclude some difficulty in effectively enforcing steady annual growth in the money supply.

Stability in Expectations and Monetary Growth. Even if a steady planned growth in the money supply were achieved, stable expectations on the part of the public and the business community would not necessarily follow. Expectations depend on many things beside the money supply. Specifically, if prices rose steadily even though money growth was doing no more than keeping pace with growth in physical production, it is strongly probable that inflationary expectations would result. On the other hand, if private production fell sharply and remained sluggish, despite a steady 4 percent increase in money supply, expectations probably would be affected adversely, despite the continued steady growth in money supply. Indeed, sharp shifts in any important variables might be expected to be reflected in business and consumer expectations.

It might be argued that sharp changes in nonmonetary variables would be unlikely in an environment of stable monetary growth. But it would seem overoptimistic to maintain that a steadily rising trend for money supply would insure stability in other major economic variables. Moreover, a steadily rising money supply does not necessarily mean a steadily rising flow of expenditure; changes in the rate of use or velocity of money could still provide a monetary stimulus to instability.

Compatibility of the Rule with Economic Needs. A discretionary monetary policy has one cardinal virtue: it enables the monetary authorities to take account of changing economic circumstances. It is extraordinarily difficult to devise an arbitrary rule which in essence endeavors in advance to provide for all the kinds of instability and problems that may arise in the distant future.[15] And if the rule does encounter unanticipated circumstances, it may prevent badly needed action. For example, if a major depression so increased liquidity preferences as to create an enormous demand for money, it would seem ridiculous to deny the satisfaction of this demand, which presumably would have to be met before economic recovery could get underway, simply because of a rule which had been designed for completely different circumstances. Yet Shaw has vigorously shut the door on exceptions to such a rule, saying, "When the nominal supply of money is growing at a stable rate, a serious recession would itself generate a very large increase in *real* money [money balances deflated by a price index]." [16]

The problem is that price rigidity might prevent any substantial price decline in recession, preventing a large increase in *real* money balances.[17] Even if real money balances did rise, and thus supplemented the 4 percent increase in nominal money balances added by the rule, the recession might still persist and perhaps even worsen.[18] If this happened, it seems dubious that an a priori rule should prevent action that might be helpful.

Application of the rule also would not have been appropriate from 1945 to 1951, a prosperous period in which the money supply rose about 3 percent a year. On Friedman's or Shaw's reckoning this is

15 Samuelson, "Reflections on Monetary Policy" *Review of Economics and Statistics,* XLII (August, 1960), 265.

16 Shaw, *United States Monetary Policy,* p. 62.

17 In some recessions, such as the 1958 business decline, prices have actually increased, reducing real money balances. Whether a really serious recession would bring substantial price declines is difficult to say in advance of the experience.

18 That is, the adverse impact of falling employment, production and perhaps prices might so worsen expectations and increase liquidity preference as to create demands for real money balances much greater than were being created by the nominal money supply additions and the decline in prices.

somewhat less than would be called for by the automatic rule. Yet
1945–1951 were years of fairly rapid inflation. Of course, even if the
money supply had been held to a lower rate of growth, or no growth
at all, the economy's accumulated store of liquid assets and current
incomes could still have financed excessive demands for goods which
had been unavailable in the war years and were still in short supply.
Thus inflation probably still would have been a problem. But it seems
plausible that a reduced creation of new money would have had some
desirable effects.

It seems difficult to escape the conclusion that central banking by
preordained rule would not permit adjustment to changing circumstances. In a world which is in a state of flux, this is a serious disadvantage.

Probability of Abandonment in Difficult Circumstances. If economic or political exigencies were to require monetary action different from that prescribed by a fixed rule, it is hard to believe that
the rule would not give way. The worst experience with discretionary
control of the money supply, as shown in Table 8, came during the
Great Depression and during World Wars I and II; these were national emergencies. Such periods of stress, in which the Government
and the people are concerned about the survival of the nation, are
the very times in which an arbitrary rule would be brushed aside if
it seemed an impediment to needed action. Thus the proposed auto-
maticity would have broken down at the very time it was needed. As
Warren Smith has said: "like the gold standard, it would be a 'fair
weather' rule, and fair weather would be unlikely to last very long." [19]

Problem of Time Lags. Time lags might well be almost as much of
a problem for a monetary policy administered by reference to a fixed
rule as for a discretionary policy. The fixed rule policy eliminates the
necessity for the central bank to recognize turns in business and accordingly shortens the "recognition" lag, that is, the period between
the need for action and the central bank's awareness of a need for
action. But the fixed rule would not at all affect the lag between the
time actions are taken and the time they have effect on the economy,
and this lag is the main reason, according to Friedman, that discretionary monetary policy has been destabilizing. Friedman said:

[19] Joint Committee, *1959 Staff Report,* p. 404.

Monetary and fiscal policy is rather like a water tap that you turn on now and that then only starts to run 6, 9, 12, 16 months from now. It is because of this long lag in the reaction to policy that you have this tendency for policy in fact to have an effect opposite to that intended.[20]

This sort of lag would be troublesome for any monetary actions, discretionary or automatic. It might be said that since all money-supply changes under the automatic rule would be at the same rate, for example, 4 percent a year, lags in their impact would be irrelevant; whenever they took effect, their impact would be the same. But what matters for the economy is not simply the amount of money created but the money conditions created by the interaction of the 4 percent increase in money supply and the incremental demand for money and these vary considerably. In prosperous periods demand for money could outrun a 4 percent increase in supply and create tight money conditions; in recessions, easy money could result from the fact that the incremental demand for money fell short of the 4 percent rise in supply. Just as with discretionary policy, lags could mean that tight money had its effect in the following recession, while easy money took effect in a prosperous period.

Thus, so far as lags are concerned, there is little to be gained from replacement of discretionary control over the money supply by a rule calling for an automatic 4 percent annual increase in money supply.

SUMMARY ON CONTROL OF MONEY SUPPLY. The critics of discretionary monetary policy have shown that the Federal Reserve has not been successful in producing countercyclical behavior of the total money supply; that is, expansion in the money supply when business is declining and vice versa. Rather the pattern has been for changes in the money supply to lag behind both changes in business conditions and changes in monetary policy. Accordingly, reduced rates of growth or even contractions of the money supply, originally aimed at slowing too-rapid business expansion, have overlapped into periods of business contraction when expansion of the money supply would have been more appropriate. Similarly, accelerated expansion of the money supply, designed to combat recession, has overlapped for some months into periods of business expansion. Thus, the critics have established that even in the area to which it has largely restricted

[20] Joint Committee, *1959 Employment Hearings*, Pt. 4, p. 615.

monetary policy—control of the money supply—the Federal Reserve's performance is open to criticism.

However, in assessing the importance of this criticism, it needs to be borne in mind that monetary policy has affected substantial and strategic parts of the money supply—deposits in New York, Chicago, and other major money centers—much more rapidly than it has affected deposits in small and medium-sized banks throughout the country. This has reduced the overlap of inappropriate movements for these sectors of the money supply. Imperfect control of the total money supply has reflected mainly the lagged impact of Federal Reserve policy on smaller banks. Moreover, this lagged impact could be substantially speeded up if the Reserve System made use of moderate increases in reserve requirements in periods of restrictive monetary policies.

The critics' proposal for better control of the money supply—adoption of a rule requiring automatic annual increases in the money supply at some given percentage rate, for example, 4 percent—would raise perplexing problems of its own. It would impose undesirable rigidity on monetary policy which might prove positively harmful at times, and would probably be abandoned whenever serious economic problems arose. The rule would make no allowance for any change in the moneyness of various types of liquid assets; over time this might make the rule obsolete or at least sharply reduce its influence on economic activity. Achieving a steady 4 percent growth in the money supply would involve many of the same problems which have made discretionary control of the money supply difficult. At the same time, many of the advantages claimed for automatic increases turn out on analysis to disappear or diminish.

To sum up: Criticism of the Federal Reserve's discretionary control of the money supply seems exaggerated and the associated proposals for replacing it with an automatized control are themselves open to criticism. Nevertheless the critics have clearly shown that Federal Reserve control over the money supply needs improvement. Somewhat better performance might be achieved by use of reserve requirement increases as a tool of credit restraint, since these could spread the impact of monetary policy throughout the banking system more rapidly and accordingly bring about a quicker response of the entire money supply to changes in monetary policy. If the portion of the money supply in small and medium-sized banks still was only sluggishly affected, implying also a delayed impact on the credit-granting abilities of such banks, this would strengthen the case for use of selective controls on consumer and mortgage credit which these banks are particularly important in supplying. When one considers the deficiencies of Federal Reserve control of the money supply and the lags in the influence of changes in the money supply on long-term interest rates or on the economy's decisions, the case for a many-sided approach to monetary policy is strengthened and the case for the Federal Reserve's single-minded policy of concentrating attention on the money supply correspondingly weakened.

MONEY SUPPLY VERSUS INTEREST RATES, LIQUIDITY, AND NONBANK CREDIT-GRANTING INSTITUTIONS

A growing number of economists have argued recently that whether the central bank can closely control the money supply is really an outmoded and peripheral issue, which has distracted attention from more important questions, such as whether the central bank should attempt instead to directly control interest rates, general liquidity, and the growth of all kinds of credit.

MONEY SUPPLY VERSUS INTEREST RATES. In what is in effect almost a complete reversal of the Federal Reserve's view that controlling the money supply is *the* task of the central bank, a number of economists have asserted that on the contrary the central bank's main task is to control rates of interest without particular regard to the money supply. As R. F. Kahn put it, "It is immaterial what changes in the quantity of money have to occur as part of the process of securing a particular desired behavior of rates of interest." [21] This point of view was adopted by the British Radcliffe Committee, which explicitly rejected the idea that the "central task of the monetary authorities is to keep a tight control on the supply of money" [22] and insisted on "the structure of interest rates rather than some notion of the 'supply of money' as the centre-piece of monetary action." [23]

Nicholas Kaldor justified exclusive emphasis on interest rates as follows:

[21] Radcliffe Committee, *Memoranda,* Pt. III, No. 19, p. 144.
[22] Radcliffe Committee, *Report,* p. 132.
[23] *Ibid.,* p. 134.

(i) Changes in the money supply do not exert any direct influence on the level of monetary demand for goods and services as such, but only through the consequential changes in interest rates which are induced by them.

(ii) The magnitude of these consequential changes in interest rates for any given percentage change in the money supply depends on the extent of inconvenience (or conversely, increased convenience) involved in any corresponding change in the average ratio of cash balances to monetary turnover. Except where this ratio is abnormally small, the elasticity of interest rates with respect to the change in the cash-balance ratio may only be a moderate one.

(iii) Since the regulatory effect of monetary policy essentially resides in the effect of changing interest rates on expenditures, it is more efficacious to concentrate on the regulation of interest rates directly through the money market and/or the gilt-edged market than indirectly through pressure exerted on the supply of bank credit.[24]

Each of these arguments will be considered in turn.

(i) Kahn spelled out Kaldor's first point more fully as follows:

If the quantity of money is increased, this means that the banks have increased their assets, and in doing so they will have bid up the prices of securities, i.e., lowered rates of interest. Until this fall in rates of interest (and any expansion in bank advances) has influenced the level of demand, and so of activity, by its effect on investment, the whole of the additional money will be held in inactive form, the rise in security prices and the fall in interest rates having precisely to be such as to induce the public to make the necessary swaps with the banks of other forms of holding wealth for deposits.[25]

The problem with this argument is that it tends to minimize well-known imperfections in the money and capital markets, and also slights the direct contribution an increased money supply could make to higher expenditures. In the first place, as studies of the securities markets have shown, prospective sellers of securities are sometimes unable to find a buyer unless they mark prices down sharply. If they are unwilling to accept such price reductions no transaction takes place. Under these circumstances, increased availability of bank reserves would permit these potential sales of securities to take place at unchanged interest rates (prices) with the banks as buyers. If the sellers of securities had planned to use the funds raised for business investment, the banks' purchases will permit investment to take place without Kahn's postulated "fall in rates of interest."

[24] Radcliffe Committee, *Memoranda,* Pt. III, No. 20, p. 148.
[25] *Ibid.,* No. 19, p. 144–45.

Imperfections in the bank credit market, namely stickiness of bank loan rates and attendant "credit rationing," also permit banks to increase the money supply and quicken economic activity without first lowering interest rates. More of the fringe of unsatisfied borrowers may be accommodated at unchanged interest rates if the availability of bank reserves increases. This might be particularly likely to occur in consumer credit extensions where loan rates are notoriously sticky.[26] Thus, even though changes in the money supply ordinarily take place through commercial bank lending or investing, this does not mean, as Kaldor and Kahn tend to assume, that money can affect spending only through interest rates.

Moreover, it would be theoretically possible to change the money supply without any preceding change in bank loans or investments. The Federal Government could create new money and pay it out directly to recipients of unemployment compensation, veterans' benefits, interest on the Federal debt or in payment of any of its bills. Money could be extinguished when received in payment of taxes.[27]

It would seem fair to conclude that changes in the money supply can influence spending and demand without changes in interest rates although normally changes in interest rates would be a significant part of the process.

(ii) The Radcliffe-Kahn-Kaldor argument also understates the influence of the money-income ratio on interest rates. Frank Paish provided considerable evidence to the Radcliffe Committee on the close relationship between the long-term rate of interest and the ratio of money to national income in the United Kingdom.[28] Paish argued that the relationship had been so close that if one knew the ratio of bank deposits to net national money income, one could predict what the rate of interest would be "almost exactly." [29] It is worth noting

[26] It is of course possible to consider that a change in banks' views of what constitutes a creditworthy customer itself is equivalent to a change in the interest rate, or that a change in down-payment requirements or maximum maturity is equivalent to a change in interest rates. But if a change in any of the terms or conditions of lending is considered equivalent to a change in interest rate, the term interest rate becomes so broad as to lose operational content.

[27] Shaw, *Money, Income and Public Policy,* p. 253; and R. F. Harrod, *Toward a Dynamic Economics* (London, Macmillan, 1948), pp. 138–42.

[28] Radcliffe Committee, *Memoranda,* Pt. III, p. 102, 184–85; and Radcliffe Committee, *Minutes of Evidence,* pars. 10431–34, 10436, 10438, 10441, 10443–53.

[29] *Ibid.,* par. 10434.

that John Gurley, who in the United States has been one of the leading exponents of greater emphasis on liquid assets other than money, took the occasion in his review of the Radcliffe Report and Evidence to say:

Altogether, there seems to be an impressive body of evidence to support the view that the money-income ratio, modified by the presence of other liquid assets, and within the context of 'real' variables, was the principal determinant of the level of interest rates in Britain during the postwar period.[30]

The relationship between the money-income ratio and interest rates has also been close in the United States during the postwar period. Gurley, in an examination of liquidity and interest rates, concluded that while the shape of the public's demand schedule for money is influenced by the volume of nonmonetary liquid assets available, this is perfectly consistent with "a 'perfect correlation' between the money supply and the interest rate." [31] Moreover, the degree of change in interest rates with a given change in the money-income ratio has been increasing during the postwar years. In other words interest rates have been becoming more sensitive to change in the money-income ratio. To avoid repetition a demonstration of this point is deferred until the next chapter on velocity which includes charts and tables on the changing and more sensitive relationship of interest rates to the income-money ratio (that is, simply the inverse of the money-income ratio).

The conclusion is that the money-income ratio is closely connected with the level of interest rates and that it is by no means obvious that the reaction of interest rates to changes in the money-income ratio will be only "moderate," as Kaldor put it.

(iii) Kaldor's point that interest rates should be influenced "directly through the money market and/or the gilt-edged market" has much to recommend it, as concluded in our study of the Federal Reserve's "bills only" policy. However, to approve conscious control of interest rates as a supplement to control of the money supply is not

[30] Gurley, "The Radcliffe Report and Evidence," *American Economic Review*, L (September, 1960), 680.

[31] U.S. Congress, Joint Economic Committee, *Employment, Growth, and Price Levels, Study Paper No. 14: Liquidity and Financial Institutions in the Postwar Period*, by John Gurley, 86th Cong., 1st Sess., 1960, p. 54. Cited hereafter as Gurley, *Study Paper*.

to recommend it as an alternative. The Radcliffe Committee, if not also Kahn and Kaldor, has apparently viewed control of the money supply and interest rates as alternatives, not as complements.

The difficulty with viewing control of the money supply and of interest rates as alternative policies is that one almost invariably involves the other. Both the liquidity preference and loanable funds theories of interest-rate determination picture the rate of interest as the price at which the supply and demand for money are equated.

The Radcliffe Committee at times seemed to deny these views of interest-rate determination in favor of the idea that interest rates reflect mainly expectations about the future level of interest rates.[32] But the Committee nevertheless here and there indicated its awareness of the importance of the money supply for interest rate determination. For example, in rejecting the idea that the monetary authorities should peg interest rates, the Committee pointed out that this could be done only by exchanging *money* for bonds at the pegged interest rate level, and that this would mean "monetization of the National Debt." [33] Again, when the Committee said that "the authorities can raise interest rates without difficulty," it supported this by referring to the "Bank of England as the ultimate source of liquidity," [34] and in this context such a statement can only mean that interest rates are raised because of restrictions on the supply of new cash the Bank of England is willing to make available. In the same paragraph the Committee objected to an official attempt to reduce interest rates rapidly because this may require the Bank of England "to pour out cash in exchange for bonds." [35]

Experience in the United States has some relevance in appraising the importance of the money supply for interest-rate determination and in appraising the possibilities of setting interest rates without influencing the money supply. The attempts by the Federal Reserve to peg interest rates from 1942 to 1951, for example, had to be backed by a readiness to buy bonds. Moreover in 1959, when the 4¼ percent legal limit on interest rates payable on new bond issues blocked the U.S. Treasury out of the market, the fact that the largest bor-

---

[32] Gurley, *American Economic Review*, L, 678–80.
[33] Radcliffe Committee, *Report*, p. 176.
[34] *Ibid.*, p. 175.
[35] *Ibid.*

rower was stopped from issuing long-term bonds and that the monetary authorities would have welcomed lower interest rates did not prevent market rates of interest from rising further.

There is, to be sure, a good deal to the Radcliffe Committee's view that expectations are important in influencing interest rates, particularly in the short run. Thus, interest rates may change considerably at times even though the money supply has remained practically unchanged.[36] But this is only to say that interest rates are not uniquely determined by the money supply. The Radcliffe Committee mounted a powerful attack on the Federal Reserve's faith in the virtues of confining the central bank's attention to money supply and letting interest rates take care of themselves, but it has not succeeded in demonstrating that only interest rates matter.

To sum up: It seems clear that direct central bank influence on interest rates would add to effectiveness of monetary policy. But a policy of concentrating central bank action only on interest rates, and ignoring or slighting the importance of controlling the money supply, might well be as harmful to an effective monetary policy as the Federal Reserve's contrary view of putting all the emphasis on controlling the money supply, and almost none on the importance of appropriate interest rate behavior. The money supply and interest rates are closely related, but there is enough "play" in the relationship (traceable largely to independent changes in the demand for money) to make control of both essential for an effective monetary policy.

MONEY SUPPLY VERSUS LIQUIDITY. A great deal of the skepticism about the usefulness of central bank control of the money supply has stemmed from recognition that the economy has many sources of liquidity besides money. An increased availability of nonmonetary liquid assets is believed to reduce the demand for money because liquid assets serve as good substitutes for money in its store-of-value function. People who decide to hold part of their accumulated savings in savings and loan shares, savings bank accounts, U.S. Savings bonds, or businesses which hold reserves in the form of Treasury bills

[36] Any number of illustrations could be adduced. Consider, for example, the precipitous drop in interest rates in the early months of 1960—yields on 91-day Treasury bills dropped 40 percent (from 4.67 percent at the peak in December, 1959, to 2.73 percent at the low in April, 1960) and longer-term bond yields declined about 11 percent in the same period—when the money supply changed less than 1 percent, and this change was a decrease.

or other short-term debt instruments are obviously freeing cash for use by others.

But acceptance of this view does not imply that liquid assets are as good as cash in all its uses. Cash can be used immediately to make payments. Liquid assets, on the other hand, ordinarily have to be converted into cash before their owner can make a payment. This may involve inconvenience, delay, and expense.

Accordingly, many students who recognize the importance of liquid assets retain an important or even primary place for the supply of money in the constellation of liquid assets. Money is not only the largest single block of liquidity but also the most liquid. Gurley, for example, calculated that a dollar of money is equivalent to at least two dollars of other liquid assets in its influence on interest rates.[37] From this point of view, central bank control of the money supply would still be important. The presence of a large volume of non-monetary liquid assets would mean only that the central bank might have to restrict the money supply somewhat further to make up for the added liquidity provided by such assets.[38]

However, this does not mean that considerable shifts between

[37] Gurley, *Study Paper,* p. 8 ff.
[38] Compare the comments of Gurley in Joint Committee, *1959 Employment Hearings,* Pt. 4, p. 855. But it should be noted that a more extreme view asserts that liquid assets can eliminate, as well as reduce, the demand for money. This minority view was expressed at the same hearings by Eisner in the following words: "money is, after all, just one of a number of things that people can use. It has substitutes. And what I become rather fond of suggesting is that we ask ourselves what would happen to the economy if the monetary authority began reducing the quantity of nickels; suppose the monetary authority said, 'We are going to make nickels really tight so that you can't get nickels,' and they would keep selling bonds for nickels and keep withdrawing nickels from circulation. What would that do to the economy, to the rate of interest? I would suggest that it would do very little, because nobody would pay a premium for nickels when he could get pennies and dimes. This seems rather obvious and perhaps ludicrous. . . . There is really no reason ultimately why business need be hamstrung by lack of money." Joint Committee, *1959 Employment Hearings,* Pt. 4, pp. 782–83.
Eisner's analogy is open to obvious objection. He has assumed away the question of whether liquid assets are good substitutes for money. Nickels, dimes, and pennies are all money; of course they are good substitutes for one another. But Treasury bills and savings and loan shares, to take two types of liquid asset, are not money and are not substitutable for it in all of its uses. They would be inappropriate and clumsy ways of paying a grocery bill, for example. And so long as money has no good substitutes as a means of payment, some quantity of money is likely to be essential for the effective functioning of the economy.

money and liquid assets would not pose some problems for the central bank. Replacement of money by liquid assets in consumers' and business firms' asset portfolios doubtless runs into limits—because of the irreducible demand for money as a means of payment and because the marginal substitution rate of assets for money will fall as more and more such exchanges take place—but in the meantime the velocity, or turnover, of the remaining money stock may increase considerably, and to an extent which it may be difficult for the central bank authorities to predict and offset.[39] How serious this could be for the central bank is examined in the next chapter.

MONEY SUPPLY AND BANKS VERSUS NONBANK FINANCIAL INTERMEDIARIES. Gurley and Shaw have been responsible for an alternative major attack on the usefulness of controlling the money supply. They have argued that rapid growth of nonbank financial intermediaries has made control of the money supply and the banking system much less important. Financial intermediaries are not a new development, of course, but the traditional view has been to regard them as essentially channels which make the savings of one set of people available for use by others. Gurley and Shaw have challenged this view and have argued that the intermediaries create credit just as the banks do but are not reached by conventional monetary controls, and accordingly need special regulation.[40]

---

[39] See the comments of Gurley and Shaw, "Financial Growth and Monetary Controls," p. 12; and Warren Smith, "Financial Intermediaries and Monetary Controls," *Quarterly Journal of Economics*, LXXIII, (November, 1959), 549.

[40] Voluminous literature on the subject has developed. See the following book and articles by John G. Gurley and Edward S. Shaw: *Money in a Theory of Finance* (Washington, Brookings Institution, 1960); "Financial Aspects of Economic Development," *American Economic Review*, XLV (September, 1955), 515–38; "Financial Intermediaries and the Savings-Investment Process," *Journal of Finance*, XI (May, 1956), 257–76; "Financial Growth and Monetary Controls"; and "The Growth of Money and Debt in the United States, 1800–1950," *Review of Economics and Statistics*, XXXIX (August, 1957), 250–62.

For comment on the Gurley-Shaw thesis, see the following technical literature: G. W. McKinley, "The Federal Home Loan Bank System and the Control of Credit," *Journal of Finance*, XII (September, 1957), 319–32; Ross N. Robertson, "The Commercial Banking System and Competing Non-monetary Intermediaries," in Federal Reserve Bank of St. Louis, *Monthly Review*, XXXIX (May, 1957), 62–69; J. M. Culbertson, 'Intermediaries and Monetary Theory: A Criticism of the Gurley-Shaw Theory," *American Economic Review*, XLVIII (March, 1958), 119–31 (Also in this issue is Gurley and Shaw's reply.); Richard S. Thorn, "Nonbank Financial Intermediaries, Credit Expansion and Monetary Policy," *Staff Papers of the International Monetary Fund*, VI (November,

The Gurley-Shaw thesis rests on four supports: (1) Intermediaries create credit just as banks do; (2) Intermediaries create claims on themselves which reduce the demand for money; (3) Intermediaries' portfolio activities may activate idle money balances; and (4) The fact that banks have become relatively smaller compared to intermediaries indicates the growing inadequacy of conventional monetary controls.

Credit Creation by Financial Intermediaries. Gurley and Shaw have argued that intermediaries are similar to commercial banks in that they engage in multiple credit expansion just as banks do. Banks, they have said, are only "one among many financial intermediaries." [41] They have admitted that intermediaries cannot create *money,* that is, means of payment, but have countered with the argument that neither can banks create savings and loan *shares* or mutual savings bank *deposits.*[42] The uniqueness of the money creation facility of the commercial banks in their opinion, has been no more important than the unique ability of intermediaries to create their own individual types of claims against themselves. It is the credit-creating activities of the intermediaries [43] which are of supreme importance because intermediaries' lending and investing expands the supply of loanable funds available to finance expenditures, regardless of whether the money supply increases. Thus, it is the intermediaries' credit-creation powers which make central bank control of the money supply inadequate.

The point can be illustrated by considering a situation in which the central bank has imposed monetary restraint which has tightened bank reserve positions and made bank credit harder to get. The argument is that the credit market offers many alternative sources of

---

1958), 369–83; Eugene A. Birnbaum, "The Growth of Financial Intermediaries as a Factor in the Effectiveness of Monetary Policy," *Staff Papers of the International Monetary Fund,* VI (November, 1958), 384–426; Donald Shelby, "Some Implications of the Growth of Financial Intermediaries," *Journal of Finance,* XIII (December, 1958), 527–41; Joseph Ascheim, "Commercial Banks and Financial Intermediaries: Fallacies and Policy Implications," *Journal of Political Economy,* LXVII (February, 1959), 59–71; Warren Smith, *Quarterly Journal of Economics,* LXXIII, 533–53; and Lindsay and Guttentag, "Financial Intermediaries and the Effectiveness of Monetary Policy."

[41] Gurley and Shaw, *American Economic Review,* XLV, 521–22.

[42] *Ibid.*

[43] In this study, as in the Gurley-Shaw analysis, "credit creation" means lending or investing. Unlimited credit creation could result from a few individuals lending back and forth among themselves. This should be distinguished from bank credit creation which adds to the monetary supply.

funds and that borrowers accordingly need only turn to the financial intermediaries for the funds they need.[44] The intermediaries' lending supplies the funds to keep economic activity rising as fast as businessmen desire, contrary to the central bank's aim of restraining the pace of activity. The remedy, Gurley and Shaw argue, is for some sort of direct controls on the ability of intermediaries to extend credit.[45]

The crucial point in this stage of discussion, that is, the credit-creation stage, is whether in fact intermediaries can, and do, extend credit in the same way as commercial banks. The answer would seem to be that they do not, that there are important differences which justify special controls on the banks.

Banks can achieve greater and faster credit expansion on a given addition to reserves available for lending than can intermediaries. The reason for this is that the reserves loaned to customers by banks ordinarily return to the banking system almost immediately because banks operate the nation's payments mechanism. When a borrower pays over the funds borrowed to another—in payment for labor, materials, securities, or whatever—the money is almost always returned to the banking system within a few days because of the general practice of depositing a check shortly after it has been received. Although the initial supply of reserves may change its resting place among individual banks, it remains in the banking system and is available for continuous relending until the successive creations of credit have created enough new deposits to absorb that amount of reserves in satisfaction of the legal reserve requirement against deposits.[46] Thus the banks' distinctive role as issuers of the means of payment and operators of the payments mechanism does give commercial banks a peculiar and unique ability to expand credit.

---

[44] The question of where the intermediaries get the funds they lend is deferred to the next section.

[45] Gurley and Shaw, "Financial Growth and Monetary Controls," pp. 17–22.

[46] As Smith has pointed out, this statement must be qualified to the extent that the recipient of a check takes some or all of the proceeds in cash or the intermediary in which the check is deposited uses the proceeds to add to its vault cash. This qualification is ordinarily not very important because under normal circumstances the marginal currency-to-demand-deposit ratios of both the public and the intermediaries are quite low. Also, if the funds are deposited in a savings accounts of member commercial banks, a small amount of member bank reserves (5 percent of the savings deposit) is drained away from the commercial banking (demand deposit) portion of the banking system. Compare Warren Smith, *Quarterly Journal of Economics*, LXXIII, p. 536.

In contrast, the funds extended by financial intermediaries in the course of their credit creation return to them in no such automatic fashion nor with such speed. This limits the amount of credit they can build on a given addition to their reserves within any given period. Funds loaned by a savings and loan association, for example, swell the total of credit created and incomes generated just as do commercial banks' credit extensions, but the savings and loan associations do not recover any of the loaned funds until incomes have been increased and income recipients have decided to put some portion of their savings from the new income receipts (the savings portion itself being a small part of income) back into the savings and loan associations. At this point the savings and loan associations have available for relending some of the funds originally loaned, but it is only a small portion (that part of savings which people decide to keep in savings and loan associations) of a small part (savings) of the income that was created by the original credit extension. It is pertinent that the recovery period for the portion of funds originally loaned is the income-period, that is, the average period which elapses between successive receipts of income in the income-expenditure process, and this is likely to be measured in terms of weeks or months.

Thus commercial bank extensions of credit make a round trip and are available for relending much more quickly than intermediaries' extensions of credit. Also, leakages out of the credit initially extended are larger for intermediaries than for banks. Accordingly banks can erect a much larger structure of credit on a given addition to reserves within a given time than can intermediaries.

Moreover, banks are more likely than intermediaries to be associated with sudden and extreme changes in the volume of credit outstanding. In part this reflects the considerations just discussed—little or no leakages and the short round trip associated with extensions of bank credit—but also involved is the special nature of banks' assets and liabilities. Banks provide the bulk of the economy's short-term, emergency-type finance and this naturally implies volatility in the demand for bank credit and in the volume of bank assets. At the same time, banks' demand deposit liabilities, because they are used by the public at large as means of payment and are withdrawable on demand, serve the economy as a buffer against sudden changes in current account surpluses and deficits and hence are subject to quick swings. Thus banks are subject to fairly quick changes in their liquidity standards and in the reserves they would voluntarily carry, and these changes are much more important for the volume of credit outstanding than would be changes in liquidity standards or reserve ratios for most intermediaries.

These theoretical expectations are borne out by an examination of the annual changes in the volume of funds advanced by commercial banks compared to the volume of funds advanced by nonbank financial intermediaries (savings and loan associations, mutual savings banks, credit unions, insurance companies, pension funds, finance companies, security dealers, mortgage companies, etc.). The banks' extensions of funds are subject to much greater cyclical instability than are extensions of the nonbank financial institutions [47] (see Chart 2).

Thus, so far as the analysis has gone, it would seem that the credit-creation potential of nonbank financial intermediaries is more limited than the credit-creation potential of commercial banks, and credit extended by banks appears to be substantially more unstable than credit extended by intermediaries. Both of these findings suggest that there is validity in the traditional view that the central bank should pay special attention to the commercial banking system and the money supply. However, it is now time to bring into the analysis the fact that the intermediaries create claims on themselves, many of which count as liquid assets and compete with money in consumer and business asset portfolios.

Financial Intermediaries and Demand for Money. We have assumed in the analysis that financial intermediaries secure the funds they lend as their normal share of consumer savings. But intermediaries may increase their share of consumers' funds by making the claims they create more attractive to hold or by advertising the advantages of placing savings with them. If they are successful in this endeavor, they not only can capture a larger share of current savings, but also can induce consumers to shift balances held on demand de-

---

[47] Robert Lindsay and Jack Guttentag have pointed out that the observed instability of bank credit reflects, in addition to the factors discussed, the influence of Federal Reserve policy. However, they add that if the Federal Reserve had not added or subtracted reserves after 1948, and banks had kept a 20 percent reserve ratio, bank loans and investments would have been even more unstable. See "Financial Intermediaries and the Effectiveness of Monetary Policy," pp. 7–15.

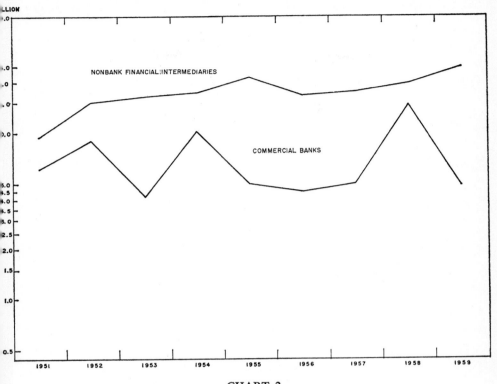

CHART 2
FUNDS ADVANCED BY NONBANK FINANCIAL INTERMEDIARIES AND
COMMERCIAL BANKS, 1951–1959
Source: Board of Governors of Federal Reserve System, "Flow-of-Funds Accounts," for 1951–
1959.

posit into, for example, savings and loan accounts. Such a shift of funds would increase the savings and loan associations' lending power correspondingly while not reducing the banks' ability to lend. This is because the savings and loan associations hold their reserves in the form of bank deposits and the switch simply shifts ownership of a given amount of deposits on the banks' books. In effect cash balances would be dishoarded and transmitted to ultimate borrowers through the intermediaries.

Over long periods, something like this undoubtedly has occurred. But such longer-run effects of the development of money substitutes by financial intermediaries can be compensated for by the central bank by simply reducing the additions to the money supply that might otherwise have been made to keep the availability of money in line with growth of the economy. The more serious problem is whether there are consistently destabilizing *cyclical* shifts between money and intermediary claims.

Some of the intermediaries, such as life insurance companies and pension funds, offer claims which are not close substitutes for money in any short-term sense and hence are not likely to give rise to sudden shifts from money to them or from them to money. However, this still leaves savings and loan shares, mutual savings bank deposits, and credit union shares as possible sources of short-term shifts, for these are good substitutes for money in its store of value function.

Many have assumed such shifts might take place in a period of credit restraint when interest rates are rising, if intermediaries raised rates offered on money placed with them and thus induced transfers of funds to them from non-interest paying demand deposits or from time deposits with commercial banks which pay lower interest rates.[48] In this way the supply of loanable funds might be increased consider-

[48] See, for example, Burns, *Prosperity Without Inflation*, p. 50; and Gurley's discussion of papers by Herbert Stein, J. W. Angell, and E. M. Bernstein, *American Economic Review*, XLVIII (May, 1958) 105. Gurley and Shaw have on occasion argued that destabilizing shifts from bank deposits to intermediary claims could take place at falling interest rates and that accordingly it is not valid to assume that monetary velocity would rise only when interest rates rise. The possibility may be granted. Whether it is a reasonable probability is quite another matter. As Lindsay and Guttentag point out, Gurley and Shaw's evidence for the possibility's actually occurring is restricted to a footnote reference to the experience during the 1920s. The more usual as well as the more recent experience has been for velocity and interest rates to be positively and indeed closely correlated. We shall take up the point in Chapter XI at greater length. Meanwhile, for Gurley and Shaw's views on velocity and intermediaries

ably despite restraint on the money supply created by commercial banks.[49]

In periods when interest rates on the primary securities which they purchase were falling, the intermediaries might reduce rates offered on the liquid assets they create. If this induced a shift out of intermediary claims and back into demand deposits, loanable funds would *decline* by about fifty-five cents for each dollar shifted out of, for example, a savings and loan association. It is clear that such shifts would tend to destabilize the economy. In periods when the economy was active, interest rates were rising, and the Federal Reserve was trying to restrict the supply of loanable funds, shifts from deposits to intermediary claims could increase the supply of loanable funds. In recessions, on the other hand, when interest rates were being encouraged to fall by Federal Reserve actions to stimulate the economy, shifts back into demand deposits could shrink the supply of loanable funds and thus counter an expansive monetary policy.

However, there is no evidence that such destabilizing shifts have occurred in any significant degree. Intermediary claims of the liquid asset type have increased more rapidly than the money supply in the postwar years, but their growth has been rather steady. There has been no perceptible acceleration of the growth of such liquid assets during periods of rising interest rates; nor has there been deceleration of growth, or even decline, in periods of falling interest rates [50] (see Table 10).

As Table 10 shows, mutual savings bank deposits increased at about the same average quarterly rate from the first quarter of 1952 to the third quarter of 1957, although this whole span embraced two periods of rising rates separated by one period of falling rates. Furthermore, the one marked acceleration in mutual savings bank deposit growth came in a period of falling interest rates, from the fourth

---

see, *American Economic Review*, XLV, 533–34; and "Financial Growth and Monetary Controls," 14–16. For Lindsay and Guttentag's critique, see "Financial Intermediaries and the Effectiveness of Monetary Policy," pp. 36–38.

[49] For some numerical calculations of the impact on credit outstanding of shifts among currency, demand deposits, time deposits and intermediary claims, see Smith, *Quarterly Journal of Economics*. LXXIII, 540.

[50] As Smith has pointed out, the reason for lack of shifting between deposits and intermediary claims in response to general movements in interest rates may be that the rates offered by savings and loan associations and mutual savings banks have risen steadily during the postwar period and have not therefore participated in the periodic declines which have characterized rates on open market paper and bank loans. See, Joint Committee, *1959 Staff Report*, p. 355.

TABLE 10

QUARTERLY AVERAGE CHANGE IN SELECTED
LIQUID ASSETS, 1952–1959

(*$ billion*)

	Mutual Savings Bank Deposits	Savings and Loan Shares	Credit Union Shares
I, 1952–II, 1953 Rising interest rates	0.45	0.83	0.07
III, 1953–II, 1954 Falling interest rates	0.45	1.03	0.08
III, 1954–III, 1957 Rising interest rates	0.44	1.15	0.10
IV, 1957–II, 1958 Falling interest rates	0.60	1.60	0.07
III, 1958–IV, 1959 Rising interest rates	0.35	1.60	0.12

Note: Roman numerals indicate the quarters; for example, "I" is first quarter.
Source: Board of Governors of the Federal Reserve System, "Flow of Funds/ Saving Estimates, Supplement #3," July 8, 1960; and *Federal Reserve Bulletin,* XLVI (April, 1960), 434.

quarter of 1957 to the second quarter of 1958, and the one deceleration in growth, from the third quarter of 1958 to the fourth quarter
of 1959, took place despite a rise in interest rates: both contrary
movements to what the theory would have indicated.

Savings and loan shares grew at an accelerating rate, in absolute
terms, until the last period shown—the third quarter of 1958 to the
fourth quarter of 1959—when, despite rising interest rates, the growth
of savings and loan shares leveled off. Again there is no evidence of
a systematic response to changes in the general level of interest rates,
and indeed, the leveling off in the absolute rate of growth in the final
period of rising rates is contrary to what the theory would lead us
to have expected.

Only in the pattern of growth of credit union shares is there support for the theory that intermediary claims are substituted for money
in a destabilizing way. As Table 10 shows, the growth of credit union
shares speeded up in the periods of rising interest rates and slowed
down in one of the two periods of falling rates. But the amounts in-

volved were rather small. In the most recent period shown, when they grew most, the dollar growth in credit union shares was only about 5 percent of the growth in mutual savings bank deposits and savings and loan shares.

Thus it seems probable that the intermediaries' ability to create liquid assets has not been cyclically destabilizing to any significant extent. The longer-run substitution of intermediary claims for money in the public's asset portfolio, evidenced by the fact that the public's holdings of these claims has been increasing faster than the money supply, has helped increase the velocity of money, but as will be brought out in the following chapter, this is only part of a general velocity problem which must be dealt with by the central bank.

Financial Intermediaries' Portfolio Shifts. Financial intermediaries may also sell Government securities to holders of idle money balances and use the funds thus procured to satisfy the loan demands of private borrowers. Thus their administration of asset portfolios could speed up the velocity of money. Such management of asset portfolios to encourage others to minimize holdings of money balances would be a parallel to their creation of new liabilities, which are substitutes for money and which serve the same purpose of speeding up monetary velocity.

There is little doubt that intermediary sales of securities have increased income velocity. Moreover, at times, such sales have assumed sizeable dimensions (as noted with respect to insurance companies and savings banks in the section on the Federal Reserve's "bills only" policy), but they do not seem to have been a major cause of the overall economizing on cash and increasing monetary velocity which traditionally has accompanied a period of high business activity and rising interest rates.

Thus, Warren Smith has shown that in the period from December 31, 1954, to June 30, 1957, when monetary policy was generally restrictive, the $47.9 billion of funds supplied to private borrowers by nonbank financial intermediaries came almost entirely from their normal inflows of funds from consumers and others (and presumably largely represented savings); only $0.8 billion, or 1.7 percent, was derived from sales of Government securities from intermediary portfolios. In contrast, commercial banks and the rest of the monetary system obtained $14.5 billion, or 64.4 percent, of the funds they advanced to the private sector from sales of Government obligations.[51] The inference is clearly that the banks' portfolio operations were a much more destabilizing influence on monetary velocity than were portfolio operations of financial intermediaries.

However, the sales of Government obligations by intermediaries, while small compared to commercial bank sales as well as to intermediaries' total credit extensions, have varied in a destabilizing fashion, being highest during periods of credit restriction and rising interest rates and lowest during periods of credit ease. During the periods of credit restriction—December, 1952, to June 30, 1953, and December, 1954, to September, 1957—intermediary sales of Government obligations averaged about $200 million a quarter, but during the June, 1953, to December, 1954, period of credit ease, when the authorities were trying to encourage spending, the intermediaries sold only $100 million a quarter. During the September, 1957, to December, 1958 period, largely if not entirely a period of credit ease, the intermediaries actually bought $200 million Governments a quarter.[52]

Thus the nonbank intermediaries' portfolio behavior would seem to have been destabilizing in a moderate degree, but much less so than the banks' portfolio operations. Certainly it might be appropriate for the central bank to attempt to influence the intermediaries' portfolio operations so that their influence was not destabilizing. But the situation is not, and has not been, so serious as to justify any major overturn of central banking procedures. The abandonment of the "bills only" policy may suffice to give the Federal Reserve more influence over the portfolios of the intermediaries and thus obviate necessity for any more radical measures.

Relative Decline of Banks in the Financial Structure. Apart from the points discussed in the preceding pages, proponents of the Gurley-Shaw thesis have argued that rapid growth of intermediaries in itself has reduced the relative importance of banks and accordingly has made central bank control of the banking system and the money supply less effective. As Gurley and Shaw have put it: "Measured

[51] Warren Smith, *Quarterly Journal of Economics*, LXXIII, 549.
[52] Joint Committee, *1959 Staff Report*, p. 355.

in terms of indirect debt, the relative size of the monetary system has
been almost halved in the past thirty or forty years. . . . The implications of this for monetary controls are as serious as they are plain." [53]
The notion clearly is that the central bank is affecting a shrinking base
if it confines its attention to the commercial banks and the money supply, and with the traditional instruments and intensity of application
it is likely to be less effective in the new environment. In short, Gurley
and Shaw say: "The authorities today limit the growth of a relatively
diminishing segment of this system, making the job of regulating
terms of lending correspondingly more difficult." [54]

As noted earlier, there is no question that nonbank intermediaries
have grown faster than banks in recent years. But it is not clear that
this means that the banking system and the money supply have diminished in importance relative to the financial structure, the gross
national product, or the purposes of monetary control. As a matter
of fact there are a number of reasons for holding that the banks and
the money supply are still of major importance in any program for
effective monetary control. For example:

1. While it is perfectly true, as Gurley and Shaw have emphasized,
that nonbank intermediaries have grown faster than commercial
banks, the banking system, including commercial banks and the Federal Reserve, still held 17.8 percent of total financial assets in 1949,
appreciably more than the 14.1 percent in 1900 and the 12.6 percent
in 1929.[55] It may be objected that the downtrend in the banking system's share of financial assets which began immediately after World
War II has continued since 1949. In a rough attempt to bring the picture up-to-date—Goldsmith's data are not published for recent years
—similar new calculations were made using the Federal Reserve's
"Flow-of-Funds" data. These show a decline in the share of the
banking system in national financial assets from 19.6 percent in 1949
(as compared with Goldsmith's 17.8 percent figure) to 13.6 percent
at the end of 1959.[56] While data from these two sources are not com-

[53] Gurley and Shaw, "Financial Growth and Monetary Controls," p. 14.
[54] *Ibid.*, p. 16.
[55] Goldsmith, *Financial Intermediaries in the American Economy Since 1900,*
calculated from pp. 321, 337, 339, 353.
[56] *Federal Reserve Bulletin,* XLVI (August, 1960), 940–46.

parable, if the Goldsmith series had declined as much as the "Flow-of-Funds" series, since 1949, the banking system's share would be down to the level of 1929. Even so, the Federal Reserve's powers over the banking system still enabled it to reach more or less directly about the same proportion of the nation's financial assets as it did in 1929 before the dramatic rise of the intermediaries.

2. Gurley and Shaw's discussion of the implications of the differing growth rates of nonbank intermediaries and banks is open to another objection. The idea that monetary policy has been weakened simply because intermediaries have grown faster than banks has reflected the assumption that banks and nonbank intermediaries are of equal importance. In fact Gurley and Shaw have said explicitly that both are "loanable funds brokers. Both create credit." [57]

But as we have seen in the discussion of credit creation, there is good reason for regarding the banking system as being more than "one among many financial intermediaries." [58] Banks can create credit faster than nonbank intermediaries. Because banks suffer almost no "leakages," they can create more credit on given initial reserves than can nonbank intermediaries. In addition, bank credit and liabilities are inherently more unstable than nonbank intermediaries' credit and liabilities and hence more likely to give rise to or facilitate destabilizing movements in the economy. All of these are reasons why the central bank needs to pay special attention to the banking system and to the money supply, regardless of whether nonbank intermediaries seem to be growing more rapidly.

3. Moreover, because intermediaries hold their reserves in the form of commercial bank liabilities, that is, demand deposits, the intermediaries' ability to expand credit is affected, indirectly it is true, by central bank actions which influence bank reserves and deposits. Assuming that the public's holdings of intermediary claims and bank deposits expand in proportion, it can be shown that the larger intermediaries are in relation to banks, the greater is the effect which central bank actions affecting bank reserves will have on the structure of intermediary claims and credit.[59] Some economists have therefore

[57] Gurley and Shaw, *American Economic Review*, XLV, 522.
[58] *Ibid.*, 521.
[59] Smith presents a formula to encompass nonbank financial intermediaries in the traditional "credit expansion multiplier." On the assumption that the pub-

argued that the growth of nonbank intermediaries has not seriously weakened monetary controls.[60] In Donald Shelby's words: "What is outmoded in applying traditional monetary restraint upon a diminishing segment of the total financial apparatus if its very diminution provides the essential ingredients of leverage?" [61]

The difficulty remains, however, that the impact of central bank actions on the nonbank intermediaries may take effect with considerable lag if it operates only through bank deposit volumes and if these are influenced, as they have been in the past, with a lag. This is yet another reason suggesting more flexible and effective use by the Federal Reserve of existing instruments. Broadened use of open market operations in all maturities might influence intermediaries' portfolio operations and their willingness to lend more promptly.

---

lic holds demand deposits, currency, and claims against intermediaries in the proportions l:c:t and expands its holdings of these claims proportionally, the multiplier would be:

$$E = \frac{1+c+t}{r_d + c + (r_t + r_d r_s)^t} X$$

where E is the combined expansion of financial claims (currency, demand deposits, and intermediary claims), or alternatively, the combined acquisition of credit instruments by banks and intermediaries; X is excess reserves of commercial banks available to support deposit expansion; r_d is reserve requirement for demand deposits; r_t and r_s are reserve requirements for intermediary claims (held in central bank deposits and currency and in demand deposits in commercial banks respectively). If, for example, $c = .25$, $t = 1.25$, $r_d = .20$, $r_t = .03$, and $r_s = .02$, the multiplier will be approximately 5, $(2.50 \div .4925)$, and $100 of commercial bank excess reserves will permit expansion of financial claims and of earning assets of banks and intermediaries combined by about $500, of which $200 will be demand deposits, $50 currency, and $250 intermediary claims.

To illustrate the point in the text, if intermediaries are larger in relation to banks and accordingly (following the proportionality assumption) the public adds correspondingly more to its holdings of intermediary claims than to deposits when total financial claims increase, then a given change in banks' excess reserves will have a greater impact on intermediary claims (and credit) than on deposits. Thus if t rises to 2.00 (as opposed to 1.25 in the foregoing illustration) the multiplier rises to 6.27, $(3.25 \div .5180)$, and $100 of commercial bank excess reserves will permit total credit expansion of $627. But now the distribution will change, with about $193 in demand deposits, $48 in currency, and $386 in intermediary claims. The central bank accordingly gets a large impact on intermediary credit through a given change in basic bank reserve positions. Shelby employs a similar approach, as do Lindsay and Guttentag.

[60] McKinley, "The Federal Home Loan Bank System and the Control of Credit," *Journal of Finance*, XII (September, 1957), 319–32; and Shelby, "Some Implications of the Growth of Financial Intermediaries," *Journal of Finance*, XIII (December, 1958), 527–41.

[61] *Ibid.*, 540.

Furthermore, supplemental use of selective controls on consumer and mortgage credit could influence demand for the types of credit intermediaries extend.

Summary on Gurley-Shaw Thesis. The analysis by Gurley-Shaw directed attention to a number of areas which had been neglected, both in monetary theory and in the practice of central banking, but the main fruits of their work suggest a redirected emphasis for monetary policy-makers and more flexibility, rather than a revolutionary shift in direction.

RADCLIFFE COMMITTEE'S VIEW: MONEY VERSUS "GENERAL LIQUIDITY." Perhaps the most uncompromising attack on the view that the money supply is an important monetary control variable came from the British Radcliffe Committee. Rejecting the orthodox view that "the supply of money holds the key position," [62] the Radcliffe Committee proposed instead that the central bank's task should be to control the "whole liquidity position." [63] Unfortunately the Committee nowhere rigorously defined or analyzed the "whole liquidity position" but the concept seems to consist of a combination of orthodox liquidity analysis, the ability of nonbank intermediaries to create credit, credit extension by nonfinancial business, and receipts of income. As the Committee put it in an indirect statement:

> spending is not limited by the amount of money in existence; but it is related to the amount of money people think they can get hold of, whether by receipts of income (for instance from sales), by disposal of capital assets or by borrowing.[64]

There is much to be said for using such a broad definition to describe the influences on an individual person's or firm's liquidity position, although the same cannot be said of the entire economy's liquidity position. Certainly an individual's or business's needs for a reserve of liquid assets will be influenced by ability to borrow on short notice or by the amount, timing, and certainty of expected income receipts. There is also some merit in recognizing that liquidity is a function of states of mind as well as of the realities of the availability of money and credit. People's economic behavior may well, at least for a time, reflect their *conceptions* of how much money they

[62] Radcliffe Committee, *Report,* p. 132.
[63] *Ibid.*
[64] *Ibid.,* p. 133.

could quickly lay their hands on, rather than the *reality* of how much actually is available to them. But it seems questionable that mere belief "in the amount of money people think they can get hold of" would persist for more than a short period if it were not supported by actual ability to raise cash quickly by the sale of capital assets or borrowing. And this reintroduces the importance of money for the concept of liquidity.

The fact is that even in people's minds capital assets are regarded as having varying degrees of liquidity, depending on the ease and the definiteness of the price at which they can be turned into cash. A home, to take one major capital asset, is ordinarily considered a poor source of liquidity. It can be sold but the price can vary within rather wide limits, depending on the circumstances of the transaction, and there can be considerable delay in finding a buyer. Common stock, to take another type of capital asset, may be highly salable at profitable prices in periods of rising stock prices, but most people would not wish to consider their stock holdings as a source of ready cash. The stock market is too volatile, too dependent on general economic conditions, for anyone to be able to count on converting a given number of shares into a given quantity of money. Thus people are not unaware that assets vary considerably in their ability to be converted into money quickly and without any considerable loss.

Borrowing as a source of liquidity for the individual person or business is subject to some of the same comments. Ironclad bank credit lines are a source of liquidity. But mere access to a bank or to the open credit markets does not guarantee that cash can be obtained under all circumstances. It is well known that banks become more selective in granting credit during periods of credit restraint and tight money. Underwriters of bond issues also become more selective and less willing to undertake the underwriting risk in periods when interest rates are rising and money is scarce. Thus whether the possibility of borrowing adds to a person's or firm's liquidity, and the degree of the contribution, depends very much on how certain the assurance is that a given amount of cash can be secured when needed. This, in turn, depends on the quantity of money in existence. Lenders, after all, lend money and their ability to accommodate borrowers depends on their ability to find money to lend.

Nevertheless, one member of the Radcliffe Committee went so far as to say that the supply of money has "already become the small change of the system." [65] This striking assertion is based essentially on two assumptions: (1) That potential credit extension is a source of liquidity independent of the supply of money or of bank reserve funds; and (2) That in all but trivial aspects, liquid assets and money are indistinguishable. In the pages that follow these views will be analyzed in an attempt to show that they are mistaken.

Lending Potential as Source of Liquidity. The Committee's emphasis on lending potential as a source of liquidity is evidenced by the survey in Chapter IV of the wide variety of institutions which "supply finance to borrowers of different kinds." [66] This special stress on "the methods, moods and resources of financial institutions and other firms which are prepared (on terms) to finance other people's spending," [67] implies, as Gurley has pointed out, that "the greater the number of potential lenders, especially institutional lenders, the greater is the public's potential liquidity." [68] Even where it considers commercial banks, the Committee states that it gives them importance as "key lenders in the system, and not . . . as 'creators of money'." [69]

This stress on lending potential as liquidity is responsible for the rather surprising assertion by Sayers that "as the boom rises, the sources of liquidity broaden." [70] The first point he puts forth in support is that: "In the course of time people devise new financial intermediaries; the efficiency of the financial system increases and this process tends to accelerate in a prolonged spell of business prosperity." [71] And the second point adduced also has to do with credit extension: "The relative attraction of nonbank debtors varies according to the general trade prospect. . . . At a time when, as an anti-inflation measure, the authorities are enforcing a restriction of bank credit, the apparently favorable position of other debtors makes the extension of nonbank credit peculiarly easy." [72]

There are some obvious inadequacies in this position, particularly

[65] Sayers, "Monetary Thought and Monetary Policy in England," *The Banker*, CX (October, 1960), 683.

[66] Radcliffe Committee, *Report*, p. 107.

[67] *Ibid.*, p. 132.

[68] Gurley, "The Radcliffe Report and Evidence," *American Economic Review*, L (September, 1960), 686.

[69] Radcliffe Committee, *Report*, p. 134.

[70] Sayers, *The Banker*, CX, 683.

[71] *Ibid.*, p. 675.   [72] *Ibid.*

with respect to the second point. It would seem to be stretching the meaning of words to assert that an increase in the number of credit-worthy borrowers is synonomous with a *broadening* of the sources of liquidity. Indeed, the contrary seems more plausible. An increase in the number of borrowers able to compete effectively for funds is likely to mean that existing sources of liquidity have to flow into more pockets with a *narrower* stream going to each.

And turning back to the first point, even an expansion in the number of intermediary lenders may not mean an addition to net liquidity if one considers the economy as a whole. It is apparent, for example, that an extension of trade credit reduces the lending firm's liquidity by as much as it increases the debtor firm's ability to buy.[73] Credit extension by a nonbank financial intermediary can be more productive of liquidity; the ultimate lender gets a claim on the intermediary which he regards as nearly money and hence he gives up less liquidity than the borrower gains. Even lending by commercial banks may not represent a net addition to liquidity if bank reserves have not been increased; sales of Government securities by banks to finance such loans decrease bank liquidity, and the buyers of the banks' Governments in turn decrease their liquidity by giving up cash for securities. Viewed in this way, credit extension by business firms and financial intermediaries is essentially a reshuffling of excess money balances, not creation of new liquidity.

To be sure, it must be granted that such a reshuffling of money balances and liquidity positions can mobilize and redistribute existing funds more efficiently and thus permit a higher level of spending without any change in the over-all total of the money supply. But this is to say only that the effectiveness of monetary policy is impaired if excess liquidity already exists in any substantial degree in the economy. It does not follow that interfirm lending and the lending of intermediaries *creates* or *is* liquidity.

The distinction between reshuffling and creating liquidity is important. The crucial point is that no matter how efficient the financial machinery for the transfer and redistribution of funds becomes, so long as only the monetary system is the "ultimate source of cash," [74]

[73] Harrod, "Is the Money Supply Important?" *Westminster Bank Review*, November, 1959, p. 4. Also note, Radcliffe Committee, *Report,* p. 103.

[74] Sayers, *Modern Banking* (5th ed.), p. 162.

the central bank can bring about a shortage of excess funds available for redistribution, and this will check spending. Acceptance of this point is incompatible with Sayer's contention that:

> restriction of the supply of bank deposits [money], if long continued, can be expected to become increasingly ineffective as a curb on total demand, because the demand for liquidity can be so well satisfied from other sources.[75]

The "Moneyness" of Liquid Assets. The Radcliffe Committee has recognized the special place of money in a few isolated passages of its *Report.* But the predominant tone of the Committee's remarks is that money is only one of many equally useful liquid assets. This is why the Committee argued that control of the money supply is no longer effective as an influence on spending and why Sayers could refer to money as the "small change of the system." The liabilities of commercial banks—demand deposits or money—and the liabilities of industrial banks, savings banks, savings and loan associations, and other financial intermediaries are considered to be "close substitutes for each other, so that a clamping down on one group will not create such an abrupt scarcity of liquidity as will have a worthwhile impact on the pressure of total demand." [76]

It has already been indicated, in the discussion of "Money Versus General Liquidity," that money is significantly different from other liquid assets. But it is instructive to examine how the Radcliffe Committee arrived at what appears to be an erroneous conclusion. Sayers pointed out that one milestone in economic theorizing about money came when "the demand for money was refashioned by looking at money primarily as one among other stores of value," [77] and not merely as a "pure medium of exchange" [78] as the Quantity Theory had postulated.

But this new approach, the liquidity preference theory of interest, still gave some importance to money as a medium of exchange by dividing the money supply into " 'active money', whose elasticity of demand was unity, and 'idle money' the utility of which behaved in the more ordinary way and had to be balanced against the interest that could be earned by holding bonds." [79]

---

[75] Sayers, *The Banker,* CX, 682.   [76] *Ibid.,* pp. 681–82.
[77] *Ibid.,* p. 680.   [78] *Ibid.*
[79] *Ibid.*

In sharp contrast, Sayers, and presumably the Committee as a whole, rejected the concept of "active money," or money as a medium of exchange, as being anything more than arbitrary and artificial.

The Radcliffe view is to concentrate attention almost exclusively on idle money, or money as a store of value. And of course money has many close substitutes in this role. It is only because of a single-minded concentration on the store of value aspect of money that the Radcliffe view can regard money and other liquid assets as the same thing. To be sure, Sayers conceded that "the former is useful for payments and the latter are not," [80] but the weight of his argument is that "the world in which we live lacks these sharp distinctions. . . . There is no clear line between purchasing power that carries no interest and interest-earning assets that have no influence on purchasing power." [81]

There would seem to be an obvious error here. The "clear line" which Sayers cannot find is simply that one asset, money, is purchasing power, that is, a medium of exchange, while other liquid assets are *not* direct purchasing power. The failure to perceive this is because the Committee and Sayers have their attention firmly fixed on the store-of-value function of money. Indeed, one might say that they have erred as much in this direction as did crude versions of the Quantity Theory in emphasizing only the medium of exchange aspect of money.

It is the demand for money as a medium of exchange—to cover transactions and to serve a precautionary function against unexpected outlay requirements—that gives money its special place in the constellation of liquid assets. For this purpose other liquid assets do not serve nearly as well. Indeed, such liquidity as other assets possess derives from the readiness with which they can be converted into cash without loss.[82] And the supply of money obviously is extremely important in determining the terms on which assets can be exchanged for cash.[83] Accordingly, it is incorrect to say that money has become "the small change of the system" and to imply that the demand for liquidity can be met indefinitely by simply creating more liquid assets.

[80] *Ibid.*, p. 681.   [81] *Ibid.*
[82] Sayers, *Modern Banking* (5th ed.), pp. 158–64.
[83] *Ibid.*, pp. 165–66.

It follows that, contrary to the Radcliffe Committee's view, shortage of money *can become* a "monetary ceiling against which a boom will bump its head." [84]

Evaluation of Radcliffe Committee Views. It is hard to escape the belief that the Radcliffe Committee went too far in downgrading the importance of the money supply. Even in a world full of lenders and nonmonetary liquid assets, the availability of money as such has great importance in the formation of economic decisions.

In the first place, the size of the money supply alone entitles it to major importance in the constellation of "general liquidity." [85] Moreover, money is the most liquid of liquid assets and accordingly should be weighted more heavily in assessing its importance in the total of liquidity.[86] Money, as the means of payment, plays a key role in influencing the utility and liquidity of the other components of "general liquidity." For example, the behavior of bank reserves and the supply of money has important influence on the "moods and resources of financial institutions and other firms which are prepared (on terms) to finance other people's spending." [87] The ease with which nonmonetary assets can be turned into cash, and hence their liquidity, depends on the supply of money and people's desire to hold cash. Gurley has said that whether a larger number of intermediary lenders means an increase in liquidity depends on whether "the growth of intermediaries reduces the public's demand for money—and so money becomes vital to the analysis." [88]

Nevertheless, there is little question that the Radcliffe Committee

[84] Sayers, *The Banker,* CX, 683.

[85] In the United States, for example, the money supply (demand deposits adjusted and currency outside banks) at the end of 1959 was almost one and one half times larger than any other component of general liquidity and accounted for 35 percent of a general liquidity total composed of: (1) the money supply; (2) time deposits in commercial, mutual savings and postal savings accounts; (3) savings and loan shares; (4) U.S. savings bonds; (5) U.S. Government marketable debt due within one year and held outside the Federal Reserve and Government agencies or trust funds; (6) credit union shares. This calculation is based on figures in the *Federal Reserve Bulletin,* XLVI (April, 1960), 386, 405; and XLVI (August, 1960), 940.

[86] Gurley, *Study Paper,* pp. 7–9. The Radcliffe Committee admits by implication at one point that nonmonetary liquid assets are *not* equivalent in liquidity to money; see, Radcliffe Committee, *Report,* pp. 170–71.

[87] Radcliffe Committee, *Report,* p. 132.

[88] Gurley, *American Economic Review,* L, 686.

has performed a signal service in so dramatically emphasizing the diversity and multiplicity of instruments and procedures for the transmission of money and liquidity from one part of the economy to another. The Committee may not have succeeded in proving that money doesn't matter. But it undoubtedly has shown that many other financial quantities besides money do matter.

CONCLUSIONS ON FEDERAL RESERVE'S CONTROL OF MONEY SUPPLY

The Federal Reserve's almost exclusive emphasis in 1951–1959 on the money supply as the means through which monetary policy should work was unfortunate. In practice this meant that the Federal Reserve tended to neglect other methods of exerting influence on the economy, which could have added appreciably to the effectiveness of monetary policy. Moreover, the Federal Reserve's choice of monetary policy instruments, heavily influenced by traditional precedents, was not designed to accomplish even the limited objective of controlling the money supply as well as it might have, had the authorities shown greater flexibility.

As a number of critics have pointed out, the money supply as a whole did not behave appropriately in relation to business conditions and the intentions of monetary policy-makers. Nevertheless, the Federal Reserve's record has not been so bad as to justify withdrawing its authority to make discretionary changes in the money supply. In the first place, the important and strategic element of the money supply held in New York and other weekly reporting member banks, amounting to almost half the total, has responded fairly quickly to changes in business conditions and monetary policy. The half of the money supply which on occasion has not responded promptly has represented deposits in small and medium-sized banks throughout the nation. Even these deposits were relatively quickly affected in recession when reserve requirement reductions were part of credit-easing monetary policies. Thus, the main problem has been the behavior of a portion of the money supply during business expansions. It is probable that deposits in small and medium-sized banks would have shown a considerably greater response to monetary policy during business expansions if reserve requirement increases had been used as a tool of credit restraint. Accordingly it would seem appropriate to make this change in the use of the instruments of monetary policy before taking the much more drastic step of abandoning discretionary central banking.

This conclusion is reinforced by an examination of some of the difficulties that might result from adoption of the suggested alternative: namely, an unvarying percentage increase, for example, 4 percent, in the money supply every year to correspond with real growth of the economy and normal change in velocity. Perhaps the major problem is that the Federal Reserve might have as much difficulty achieving a 4 percent growth in money every year as it has had in achieving varying growth rates under a discretionary policy. The difficulty is that the money supply is affected by a variety of influences which are subject to only imperfect control by the Federal Reserve. Moreover, even if a steady 4 percent growth rate in money could be achieved, there may well be occasions in the future when it would not be appropriate to the economic circumstances—deep depression and raging inflation are the obvious extreme examples. Such a fixed rule does not permit the adjustments to changing circumstances that are possible with a discretionary policy. Thus it is doubtful that the Federal Reserve's discretion in monetary policy-making should be given up in favor of a fixed rule.

A more serious view must be taken, however, of the Federal Reserve's tendency in 1953–1959 to neglect other important monetary magnitudes and financial variables at the same time that it emphasized control of the money supply. Important consequences—most of them adverse to the effectiveness of monetary policy—followed from the rejection of direct influence over interest rates and capital values; the less than adequate attention paid to liquidity positions, velocity of money and the growth of nonbank financial intermediaries. In short, the Federal Reserve tended to confine itself to the use of monetary instruments which were suited best to control of the money supply, even though this meant rejection of instruments and techniques which could have increased the effectiveness of monetary policy.

The point is not, as some of the Federal Reserve's critics have maintained, that the money supply is unimportant or that interest rates, liquidity, or nonbank financial intermediaries are the only important quantities deserving central bank attention. These views are as simplistic as the Federal Reserve's implication that only the money supply mattered. Control of the money supply remains essential to any effective monetary policy. What many critics have tended to overlook or minimize is that the money supply is an important, though indirect, influence on interest rates, liquidity, and even the activities of nonbank financial intermediaries. Effective control over interest rates, liquidity, and intermediaries *involves,* rather than is an alternative to, control of the money supply.

But what the Federal Reserve seems not to have appreciated is that mere control over the volume of money is not sufficient to provide the sensitive monetary control needed in the complex financial environment characteristic of a modern economy. For one thing, the money supply, while influential, does not uniquely determine either the level or structure of interest rates, and both of these can exercise a significant independent influence on economic activity. Moreover, the Federal Reserve's control of the money supply has been largely limited to making marginal additions or subtractions. While having important effects in themselves, these have not purposefully affected the economy's access to the balance of the mony supply, or what might be called *existing* money. Access to *existing* money—the great bulk of the money supply which remains after Federal Reserve actions have added or subtracted marginal amounts—depends on holdings of liquid assets and bonds, interest rates (that is, the terms on which liquid assets and bonds can be converted into money), and the ability of nonbank financial intermediaries to capture idle money balances and channel them to potential borrowers and spenders. But it was precisely these factors which did not seem to be important considerations to Federal Reserve policy-makers. Accordingly, increased turnover of *existing* money—or in other words, a higher income velocity of money—served to offset, at least partly, the impact on the economy of the Federal Reserve's control of the money supply in the 1953–1959 period.

The evidence suggests strongly that the Federal Reserve needs to take considerably greater account, in developing and applying monetary policy, of interest rates as such, of the volume and types of liquidity available to the economy, and of the varieties and activities of nonbank financial institutions. This would not mean abandonment of the money supply as an important focus of central bank attention. But it would mean much greater flexibility in the use of monetary instruments than was required when the central bank's only immediate task was to control the money supply. Accordingly, the abandonment of "bills only" and the return to open market operations in all maturities of the Government securities market was a highly constructive move toward greater Federal Reserve influence over interest rates, liquidity, and the activities of nonbank financial intermediaries. Selective controls on consumer and mortgage credit might also at times be useful in affecting consumer liquidity as well as in influencing the demand for intermediary credit, the latter serving indirectly to influence the pressure on intermediaries to mobilize existing money balances.

In other words the Federal Reserve needs to employ a many-sided approach to monetary control, rather than to rely on one approach as it tended to do in the past. There is no one magic key to control of the complex mechanisms which modern economies have become.

XI

THE PROBLEM OF THE VELOCITY

OF MONEY

THE ABILITY, or inability, of the monetary authorities to control the money supply is only one aspect of their ability to influence appropriately the total flow of spending. A given change in the money supply can have widely varying effects on production and prices, depending on the behavior of the income velocity of money.[1] A change in the income velocity or turnover of the money supply can be regarded as, in effect, the same thing as a change in the size of the money supply with velocity unchanged. For example, the economy may produce a gross national product (GNP) of $300 billion with a money supply of $100 billion, in which case the GNP or income velocity of money is said to be 3. Alternatively, if each dollar of the money supply had turned over faster, for example, 4 times, a $300 billion GNP might have been possible with a money supply of only $75 billion. Thus, a one-third rise in income velocity from 3 to 4 can be regarded as equivalent to a one-third increase in money supply from $75 billion to $100 billion in financing an increase in GNP.

It follows that the total flow of spending can change either as a re-

[1] In the present study, attention is focused on the behavior of *income velocity:* specifically the ratio of gross national product to a money stock defined as currency in circulation outside banks, the Federal Reserve System and the Treasury, plus demand deposits adjusted to exclude cash items in process of collection, interbank deposits, and U.S. Treasury deposits. This concept is consistent with the usage of critics of the monetary policy discussed in this chapter and has the merit of focusing attention on GNP or national income, both of central significance to monetary policy. Other definitions of velocity may use different money flows—total money transactions as in Irving Fisher's conception, or even the money income or expenditure of a specific industry or part of the economy as in computations of sector velocities—or may enlarge the money stock to include savings and time deposits, U.S. Treasury deposits, and even savings and loan shares. For a discussion of various concepts of velocity, see Selden, "Monetary Velocity in the United States," in *Studies in the Quantity Theory of Money,* ed. by Friedman, pp. 180–82, 234–51.

sult of a change in the amount of money in people's hands, or as a result of a change in the rapidity with which the existing supply of money is spent. Thus the importance of income velocity for monetary policy is obvious.

VIEWS ON VELOCITY

Awareness of velocity of the money supply as an economic quantity dates from as far back as 1664.[2] The interchangeability of an increase in velocity and an increase in money supply in achieving a larger flow of expenditures was discussed in the eighteenth and early nineteenth centuries.[3] The literature on velocity, however, is full of disagreement on the relationship of movements in velocity to movements in money supply; on whether there is a secular trend in velocity and, if so, what it is; and on the nature of velocity itself.[4] It may be helpful, in assessing the recent arguments of those who have stressed velocity in their criticisms of monetary policy, to sketch in some of the diverse paths which thinking on velocity has taken over the years.

There has hardly ever been agreement on just how velocity behaves. Rist has pointed out that Cantillon's and Thornton's views that velocity rises and falls with the quantity of money was followed in due course by Ricardo's idea that changes in velocity automatically offset or compensate for changes in the quantity of money.[5] The tendency of the quantity theorists was to assume stability in velocity, though Fisher granted that in transitional periods transactions velocity tends to change in the same direction as the money supply.[6] Angell's pioneer empirical investigation in the early 1930s provided statistical evidence that income velocity moves up and down with

[2] Holtrop, "Theories of the Velocity of Circulation of Money in Earlier Economic Literature," *Economic History,* I (January, 1929), 503–34. Holtrop asserts that Petty (*Verbum Sapiente,* 1664) was the first to discuss velocity.

[3] See Richard Cantillon, *Essai sur la Nature du Commerce en General* (English ed.; London, Macmillan, 1931), p. 160 for an early (1755) expression of this view: "I have already remarked that an acceleration or greater rapidity in circulation of money in exchange is equivalent to an increase of actual money up to a point." Also, see Thornton, *An Enquiry into the Nature and Effects of the Paper Credit of Great Britain,* ed. by Hayek, p. 267.

[4] For example, Marget, *The Theory of Prices* I, 290–478. Rist, *History,* pp. 34–43, 86–87, 110–30, 134–49, 170–76, 220–22, 248–66, 337–53; and Botha, *A Study in the Theory of Monetary Equilibrium,* pp. 1–54.

[5] Rist, *History,* pp. 171, 264.

[6] Fisher, *Purchasing Power of Money,* pp. 159–60.

business activity, and led him to conclude that this reflects the decline in idle money balances in prosperity and the growth of idle balances in recession.[7] So long as the money supply is free to respond to the tides in business, it too would tend to rise and fall with business activity, so that Angell's investigation tended to confirm the earlier views of Cantillon and Thornton.

Nevertheless, the idea that income velocity passively changes in a direction opposite to changes in the money supply and thus merely offsets or compensates for changes in the money supply still has its proponents. Robert Eisner expressed this view before the Congressional Joint Economic Committee in May 1959.

> I think there is little evidence that an increase in the quantity of money or credit or potential credit would do anything other than involve a corresponding drop in velocity.
> I might point out that velocity is simply defined, usually, as something like the total expenditures divided by the quantity of money. And if one therefore increases the quantity of money, unless we can say that that will increase the quantity of expenditures, then increasing the quantity of money by raising the denominator of the fraction must decrease the velocity.[8]

Eisner's view is in the Keynesian tradition, which prefers to view the influence of money in terms of its impact on liquidity preference and the rate of interest.[9] But liquidity preference theory is consistent with the idea that income velocity might rise with an increase in the supply of money. For example, an increased money supply which resulted in a lower rate of interest might stimulate investment and raise the "quantity of expenditures." Velocity would increase if the in-

---

[7] Angell, *Behavior of Money*, pp. 136–44.

[8] Joint Economic Committee, *1959 Employment Hearings*, Pt. IV, p. 790.

[9] For some early postwar controversy concerning Keynesian and anti-Keynesian views on velocity, see: Clark Warburton, "The Monetary Theory of Deficit Spending," *Review of Economic Statistics*, XXVII (May, 1945), 74–84; Arndt, "The Monetary Theory of Deficit Spending, A Comment on Dr. Clark Warburton's Article," *Review of Economic Statistics*, XXVIII (May, 1946), 90–94; Tobin, "Liquidity Preference and Monetary Policy," *Review of Economic Statistics*, XXIX (May, 1947), 124–31; Fellner, "Monetary Policy and the Elasticity of Liquidity Functions," *Review of Economics and Statistics*, XXX (February, 1948), 42–44; Warburton, "Monetary Velocity and Monetary Policy," *Review of Economics and Statistics*, XXX (November, 1948), 304–17; Warburton, "The Secular Trend in Monetary Velocity," *Quarterly Journal of Economics*, LXIII (February, 1949), 86–90; also, see Hansen, *Monetary Theory and Fiscal Policy* (New York, McGraw-Hill, 1949), Chapter 4; and Tobin, "The Interest-Elasticity of Transactions Demand for Cash," *Review of Economics and Statistics*, XXXVIII (August, 1956), 240–47.

crease in expenditure were relatively larger than the increase in money supply. This in turn would depend on the shape of the liquidity preference curve and the interest elasticity of investment spending. Eisner's idea that increasing the quantity of money could *only* "involve a corresponding drop in velocity" would imply that liquidity preference had become, as Keynes put it, "virtually absolute" so that "the monetary authority would have lost effective control over the rate of interest" and hence over the rate of investment expenditures. But as Keynes said, "whilst this limiting case might become practically important in future, I know of no example of it hitherto." [10] To be sure, even if interest rates did fall, investment might be interest inelastic; but recent discussions have suggested that earlier skepticism on this point was overdone.[11] Moreover, concentration on the rate of interest alone overlooks the independent importance of the availability of money.

Another area of disagreement has been over whether there is a trend in the longer-term movements of velocity, and if so, what it is. Studies in the early 1930s produced the view that over longer periods income velocity was essentially a stable magnitude. Thus, Angell's study of data for 1909–1929 led him to the conclusion that, while cyclical changes in the proportion of money balances held idle might produce "substantial year-to-year fluctuations" in the short run, over longer periods there existed "a remarkably high degree of stability" which could be expressed by a "nearly horizontal" trend.[12] However, a number of later investigations found a long-term downtrend in velocity. Selden, in his analysis of velocity studies, concluded that if the various studies had been made on a comparable basis (covering the same time period and using the same definitions), they would probably have agreed on a falling trend as the most fitting description of velocity's secular movement.[13]

However, there still remained no agreement on why the trend of

---

[10] Keynes, *General Theory*, p. 207.

[11] White, "Interest Inelasticity of Investment Demand," *American Economic Review*, XLVI (September, 1956), 565–87; and Gehrels and Wiggins, "Interest Rates and Manufacturers' Fixed Investment," *American Economic Review*, XLVII (October, 1957), 79–92.

[12] Angell, *The Behavior of Money*, pp. 140, 153.

[13] Selden, *Studies in the Quantity Theory*, pp. 187–90.

velocity had fallen. Traditional analysis of reasons for trend, or the lack of it, in income velocity has tended to focus on habitual practices of the community with respect to savings, hoarding, the duration of payment periods, and the concept of a normal average money stock.[14] Economists with a Keynesian orientation have tended to place more emphasis on movements in the rate of interest as an explanation of the falling velocity trend. For example, James Tobin in his discussion with Clark Warburton in 1947 said:

this secular decline in velocity can be interpreted in a manner completely contradictory to Dr. Warburton's thesis. During most of the period, interest rates were declining; and at the extremely low rates of the 1930's the demand for cash balances may be so elastic with respect to the rate of interest that almost indefinite quantities of cash will be willingly held idle. This is what seems to have happened to the additions to the money supply during that decade. If this interpretation is correct, the only result of following Dr. Warburton's advice to keep the quantity of money increasing fast enough to offset the "secular" decline in velocity would be to accelerate the decline in velocity itself.[15]

While this seems to come very close to Eisner's view, Tobin is talking of an extremely special situation, the so-called "liquidity trap" where the demand for money is perfectly elastic with respect to the rate of interest.

Much of the controversy about velocity over the years has centered on which concept of velocity is most useful for economic analysis. Transactions velocity, the concept used by Fisher, has been severely criticized on the grounds that the *total* volume of transactions in the economy includes financial transactions in existing rights, claims, and titles which may vary substantially without affecting *real* economic activity very much. Income velocity, the concept used in this study, has seemed free from many of the objections to transactions velocity and accordingly has been used, in one or another of its variants, by many students of monetary economics in recent years.[16]

However, there is a body of economic opinion which denies the

[14] Fisher, *Purchasing Power of Money*, p. 79; Angell, *Investment and Business Cycles*, p. 139; Lester V. Chandler, *The Economics of Money and Banking* (New York, Harpers, 1948), p. 546.

[15] Tobin, "Liquidity Preference and Monetary Policy," *Review of Economics and Statistics*, XXIX (May, 1947), 127.

[16] See, Angell, *The Behavior of Money*, pp. 93–94, 129–55.

validity and meaningfulness of any concept of velocity. This view would, as Hansen has put it, "eliminate the term 'velocity of circulation' from our vocabulary." [17] To R. F. Kahn it is "an entirely bogus concept." [18] Supporting critics of the velocity concept, Kaldor has said:

I believe that they are fundamentally correct in the view that the hypothesis of any independently given velocity, grounded on things like the frequency of various kinds of payments—i.e., that wages are paid weekly, salaries monthly, business accounts quarterly, etc.—is a mirage and that velocity can be speeded up or slowed down to an almost indefinite extent without any alteration in the habitual frequency of various types of money payment.[19]

Critics of the concept of velocity have made the following points:

1. The velocity of money is merely an arithmetic ratio and hence has no independent significance. The Radcliffe Committee has said that it is merely a "statistical concept that tells us nothing of the motivation that influences the level of total demand." [20] In Kaldor's words:

The velocity of circulation of money (or what comes to the same thing, the ratio which cash balances bear to the volume of turnover of money payments per unit of time) is not determined by factors that are independent either of the supply of money or the volume of money payments; it simply reflects the relationship between these two magnitudes.[21]

2. Accordingly velocity is said to be a purely passive factor, which simply adjusts automatically to offset changes in the money supply and can have no influence of its own. Thus, Eisner argues, "there is little evidence that an increase in the quantity of money or credit or potential credit would do anything other than involve a corresponding drop in velocity." [22] And Kaldor claims, with respect to increases in velocity, "If the supply of money had not been restricted, the increase in the velocity of circulation would not have taken place." [23]

3. In support of the view that increases in velocity could offset

---

[17] Hansen, *The American Economy*, p. 50.
[18] Radcliffe Committee, *Memoranda*, Vol. III, No. 19, p. 144.
[19] Kaldor, "The Radcliffe Report," *Review of Economics and Statistics,* XLII (February, 1960), 19.
[20] Radcliffe Committee, *Report*, p. 133.
[21] Radcliffe Committee, *Memoranda*, Vol. III, No. 20, p. 146.
[22] Joint Committee, *1959 Employment Hearings,* Pt. IV, p. 790.
[23] Radcliffe Commitee, *Memoranda*, Vol. III, No. 20, p. 146.

almost any reduction in the money supply, Kaldor cites the very high levels of velocity reached in hyperinflations.

> As the experience of Germany and other countries during the great inflations has shown, the economic system in case of need can be "run" on a very small fraction of its normal cash requirements. (In Germany in 1923 money in circulation amounted to less than ½ per cent of the current level of incomes expressed at annual rates.) [24]

These are strong statements. Indeed, they go a good deal too far in denying significance to velocity. Accordingly, the entire argument is open to serious question. This is best seen by taking up the points made step by step.

1. The velocity of money is, of course, an arithmetic ratio. But this does not deny it economic significance. Kaldor and his fellow critics of velocity are disregarding the fact that velocity (income expenditure/money) is merely the inverse of the Cambridge k (money/income expenditure), the ratio of money which people and firms wish to carry in relation to income and expenditure. The Cambridge k, as Robertson has said, is associated with desires for liquidity.[25] A vote to eliminate the concept of velocity would seem to involve also a vote to eliminate the concept of liquidity, its inverse.

It can be questioned, of course, whether people really do carry some normal proportion of their expenditures or income in cash to bridge receipts of incomes and meet expenditure needs. Whatever the answer for individuals, the concern of bankers and accountants with financial ratios certainly suggests that business firms must do more than pay lip service to conventional ratios of cash and liquid assets to current liabilities and expenditures if they wish good credit ratings and access to loan funds.

Moreover, Kaldor's assertion that the concept of income velocity is useless because it is not determined by factors that are independent of the terms which make it up would condemn to oblivion many other useful economic concepts. The consumption function, for example, commonly measured by the relationship of consumption to income, is also influenced by a number of factors which are not independent of the terms which make it up. With velocity, as with the

---

[24] *Ibid.*, p. 147.
[25] Robertson, "A Squeak from Aunt Sally," *The Banker,* CIX (December, 1959), 720.

consumption function, the way to understanding would seem to be more study, not banishment of the term to oblivion.

2. Part of the rebuttal to the argument that velocity is merely passive stems from the preceding paragraphs. If individuals, businessmen, bankers, and accountants have even roughly conventional ideas on proper ratios of cash to outlays, then velocity would have at least some independent influence on economic activity. Moreover, the view that changes in income velocity merely offset changes in the money supply conflicts with the empirical evidence. If this were the case, one would expect that changes in velocity ordinarily would be of different algebraic sign from changes in the money supply. In fact, during the fifty years from 1910 to 1959 inclusive, there were thirty-two years in which the change in annual GNP velocity was in the same direction as the change in the money supply and only eighteen years in which the change was in the opposite (that is offsetting) direction. Since 1945 the tendency for velocity to move in the same direction as the money supply has been even more marked. There is little support in this record for the Kaldor-Kahn-Eisner thesis. Rather the evidence seems to support Samuelson's conviction that "it seems unwise to expect that induced changes in V [velocity] will largely undo the effects of central bank operations; at times they could be reinforcing." [26]

3. Kaldor's reference to the heights to which income velocity has risen during hyperinflations has no relevance to the assertion that velocity increases could offset almost any restriction on the money supply. In inflation, velocity rises because there is *no* restriction of the money supply, and people spend rapidly to get rid of money before further increases in its supply erode its value still further. The velocity increases during credit restriction, however, are of a very different nature. Such velocity increases reflect economizing on a scarce quantity, not frantic efforts to unload something which everyone has too much of. The result is that the velocity increases of inflation are far, far greater than any that ever took place in periods of credit restraint. Thus Kaldor's illustration of a velocity figure of 200 during the German inflation of 1923 compares with an alltime peak of about 4¼ in the United States in 1918.

[26] Samuelson, "Reflections on Monetary Policy," *Review of Economics and Statistics,* XLII (August, 1960), 268.

It can hardly be doubted that if the Federal Reserve imposed a 50 percent contraction of the money supply, the result would be a crisis in the economy, and not a mere painless and offsetting rise in velocity. In this connection it is worth remembering that the money panics of the nineteenth century, which were due to shortages of cash in relation to needs, led to downturns in real economic activity, not to automatic increases in the velocity of the existing money supply to maintain activity at existing levels.

Thus, the view that velocity is a meaningless statistical abstraction seems unwarranted. It seems closer to the truth to assume that payment periods and real balance requirements in relation to expenditure needs *do* impose some constraints on the ability of velocity to vary and give it some independent significance.

VELOCITY AND RECENT CRITICISMS OF MONETARY POLICY

The mounting wave of criticism of United States monetary policy in 1951–1959 was accompanied by a resurgence of interest in the velocity of money. To a considerable extent this reflected the belief that the postwar updrift in income velocity was an important roadblock to the effectiveness of restrictive monetary policies. Monetary restraint was said to be ineffective in checking inflation and maintaining economic stability because it automatically stimulated increases in the velocity of money.[27]

Ellis summarized recent criticisms involving velocity as follows:

The conviction of a number of economists is that monetary control of inflation, at least of the conventional sort, has been reduced nearly to impotence by offsetting increases in the velocity of money. In part this involves the shift of securities from banks and other financial institutions to individuals and non-financial corporations and the attendant acceleration of velocity. . . . In part, however, it represents the idea that other financial institutions have grown relatively to banks, that their securities serve as near-moneys to asset-holders, increasing their feeling of liquidity and their propensities to spend, while—on the other hand—these institu-

[27] Smith, "On the Effectiveness of Monetary Policy," *American Economic Review,* XLVI (September, 1956), 588–606; Minsky, "Central Banking and Money Market Changes," *Quarterly Journal of Economics,* LXXI (May, 1957), 171–82; Kareken, "Post Accord Monetary Developments in the United States," *Banca Nazionale Del Lavoro Quarterly Review,* X (September, 1957), 322–51; Angell, "The Monetary Standard: Objectives and Limitations," *American Economic Review,* XLVIII (May, 1958), 76–87; and Rousseas, "Velocity Changes and the Effectiveness of Monetary Policy," *Review of Economics and Statistics,* XLII (February, 1960), 27–36.

tions perfect various money-economizing devices, such as sale and re-purchase agreements with the government bond houses, etc. An extreme form of this line of thought, as the London *Economist* has pointed out, is that "either the cushion of velocity is of nearly infinite extent in modern conditions, in which case . . . nothing can be done about it; or the limit to the increases in velocity will not be reached until the 'bite' of restraint on the money supply becomes so severe that a really sharp contraction in activity becomes inevitable." [28]

The critics have tended to link increases in velocity directly or indirectly to higher interest rates. Higher yields on Government securities, for example, are said to draw idle money balances into use. The development of new financial institutions which have economized on money and increased velocity is said to be associated with, if not caused by, scarcity of money or higher interest rates. In any case, the idea is that restrictive monetary policies are likely to be frustrated because they stimulate more intensive use of money, permitting the total flow of spending to go forward practically, if not completely, unchecked.

It is fairly common for such critics to assume an indefinitely rising income velocity implicitly, if not explicitly, at least as long as restraint on the money supply and rising interest rates prevail. Such a view owes much, of course, to the upward sweep of velocity in the postwar years. (The GNP velocity of money rose from 1.99 in 1946 to 3.43 in 1959 while interest rates on 91-day Treasury bills were rising from .375 to 3.41 percent.)

The minority view (minority at least in the sense of representation in the professional journals) has been that

as interest rates continue to rise, due to continued monetary restraint and persistent demands for funds, idle balances are likely to approach minimum levels. Correspondingly, velocity is likely to encounter an upper limit, a rough and perhaps flexible ceiling, but a ceiling nevertheless.[29]

The crux of the matter would seem to be whether it is valid to assume that interest rates and velocity will continue to rise in the future as they have in the past postwar years. If not, then monetary policy in the future may be less hampered by offsetting rises in velocity and hence more effective.

[28] Howard S. Ellis, "Limitations of Monetary Policy," in *United States Monetary Policy,* p. 157.

[29] Ritter, "Income Velocity and Anti-inflationary Monetary Policy," *American Economic Review,* XLIX (March, 1959), 128.

It can be argued that the changes in velocity which created such problems for the monetary authorities in the past were largely traceable to the drawing into use of the huge volume of idle money balances built up in World War II and that much, if not all, of the rise in velocity which was experienced in the thirteen years from 1946 to 1959 might well have been a once and for all recovery from the abnormally depressed levels which accompanied the Great Depression and World War II.

But critics of monetary policy have not accepted this view. Smith, while not neglecting other explanations for increasing velocity, laid stress on the inherent ability of commercial banks to raise funds for lending by attracting previously idle money through the sale of securities from their portfolios at rising yields:

When these securities are purchased by nonbank investors, deposits are liquidated, and when the banks make loans to customers, the deposits are recreated. The deposits destroyed as a result of the sale of securities are idle balances. . . . On the other hand, the deposits created through the making of loans are, almost by definition, active deposits. Thus, although the money supply is unchanged as a result of such operations, the proportion of the money supply in active circulation is increased and a rise in velocity occurs.[30]

As a practical illustration, Smith pointed out that this sort of process permitted a record $8.9 billion expansion in commercial bank loans from January to September, 1955, even though aggregate member bank reserve funds were reduced by $600 million, and the money supply was decreased by $2.3 billion. He further argued that the interest elasticity of demand for the banks' portfolio of securities may be large enough to permit sizable shifts without requiring large increases in yields on the securities sold. In light of these and other considerations, he suggested that:

when credit conditions are tightened and the creation of new money through the banking system is restricted, the financial machinery of the country automatically begins to work in such a way as to mobilize the existing supply of money more effectively, thus permitting it to do most of the work that would have been done by newly created money had credit conditions been easier.[31]

[30] Warren Smith, *American Economic Review*, XLVI, 601–2. Smith's views take on additional weight because in 1959 they were incorporated in the Joint Economic Committee, *Staff Report on Employment, Growth, and Price Levels*, Chapter 9. Similar views have been expressed by other economists. See Burns, *Prosperity Without Inflation*, pp. 6–7.

[31] Warren Smith, *American Economic Review*, XLVI, 601.

Smith emphasized the importance of increases in velocity by pointing out that they have been much more important in recent years in financing increases in GNP than have been increases in the money supply, which have been slowed by restrictive Federal Reserve policies. This is shown in table 11 which compares the relative gains in GNP, money supply, and income velocity in recent expansions.

TABLE 11

COMPARISON OF PERCENTAGE CHANGES IN GNP, MONEY SUPPLY, AND INCOME VELOCITY DURING EXPANSIONS IN GNP, 1949–1960

(*percent*)

Period of Expansion	GNP	Money Supply	Income Velocity
I, 1949–III, 1953	41.3	15.6	22.2
II, 1954–III, 1957	24.8	6.2	17.3
I, 1958– I, 1960	16.3	4.6	11.1

Roman numerals indicate the quarters. Percentage changes computed from seasonally adjusted GNP and money supply figures. Money supply is demand deposits adjusted plus currency outside banks.

Another of the critics, Hyman Minsky, went so far as to charge that the effectiveness of monetary policy was being completely destroyed by institutional changes in the financial markets which have economized on the use of money during periods of credit restraint. Minsky would grant that, when velocity increases are brought about by higher interest rates in an unchanged institutional setting, the expansive effects of the velocity increase may be largely offset by the restrictive effect of the higher rates. But, he argued, the fact is that the financial structure changed during periods of tight money and changed in such a way as to permit large increases in velocity without any change in interest rates. Thus, when the velocity/interest rate relation was being shifted to the right by such institutional changes, there was no effective offset to the increases in velocity in the form of higher interest rates. As examples Minsky cited the growth of the *federal funds market,* in which banks buy and sell (borrow and lend) excess reserve balances among themselves, and the development of repurchase agreements with government security dealers as vehicles for the temporary investment of idle balances of business corporations.[32] These automatic responses of the money

[32] It might be objected that the federal funds market dates back to the 1920s, and borrowing by security dealers from business corporations was notorious in

market have economized money and reserve balances and thus offset the restrictive impact of Federal Reserve monetary policies. Minsky concluded: "The asserted asymmetry of monetary policy (that it is effective in constraining an inflation and ineffective in constraining a depression) is not true; monetary policy is of very limited effectiveness both in constraining an inflation and in counteracting a depression." [33]

An empirical study of the relationship of income velocity to changes in short-term interest rates from 1951 to 1957 by Stephen W. Rousseas broadly confirmed Minsky's view that rising interest rates bring about a shift to the right in the velocity/interest rate curve. To be sure, it is significant, as will be pointed out later in this chapter, that Rousseas found the shift occurring, not in periods of rising interest rates, but in recessionary periods when interest rates had fallen. But Rousseas did not find this a serious objection and agreed that "rapidly rising interest rates served to activate idle balances with a resulting . . . increase in the velocity of money." [34] He drew this conclusion:

Whether we look at the problem as the response of idle balances to large and rapid increases in short-term interest rates or as large increases in the relative supply of money [that is, the money supply equivalent of increases in velocity], it seems reasonable to conclude that a tight money policy increases the willingness of individuals and institutions to dishoard their cash balances. Under the circumstances, it is not unreasonable to question, once again, the ability of monetary policy to contain inflations within tolerable limits. [35]

Another criticism which involves velocity is traceable to the fundamental restatement of monetary and banking theory made by John Gurley and Edward Shaw in recent years. As indicated in Chapter X, a significant part of their criticism can be translated into an argument that institutional changes, mainly the rapid growth of nonbank financial intermediaries, have made it possible for the economy to get along with a relatively smaller money supply. The growth of financial intermediaries was attributed by Gurley and Shaw not only to individuals' desire to diversify their asset holdings but also to nonbank

---

the late 1920s. This illustrates how difficult it is to identify precisely the moment when institutional innovations take place. Nevertheless, it is probably true that these practices expanded greatly in the 1950s.

[33] Minsky, *Quarterly Journal of Economics*, LXXI, 184.
[34] Rousseas, *Review of Economics and Statistics*, XLII, 32.
[35] *Ibid.*, p. 35.

financial institutions ability to pay higher interest rates on savings accounts than commercial banks could.[36] Thus, here too interest rates were felt to play a role in influencing velocity.

The influence of nonbank financial intermediaries in increasing the velocity of money was described from two points of view. On the one hand, there was the argument that lending by nonbank financial intermediaries activates existing idle deposits and thus increased the turnover, or velocity, of the money supply. On the other hand, looking at the situation from the point of view of the individual saver or depositor, the rising volume of intermediary claims substantially increased the volume of close substitutes for money, permitting people to hold more of their liquid assets in the form of savings shares or savings deposits and relatively less in currency or demand deposits. In practice this is, of course, equivalent to getting more use out of a given money supply.

The consensus of the critics was that restrictive monetary policies failed in the past and will fail in the future because they automatically stimulated offsetting increases in the turnover, or velocity, of a given money supply.

It might be argued, of course, that the Federal Reserve authorities could take account of the possibility that velocity would increase by simply imposing more restraint on the money supply. But the critics of monetary policy have replied that this would risk so severe a monetary stringency as to threaten economic crisis and depression.

The curious picture of an ineffective monetary policy suddenly becoming so tight as to bring the economy to an abrupt halt has been painted vividly by Minsky

The reverse side of the coin to the increase in velocity is that every institutional innovation which results in new ways to finance business and new substitutes for cash assets decreases the liquidity of the economy. That is, even though the amount of money does not change, the liquidity of the community decreases when government debt is replaced by private debt in the portfolios of the commercial banks. Also, when nonfinancial corporations replace cash with government bonds and then government

[36] The ability of nonbank financial institutions to pay higher rates on savings accounts than commercial banks reflected: (1) the concentration of their assets in higher-yielding mortgages and corporate bonds; (2) their more favorable tax position; and (3) the fact that until January 1, 1962 commercial banks were prevented from paying more than 3 percent on savings by Federal Reserve and Federal Deposit Insurance Corporation regulations which do not apply to other financial institutions.

bonds with debts of bond houses, liquidity decreases. Such a pyramiding of liquid assets implies that the risks to the economy increase, for insolvency or even temporary illiquidity of a key nonbank organization can have a chain reaction and affect the solvency or liquidity of many organizations.

If during a long prosperity, monetary policy is used to restrain inflation, a number of such velocity-increasing and liquidity-decreasing money-market innovations will take place. As a result the decrease in liquidity is compounded. In time, these compounded changes will result in an inherently unstable money market so that a slight reversal of prosperity can trigger a financial crisis.[37]

These criticisms obviously deny the usefulness of restrictive general credit policies which work through limiting the size of the money supply and inducing increases in interest rates. It is only natural then that the critics would supplement or replace general credit controls with selective direct controls of various kinds. As Rousseas put it:

A re-examination of monetary techniques and central bank structure has become critical. It would help if the widespread attitude against selective financial controls was recognized for the prejudice it is. It never helps economic analysis to deal in terms of the untenable dualism of freedom versus control. Indeed, control in many instances is a pre-condition for the realization of freedom in the larger sense.[38]

However, recommendations to reject general monetary policies and institute a system of selective controls cannot be taken lightly by a nation which still relies on decentralized private enterprise and initiative to supply much of the driving force in its economy. In light of the seriousness of these criticisms and the fundamental character of the changes in policy they propose, it is surprising how little concern the Federal Reserve displayed about velocity or about the criticisms involving it. Before evaluating the criticisms based on the behavior of velocity, it seems appropriate to examine Federal Reserve views.

FEDERAL RESERVE VIEWS ON VELOCITY

The Federal Reserve's lack of concern about velocity was so marked that one has to go back many years to find a statement forthrightly admitting that untoward movements in velocity could frustrate monetary policy. For example, it is more than twenty years

[37] Minsky, *Quarterly Journal of Economics*, LXXI, 184.
[38] Rousseas, *Review of Economics and Statistics*, XLII, 36.

since W. Randolph Burgess of the Federal Reserve Bank of New York said:

in 1928 and 1929 and later in the depression even the most vigorous measures taken by the Reserve System had relatively little effect. Member bank borrowing, interest rates, and the growth of bank credit did indeed respond in a measure but these in their turn failed to influence the country's economy. The expansion of bank credit was checked in 1928 and 1929, but other lenders appeared and the increased rate of turnover or "velocity" of bank credit made up for lack of growth in volume.[39]

In the 1951–1959 period there was no such direct statement that velocity movements might frustrate monetary policy. Rather, the Federal Reserve authorities indicated that changes in velocity might complicate the administration of monetary policy but could be dealt with by appropriate Federal Reserve actions. In replying to the Patman Committee's questionnaire in 1952, Federal Reserve Board Chairman Martin said that appropriate changes in the volume of the money supply should be used to compensate for changes in the velocity of money:

Ideally, the amount of money should adjust itself to the periodic waves of pressure for increased or decreased holdings of money on the part of the public. For example, at times businesses and consumers may increase their expenditures by using existing cash balances more intensively (what economists call "increasing outlays relative to cash balances" or "increasing the velocity of circulation of money"). If this happens when productive resources are fully utilized and prices are tending to rise, it is desirable that pressure be exerted to restrain so far as possible further expansion in the amount of money in the economy. Conversely, if heightened uncertainty should cause businesses and consumers to demand higher cash balances in relation to their expenditures, the demand should be met with an increasing supply of money rather than allowed to have its reflection in decreased spending and economic activity and in unemployment.[40]

The same view was restated in an article in the February, 1953 *Federal Reserve Bulletin*.[41] These statements recognized the existence of a velocity problem. But other Federal Reserve statements published only a short time later have been cited as evidence of undue complacency toward velocity changes. For example, Smith argued:

In discussions of credit policy, the Federal Reserve System and its representatives are inclined to put almost exclusive emphasis on the control of aggregate member-bank reserves and the resulting control of the

[39] Burgess, *The Reserve Banks and the Money Market*, pp. 250–51.
[40] Patman, *Compendium*, Pt. I, pp. 342–43.
[41] *Federal Reserve Bulletin*, XXXIX (February, 1953), 107.

money supply and the total quantity of bank credit. Asset transformations which result in a more intensive utilization of the existing money supply are neglected almost entirely. Discussions of bank loan expansion are often couched in phrases which leave the impression that the inflationary effects of such expansion are practically nil when the expansion of loans is offset by bank liquidation of government security holdings. Such an approach tends to obscure some of the most important issues involved and is likely to lead to an overoptimistic evaluation of the effectiveness of monetary policy.[42]

As evidence, Smith cited a statement in the article, "Influence of Credit and Monetary Measures on Economic Stability" in the March, 1953 *Federal Reserve Bulletin:* "Individual banks can get additional funds to lend by selling Government or other securities or by permitting maturing issues to run off. As a group, however, banks cannot expand their total supply of loanable funds in this way except when such paper is being bought by the Federal Reserve System." [43] Smith noted: "The statement is correct enough, but no reference is made to the fact that shifts in the composition of bank assets, such as those referred to, may result in more intensive use of the existing supply of loanable funds." [44]

A little later in this *Federal Reserve Bulletin* article some reference is made to the possibility that sales of securities by banks might increase velocity but the emphasis again is put on the point that "such sales will not increase total bank credit and deposits." [45] Thus, the implication is that so long as the money supply does not increase, changes in velocity need not be taken seriously.

In 1957 the presidents of the twelve Federal Reserve banks took more explicit notice of the velocity problem but denied that there was any reason for concern:

It is true that demand balances in the commercial banks may be activated as funds are recirculated by the intermediaries through their investment operation, and that the velocity of deposits may thus be increased. . . . But that is not a new development, and present institutional arrangements in the United States seem adequate to prevent serious interference with credit policy arising from changes in velocity.[46]

In October, 1958, Ralph Young, then director of the Division of Research and Statistics for the Federal Reserve Board, expressed his

[42] Warren Smith, *American Economic Review,* XLVI, 604.
[43] *Federal Reserve Bulletin,* XXXIX (March, 1953), 221.
[44] Smith, *American Economic Review,* XLVI, 604, footnote 48.
[45] *Federal Reserve Bulletin,* XXXIX (March, 1953), 222.
[46] Byrd Committee, *1958 Compendium,* pp. 57–58.

views on velocity in a paper read before the American Assembly, under the auspices of Columbia University:

> To what extent do swings in money turnover negate the actions of monetary management? A reply to this question must recognize, in the first place, that changes in velocity are self-limiting. Especially on the upside, there are limits beyond which velocity cannot be increased without great inconvenience. In other words, there is a basic minimum below which cash balances of the public are not likely to be reduced, without also reducing spending.
>
> Secondly, monetary action can influence in some degree the speed with which velocity approaches its maximum and can offset the effects of increasing velocity. The more vigorous and persistent the monetary action, the more quickly and completely will there be an absorption of the idle cash balances that can potentially be activated.[47]

These assurances are persuasive in many respects but they are not convincing. Even if changes in velocity are self-limiting, the question remains how far velocity could increase before the limits came into effect. Moreover, even if monetary policy could "offset the effects of increasing velocity," the fact remains that, for one reason or another, it did not do so in the past. Assurances such as these are not likely to quiet concern about the problem of velocity.

Moreover, the Federal Reserve has gone beyond unconcern about velocity. Some statements suggested that velocity has been a positive help in the carrying out of monetary policy. Thus, Alfred Hayes, president of the Federal Reserve Bank of New York, in 1957 said:

> Certainly it would be foolish to provide mechanically for a fixed annual increase in money supply, say 3 to 4%, without regard to the intensity of use of money. On the other hand . . . at some point it may reasonably be asked whether liquidity has reached a dangerously low level, so that we may not, or perhaps should not, any longer *expect higher velocity to do a major part of the job for us.*[48]

The idea that velocity changes were helpful, not harmful, was expressed most strongly by Lawrence Ritter, then chief of the Domestic Research Division, Federal Reserve Bank of New York. Ritter argued that velocity changes serve as an essential shock absorber for monetary policy, providing the central bank with "a necessary margin of flexibility and safety, allowing it to restrain the growth of the money

[47] Ralph Young, "Tools and Processes of Monetary Policy," in *United States Monetary Policy*, pp. 40–41.

[48] Hayes, speech before the New York State Bankers Association January 21, 1957, pp. 2–3. Italics supplied by the writer.

supply (within limits) without continuous fear that a sudden financial crisis will occur." [49] Ritter pointed out:

> In view of the usual uncertainty regarding the actual state of business conditions, it is doubtful whether the authorities would ever have the courage (or the foolhardiness) to impose any significant degree of monetary restraint were it not for the built-in shock absorber represented by variations in velocity. Increases in velocity are thus to be expected in the course of an upward movement and in a real sense are an integral part of the mechanism of monetary control, in effect being merely the other side of the squeeze on liquidity which assists in transmitting the effects of a restrictive monetary policy throughout the economy. . . . Without these fluctuations in velocity the central bank would be forever at the brink of a precipice, fearing that the slightest wrong move would bring disaster; as a result, it would be most likely to do nothing at all. . . .
>
> Aggregate economic policy rarely seeks to achieve stability, but instead usually aims at "controlled" expansion. Within limits, monetary policy can make a positive contribution toward this end, in part because of—rather than in spite of—fluctuations in velocity.[50]

While Ritter's article was accompanied by the usual disclaimer releasing the Federal Bank of New York from any responsibility for the views expressed, a similar view of the role of velocity was taken in an official publication of the New York Reserve Bank less than one year later.[51]

The Federal Reserve's view of the significance of velocity movements and that of the critics of monetary policy obviously contrasted sharply.

EMPIRICAL EVIDENCE: INCOME VELOCITY AND INTEREST RATES

There is no question that both income velocity and interest rates have risen a great deal from their levels in 1946. Further, the rise in velocity offset much of the Federal Reserve's restraint on the money supply. The total flow of spending on gross national product in the postwar years was maintained by increases in the velocity of money more than by growth in the money supply, particularly in the late 1950's when the Federal Reserve curbed the latter in an effort to bring inflation under control. Moreover, it seems fair to conclude that the combined effect of increases in velocity and in money supply re-

[49] Ritter, *American Economic Review*, XLIX, 127.
[50] *Ibid.*, pp. 127, 129.
[51] Garvy, *Deposit Velocity and Its Significance*, pp. 13, 86–87.

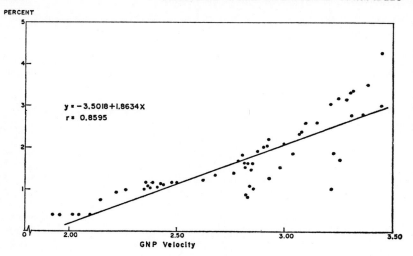

PERCENT

$$y = -3.5018 + 1.8634X$$
$$r = 0.8595$$

GNP Velocity

CHART 3

CORRELATION BETWEEN GNP VELOCITY AND 91-DAY TREASURY
BILL YIELDS, QUARTERLY, 1946–1959

sulted—whatever the Federal Reserve's intention—in an excessive
flow of expenditure: not only did prices rise but also Federal Reserve
officials repeatedly warned of inflationary pressures.

Increases in GNP velocity or income velocity were rather closely
correlated with increases in interest rates in 1946–1959. Chart 3
shows the relationship for GNP velocity and 91-day Treasury bills.
The coefficient of correlation between quarterly GNP velocity and
quarterly averages of 91-day Treasury bill yields from 1946 to 1959
was .8595. But this included periods when interest rates were falling.
For the three major subperiods when interest rates were rising, the
relationship was even closer; the value of the correlation coefficient
was .9469 from the second quarter of 1947 to the second quarter
of 1953, .9829 from the second quarter of 1954 to the third quarter
of 1957, and .8890 from the second quarter of 1958 to the fourth
quarter of 1959. This lends support to the contention that higher
interest rates automatically stimulated increases in velocity, in other
words that restrictive monetary policies in part frustrated themselves.
However, this record does not justify the conclusion that monetary
policy will be ineffective in the future because of increases in velocity.

What the critics ignored, or tended to minimize, is that the upward
thrust of velocity in response to the stimulus of higher interest rates

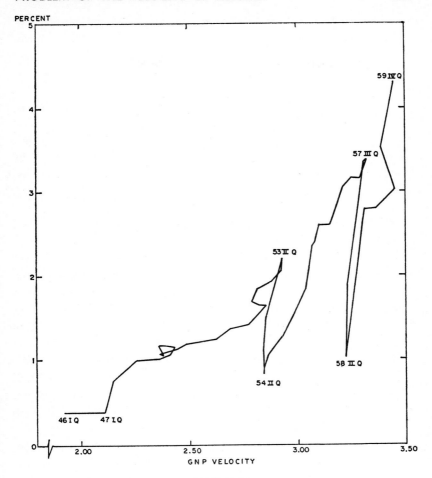

CHART 4
GNP VELOCITY AND 91-DAY TREASURY BILL YIELDS, QUARTERLY,
1946–1959
Roman numerals indicate quarters.

during the postwar years has been progressively weakening. Ironically, it is possible to see this tendency in the chart (of which Chart 4 is an updated version) which Rousseas presented in his article, "Velocity Changes and the Effectiveness of Monetary Policy," charging that velocity was out of control. Rousseas was most interested in the fact that the chart provided some evidence for Minsky's hypothesis of shifts in the velocity/interest rate function. But, as Chart 4 shows, the shifts came in recession periods, not during prosperous periods of high rates as Minsky had suggested. Moreover, the velocity/interest rate curve became successively steeper in each of its three shifts; that is, larger and larger interest-rate increases were needed to induce the same increases in velocity.

Of course, even if the velocity/interest curve was vertical, that is, if velocity was a constant regardless of the level of interest rates, it would be *theoretically* possible for the whole velocity curve to shift to the right—velocity would then be higher for each level of the interest rate. But, looking at the relationship of velocity to interest rates shown in Chart 4, this does not seem to be the way in which the velocity/interest curve shifted in the past.

The recession shifts in the velocity interest rate function seem to have worked as follows: In a period of rising interest rates, velocity rose too. Then, as conditions changed and interest rates declined sharply, velocity did not decline appreciably; instead of falling back along the same curve on which it had risen in conformity with interest rates, it remained nearly constant. At the new low level of interest rates, velocity was still at or near the peak it had reached at a high interest rate level on the old velocity/interest rate curve. In effect the shift to a new velocity/interest rate curve came at this point, because a higher level of velocity was now matched to each interest rate level. When interest rates rose again, velocity also began to move up, but with a higher level of velocity corresponding to each interest rate level than would have been appropriate on the old curve.

This is reasonable in light of what we know about the institutional innovations which Minsky has regarded as the explanation for increased velocity. Banks become aware of the federal funds market in periods of tight money either because they need funds or because they are solicited by other banks that need funds. But when money conditions ease banks do not leave the federal funds market; on the contrary they have a larger volume of funds on which they can practice what they learned in tight money periods, though the trading takes place at lower yields, of course. In the same way, the lure of attractive rates of interest may induce corporations to hire specialists to invest their money in Treasury bills or repurchase agreements with government security dealers, thus economizing on idle cash. But when interest rates decline, these men (sometimes comprising whole departments of the Treasurer's office) are not dismissed; they continue to economize on cash and maintain a higher level of velocity even though interest rates are lower. So it is that when interest rates drop, velocity does not drop back along the same curve.

This pattern raises the question of just how the shift to a new curve would be made if the velocity/interest relation became vertical, that is, if velocity became perfectly inelastic with respect to interest rates. In this case rising interest rates would not be accompanied by increases in velocity. Moreover, a failure of velocity to decline when interest rates fell would not represent a shift to a new velocity/interest rate curve. Of course, it is conceivable that every holder of money might suddenly hold smaller cash balances at every interest rate, thus shifting the vertical velocity/interest rate function to the right, but it is not clear how or why this should occur. It would seem equally conceivable that the velocity/interest rate curve's successive transformations represent an approach to a limiting value or asymptote, perhaps a moderately flexible limit but a limit nonetheless.

Annual data on velocity and rates on 91-day Treasury bills during the postwar years lend some support to the idea of a gradually approaching limit to velocity. Thus, velocity rose 0.20 in 1959, from 3.23 to 3.43 which was a little more than the 0.15 rise in 1957, from 3.14 to 3.29. But it required a 1.57 percentage point rise in bill yields to induce the 1959 gain in velocity, almost three times the 0.61 point rise in bill yield which accompanied the 1957 velocity increase. The declining sensitivity of velocity to changes in 91-day Treasury bill yields is shown in Table 12. The table also shows how many points increase in velocity were stimulated by one percentage point increase in Treasury bill yields in each of the postwar years.

Rousseas, briefly commenting on a suggestion by Hart that velocity may be approaching an asymptote, dismissed the possibility as unimportant even if true: "What I maintain is that what matters is not the asymptote itself but the gradually accumulating financial changes; for example, the evolution of nonbank financial intermediaries." [52]

This would seem to beg the whole question. Financial changes are of interest to Rousseas, Minsky, and many others because of their alleged importance in enabling the economy to evade restrictive

[52] Rousseas, *Review of Economics and Statistics,* XLII, 33.

TABLE 12

YIELDS ON 91-DAY TREASURY BILLS AND GNP VELOCITY ANNUALLY, 1946–1959

(*percent*)

	91-Day Treasury Bills [a]	GNP Velocity [b]	ANNUAL CHANGE		Number of Points Change in Velocity per Percent Change in 91-Day Treasury Bills
			91-Day Treasury Bills	GNP Velocity	
1946	0.38	1.99			
1947	0.59	2.14	0.21	0.15	0.68
1948	1.04	2.36	0.45	0.22	0.49
1949	1.10	2.37	0.06	0.01	0.16
1950	1.22	2.55	0.12	0.18	1.55
1951	1.55	2.82	0.33	0.27	0.78
1952	1.77	2.82	0.22	0.00	0.00
1953	1.93	2.90	0.16	0.08	0.48
1954	0.95	2.84	− 0.98	− 0.06	0.06
1955	1.75	3.00	0.80	0.16	0.20
1956	2.66	3.14	0.91	0.14	0.15
1957	3.26	3.29	0.60	0.15	0.25
1958	1.85	3.23	− 1.41	− 0.06	0.04
1959	3.41	3.43	1.56	0.20	0.13

[a] Annual average yield on weekly new issues.
[b] Computed by dividing annual GNP by average volume of money supply during year.

monetary policies, in a word because of their efficacy in speeding up the velocity of the money supply. Existence of an upper asymptote to the velocity curve would mean that, at least so far as velocity was concerned, the monetary economist need no longer be concerned about the evolution of nonbank financial intermediaries for they would have reached the limit of their influence on velocity.

It must be granted that strictly speaking, an asymptote is a mathematical limit, which logically has to hold without exception so long as the function which defines it is left unchanged. In the real world, the existence of a velocity asymptote can only be inferred. In other words, the fact that something has happened again and again does not prove that it logically has to happen that way forever. Nevertheless, regularities in the way things happen or don't happen are useful practical guides, and in this sense it is appropriate to speak of upper and lower limits to values of observed phenomena.

With this caution in mind, it may be worth considering whether a substantial part of the postwar rise in interest rates and velocity perhaps reflected a once-and-for-all rebound from the unusually depressed levels which resulted from the vast expansion of the money supply and liquidity during the Great Depression and World War II. There is some support for this hypothesis in the fact that commercial bank sales of Government securities, which Smith and others have argued were particularly important in drawing idle cash balances into circulation in the years after 1945, will be unlikely to provide as much of a stimulus to velocity in the future. The postwar movement by banks out of Government securities and into loans was itself a product of unusual circumstances which no longer exist. In 1945, as a result of the diminution of loan demands during the Great Depression and concentration by banks on financing the Treasury during World War II, commercial banks in the United States had only 18 percent of their net deposits in loans, compared with loan-deposit ratios of 70 to 80 percent in the 1920s.[53] Since loans are generally more profitable than investments and also involve depositor relationships favorable to future growth, the banks clearly had a strong incentive to sell securities in order to rebuild loan portfolios in the postwar years.

The substantial sales of Government securities and the concentration on lending by the banks after 1945 raised the ratio of loans to net deposits by June 15, 1960, to 58 percent for all commercial banks and 73 percent for New York City banks.[54] Moreover, several considerations make it doubtful that as much room for further increase in the ratio exists as a simple comparison with the high ratios of the 1920s would indicate. For one thing, about 13 percent of all insured commercial bank deposits in recent years has represented investments which are pledged to secure various types of deposits, bank borrowings from the Federal Reserve Banks, or are loaned.[55] The bulk of

[53] Calculations based on statistics presented in Board of Governors of the Federal Reserve System, *All-Bank Statistics, United States, 1896–1955*, pp. 34–35. Net deposits are gross deposits less cash items in process of collection.

[54] Calculations based on statistics presented in *Federal Reserve Bulletin*, XLVII (March, 1961), 319–23.

[55] Federal Deposit Insurance Corporation, *Report No. 52, Assets, Liabilities and Capital Accounts, Commercial and Mutual Savings Banks, December 31, 1959*, p. 15. On December 31, 1959, no less than $27 billion, or about half, of insured commercial banks' investments were so pledged to secure Treasury Tax and Loan deposits, deposits of states and local governments, trust deposits, borrowings from the Federal Reserve or were loaned to others or sold under

these investments are not easily available for sale to raise funds for lending. Another 11 percent of all commercial banks' deposits represents required cash reserves and working balances and is also unavailable for lending.[56] Finally, both bankers and high Federal Reserve officials have indicated that recent ratios of loans to deposits have been considered a cause for concern,[57] and in some cases excessive.[58] Thus, while banks' ratios of loans to deposits could perhaps be increased somewhat further, it is clear that the scope for velocity-increasing shifts from Government securities into loans has been considerably reduced.

If this is so, then the postwar rise in interest rates and velocity may well have been largely a return to more *normal* levels and the future potential for velocity increases would be considerably less than an uncritical extrapolation of the experience of the 1946–1959 period would suggest. Indeed, it may be worth spelling out what extrapolation of the postwar experience with velocity and interest rates would mean. For velocity to rise as much (71 percent) in the thirteen years after 1959 as it had from 1946 to 1959, it would have to reach 5.84 by 1972. This level of velocity would imply a 91-day Treasury bill rate of 9.44 percent, if the same relationship held in the future as had prevailed in the past postwar years. Neither of these figures is impossible of attainment, of course, but it does not seem unreasonable to call them improbable.

---

repurchase agreements. Figures on the breakdown of the total into these categories are unavailable. Conversations with Charles J. Gable, Jr., former Under-Secretary of the Treasury and senior vice president of the First Pennsylvania Banking and Trust Company, indicate that by far the greatest proportion would represent pledges against deposits which must be maintained (and in many cases are legally required) if banks are to keep the deposit accounts involved. At any one time some portion of these pledges might appear excess since banks try to qualify for maximum levels of, say, state or Treasury deposits.

[56] *Federal Reserve Bulletin*, XLVII, 319–23.

[57] Thus Alfred Hayes, president of the Federal Reserve Bank of New York, told the annual meeting of the New Jersey Bankers Association on May 19, 1960: "At some point, banks and their customers quite naturally feel a bit uneasy with their high loan-deposit ratios." Hayes, "A Breathing Spell for Monetary Policy," p. 4. And Murray Kyger, president of the First National Bank of Fort Worth, Texas, said in early 1960: "We as bankers feel that in general, the deposit to loan ratio is high enough." See *Bulletin of the Robert Morris Associates*, XLII, No. 7, (March, 1960), 224.

[58] James E. Hellier, vice president of Chemical Bank New York Trust, as reported in the *Bulletin of the Robert Morris Associates*, XLIII, No. 4 (December, 1960), 102.

The suggestion that the postwar increase in velocity was largely a rebound is strengthened if it is examined in the perspective of annual changes in GNP velocity over the fifty-one years from 1909 to 1959. As Chart 5 shows, for long stretches of time before the Great Depression, the GNP velocity of money showed fairly narrow cyclical fluctuations around a nearly horizontal trend. When one considers that this velocity is a composite of the velocity of money actively circulating in the income stream and of hoarded money (having much lower velocity), which vary in absolute and relative size depending on cyclical and other factors, such stability is remarkable. The presumption of many students of velocity has been that stability in the velocity of the total money supply reflected the relative slowness of change in people's habits in the use of active money and in business' cash management and payment practices. It is undoubtedly true that many economies in cash management have been made in recent years —individuals' expanded use of credit cards and corporates' use of regional cash-collection points, better inventory control, investment of excess cash in Treasury bills or repurchase agreements with Government security dealers, for example—but these took place against the background of excess liquidity which resulted from Treasury deficit financing during World War II. Thus, they may not be a trustworthy guide to how much further the economy could economize on cash once velocity returned to the range of values which were usual before the Great Depression.

Chart 5 shows that, in the fifty-one years from 1909 to 1959 GNP velocity calculated annually never exceeded 4.26 (touched only once in 1918) and reached 4 in only one year (1919). Of course, velocity could still rise considerably from the 3.43 1959 level even if it were only to duplicate these earlier peaks. Moreover, the economy has changed greatly in the past thirty or forty years and it would be rash, indeed, to rule out the possibility that velocity might rise to still higher peaks in the future. The critics of monetary policy would argue that the sharp rise in the volume of liquidity instruments—savings and time deposits, savings and loan shares, credit union shares, short-term Treasury securities, etc.—since the 1920s has lowered the amount of actual money needed by the economy and correspondingly raised velocity potentials beyond the historical peaks.

But there are two considerations which weaken these objections,

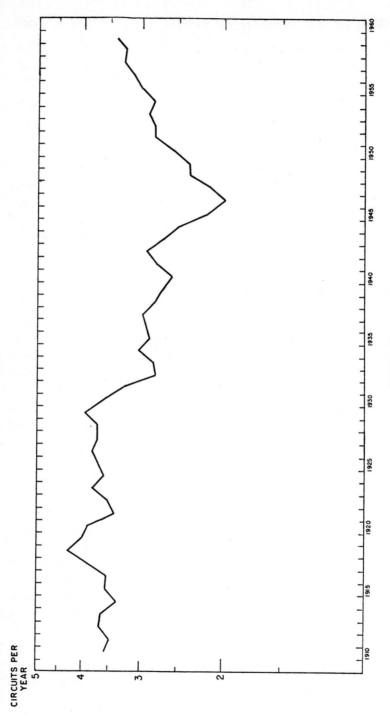

CIRCUITS PER
YEAR

CHART 5
GNP VELOCITY, 1909–1959

at least to some extent. First, Angell has warned that the historical velocity figures calculated for years before 1933, and especially before 1930, may be too high. Prior to those years:

many banks permitted a substantial though unknown proportion of their time deposits to be checked against, or at least to be converted into demand deposits (which were then at once checked against) without notice. In consequence, the category of demand deposits as reported was really "too small," and the velocity figures computed from them too high.[59]

Thus, a velocity figure of 3.43 for 1959 may be closer to the true velocity peaks of the 1920s than the recorded figures suggest. If the peaks of the 1920s did represent some sort of ceiling value, the scope for further expansion in velocity might be limited correspondingly. Second, past experience suggests caution in appraising the influence on GNP velocity of expansion in the volume of liquid assets other than demand deposits and currency. For example, a doubling in the outstanding volume of such assets from 1912 to 1922 [60] was consistent with a 5 percent decline in GNP velocity. Moreover, as noted earlier, GNP velocity in 1959 was still below levels touched in the 1920s despite the vast expansion in liquid assets since then.

Of course, it must always be borne in mind that the patterns of the past may not be a safe guide to the future. The critics of monetary policy may be correct; and velocity in the years ahead may touch new peaks not dreamed of now. But one can doubt that we should revamp our entire monetary control structure today on the assumption that this will occur in the future.

CONCLUSION ON VELOCITY, LIQUIDITY, AND MONETARY POLICY

The critics' view of velocity as an escape from monetary restraint has some validity but has been overemphasized. Equally valid, but neglected, is the point that velocity increases involve cost and inconvenience to the economy and, since they are largely a result of declining liquidity, also have some restraining effect. Every individual, firm, and the economy at large must take into account that its ease of operation and margin of safety against unexpected cash needs are reduced when it reduces its liquidity.

Looking at the liquidity aspects helps bring velocity increases back

[59] Angell, *Investment and Business Cycles*, p. 144.
[60] Goldsmith, *Financial Intermediaries in the American Economy since 1900*, p. 74.

into perspective. When rising velocity is recognized as declining liquidity, it becomes obvious that velocity cannot rise indefinitely as some of the critics have seemed to fear. For at some point, liquidity would decline to a level which would be insufficient for the effective functioning of the economy.

It is, of course, true that Minsky singled out the decreasing liquidity aspect of rising velocity and most dramatically. But Minsky regards the progressive reduction of liquidity as having little or no restraining effect on the economy until, suddenly, the economy is at the point where a liquidity crisis suddenly touches off deflation: "In time these compounded changes [decreases in liquidity] will result in an inherently unstable money market so that a slight reversal of prosperity can trigger a financial crisis." [61]

The question is whether this view is more persuasive than the assumption that velocity can increase and liquidity decrease indefinitely. Progressively declining liquidity, one would think, would be most likely *gradually* to introduce a note of caution into the behavior of individuals and business firms. Once liquidity falls below some habitual value in relation to expenditure needs, it creates a risk of not having enough cash, marketable securities, or quick borrowing power to meet unexpected needs. This inhibits expenditure as anyone knows who has gone through a weekend (when the banks are closed) with a lower than normal supply of cash in his billfold. Moreover, the effect is likely to grow as liquidity decreases: the man who has 20 percent less cash than usual over a weekend is not nearly as inhibited in his expenditures as is the man who has 50 percent less than he usually carries. Thus, as liquidity declines (including for business and the economy as a whole decreased value and lessened price stability of interest-bearing securities and reduced ease of borrowing from banks and other lenders), the effect is likely to be a progressive and gradual reduction of the willingness to spend, not a frantic scrambling at the last minute to restore liquidity positions.

To the extent that individuals and business react in this way to progressive reduction in their liquidity, there is not likely to be a sudden liquidity crisis which brings financial panic and depression. Rather, plans to spend would gradually be whittled down—by lack of cash or

[61] Minsky, *Quarterly Journal of Economics*, LXXI, 184.

by desire to maintain or rebuild liquidity positions—and the Federal Reserve authorities would be put on notice that the economy was losing some of its forward thrust and was in need of more liquidity. This explanation has in its favor the record of the 1946–1959 years, for this is the way the economy behaved.

It is worth noting that a "slight reversal of prosperity" which Minsky fears as the trigger to financial crisis has usually increased liquidity in the postwar years rather than decreased it. This is so generally recognized in the financial markets that it has become common for the prices and salability of debt instruments to rise substantially on the mere rumor that the economy is slowing down. The basis for this is the belief that recession would reduce the supply of bonds and other debt instruments created by private borrowers and at the same time cause the Federal Reserve to embark on easy money policies designed to reduce interest rates, increase the money supply, and generally increase liquidity. By and large, these expectations have rested on the experience since World War II.

Moreover, each "slight reversal of prosperity" from 1946 to 1959 was also reflected in a reduction of the total volume of expenditure, thus reducing the amount of liquidity needed. This is not to say that the financial crises feared by Minsky could not happen but merely that they are more likely to result from the collapse of a speculative bubble, as in 1929, than from a gradual shrinkage of liquidity positions. And if crises were to occur, the Federal Reserve has the powers and the task—indeed, this was its original task—to function as a lender of last resort and supply liquidity massively.

To sum up: The critics who charged that monetary policy is inherently ineffective because of rising velocity took too narrow a view. They concentrated overmuch on velocity, the rising quantity, and paid too little attention to liquidity, the declining quantity. They failed to recognize that the central bank's task after the liquidity inflation of World War II was to reduce liquidity gradually to more normal levels and that this unavoidably involved a rise in velocity. Indeed, the rise in velocity is a measure of the central bank's success in reducing liquidity, not of its failure. In their fears of a liquidity crisis arising out of central bank restraint on the money supply, the critics were overly pessimistic about the economy's ability gradually to adjust to liquidity reductions without crises, and ignored the powerful ability of the central bank to create liquidity whenever needed to fight crisis conditions. Finally, whether or not velocity is approaching an asymptote remains for the future to confirm or deny. But the decreasing sensitivity of velocity to changes in interest rates is a fact which suggests an increased effectiveness of monetary policy in the future.

XII

THE INFLUENCE OF CHANGING LONG-TERM
INTEREST RATES AND CAPITAL VALUES
ON FINANCIAL INSTITUTIONS

THE DISCUSSION of central banking techniques in the preceding chapters has touched repeatedly on the allegation that monetary policy might have been more effective if the Federal Reserve had also tried to influence interest rates and capital values directly. This point of view was a significant part of Roosa's conception of the scope of monetary policy, as expressed in 1950–1951, and was implicitly or explicitly adopted by most critics of the Federal Reserve's "bills only" policy of open market operations. The British Radcliffe Committee stressed the importance of direct central bank influence on interest rates. The growth of financial intermediaries, not directly affected by central bank operations in short-term securities and bank reserve funds, and the substantial amounts of more or less liquid assets available for conversion into cash for spending have made control of interest rates—that is, the terms on which assets can be converted into cash by both intermediaries and other economic entities—seem increasingly important as a means of economic control.

However, a number of economists have opposed direct central bank manipulation of interest rates. While a wide variety of arguments have been advanced, this opposition has seemed to focus on the contentions that fluctuations in interest rates and capital values are either dangerous or vastly overrated as a means of monetary control.

DANGERS OF LARGE CHANGES IN INTEREST RATES

What might be called the fundamentalist opposition to the aggressive use of flexibly changing interest rates as a weapon of monetary policy has put forth two main objections: (1) Even if such a monetary policy were to succeed in stabilizing production and prices, it could do so only by introducing instability into interest rates and capital values, and it is not clear that achievement of stable production and prices is worth instability in the financial markets. (2) There is a real risk that fluctuating interest rates could bring about a collapse of capital values which, in view of the widespread holdings of financial assets, could bring about general economic demoralization and collapse. In this eventuality, the presumption is that the goals of price and production stability would also be imperiled. Thus nothing would have been gained to offset the losses.

OBJECTIONS TO INSTABILITY IN FINANCIAL MARKETS. Miller has said:

Conventional views on interest rate policy hold today—as they have for long years in the past—that price level instability (i.e., inflation and deflation) and the general economic instability likely to accompany it should be minimized by manipulation (i.e., administrative instability) of the price-level of loanable funds (i.e., of interest rates and their corollaries, bond prices). One form of instability is used to fight another, and the instability deliberately introduced is allegedly unobjectionable—despite the vast change in society's economic fabric—since it presumably helps to produce a "higher" stability.[1]

In Miller's view this is a " 'casino' approach to economic control" [2] and ought to be replaced by the adoption of alternative selective control devices [3] which take account of "the growth of an economy of big government and big government debt, the changing importance of various types of credit granted, the changing importance and functions of credit-granting institutions, the changing character of production and consumption" [4] and which can "act restrictively without placing pressures on capital values." [5]

A similar view has been taken by Hansen.

In this kind of a world, primary reliance on interest rate policy as a means of stabilizing commodity prices is out of date. In our kind of world, the chief impact of sharp fluctuations in the rate of interest is on capital values. No longer is it possible, as formerly was the case, to influence commodity prices via interest rate policy without affecting capital values.

[1] Miller, "Monetary Policy in a Changing World," *Quarterly Journal of Economics,* LXX (February, 1956), 23.
[2] *Ibid.,* p. 42.
[3] Miller mentions selective controls on consumer and mortgage credit and special security reserve requirements for financial institutions.
[4] Miller, *Quarterly Journal of Economics,* LXX, 43.
[5] *Ibid.,* p. 41.

In our kind of world, the policy of sharp changes in interest rates cannot reach its goal, namely, the stability of commodity prices, without creating a degree of instability in capital values commensurate with the vigor of the policy pursued. Nowadays it is not possible, I repeat, to stabilize commodity prices via interest rate policy without causing instability in capital values.[6]

These quotations evidence a substantial degree of distaste for fluctuations in interest rates and capital values as a means of achieving monetary policy objectives. But the critics have not shown *why* some instability of capital values (short of crisis or complete collapse) is objectionable except perhaps for security dealers and necessitous sellers of securities in depressed markets. Skillfully managed fluctuations in interest rates and capital values could be designed to maintain stability and growth in such *real* economic quantities as gross national product, employment, and capital stock; and without sharp fluctuations in these latter quantities even such partly monetary variables as prices of current inputs and outputs would not be adversely influenced. Before mere distaste for capital value fluctuations can be accepted as grounds for ruling out appreciable changes in interest rates as a tool of monetary policy, it would seem necessary to examine the grounds behind the distaste. These seem to be: (1) a preference for stability, as such, over instability; (2) skepticism that stability in production and prices is worth instability in capital values; and (3) a belief that alternative controls can produce stability in both capital values and production.

While instability is often harmful, it does not follow that stability is a good to be sought at all times and everywhere. Change is the order of the universe and any organism, including a nation's economy, which is prevented from adapting to change is more likely to wither and die than to grow and thrive. A dynamic economy which is free to adjust to changes in income, wealth, tastes, and technology will inevitably be unstable in some aspects and at some times as resources are shifted in response to such changes. Many such changes increase economic welfare and are thus desirable. The task of the national economic policy-makers, accordingly, is not to prevent all instability but to channel destabilizing forces so that they do not do more harm than good. A decline in production of obsolete goods would be a desirable instability but the economic authority would act to combat any tend-

[6] Hansen, *The American Economy,* pp. 53–54.

ency for this to cumulate into a general economic decline. The point is that any particular instability must be judged in relation to the goals of the economy; it cannot be regarded as good or bad per se. Thus to assert that some policy might result in instability in capital values is not to condemn it.

Moreover, if it is accepted that the nation's economic goals are high and stable employment and production coupled with economic growth and relatively stable prices, it would seem that the achievement of stability in production *should* take precedence over stability in capital values. The instability of economic recession causes real losses of production which are irrecoverable and which result in lower levels of welfare than would otherwise have been attained. Most people, it seems fair to say, would rather experience some decline in the value of their bond or stock holdings than the loss of their jobs. Moreover, much fluctuation in interest rates and capital values is temporary. Real losses are taken only by those who borrow or sell assets in periods of restrictive monetary policy and this is a decision freely entered into. Indeed, a monetary policy of high interest rates and low bond prices is most effective if it inflicts few real losses, i.e., if most would-be spenders are discouraged by high borrowing costs and prospective capital losses and hence do not incur them.[7]

The idea that direct controls on borrowing, spending, and lending could permit both production and capital values to be held stable is seductive but doubtful. One such proposal, mentioned by Miller, would require banks and other financial institutions to hold specified amounts, or proportions of their assets, in Government securities. It seems obvious that the resultant relative shortage of funds for private borrowers would be expressed in higher interest rates on private loans and lower capital values on private securities, though the degree of change would depend on the elasticity of private demand for funds. And apart from impacts on interest rates and capital values, if one

[7] This is not to say that no one is harmed by fluctuations in interest rates and capital values. Some borrowers pay more, and some necessitous sellers suffer capital losses on sales of securities. Moreover, in the postwar perspective, at least, upswings in interest rates and declines in the value of outstanding bonds with given interest coupons have not been completely offset by opposite movements in periods of easy monetary policy. Thus on balance net capital losses on bonds may well have been incurred. But if this helped economic stability in terms of production, such losses may have been worthwhile. They cannot be considered objectionable, per se.

prizes stability as a value, it is surely incorrect to ignore the impact of such direct controls on the stability of the availability of credit to private borrowers. If fluctuations in interest rates were to be replaced by fluctuations in credit terms—down payments and maximum maturities, for example—there would be times when some borrowers were unable to secure access to credit on any terms and at any rate at all. Instability in access to credit might well be more upsetting to borrowers than instability in the cost of credit, for this could mean sudden interruption in the ability to produce rather than merely an increase in the cost of producing.

When all of these considerations are taken into account, it is difficult to agree that the test of any monetary policy should be its impact on capital values. Rather, the issue should be how effective a given policy is in achieving policy objectives, viewed in terms of employment, production, prices, and growth.

COLLAPSE OF CAPITAL VALUES. It must be granted that the impact of monetary policy on capital values can assume overriding importance in the limiting case—that is, if monetary policy were to bring about a collapse of capital values, or so impair capital values as to create a crisis of confidence. In this event, as noted earlier, the central bank would not be "trading" instability of capital values for stability of production and prices; collapse of capital values would probably be inconsistent with stability in real economic activity. It is by no means clear, however, that the financial structure is so sensitive as to give way easily before a restrictive monetary policy, even though some eminent economists have asserted this.

Hansen has been a vigorous exponent of the idea that capital values might collapse in the face of a stern monetary policy. Indeed, Hansen has argued that:

This is the basic underlying reason why monetary policy is compelled to assume, in modern times, a subsidiary role in the arsenal of stabilization weapons. Central bankers are thoroughly aware of this fact. No central banker is prepared to bring down upon the economy a collapse of capital values. He is perfectly aware that it is no longer possible to penetrate effectively into the area of commodity prices without first making a devastating assault on capital values. This he is not prepared to do, and rightly so. The modern central banker is cautious lest in the effort to stabilize commodity prices he destroy capital values.[8]

[8] Hansen, *The American Economy*, p. 54.

Even the British Radcliffe Committee, contrary to its recommendation that the central bank place more stress on interest rates and less on the money supply, cautioned in its *Report* against "any suggestion that the rate of interest weapon should be made more effective by being used much more violently than hitherto." [9] The Committee argued:

The intricate and highly developed network of financial institutions bases some of its strength on the existence of a large body of highly marketable Government bonds whose market values are assumed to have a considerable measure of stability.[10]

There is little doubt that there is the possibility that monetary policy at some point might inadvertently be carried too far and precipitate a financial panic. But this possibility has not and should not be permitted to cripple the administration of monetary policy. Responsible policy makers cannot deal in possibilities if monetary policies are to be effective; they must confine themselves to probabilities. And the probability that an active interest rate policy will bring a collapse of confidence and capital values must be reckoned as small. After all, similar fears were expressed in 1945–1946 when one of the main arguments against flexibility in interest rates was that "the vast holdings of government bonds by financial institutions, business, and the public generally preclude the use of this monetary weapon" because of "the effects on the economy of a substantial fall in bond values." [11]

Yet bond values did fall dramatically in the period from 1946 to 1959 without causing any general collapse in either capital values or confidence. The 2½ percent U.S. Treasury bonds issued in World War II and due in 1972, which traded as high as 106½ in April, 1946, dropped as low as 79¼ in December, 1959. This was the lowest price on a U.S. Government obligation since August, 1921, when the fully tax exempt Panama Canal 3 percent bonds touched 74½. In the United Kingdom, 2½ percent Consols (irredeemable bonds), which had traded as high as 100 in 1946, traded as low as 40 in 1959.

Shorter-term swings in bond prices, perhaps more significant in their impact on the psychology of the market, have also been striking.

[9] Radcliffe Committee, *Report,* p. 175.
[10] *Ibid.*
[11] Alvin Hansen, "Stability and Expansion," in *Financing American Prosperity,* pp. 250–51.

Thus the U.S. Treasury 2½s of 1972 dropped from 98 in June, 1952, to 90 by May, 1953, and then recovered to 100 by April, 1954. In the next downswing, their price fell from 100 in July, 1954, to 86 by October, 1957. The most rapid and extreme fluctuations came in 1957–1958 when the 2½s of 1972 rose 10 points in only six months, from 86 in October, 1957, to 96 in April, 1958, and then fell 11 points to a price of 85 by December, 1958.

The, economy's demonstrated ability to withstand substantial declines in bond values can be explained in a number of ways. Financial institutions generally have been sophisticated enough not to panic when the market values of their bond holdings declined. Many have had such strong cash inflows that they were under no pressure to sell securities at losses and hence did not need to weaken their capital positions; they could wait for securities to approach maturity when they would be redeemable at 100 cents on the dollar or wait for easier money conditions to bring increases in market values. Moreover, as the discussion in the next section brings out, declines in bond prices are more likely to lessen selling by institutions than to increase it. Thus market forces in periods of declining bond prices have worked against an acceleration of selling pressure and the panic conditions which this would have brought.

To be sure, the past is not always a safe guide to the future. But the fact that financial institutions and the economy generally have become accustomed to considerable fluctuations in interest rates and capital values suggests increased, not decreased, immunity to financial panics growing out of swings in capital values. Certainly there has been nothing in the postwar experience of Great Britain or the United States to justify the belief that a nation would face financial collapse if its bonds fell 10, 20, or even 60 percent below par because of variations in interest rates. Trepidation about the impact of fluctuations in interest rates on financial stability has been much exaggerated and should not be permitted to inhibit the effective application of monetary policy.

CHANGES IN INTEREST RATES, CAPITAL VALUES, AND LENDERS' BEHAVIOR

A conclusion that fluctuations in interest rates need not have calamitous effects on capital values and economic activity does not, of course, constitute an endorsement of Roosa's thesis that changes in interest rates and capital values could be useful and even powerful influences on the willingness and ability of financial institutions to extend credit to private borrowers. Roosa's view has been endorsed by the Federal Reserve System (though, as noted previously, the Open Market Committee for a number of years was most reluctant to take the measures necessary to implement it), as well as by the Radcliffe Committee in the United Kingdom, but it has also met with considerable skepticism from economists. A brief review of the opposing opinions and theoretical assumptions will be helpful to set the stage for an examination of data which bear on the question.

THEORETICAL DISPUTE. Roosa's thesis, it will be recalled from the discussion in Chapter III, was that rising yields on Government securities, and particularly on long-term Governments, would deter banks and other lenders from selling them to finance loans to private borrowers. This view rested on a number of assumptions: (1) Bond prices decline in periods of rising interest rates and financial institutions are (admittedly, perhaps irrationally) reluctant to take capital losses on Government securities, even if alternative assets offer higher yields; (2) Increased yields would make Government bonds more attractive to hold, particularly since institutional rigidities might prevent prompt upward adjustment of yields on private loans and securities; (3) Rising interest yields contribute to an atmosphere of uncertainty in the financial markets, tend to cause lenders to adopt a "wait and see" attitude, and cause at least a temporary slowdown in the pace of credit extension.

The critics of Roosa's thesis challenged this analysis at almost every point. Taking the points up in turn:

(1) The importance of the alleged reluctance of financial institutions to accept capital losses has been questioned on a wide variety of grounds. First, it has been pointed out that capital losses are significant considerations mainly on longer-term securities, and hence could not be expected to appreciably influence the behavior of institutions, such as commercial banks, which are mainly holders of short- and intermediate-term obligations.[12] Second, it has been asserted that even in the case of long-term securities, institutions which refuse to accept a capital loss on Governments in order to switch into higher-yielding

[12] Warren Smith, "On the Effectiveness of Monetary Policy," *American Economic Review*, XLVI (September, 1956), 589–90.

private assets are acting irrationally and such irrational behavior cannot be expected to persist, if indeed it exists at all.[13] Third, it has been said that the emphasis on the deterrent effects of prospective capital losses in curbing bond sales ignores important tax considerations which considerably reduce the impact of capital losses on the institutions involved.[14] Some institutions, it has been argued, may deliberately choose to establish a loss to offset a capital gain elsewhere and thus gain a tax advantage. More important, the special tax treatment of capital losses of commercial banks makes them insensitive to capital losses since, for a profitable bank earning more than $25,000, 52 percent of the loss is borne by the United States Treasury in the form of reduced income-tax receipts. Finally, critics have argued, the Roosa analysis fails to allow for the influence of expectations about the future course of security prices.[15] If an initial decline in bond prices were to give rise to an expectation of further declines, it might well stimulate anticipatory selling of bonds which would drive prices down further and make expectations about bond prices still more bearish. Thus a moderate rise in interest yields and decline in bond prices might stimulate a cumulative wave of selling, rather than create an incentive to buy.

(2) The critics also have argued that the emphasis on the attraction of rising interest yields as an incentive to hold long-term Governments ignores several offsetting considerations. For one thing, as noted in the preceding paragraph, if increases in interest yields (and declines in bond prices) gave rise to expectations of more of the same, financial institutions could become less, rather than more, willing to buy and hold Government bonds. Like other prospective buyers, they might choose to wait for still higher yields and lower prices. If they had planned to sell, they might accelerate their sales to get them accomplished before prices dropped still further. In addition, critics have asserted, even if interest rates on Treasuries were not expected to rise further, an increase in the yield on Governments would not be attractive to lenders if yields on competing investments rose as much

[13] Tobin, "Monetary Policy and the Management of the Public Debt: The Patman Inquiry," *Review of Economics and Statistics,* XXXV (May, 1953), 122–24.

[14] Whittlesey, "Monetary Policy and Economic Change," *Review of Economics and Statistics,* XXXIX (February, 1957), 36.

[15] *Ibid.*

or more.[16] Indeed, under these circumstances financial institutions would have an incentive to sell Treasuries and switch into these other higher-yielding private assets, despite the increase in Government bond yields. It may be noted here that many of the critics have been inclined to view institutional rigidities of rates on private loans and investments as essentially transitional, and therefore as no more than temporary helps to the demand for Treasury bonds.[17]

(3) Skepticism has also been expressed about the idea that rising yields on Government bonds contribute to a feeling of uncertainty in the financial markets, and that this in turn will tend to slow institutions' sales of Governments or even, because of increased liquidity preference, lead them to increase their purchases.[18] It has been pointed out that rising interest rates and restrictive monetary policies usually are associated with business prosperity and accordingly may be taken as signs that needs for liquidity and risk protection can be reduced for a time at least. This could involve an increased flow of lenders' funds into private securities even though Government bond yields were rising.

To sum up: It seems clear that the critics' view of the interrelationship between Government bond yields and financial institutions' willingness to buy and hold Government bonds is very different from Roosa's views and has opposite implications for institutional investment behavior. The Roosa doctrine suggests that rising yields on long-term Government securities will quicken institutional purchases of Government bonds and slow sales, even in the face of the attraction of higher yields on corporate securities or mortgages. In sharp contrast, Roosa's critics suggest that rising yields on Government bonds may not only fail to stimulate buying or slow down selling but, if expectations are adverse, may even give rise to increased selling by institutions. In any case, the critics say, institutional willingness to

[16] Warren Smith, *American Economic Review,* XLVI, 589–93; and Whittlesey, *Review of Economics and Statistics,* XXXIX, 35–36.

[17] Paul Samuelson took this point of view, for example, in his testimony before the Patman Committee in 1952. Patman Committee, *Hearings,* pp. 695–97. Also, see Tobin, *Review of Economics and Statistics,* XXXV, 123–24.

[18] Samuelson, "Reflections on Monetary Policy," *Review of Economics and Statistics,* XLII, 268; and "Recent American Monetary Controversy," *Three Banks Review,* March, 1956, pp. 10–11. Whittlesey has commented to the same general effect though not precisely on the point at issue here. See Whittlesey, *Review of Economics and Statistics,* XXXIX, 38.

buy Governments is strongly influenced by yields on alternative investments; if the yield on new corporate securities should rise more than that on Treasuries, sales of Government bonds by institutions would increase despite their increased yield.

These are mutually exclusive points of view. A definitive answer as to which is closest to the truth could be obtained only from a detailed examination of the actual investment behavior of a large number of individual financial institutions. But in the absence of such data, useful clues can be gained from an examination of Treasury data on holdings of long-term Government securities by broad categories of institutions in relation to Treasury bond yields and yields on competing investments.

STATISTICAL EVIDENCE. The analysis in the pages which follow examines the behavior of long-term Government bond holdings [19] of commercial banks, mutual savings banks, life insurance companies, fire, marine and casualty insurance companies, and corporate pension trust funds during the years from June, 1951, to December, 1959. These data—monthly except for holdings of corporate pension trusts which are reported quarterly—were calculated from the United States Treasury's "Survey of Ownership" of securities issued by the United States Government and Federal agencies and published monthly in the *Treasury Bulletin*. The Treasury Survey, while by no means inclusive of every institution in the categories mentioned above, does include the larger institutions which hold the bulk of Government securities. According to the Treasury, the Survey covers "approximately 95 percent of such securities held by all banks and insurance companies in the United States." [20] We have defined long-term securities for the purpose of this study to include all issues maturing in or after June, 1969, including such new issues as were acquired in the years after June, 1951.[21]

[19] Roosa actually was concerned with the tendency of changes in interest rates and capital values in influencing the *total* holdings of Government securities, short-term as well as long-term, of financial institutions. But this discussion concerns only long-term holdings because they exhibit the largest changes in capital value and hence are most likely to exhibit the "Roosa effect," if one exists.

[20] *Treasury Bulletin,* August, 1960, p. 56.

[21] An alternative procedure would have been to define long-term securities as those maturing after a certain number of years, for example, to include all those maturing after ten years. The drawback of this procedure is that with

The first step in the study is to compare the behavior of each institution's holdings of long-term Governments with fluctuations in yields on long-term Government bonds from June, 1951, to December, 1959. Next scatter diagrams are used to determine, for each institution individually, the extent and nature of the relationship between monthly changes in holdings of long-term Governments and (1) long-term Treasury bond yields, (2) the margin of corporate bond yields over Treasury bond yields, and (3) the margin of mortgage yields over Treasury bond yields. Finally, for one institution, life insurance companies, multiple correlation techniques are applied to explore the relationship between changes in holdings of long-term Government bonds and a number of possible explanatory variables.[22]

Holdings and Yields, 1951–1959. A panoramic view of the relationship between holdings of long-term Government securities by various institutions and interest yields on long-term Government bonds is presented in Chart 6. The chart shows the long-term Government bond holdings of life insurance companies, mutual savings banks, commercial banks, fire, marine and casualty insurance com-

---

the passage of time some securities would become so short as to move out of the sample, creating apparent changes in long-term holdings which would befog the analysis since they have nothing to do with the institutions' purchases and sales. In contrast, the procedure used in this study keeps the securities selected in the sample portfolios despite gradual shortening in maturity unless they are actually sold by the institutions. The shortest term securities included, the 2½ percent bonds due in June, 1964–69, were 18½-year securities in June, 1951, and 9½-year obligations in December, 1959. Total portfolios did not shorten this much because institutions added new issues to their holdings of long-term Treasuries.

[22] The figures on Treasury bond holdings come from various issues of the *Treasury Bulletin,* "Survey of Ownership." The figures on yields have the following sources: The yield on long-term Government bonds is the average published in the *Federal Reserve Bulletin,* currently for all issues maturing or callable in ten years or more; the yield on new corporate bonds, adjusted to a Aaa rating basis, is that compiled by the First National City Bank of New York; the yield on FHA mortgages is that computed by the Federal Reserve Board. However the Federal Reserve Board's mortgage yield index is available monthly only back to June, 1955, and there are six months within this period (December, 1956, and January, 1957, August and September, 1957, and September and October, 1959) for which no yield is given because contract rates on FHA mortgages were changing. Straightline interpolations were made to obtain yields for the missing six months. To obtain yields for the June, 1951, to June, 1955 months (when the Federal Reserve Board gives only quarterly figures) interpolations were made by using percentage changes in an FHA mortgage yield index computed by J. M. Guttentag of the Federal Reserve Bank of New York and reproduced in Leo Grebler, *Housing Issues in Economic Stabilization* (New York, National Bureau of Economic Research, 1960), Occasional Paper No. 72, p. 117.

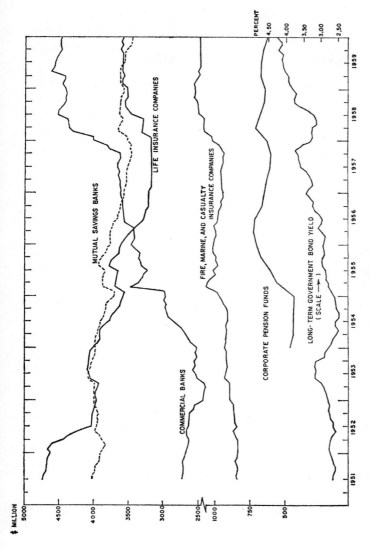

CHART 6

HOLDINGS OF GOVERNMENT SECURITIES DUE AFTER MAY, 1969, OF VARIOUS
INVESTOR GROUPS AND YIELD ON LONG-TERM GOVERNMENT BONDS,
MONTHLY, JUNE, 1951–DECEMBER, 1959

Source: United States Treasury Department, "Survey of Ownership," *Treasury Bulletin* for
years 1951–1959.

panies, and corporate pension trust funds for the period June, 1951, to December, 1959, together with the Federal Reserve's index of yields on long-term Government bonds. The significant points brought out by the chart are as follows:

1. Broadly speaking, Roosa's theory about the reactions of institutions to changes in Government bond yields is borne out by the behavior of life insurance companies and mutual savings banks. Both institutions, with some lags and exceptions, tended to slow their sales of long-term Governments in periods of rising interest yields and falling prices and to accelerate their sales when interest rates were falling and bond prices rising. Note, for example, that the sharp decline in life insurance company bond holdings from February, 1952, to July, 1952, when Government bond yields were declining, leveled off from August, 1952, to July, 1953, when interest rates generally were rising. Note, too, that both life insurance companies and mutual savings banks resumed sales of Government bonds in late 1953 and throughout 1954, when interest yields were declining and bond prices rising, but stopped their sales and even added to their holdings in the first seven months of 1955, when interest rates were rising again. In the latter part of 1955 a leveling out of the rise in interest yields and decline in bond prices gave the savings banks and life insurance companies opportunity to resume their sales of Government bonds, and these sales were not halted until the last few months of 1956 when, significantly, yields on long-term Government bonds rose rapidly and prices dropped sharply.

However, 1958 represents a major exception to the pattern suggested by Roosa. In 1958, unlike 1954, the life insurance companies and savings banks did not take advantage of declining interest rates and rising bond prices to sell Government bonds but rather added to their holdings. The explanation appears to be that the insurance companies and mutual savings banks were attracted by the opportunity to subscribe to new issues of long-term Treasury securities and their acquisitions of the 3½ percent bonds of 1990 and 3¼ percent bonds due in 1985 offset sales of already outstanding long-term Treasury issues from their portfolios. In 1954 the Treasury did not offer any new long-term bonds so the influence on life insurance company and savings banks' bonds' portfolios of the availability of new Treasuries on original issue was not felt.

2. Commercial banks' holdings of long-term Government bonds, on the other hand, have not fluctuated in accordance with what Roosa's analysis suggested. However, they also have not fluctuated in accordance with what might have been expected on the basis of some critics' fears; that is, rising interest rates and falling bond prices have not brought an acceleration of commercial bank selling of long-term Governments nor do the banks appear to have made net sales of long-term Governments to make customer loans or to take advantage of the favorable tax treatment of capital losses.[23]

Chart 6 shows that the commercial banks exhibited rather continuous demand for long-term Government bonds since early 1953 and by early 1959 had almost doubled their $2.3 billion level of holdings in March, 1953. As the chart also indicates, the major additions to the banks' holdings of long-term Governments took place in recession years or in the first year of economic recovery, that is, in 1954, 1955, and 1958, but the banks also added to their holdings, albeit in lesser amounts, in years of prosperity and rising interest rates.

While the pattern displayed by commercial banks' holdings of long-term Government securities may not fit the preconceptions of Roosa or his critics, it is consistent with the nature of the banking business.[24] Banks are essentially lenders; their investment portfolios serve as reservoirs of potential loan funds and as protection against needs for liquidity and income. Long-term bonds ordinarily provide more income than short-terms and also insure some stable income in the event that loan demands, loan rates, and interest earnings on short-term securities decline. Banks are most likely to add to their investment portfolios, including long-term Governments, at times when, as in 1954 and 1958, they have large amounts of surplus funds (excess reserves) and loan demands are relatively low. However, the availability of long-term Governments on original issue is

---

[23] The banks have sold large amounts of Government securities in periods of rising interest rates and credit restraint, but these were short-term obligations and subject to smaller capital losses.

[24] The view of the banking business which is taken here rests on the writer's experience with the First National City Bank of New York and on the descriptions and analysis provided in the following works: Robinson, *The Management of Bank Funds;* Alhadeff, *Monopoly and Competition in Banking;* Warren Smith, *American Economic Review,* XLVI, 588–606; Gaines, "Management of the Public Debt."

also a consideration—although banks have shown more willingness to buy long-term Governments in thin open markets than have other financial institutions—and Treasury new issues of long-term bonds have been a significant inducement to banks to add to their holdings of long-terms even in years such as 1955, when tightening reserve positions and rapidly growing customer loan demands, taken by themselves, would have indicated lessened bank purchases of long-terms.

However, the fact that commercial bank investment decisions are importantly influenced by reserve positions and by the strength of customer loan demand does not mean that fluctuations in long-term interest rates and capital losses on sales of bonds have no meaning for bankers. There are a number of indications to the contrary. It is significant for example that in periods of strong credit demand when banks have sold billions of dollars of securities to finance customer loans, they have concentrated these sales in relatively short-term issues which generally involved smaller capital losses than would have been incurred on sales of longer-term bonds.[25] Sales of long-term securities at substantial capital losses may, of course, occur but banks are generally reluctant to raise funds for short-term loans in this manner because loan rates may decline before the added interest income has compensated for the capital loss.

Bankers themselves have frequently mentioned an aversion to incurring capital losses on securities sales. A portfolio officer of one leading bank has said that capital losses do discourage bank selling of bonds

for the simple reason that a loss is a loss regardless of whether there is a tax palliative. The tax offset admittedly softens the loss by cutting it in half but does not make senior management (or portfolio officers) ready, willing and happy to sell out. As to the fact that a higher interest rate will be obtained on loans, it is true that this has entered into our thinking but probably only incidentally. Many loans are short-term and there is, therefore, no assurance that the interest rate differential will continue for a sufficient number of years to offset the capital loss on bonds.[26]

[25] For example, the $9.7 billion reduction in Government security holdings of banks covered in the *Treasury Bulletin*, "Survey of Ownership" from December, 1954, to September, 1957, a period when loan demands were strong and credit policy restrictive, was all in shorter-term obligations. Indeed, as Chart 6 indicates, the banks' holdings of long-term Government securities, that is, those due after May, 1969, actually rose by $669 million in this period.

[26] Joseph H. Fleiss, vice president of the First National City Bank of New York, in a letter to the writer, November 21, 1960.

The same investment officer commented on the idea that a decline in bond prices could stimulate an avalanche of selling by saying that "the preference would be to sell longer issues if one were convinced of a sustained downtrend in prices" but, he added, "this has merit . . . only if the investor is sufficiently clairvoyant." [27]

Moreover the gains from outguessing the market must be balanced against the risk of permanently impairing bank capital positions by incurring losses which may represent only temporary downswings in security prices. Unrealized losses on securities in bank portfolios can bulk fairly large in relation to bank capital, since the latter is ordinarily only a small proportion of total loans and investments. For example, on December 31, 1959, unrealized losses on Treasury notes and bonds amounted to 11.3 percent of total capital accounts for Reserve City member banks and 5.4 percent for Central Reserve City member banks.[28] These are significant proportions but the percentage in all probability would be considerably greater for Country member banks because these smaller institutions traditionally carry a larger proportion of their investments at longer term where prospective capital losses would be greatest.[29]

To be sure, tax "switches" by banks out of one Government security selling at a discount and into another at a discount do, as critics have emphasized, indicate some willingness on the part of banks to accept and, indeed, to seek capital losses for the tax benefits involved. But this needs to be considered in perspective if its significance is properly to be appreciated. In the first place, many tax switches are made into securities which are about the same or longer maturity as those on which the loss has been taken. While this is not, of course, an invariable rule, there are profit considerations which encourage it.[30]

[27] *Ibid.*

[28] My calculation is based on figures showing unrealized capital losses on notes and bonds for Central Reserve City and Reserve City member banks published by the Federal Reserve Bank of Kansas City in "Bank Reactions to Security Losses," *Monthly Review,* June, 1960, p. 15; and the data on capital accounts for these classes of banks shown in the *Federal Reserve Bulletin,* XLVI (April, 1960), 391. Both numerator and denominator were of course for the same date, December 31, 1959.

[29] The unavailability of data on the unrealized note and bond capital losses for Country member banks made it impossible to compute a percentage to their capital accounts. It is worth mentioning, however, that their greater exposure to capital loss, because of longer average maturity of portfolio, is not compensated by stronger capital positions on the average. Their ratio of capital accounts to total loans and investments is relatively low.

[30] Banks are permitted to deduct capital losses on securities from taxable

To the extent that this is the case, total bank holdings of long-term Governments might be little affected by such switches.[31] Moreover, there is some evidence that even tax-switching transactions are engaged in only by a minority of the larger more sophisticated banks.[32] A study by the Federal Reserve Bank of Kansas City of bank reactions to security losses in the Tenth Federal Reserve District concluded

a majority of banks appear to have been reluctant to establish sizable net losses on securities, and it would seem correct to conclude that in these cases their willingness to extend additional loan credit was to some extent correspondingly tempered. Thus, the evidence appears to indicate that the "lock-in" effect, though it is far from being a universal influence, is an important one.[33]

3. Fire, marine and casualty insurance companies' and corporate pension trust funds' holdings of long-term Government bonds have not shown any consistent relationship with the movement of yields on Treasury bonds. Chart 6 indicates that Government bond

---

income, thus saving 52 percent (the corporate tax rate on income over $25,000) of the loss and are taxed at no more than 25 percent (maximum capital gains tax rate) on capital gains on the securities which are bought to replace the bonds sold. A bank which sold $100,000 of securities at a 10 point discount would thus suffer a net after-tax loss of $4,800 ($10,000 less the $5,200 saving on income tax). Reinvestment of $100,000 in different securities also at a 10 point discount would promise a $10,000 capital gain at maturity when the obligations would be redeemable at par, less $2,500 capital gains tax. On the entire switch transaction, there would be a net after-tax profit of $2,700 in prospect (the $7,500 after-tax gain less the initial $4,800 after-tax loss on the securities sold to initiate the transaction).

But note that the profitability of the switch depends directly on the size of the discount on the security purchased, for this governs the amount of capital gain at maturity. This discount in turn is directly related to the maturity of the security purchased; given interest rates, the longer the term the larger the discount. To be sure, if the security purchased had a very low coupon it could be a short-term obligation and still offer a discount comparable to those on long-term securities but an examination of Government security dealers' quotation sheets reveals very few such opportunities in recent years. To insure comparable discounts, and thus the profitability of switch transactions, banks are likely to have to switch between securities of comparable maturity. For a description of the tax provisions governing banks' security transactions, see R. H. Parks, "Income and Tax Aspects of Commercial Bank Portfolio Operations in Treasury Securities," *National Tax Journal*, XI (March, 1958), 21–34.

[31] To be sure, banks might switch into comparable term corporate bonds but banks are not generally important buyers of corporate bonds. Poor loss experience in the early 1930s, the growth of the term loan as the preferred vehicle of intermediate and longer term lending to corporations, and the failure of corporate bonds to meet banks' maturity needs and protect against early call are some of the reasons for reluctance to buy corporate securities.

[32] Federal Reserve Bank of Kansas City, *Monthly Review*, pp. 14–15.

[33] *Ibid.*, p. 16.

holdings of the nonlife insurance companies rose almost 40 percent from January, 1952, to December, 1959, but the bulk of the rise came in late 1954 and early 1955 and in 1958, all periods in which the important influence was Treasury offerings of new long-term issues. During the restrictive credit policy periods of 1956, 1957, and 1959, when interest rates were rising and bond prices were falling, the nonlife insurance companies reduced their holdings of long-term Governments to some extent but not to a degree which would support the view that they were selling in anticipation of price declines. One student, arguing from data through 1957, said that Government securities holdings of these companies appeared to be essentially liquidity reserves necessitated by relatively large fluctuations in loss claims and payments and he drew the conclusion that there is little likelihood of growth in their demand for long-term Governments.[34] However, as the chart shows, 1958 brought a substantial rise in the nonlife insurance companies' holdings of long-term Governments, reemphasizing the importance of the opportunity to buy Treasuries on original issue.

Corporate pension trust funds' holdings of long-term Government securities at the close of 1959 were lower than they were in early 1956 despite the increase in interest rates. In contrast, pension funds' holdings of short-term Government securities (not shown in the chart) rose by almost 100 percent to $1.2 billion in the same period, indicating that for pension funds, Governments were held mainly as liquidity instruments. Again, however, it is worth noting that the increases in pension funds' long-term holdings which did take place came during periods when the Treasury was offering new issues of long-term bonds, suggesting that greater opportunity to buy such bonds might make yields on them more of an influence on the pension funds' activities.

4. A striking aspect of Chart 6, touched on repeatedly in the foregoing paragraphs, is the importance of new offerings of Treasury long-term bonds in inducing institutions to increase their holdings. The Treasury issued new long-term bonds on nine separate occasions from 1951 to 1959 (see Table 13).

As a glance at Chart 6 will confirm, the long-term Government bond holdings of every group of institutions shown rose appreciably in almost every month in which the Treasury issued new long-term

[34] Gaines, "Management of the Public Debt," pp. 348–50.

TABLE 13

UNITED STATES TREASURY LONG-TERM BOND ISSUES,
1951–1959

Issue Date	Description of Security	Term
May 1, 1953	3¼ % bonds due June 15, 1978–83	30 yrs. 1½ mos.
Feb. 15, 1955	3% bonds due Feb. 15, 1995	40 yrs.
July 20, 1955	3% bonds due Feb. 15, 1995	39 yrs. 7 mos.
Oct. 1, 1957	4% bonds due Oct. 1, 1969	12 yrs.
Dec. 2, 1957	3⅞ % bonds due Nov. 15, 1974	16 yrs. 11½ mos.
Feb. 14, 1958	3½ % bonds due Feb. 15, 1990	32 yrs.
June 3, 1958	3¼ % bonds due May 15, 1985	26 yrs. 11 mos.
Jan. 23, 1959	4% bonds due Feb. 15, 1980	21 yrs. 1 mo.
April 1, 1959	4% bonds due Oct. 1, 1969	10 yrs. 6 mos.

Source: *Treasury Bulletin,* August, 1960, pp. 36–38.

bonds. Examination of these holdings by issue confirms that the increases reflected subscriptions for the new securities being offered. This occurred even in those cases where institutions up to then had been liquidating long-term Treasury bonds, as for the life insurance companies and mutual savings banks in February and July, 1955, and for the commercial banks in January and April, 1959.

The implication is that the institutions view opportunities to buy long-term Treasuries on original issue as being different in kind from the day to day opportunities to buy Government securities in the dealer market. This is confirmed, as will be shown in the next section, by scatter diagrams relating institutions' changes in their long-term Government security holdings to the yield on long-term Government bonds. The scatter diagrams show that the willingness of institutions to buy long-term Governments on original issue is much greater, measured by readiness to accept lower yields, than is their willingness to buy Governments in the market.[35] Institutional purchases of Governments on original issue would seem to represent a different "universe" from purchases in the dealer market. While there doubtless are a number of reasons for this,[36] part of the explanation is that the day

[35] The readiness to buy long-term Governments on original issue is not due to the fact that the Treasury has tended to concentrate bond offerings in easy money periods. Institutions also took substantial amounts of the bonds offered in May, 1953, February and July, 1955, and January and April, 1959, all periods of rising rates.

[36] For example, surprising as it may seem, financial institutions feel an obligation, for patriotic reasons, to support new Treasury issues by subscribing. Another reason, less altruistic, is that to encourage purchases, the Treasury customarily prices its new issues to yield a little more than comparable outstanding issues.

to day dealer market in Government bonds is notoriously thin; prospective buyers as well as sellers find that to conduct any substantial volume of transactions they must make considerable price concessions, engage in a number of transactions, and be willing to spend considerable time in the process. Buying Governments on original issue, on the other hand, is a relatively simple matter and the price paid is independent of the volume sought.[37]

If this analysis is correct, the effectiveness of monetary policy might well be increased by more frequent issues of Treasury bonds when it is desired to curb institutions' extensions of credit to private borrowers. In other words, because of imperfection in the Government bond market, the interest rate attraction might need to be supplemented by increasing the availability of bonds. An alternative approach would be for the Federal Reserve to deal frequently in long-term Governments with the aim of broadening the market. While a broader and more active market in outstanding long-term Government bonds might not increase institutional demand for Governments, the possibility that it would—by increasing the availability and salability of Governments—deserves some exploration.

The Evidence of Scatter Diagrams. The form of the relationship between long-term interest yields and institutions' willingness to hold Government securities may be shown by plotting changes in institutions' holdings of long-term Governments against the yield on long-term Governments. Roosa's conception of the relationship would tend to be borne out if such scatter diagrams revealed that the institutions sold Governments at low interest rates and reduced their sales or even bought Governments as interest yields rose. If there appeared to be no consistent relationship at all, Roosa's theory would suffer and the critics' skepticism would gain support. However, lack of a consistent relationship would not justify the more extreme critical views: that increases in interest rates can touch off cumulative selling and that institutions' holdings of Governments are keyed not to their yield but to the spread between their yield and yields available on competitive investments. These would be borne out only if institutions' sales increased and purchases decreased as Government bond yields rose; or if institutions' sales increased as the yield advantage of competitive

---

[37] Original issue subscriptions involve some problems but they are not serious. A subscriber does not know in advance what the allotment percentage will be and hence must guess in padding his subscription.

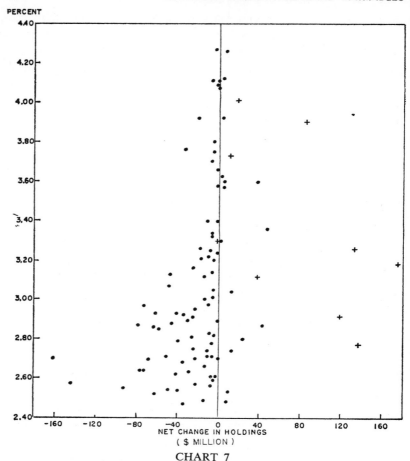

CHART 7

CHANGES IN LIFE INSURANCE COMPANIES' HOLDINGS OF LONG-
TERM GOVERNMENT BONDS DUE AFTER MAY, 1969, AND YIELDS
ON LONG-TERM GOVERNMENT BONDS, JUNE, 1951–DECEMBER, 1959
Note: Crosses indicate months in which the Treasury offered new long-term
securities.

investments over Treasury bonds increased, regardless of what was
happening to the level of Treasury bond yields.

1. Life Insurance Companies. The relationship between life insurance companies' purchases and sales of long-term Governments and
yields on long-term Governments is shown in Chart 7, covering
monthly changes from June, 1951, to December, 1959.[38] It is ap-

[38] The scatter diagrams, and the multiple correlations based on these data,
omit June, 1952, when the Treasury exchanged nonmarketable 2¾ percent
bonds due in 1975–80 for outstanding long-term 2½ percent bonds.

parent from the chart that life insurance companies reduced their sales of long-term Governments as long-term yields rose. Thus, Roosa's thesis gains some support. However, the relationship between insurance companies' purchases and sales and Governments bond yields was rather loose with a considerable degree of scatter. Accordingly, it is difficult to say whether the relationship is linear or curvilinear in form, though the diagram suggests some curvilinearity. A curvilinear relationship would have logic in its favor, that is, it is reasonable that as interest rates fall and insurance companies sell Governments, their willingness to sell should increase as interest rates reach what are considered unusually low levels and bond prices touch unusually high levels. This tendency would be reinforced by the fact that insurance company requirements for Governments as a source of liquidity are relatively low, since premium income and amortization payments on mortgages and other loans provide a strong and steady cash flow. The fact that sales did decline to an asymptote around zero as interest rates rose and bond prices declined suggests that the main factor involved was the prospect of capital losses. If the interest yield to be gained on Governments were an important factor, one might have expected rising rates to have encouraged more net purchases of Government securities at high rates.

It is interesting to note how Chart 7 confirms the suggestion in Chart 6 that the opportunity to buy Treasury securities on original issue was an important influence explaining institutional acquisitions. The insurance companies' major acquisitions of long-term Treasury's took place in months in which new issues were being sold.

To test the critics' contention that institutions buy and sell long-term Governments in accordance, not with Government bond yields, but with the relation of these yields to yields on competitive investments, Chart 8 shows life insurance company changes in holdings of long-term Government bonds plotted against the spread, or excess, of yields on new issues of corporate bonds over the yield on long-term Treasuries. If the critics were correct, insurance company sales of Governments would rise as the margin of corporate bond yields over Treasury bond yields rose, that is, as the advantage of selling Governments to switch into corporate bonds increased. In fact, however, life insurance company transactions in long-term Governments behaved in the opposite manner. Their sales of Governments declined rather than rose as the yield margin of corporate bonds over Gov-

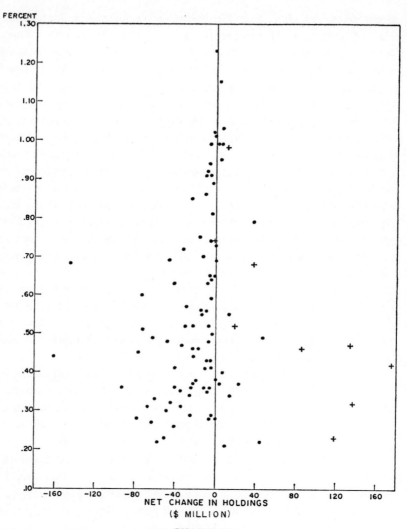

CHART 8

CHANGES IN LIFE INSURANCE COMPANIES' HOLDINGS OF LONG-
TERM GOVERNMENT BONDS DUE AFTER MAY, 1969, AND SPREAD
OF YIELDS OF NEW CORPORATE BONDS OVER LONG-TERM
GOVERNMENT BONDS, JUNE, 1951–DECEMBER, 1959

Note: Crosses indicate months in which the Treasury offered new long-term
securities.

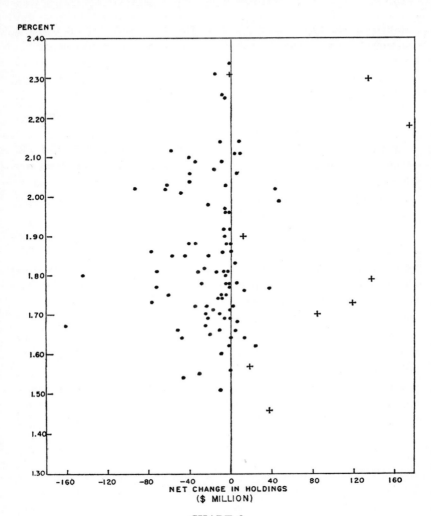

CHART 9

CHANGES IN LIFE INSURANCE COMPANIES' HOLDINGS OF LONG-
TERM GOVERNMENT BONDS DUE AFTER MAY, 1969, AND THE
SPREAD OF FHA MORTGAGE YIELDS OVER LONG-TERM
GOVERNMENT BONDS, JUNE, 1951–DECEMBER, 1959

Note: Crosses indicate months in which the Treasury offered new long-term
securities.

ernment bonds rose. The explanation for this, apparently, is that the margin of corporate yields over Treasury yields was widest at periods of high interest rates and money market pressure and this was precisely the time when Treasury bond yields were most attractive and capital losses on sales of Treasuries most punitive. The latter considerations evidently outweighed the attractions of more yield on corporate bonds.

Mortgages are an extremely important investment outlet for life insurance company funds. Chart 9 shows life insurance company changes in holdings of long-term Government bonds plotted against the spread of FHA mortgage yields over long-term Treasuries. This gives more ambiguous results. The companies apparently were more willing to sell Governments when the spread of mortgage yields over Government yields was wide than when the spread of corporate yields over Governments was wide. But this does not conflict with Roosa's thesis. The key point is that the sluggishness of mortgage yields has made movements in Government bond yields the active element in changing the spread. The spread of mortgage yields has been widest when Treasury bond yields have fallen, Treasury bond prices have risen, and the penalty for selling Treasuries to buy mortgages has been minimal or nonexistent. However, many mortgage acquisitions are arranged long in advance through the forward commitment process, and this tends to reduce the significance of current yield relationships.

2. Mutual Savings Banks. The relationship between mutual savings banks' purchases and sales of long-term Governments and the yields on long-term Governments is shown in Chart 10, covering monthly changes from June, 1951, to December, 1959. This also tends to support Roosa's thesis rather than his critics'. That is, to the extent that there is a relationship, it seems to be one in which the savings banks became more willing to hold Government bonds as their yields rose. However, this relationship is looser than that shown for the insurance companies, and it is even more difficult to say whether the form of the relationship is linear or curvilinear. As in the case of the life insurance companies, the mutual savings banks' major acquisitions of Government bonds were largely in months in which the Treasury issued new long-term bonds.

Like the life insurance companies, the savings banks showed no tendency to increase sales of Governments as the margin of yields on competing new corporate bonds over Treasury bond yields rose.

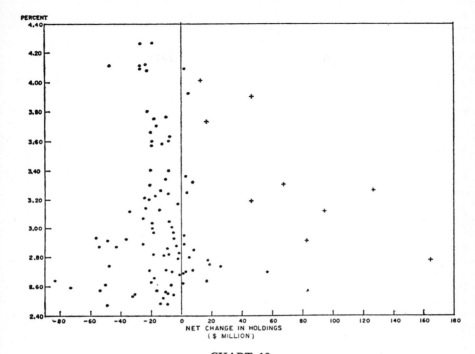

CHART 10

CHANGES IN MUTUAL SAVINGS BANKS' HOLDINGS OF LONG-TERM GOVERN-
MENT BONDS DUE AFTER MAY, 1969, AND YIELDS ON LONG-TERM
GOVERNMENT BONDS, JUNE, 1951–DECEMBER, 1959

Note: Crosses indicate months in which the Treasury offered new long-term securities.

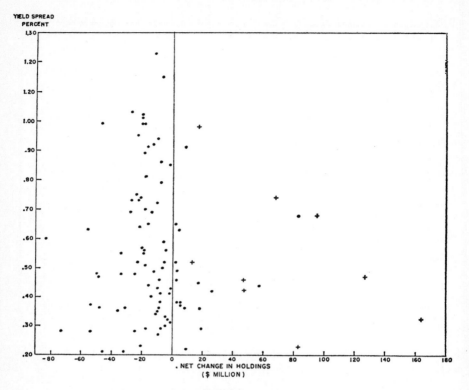

CHART 11
CHANGES IN MUTUAL SAVINGS BANKS' HOLDINGS OF LONG-TERM GOVERN-
MENT BONDS DUE AFTER MAY, 1969, AND SPREAD OF YIELDS ON NEW
CORPORATE BONDS OVER LONG-TERM GOVERNMENT BONDS,
JUNE, 1951–DECEMBER, 1959
Note: Crosses indicate months in which the Treasury offered new long-term securities.

However, as Chart 11 indicates, there is less evidence, compared with the life insurance companies' behavior, of a tendency to reduce sales of Governments in spite of an increase in the yield advantage of corporate bonds. This would be consistent with a view sometimes heard that savings banks are more aggressive traders and more aware of yield differentials.[39] However, the evidence clearly does not support the idea that a rising margin of corporate yields over Treasury yields would bring an increase in sales of Governments.

To avoid repetition, we shall not present a chart to show the influence of the spread of FHA mortgage yields over Government bond yields on changes in savings banks' holdings of long-term Governments, there is a noticeable lack of correlation.

3. Commercial Banks. It has already been suggested in a preceding section that changes in commercial banks' holdings of long-term Government bonds have not seemed to be significantly related to long-term yields or that, if there is a relationship, it has been overpowered by the influence of other considerations. Chart 12, showing changes in commercial bank holdings plotted against yields of long-term Government bonds, confirms this judgment. It may be noted that an attempt (not shown) was made to study the relationship in shorter periods—cyclically and in terms of interest yield movements—but that no consistent patterns emerged.

However Chart 12 is not devoid of implications. It tends to refute the theory that increases in yields and declines in bond prices act to accelerate selling of long-term Government bonds, for sales seem to show very little correlation of any kind with yields. Also, the diagram provides further evidence of the attraction of the opportunity to buy Governments on original issues; major acquisitions of Treasuries by the banks took place in months in which the Treasury was offering new long-term bonds.

4. Fire, Marine and Casualty Insurance Companies, and Corporate Pension Trusts. Long-term Government bond holdings of these institutions have shown practically no correlation with the level of yields on Government bonds. Their purchases and sales have apparently been related to factors other than yields. Accordingly, no scatter diagrams are shown. It should be noted that, just as in the case of

---

[39] For a description which suggests the sharp trading engaged in by savings banks, see the testimony of John M. Ohlenbusch, vice president of the Bowery Savings Bank, in 1959. Joint Committee, *1959 Employment Hearings*, Pt. 6A, pp. 1410–22.

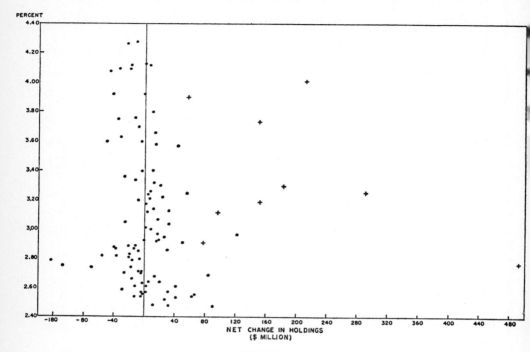

CHART 12
CHANGES IN COMMERCIAL BANKS' HOLDINGS OF LONG-TERM GOVERNMENT
BONDS DUE AFTER MAY, 1969, AND YIELDS ON LONG-TERM
GOVERNMENT BONDS, JUNE, 1951–DECEMBER, 1959
Note: Crosses indicate months in which the Treasury offered new long-term securities.

the other institutions, the major purchase of Governments by nonlife insurance companies and corporate pension funds came in periods when the Treasury made new long-term securities available on original issue.

Experiment with Multiple Correlation. Significant relationships between economic quantities sometimes are concealed because a number of influences are operative at the same time, clouding the relationship between the dependent variable and any one of the explanatory or independent variables taken alone. With the thought that this kind of interference might have confused the relationship between institutions' changes in holdings of Government bonds and yields on Government bonds, it seemed worthwhile to make at least one attempt to use multiple correlation techniques to see whether they could improve the explanation of movements in Government bond holdings. The life insurance companies' holdings of Government securities were chosen for this study because they seemed to show the best gross relation to Government bond yields.

As noted earlier, the life insurance company scatter diagram, Chart 7, suggests that the gross relation between Government bond holdings and yields might best be explained by a curvilinear function. But this is only suggested; the data does not clearly show a curvilinear relation. Moreover, the indicated curvilinearity might have been due to the net effect of a number of influencing variables, each of which could have been linearly related to changes in holdings. Taking all this into account, along with the fact that curvilinear multiple correlation involves substantially greater difficulty of calculation, it was decided to use linear multiple correlation procedures.[40]

The change in life insurance companies' holdings of long-term Government bonds was treated as the dependent variable to be explained by variations in seven independent variables: (1) a time trend; (2) changes in the consumer price index of the Bureau of Labor Statistics (assumed to measure the effect of concern about inflation on the demand for bonds); (3) offerings by the Treasury of new long-term bonds (the months of such offerings being considered as the "dummy" variable); (4) the Federal Reserve's index of yields

[40] Also, as Klein puts it: "Very often linear approximation is adequate . . . a series of linear segments, if divided finely enough, can be used to approach curved surfaces as closely as we please." Klein, *A Textbook of Econometrics,* p. 15.

on long-term Government bonds; (5) the Federal Reserve Board's index of yields on FHA mortgages in secondary markets, extrapolated as noted earlier; (6) the First National City Bank's index of yields on new issues of corporate bonds adjusted to an Aaa-rating basis; (7) Standard and Poor's index of yields on 500 common stocks. The period analyzed in this manner extended from June, 1951, to December, 1959, with June, 1952 excluded because of the exchange in that month of nonmarketable 2¾ percent Treasury bonds due in 1975–1980 for outstanding long-term 2½ percent bonds.

The results were not especially illuminating. To be sure, changes in the life insurance companies' Government bond holdings were clearly significantly related to the combined influence of the seven independent variables. But the coefficient of multiple correlation, adjusted for the number of degrees of freedom, amounted to only .6353, indicating that no more than 40 percent of the variation in life insurance companies' holdings was "explained" by movements in these seven variables. Moreover, of the independent variables only the regression coefficients of new Treasury bond offerings and yields on new corporate bond offerings proved statistically significant. The regression coefficients of all the other independent variables, including the long-term Government bond yield, proved not to be significantly greater than their standard errors.[41] It is interesting, however, that the corporate bond yield, and not the Treasury bond yield, proved significant in the equation. This tends to support the critics of Roosa who have argued that alternative investment opportunities are more important to institutional investment policy than yields on Treasury bonds themselves.

However this indication vanished when an attempt to improve and sharpen the relationships was made by dropping common stock yields

[41] The equation of relationship obtained in the first attempt is given below with the standard error of each regression coefficient below it in parenthesis:

$$GB_h = -125.55 - .05t + .32p + 92.41z + .16i_g + .30i_m - .21i_e - .03i_e$$
$$\quad\quad\quad\quad (.80)(1.28)\ \ (12.95)\ \ (.24)\ \ (.36)\ \ (.07)\ (.15)$$

GB_h = changes in Government bond holdings; t = time; p = change in consumer price index; z = new Treasury offering dummy variable; i_g = Government bond yield; i_m = FHA mortgage yield; i_e = new corporate bond yield; i_e = common stock yield.

$R = .6353$
$R^2 = .4450$
$\overline{R^2} = .4037$ (adjusted for degrees of freedom)
$\overline{S} = 129,465$

and mortgage yields from the explanatory equation and trying another multiple correlation with the five remaining independent variables: (1) a time trend; (2) changes in consumer prices; (3) Treasury offerings of new securities; (4) long-term Government bond
yields; and (5) yields on new corporate bonds. This approach improved the coefficient of multiple correlation marginally to .6447,
with the percentage of "explained" variation in Government bond
holdings rising from 40 to 42 percent. But the standard errors and
the statistical significance of the various independent variables shifted
erratically. The regression coefficient of the corporate bond yield
which had been statistically significant became insignificant as its
standard error tripled. The only statistically significant explanatory
variable left in the equation was the term representing new offerings
of Treasury securities.[42] Thus the evidence for the importance of the
corporate bond yield afforded by the first multiple regression equation
disappeared in the second equation. Accordingly, the multiple correlation technique, so far as it was taken, provided support neither to
Roosa nor to his critics.

The influence of the opportunity to buy new Treasury securities on
original issue was brought out strongly by the multiple correlation
technique, confirming the evidence of the charts. But the results do
not support the view that even the seven variables combined exert a
predominant influence on institutions' holdings of Government bonds.
Nevertheless, it would be invalid to conclude that these results show
that Government bond yields or the other independent variables included in the equation do not affect, or are not related to, institutions'
holdings of Government bonds. Multicollinearity could be responsible
for the relatively low coefficient of multiple correlation and this is a
common problem with interest rate series, or indeed with time series

[42] The equation of relationship obtained in the second correlation is as
follows:

$$GB_h = -52.43 + .30t + .40p + 92.18z + .27i_g - .18i_c$$
$$(.24)\ (1.27)\ \ (12.67)\ \ (.32)\ \ (.20)$$

GB_h = changes in Government bond holdings; t = time; p = change in consumer
price index; z = new Treasury offering dummy variable; i_g = Government bond
yield; i_c = new corporate bond yield.
$R = .6447$
$R^2 = .4388$
$\overline{R^2} = .4157$
$\overline{S} = 126,853$

in general. The fact that the standard errors of many of the regression coefficients were altered so considerably by omission of two of the independent variables suggests a considerable amount of multicollinearity or intercorrelation.[43]

Moreover, if, as noted earlier, the true relationships between Government bond holdings and some or all of the independent variables, including Government bond yields, were curvilinear, a linear multiple correlation might fail to show significant relationships, even though these actually existed.

It seems clear that further experimentation with multiple correlation, including lagged variables and curvilinear functions, is indicated. Unfortunately, in the absence of access to an electronic computer and without statistical and clerical help, a thoroughgoing investigation of this type was impractical in terms of time and resources available for this portion of the study.

CONCLUSIONS ON INFLUENCE OF CHANGING INTEREST RATES AND CAPITAL VALUES ON FINANCIAL INSTITUTIONS

Fluctuations in interest rates and bond prices need not be ruled out as legitimate weapons of central bank monetary control. An investigation of the postwar economic record discloses nothing to suggest that even fairly wide fluctuations in long-term interest rates and capital values would have explosively undesirable results or lead to a collapse of capital values and consequently disrupt the economy. Such fears seem as ill founded as the earlier fears that abandonment of the policy of supporting Government bond prices would bring chaos in the financial markets.

However, the record of 1951–1959 also suggests that changes in long-term interest rates and bond prices (at least those which occurred under a monetary policy which refused to influence them directly) were not as potent an influence on financial institutions' behavior as Roosa had suggested.[44]

[43] For a good discussion of some of the hazards involved in multiple correlation procedures, see Herman Wold, *Demand Analysis, A Study in Econometrics,* Ch. 2 and particularly pp. 46–47; and also, Davies, *Statistical Methods in Research and Production,* Ch. 8 and particularly pp. 234–36.

[44] Roosa had suggested that yields on long-term Government securities might have to fluctuate only $\frac{1}{8}$ percent or thereabouts to exert considerable influence on financial institutions' willingness to extend credit to private borrowers. Roosa, *Money, Trade, and Economic Growth,* pp. 288–90. Actually, the 1951–1959 fluctuations in long-term yields have been ten times this size. A number

The exploratory examination of the record made in this study indicates that only life insurance companies and mutual savings banks were obviously influenced in their willingness to hold long-term Government securities by fluctuations in their yields and prices in the way Roosa had suggested. In other words, only these institutions exhibited an increased willingness to hold Government bonds as their yields rose and their prices declined, and showed a decreased willingness to hold them as their yields fell and prices rose.

To be sure, there is reason to believe that long-term interest rates and bond prices have some influence on commercial banks' loan and investment decisions, but there is no evidence in the data examined that Government bond yields had any influence on banks' willingness to hold long-term Governments, perhaps because such influence was submerged by stronger influences associated with bank reserve positions and customer loan demands. There is also apparently little relation between Government bond yields and holdings of long-term Government securities of fire, marine and casualty insurance companies and corporate pension trust funds.

Nevertheless, it is significant that the data examined tend to support Roosa's view rather than that of his critics. That is, if any relationship at all exists between long-term Government bond yields and institution's holdings of such securities, it seems to be the one Roosa postulated: institutions' willingness to hold Governments rises when their yields rise and readiness to sell Governments declines as their yields rise.

The more extreme criticisms of Roosa's doctrine, on the other hand, find little or no support in the data: There is no evidence that increases in Treasury bond yields and declines in prices touched off cumulative waves of selling of Government securities in anticipation of still further yield increases and price declines. The data also do not support the idea that increases in Treasury bond yields would have little effect in keeping institutions invested in Treasury bonds if the spread of yields on private loans and investments in excess of Treasury yields also increased as much or more. For life insurance companies and mutual savings banks, at least, sales of Government

---

of observers have suggested, however, that the modest yield changes envisaged back in 1950–1951 by Federal Reserve spokesmen were mainly wishful thinking designed to allay the fears of those who were concerned about the impact of large interest rate changes on capital values. See, for example, Robertson, *Economic Commentaries*, p. 70.

bonds actually decreased when the spread of corporate bond yields over Treasury bond yields increased.

However, this is not to say that institutions ignore opportunities to earn higher yields on private securities. The testimony of institutional spokesmen indicates that they do consider yield alternatives; [45] and it will be recalled that the first multiple correlation analysis of life insurance company behavior indicated that corporate bond yields were a statistically significant influence on the insurance companies' willingness to buy or sell long-term Government bonds. Nevertheless, when all considerations are taken into account the evidence indicates that while the attraction of higher yields on private securities may have induced institutions to put more of the flow of new savings into them, this was not reflected in switches out of Government bonds and into corporate bonds as the yield advantage of corporate bonds widened.

Moreover, consideration should be given to the possibility that the failure of the data to support Roosa's thesis more fully is due to the refusal of the Federal Reserve authorities, during the period studied, to influence bond yields and prices directly, as Roosa had suggested. Leaving the long-term markets "on their own" meant that movements in Treasury bond yields largely reflected movements in yields of private securities such as corporate bonds. When private demand for credit rose, pushing up corporate bond yields, Treasury bond yields were dragged up too by a sort of arbitrage process. But this procedure meant that the spread of corporate bond yields over Treasuries widened markedly in tight money periods, a fact that not only worked against Roosa's conception of Government bond yields as the dynamic factor but also against economic stability. A widened corporate-Treasury bond yield spread in tight money periods encouraged shifting out of Governments into private securities at a time when monetary policy was trying to slow the rate of growth of private borrowing and spending. In recessions, the spread of corporate yields over Treasuries narrowed; corporate yields fell faster than Treasury yields, the latter being held up by the Treasury's practice of increasing the supply of bonds in recession periods.[46] This too was contrary to

[45] Joint Committee, *1959 Employment Hearings*, Pt. 6A, pp. 1410–22.
[46] The Treasury has found it difficult to market bonds in periods of credit restraint and has also not wanted to interfere with the supply of long-term

the aim of monetary policy since it discouraged shifts out of Governments into private securities at a time when the aim of policy was to stimulate private borrowing and spending.

A Federal Reserve and Treasury policy aimed at making Government bond yields and prices a more active element in the securities markets might well increase the influence of Government bond yields on institutions' willingness to hold Governments and accordingly strengthen the effect of monetary policy. If Government bond yields moved up first in periods of credit restraint, they would help push up corporate bond yields rather than themselves being pulled up by corporate bond yields, and the spread between Governments and corporates would narrow in the process.[47] In recessions, Federal Reserve purchases of long-term Government bonds could push Treasury yields down, the falling Government bond yields in turn exerting a down pull on corporate bond yields with the yield spread widening in the process. This pattern of behavior of yield spreads would tend to encourage institutions, such as life insurance companies and savings banks, to stay in Governments during periods of credit restraint but to shift into private loans in periods of credit ease, both being more consistent with monetary policy goals than the contrary influence exerted by spreads in recent years.

A broad program of regular Federal Reserve operations in long-term Government securities might increase the responsiveness of commercial bank holdings of long-term Governments to changes in their yields. But whether or not this occurred it should be remembered that a failure of banks' long-term investment operations to reflect changes in long-term yields need not mean that they are unaffected by monetary policy. The banks, after all, are directly subject to the Federal Reserve's control of their reserve positions; these are the main deter-

---

funds for business, state and local governments, and home buyers. See the remarks of George M. Humphrey, then Secretary of the Treasury, in Byrd Committee, *1957 Hearings*, Pt. I, pp. 163, 170. This has left years of recession and early recovery as the periods when Treasury bonds have been marketed.

[47] It can be argued that the narrowing would be only a temporary phenomenon, that corporate borrowers and underwriters would quickly adjust yields on new corporate bonds upward to restore a normal spread. But this ignores the fact that an aggressive Federal Reserve policy would have the initiative, and each adjustment by underwriters could be met by a further adjustment of yields on Government bonds by the Federal Reserve. The chilling effect of rising yields on underwriters' willingness to offer securities would increase the effectiveness of such a Federal Reserve policy.

minant of banks' loan and investment behavior. Federal Reserve operations in long-term securities would be designed to affect primarily the behavior of nonbank financial institutions which are not subject to direct Federal Reserve control. But within the context of reserve positions and customers' loan demands, Federal Reserve influence on long-term Government security yields and prices might also have useful supplementary effect on banks' behavior which should not be ignored.

To sum up: So far as the investigation has gone [48] the data studied have provided some support for Roosa's general position that conscious central bank influence on long-term interest rates and bond prices could have useful effects in guiding financial institutions' lending and investing along lines consistent with the aims of monetary policy. This is not to say that the effects would be as powerful as Roosa originally envisaged them, nor is it to deny that long-term yields and capital values of Government bonds are only some of the considerations which institutional investors and lenders take into account in formulating policy. But there seems little question that the effects of such a central bank policy would work in the right direction and would tend to reach institutions, the so-called nonbank financial intermediaries, which are largely outside the scope of traditional central bank controls over bank reserve positions. Accordingly a central bank which eschews direct influence over the long-term Government bond market as an avenue of making its influence felt is not utilizing its powers in the most effective way possible.

---

[48] This investigation has been little more than a preliminary survey. The behavior of financial institutions with respect to the significance of interest rates, capital values, types of investment instruments and loans preferred, etc. deserves a great deal more study with more resources and tools of investigation than were at the disposal of this writer. I commend it to the attention of research institutions with large staffs and access to electronic computers.

Part IV
SUMMARY

XIII

FINDINGS AND CONCLUSIONS OF THE STUDY

MONETARY MANAGEMENT TECHNIQUES

When flexible monetary policies were reintroduced in 1951, the Federal Reserve was free to implement them as it wished. On the one hand, it could have decided to use all that had been learned of monetary techniques during the pegging period in order to make flexible monetary policy as effective as possible. On the other hand, it could have turned its back on the pegging experience and everything associated with it, banishing all instruments and techniques connected with pegging. In effect, Roosa and his associates at the Federal Reserve Bank of New York argued for the first course on the ground that open market operations in long-term securities, direct influence on interest rates, and use of selective credit controls—all associated with the pegging period—could make useful and substantial contributions to the effectiveness of flexible monetary policy. But this view was rejected by the majority of the Federal Reserve Board and Open Market Committee.

Hence the Federal Reserve entered upon the 1951–1959 period of flexible monetary policy with a divided purpose. It certainly wished to prove the effectiveness of flexible monetary policy. But, judging from its pronouncements and actions, it wanted even more to avoid any possibility of a return to the practices of the pegging period, including all instruments and techniques connected with pegging. As a result it tried to leap back beyond the pegging era to the days of traditional central banking. The central bank's role was to be confined to influencing bank reserve positions and the money supply. Monetary policy instruments and techniques which did not have classical precedents were viewed with suspicion or rejected.

But at the same time that it was cutting down the number and variety of means by which it could make monetary policy effective, the Federal Reserve was accepting more responsibilities for monetary policy than it had ever shouldered before. Whereas the classical central bank had acted only to protect the gold reserve and prevent money panics, the Federal Reserve in the postwar years committed itself to the promotion of high employment, stable prices, stable production, protection of the gold reserve, and encouragement of a high rate of economic growth. Thus the Federal Reserve's attachment to traditional techniques and instruments of monetary policy was not accompanied by a parallel attachment to the limited objectives of traditional monetary policy. Indeed it could not have been, for the widening tasks of the Federal Reserve had been thrust upon it by forces outside itself. As Roosa put it:

> The public eye has shifted from the early conception of a Federal Reserve System that should determinedly "keep money out of the way" by making the monetary machinery work smoothly, and has passed over to one that demands aggressive use of the central bank's influence on money and credit to help promote economic growth and to help limit or counteract the inflationary or deflationary disturbances that are generated from time to time by an ever-changing constellation of widely varying economic forces.[1]

It is difficult to escape the conclusion that this narrowing of the means by which monetary policy might be made effective, at the same time that the goals of monetary policy were being broadened, was a serious mistake that was bound to impair the effectiveness of monetary policy.

MONETARY POLICY INSTRUMENTS

Conceptions of what were "proper" means of implementing monetary policy evidently had a strong influence on the Federal Reserve's choice of monetary policy instruments. Instruments and techniques which had traditional standing, such as the discount mechanism, were emphasized initially, regardless of whether they were suited to the task at hand. Open market operations were restricted to very short-term Government securities, giving them a classical cast and at the same time avoiding any parallel to the pegging period, when vast quantities of long-term obligations had been bought. Changes in reserve requirements were made sparingly and only in a downward direction, permitting requirements to move gradually down toward

[1] Roosa, *Federal Reserve Operations in the Money and Government Securities Markets,* p. 8.

what was evidently deemed a more "natural" level. Selective credit controls on consumer and mortgage credit, used during the pegging period largely because the pegging commitment made general credit restraint difficult, were not used at all. Since the criteria for the use, or the lack of use, of an instrument went beyond its effectiveness and gave weight to whether it had traditional standing or had been associated with the pegging period, it is not surprising that the effectiveness of monetary policy suffered.

OPEN MARKET OPERATIONS. Perhaps the most important impairment of the effectiveness of monetary policy was the restriction of open market operations to dealings in short-term Government securities, the so-called "bills only" policy. This denied the Federal Reserve direct influence on long-term, or even intermediate-term, security yields and prices and made it impossible for monetary policy to influence short- and long-term yields differentially or in opposite directions, thus limiting both the range and the flexibility of monetary policy.

The Federal Reserve supported its adoption of the "bills only" policy with a wide variety of arguments, but most of them fail to stand up to analysis or to the test of experience. The argument that "bills only" would improve the functioning of the long-term Government securities market was not borne out by experience. Bond prices and yields fluctuated more widely after adoption of "bills only" than they did before, dealers' spreads increased, dealer positions in long-term bonds remained painfully thin, and both dealers and other market participants continued to complain that it was exceedingly difficult to execute transactions without causing unduly wide price fluctuations.

The contention that control over short-term rates would afford adequate influence over long-term interest yields proved faulty. The relation between short-term and long-term rates of interest turned out to be highly variable, particularly in the short-run, so that it proved difficult to predict the influence on long-term rates of any given change in short-term yields.

Contrary to Federal Reserve assertions, the evidence strongly suggested that direct dealings in long-term bonds, or swaps of long- for short-term securities, could appreciably affect the structure of yields. A variety of Federal Reserve arguments to the effect that open market dealings in long-term bonds would seriously impair or destroy the private Government securities market found no support in foreign experience, where several central banks have dealt in long-term obligations for many years, or in the American experience following the discontinuing of "bills only" in late 1960 and early 1961.

But the most important objection to "bills only" was, and is, that it significantly impaired the effectiveness of monetary policy. In periods of credit restraint, the response of long-term interest rates to credit restriction in the short-term market was unpredictable and often inappropriate. In the 1955–1957 business expansion, for example, the amount of pressure exerted by a "bills only" monetary policy on the bond market was modest in the first half of the period when the boom was strong but large in the last year when business was already weakening, just the opposite of what might be considered appropriate.

A still bigger disadvantage of "bills only" was that, because of the unpredictable and sometimes weak response of long-term rates to credit policy actions in the short-term markets, it led the Federal Reserve to create excessively easy conditions in the money market during the 1954 and 1958 recessions in order to ensure that long-term yields would decline sufficiently to stimulate investment. The excessive liquidity thus built up severely handicapped Federal Reserve efforts to apply restraint in the subsequent economic recoveries.

Equally important, the "bills only" policy made it impossible for the Federal Reserve to influence long- and short-term interest rates differentially or in opposite directions, thus denying needed flexibility to the central bank. This was emphasized by the bond market collapse in June, 1958, which occurred at the same time that business recovery was beginning, the one development suggesting some easing action to slow the chaotic decline in bond prices while the other called for restraint on bank reserves to prevent recovery from turning into inflation. The entire episode provided a perfect opportunity for use of a massive swap operation in which large-scale Federal Reserve bond purchases could have given needed support to the bond market, while simultaneous sales of Treasury bills could have reabsorbed the reserve funds released by the bond purchases. Indeed, the Reserve authorities could actually have exerted some modest pressure on reserve positions by making their sales of bills exceed their bond purchases. But such a swap was ruled out by "bills only," and the effectiveness of monetary policy suffered accordingly.

The need for flexibility led to the progressive abandonment of the "bills only" policy in late 1960 and early 1961. "Bills only" open market purchases in the 1960 recession would have involved creation of excessive short-term ease and exceedingly low short-term rates of interest. Both of these conditions would have accelerated the outward movement of short-term foreign dollar holdings which was already reducing the U.S. gold stock and impairing confidence in the dollar both here and abroad. What was needed was an ability to maintain short-term rates of interest well above previous recession levels while at the same time bringing down long-term rates of interest. Purchases of long-term bonds were indicated. They would supply bank reserves without putting direct pressure on short-term yields and at the same time nudge long-term yields downward. Having abandoned "bills only," the Federal Reserve had the flexibility required to deal separately with long-term and short-term rates at a time when the domestic business situation and the gold outflow called for such differential treatment.

In view of the deficiencies in the Federal Reserve's theoretical arguments for the "bills only" policy and the obvious impairment of the effectiveness of monetary policy, it is hard to escape the conclusion that the abandonment of the "bills only" policy was long overdue. Rigid adherence to "bills only" might have been appropriate in a simpler age but it did not suit the needs of a modern central bank or a modern economy.

DISCOUNT MECHANISM. The main criticism of the Federal Reserve's use of the discount mechanism concerns the initial effort to make it a leading weapon of monetary policy, a role for which its nature poorly suited it. But this attempt was made and failed in 1952 and 1953. Thereafter the authorities relegated the discount mechanism to a more subordinate but still useful role, for which it was eminently suited.

The 1952–1953 attempt to make discounting a major weapon, even in periods of credit restraint, evidently reflected a desire to restore it to its traditional importance, for the classic central banking weapon was discounting and the discount rate. What this attempt overlooked was that the role of the central bank had changed considerably—from that of being largely a lender of last resort, in which function discounting had pre-eminence to that of being a regulator of the use of credit and money, a role in which discounting is not as efficient a weapon as some more recently developed instruments of monetary control.

But rejection of the discount mechanism as an aggressive weapon of monetary policy does not mean that it can serve no role at all. Indeed, the fact that discounting supplies funds to the market but only at the cost of introducing some constraint, because of the banks' reluctance to borrow, gives it a special value as a safety valve, preventing sudden liquidity gaps in the banking system, but only at a price and under administrative terms which prevent it from becoming an escape from credit restraint. This is a needed facility in a nation with thousands of unit banks, among which funds are shifting constantly. With discounting available as a buffer against other weapons of monetary policy, the market is protected against violent shocks, perhaps arising out of a credit-policy miscalculation, and the Reserve System in turn is able to act aggressively without fear that a miscalculation would panic the market. Moreover, as a temporary source of funds to the banking system, discounting has contributed to the elasticity of the Government securities market, and thus to the ability of the Treasury to market its new issues without disruption to the market.

Proposals for the abolition of discounting hence seem ill considered. They overemphasize discounting as an escape from credit restraint while slighting or ignoring the constructive contribution it makes to the smooth functioning of the banking system and monetary policy. Some improvement in the functioning of the discount mechanism might be achieved, however, by changing the way in which the discount rate is set. Under present arrangements, the money market occasionally has had trouble in distinguishing technical adjustments in the rate from more basic changes intended to signal credit-policy intentions, since all discount rate adjustments are made in the same way. This apparently has inhibited the Federal Reserve from making needed technical adjustments. Accordingly, it might be worth trying an arrangement under which the discount rate ordinarily would be set at a stipulated margin above or below the weekly Treasury bill rate, but which would permit the Reserve authorities to change the relationship of the discount rate to the bill rate whenever this seemed necessary.

To sum up: Discounting cannot be an aggressive weapon of monetary control because it gives the initiative in deciding when funds are to be released to the banks which are to be controlled. But as a supplementary weapon of monetary policy, and as an important aid to the banking system and financial structure, discounting is very important indeed.

CHANGES IN RESERVE REQUIREMENTS. It is probable that more flexible use of changes in bank reserve requirements, specifically increases in reserve requirements, could appreciably improve the effectiveness of monetary policy. But it is only fair to recognize that this conclusion clashes both with the view of the Federal Reserve and with the views of critics of the Federal Reserve. The Federal Reserve authorities have rejected reserve-requirement increases as a tool of credit restraint because they are too powerful, too blunt, and, moreover, would reduce the profitability of banking and thus impair the ability of the banking system to build capital and grow along with the rest of the economy.

Critics of the Federal Reserve's handling of the reserve requirement instrument, on the other hand, have argued that the System has been too concerned about the impact of changes in reserve requirements on bank profits. But they have not argued that reserve requirement increases should be used as a tool of credit restraint. Rather, they have suggested that the Reserve System should no longer make use of decreases in reserve requirements to combat recession. The idea is that needed reserve funds should instead be supplied through open market purchases of Government securities on which the Reserve System would earn interest which could be turned over to the Treasury. The result would be little or no use of the power to change reserve requirements.

Yet the evidence suggests need for more, rather than less, use of the reserve requirements tool. It seems clear that the Federal Reserve's practice of lowering reserve requirements in recession has had a salutary effect of spreading the impact of easier credit policies very rapidly throughout the banking system and economy, correspondingly increasing the likelihood of early recovery from recession. Eliminating reserve requirement reductions would very likely reduce the effectiveness of general monetary policy in recession, a rather important sacrifice to be contemplated for the sake of a some extra millions of dollars of interest earnings on the Federal Reserve portfolio. It bears repetition that the central banks' main task is to promote the national welfare, stability, and growth, not to add marginally to the Treasury's revenues.

What needs to be done, therefore, is to make use of increases in reserve requirements in periods of prosperity. This would speed the transmission of restrictive credit policies throughout the banking system and economy, a badly needed improvement. The failure of the Federal Reserve to use increases in reserve requirements as a tool of credit restriction during 1951–1959 was one reason for the relatively slow spread of credit restraint throughout the economy and in particular for the sluggish response of the money supply.

This recommendation does not deny that the health of the banking system is a proper concern of the Federal Reserve authorities. But it does imply that the effectiveness of monetary policy should be the overriding concern of the monetary authorities. Within this framework, increases in reserve requirements could be and should be handled to minimize their adverse impact on the banks. They should, for example, be relatively small—perhaps on the order of ¼ or ½ percentage point at a time or $250 to $500 million—but come relatively quickly in the economic expansion. Prompt impact might reduce the intensity of the restraint that would otherwise be needed with slower-acting instruments applied over a longer period. What is desired is quick diffusion of credit restraint, not necessarily a more massive impact than open market sales of Government securities could provide. Large increases in reserve requirements are not likely to be needed unless the economy were to embark on a major inflationary surge which required the therapy of a drastic shock.

SELECTIVE CREDIT CONTROLS. The Federal Reserve can fairly be criticized for not asking Congress for authority to impose selective credit controls during the 1953–1959 period. The effectiveness of monetary policy in 1955, for example, might well have been appreciably increased if the authorities had been able to slow the boom in automobile production and home building with selective controls of the Regulation W or Regulation X type. As it was, the 1955 auto and home-building boom sparked an unsustainable rate of expansion in the economy and also encouraged businessmen to undertake excessive capital investment in the belief that a new era of rapid growth in consumer markets was beginning. The situation would have been even worse if general credit controls had not had some influence on home building because of the fixed interest rates on Government-underwritten mortgages.

While we have not yet had a repetition of the 1955 experience, it would be decidedly premature to exclude the possibility. And if one occurred, it is worth emphasizing, policy would be little better fitted to deal with it today than it was in 1955. Indeed, if interest rates on FHA and VA-underwritten mortgages were made flexible, as many economists and industry spokesmen have proposed, monetary policy would be even worse equipped to deal with a boom of the 1955 type.

Moreover, it can be argued that selective controls might be useful on occasion—with due regard to the interests of the industries directly affected—to relieve some of the burden on general credit policy. The point is that if some areas of the economy, such as consumer buying, are relatively insensitive to general credit conditions, then general credit-policy measures must be all the more intense, in terms of restraint on credit availability and the height of interest rates, to achieve the desired over-all restraint. This in turn could produce crisis conditions in the capital market, excessive difficulties in Treasury financing, and a degree of public dissatisfaction with monetary policy which could threaten its replacement with a network of direct controls. Or alternatively, the fear of these developments might inhibit the Federal Reserve authorities from pressing general credit policies as far as the economic situation really required with a consequent impairment of the effectiveness of monetary policy.

The major objections to selective credit controls have related to their administrative feasibility, including possibilities of massive evasion, and allegations that they have a peculiar tendency to arouse opposition and resentment. But these objections have been carried too far. It is significant, for example that when selective controls on consumer and mortgage credit were actually in effect, Federal Reserve officials appeared to be satisfied with them and were not concerned about evasion. In addition, the idea that selective controls are unique in their ability to arouse resentment from regulated groups seems mistaken. Past resentments against selective controls in force before mid-1952 represented in good part resentment against credit restraint; general credit controls at that time were devoted either wholly or largely to maintaining stability in the bond market, not to credit restriction.

In recent years, general credit controls suffered from a veritable storm of criticism, because they had become the vehicle of credit restraint. But the economy's dislike for restraint cannot be a justification for not applying it. As a matter of fact, it is possible to argue that selective credit controls, by reducing the burden on general credit controls and hence on interest rates, might split and even reduce the opposition to monetary restraint. As things now stand, the Reserve System has no effective defense against charges that interest rates are too high or that general restraint bears too heavily on particular industries. With selective controls in force, the Reserve authorities could point to them as evidence of attempts to spread the burden of credit restraint and reduce upward pressures on interest rates.

Thus the Federal Reserve should have authority to impose selective credit controls and perhaps should even keep them continuously in effect in order to insure quick availability when needed. Normally, however, selective controls should be kept at levels which merely formalize credit terms set by the major lenders themselves, because constant interference with consumer preferences and the market's allocation of resources is undesirable.

CONTROL OF FINANCIAL VARIABLES

Federal Reserve policy in 1951–1959 failed to take full advantage of all the ways in which it could have exerted its influence. Business firms and individuals react to a variety of monetary and financial influences, such as changes in money balances, liquidity positions, interest rates, the capital value of asset holdings, and others. But the Federal Reserve rejected any attempt to exert direct influence on most of these variables in the belief that control of the money supply and bank reserve positions was all that was necessary to achieve effective monetary control. The result was an over-all impairment of the effectiveness of monetary policy. For one thing, the factors not directly influenced by the Reserve System facilitated a speed-up in velocity of money which offset the Federal Reserve's restrictions on its supply. For another, the Reserve System's attachment to traditional monetary instruments and minimum intervention in the economy, ironically prevented it from achieving close control of the supply of money, its major proximate objective.

CONTROL OF MONEY SUPPLY. A number of leading economists have considered the Federal Reserve's record in controlling the money supply to be so bad as to justify withdrawing the Federal Reserve's power to make discretionary changes in the money supply. We are inclined to reject this suggestion as too drastic. In the first place, an important and strategic segment of the money supply—demand deposits in New York and other weekly reporting member banks, amounting to almost half the total—has responded fairly quickly to changes in business conditions and monetary policy. Moreover, the half of the money supply which on occasion has not responded promptly—deposits in small- and medium-sized banks throughout the nation—has been affected relatively quickly by monetary policy in recessions when the reserve requirement weapon was used. The main problem has been the tardy response of only a portion of the money supply to credit restraint during business expansions.

We believe that a considerably more prompt response of deposits in small banks would occur if reserve requirement increases were used as a tool of credit restraint. Accordingly we would recommend this change in the use of the instruments of monetary policy before taking the drastic step of abandoning discretionary central banking.

This conclusion draws support from examination of some of the difficulties that might be met in adopting the suggested alternative to discretionary Federal Reserve control of the money supply; namely a 4 percent a year increase in the money supply to correspond with the real growth of the economy and the normal change in velocity. If the Federal Reserve has had difficulty in achieving appropriate behavior of the money supply with respect to the business cycle, is there markedly greater assurance that it could maintain a steady 4 percent a year increase in money? The money supply, after all, is affected by the willingness of banks to lend or invest, the willingness of businesses and individuals to borrow, and the asset preferences of nonbank investors—all of which are subject to only imperfect control by the Federal Reserve.

Moreover, even if achieved, such a 4 percent money-growth rule would undoubtedly be inappropriate at some point. In velocity-financed inflation, for example, restraint on the money supply would be more appropriate than a 4 percent annual increase. In depression, on the other hand, increased liquidity preference might make a more than 4 percent increase in the money supply appropriate. A fixed rule makes no allowance for changing circumstances. It would seem inadvisable that the central bank should so tie its hands. Rejection of flexibility in this area would be likely to lead to an impairment of the effectiveness of monetary policy just as did the "bills only" policy.

OVEREMPHASIS ON MONEY SUPPLY. There is no doubt that the Federal Reserve permitted itself to concentrate overmuch on the money supply and to neglect the importance of other monetary and financial variables for an effective monetary policy. But much of the criticism of the Federal Reserve's emphasis on the money supply has gone beyond charges of overemphasis to charges of misdirection. A growing number of critics have asserted that it is really not very important that a central bank control the money supply; that control of interest rates, liquidity, or nonbank financial intermediaries are the essentials of monetary policy. These charges seem extreme, however much one may agree that the Reserve System's failure to give adequate attention to these other variables and institutions has been unfortunate and has impaired the effectiveness of monetary policy.

These criticisms of the Federal Reserve's emphasis on the money supply, and also the Federal Reserve's case for exclusive emphasis on the money supply share a common defect. They all take too doctrinaire a view. Whereas decisions on important policy issues seem to be essentially matters of emphasis, both the critics and the defenders of concentration on the money supply argue in terms of mutually exclusive alternatives. For example, if the money supply is viewed as important, then says the Federal Reserve, interest rates can be determined as the market wishes. On the other hand, if interest rates are viewed as the key monetary variable, then, in Kahn's opinion, the money supply need be of no particular concern. A similar tendency to a "black and white" type of discussion is commonly found in the controversies over the relative importance of money and liquid assets, or in the dispute over whether banks are more or less significant to monetary control than nonbank financial intermediaries.

It seems more persuasive to view the economy as an increasingly complex mechanism to which there is no one magic key. Moreover, we think it useful to recognize that the quantities and variables in dispute are related, often closely related, but that there is also some range of independent variation in the relationships.

Thus the conclusion follows that the Federal Reserve should take considerably greater account of the influence of changes in interest rates as such, of the volume and types of liquidity available in the markets, and of the variety and number of specific characteristics of nonbank financial institutions; and that it should increase the variety of its approaches to monetary control accordingly. But all this should be added to its control of the money supply to give additional influence, not substituted for it. For after all, money is extremely important for interest rate determination, liquidity positions, and for the ability of nonbank lenders to extend credit. Similarly, the Federal Reserve should continue to give major attention to controlling member bank reserve positions, for banks are particularly volatile lenders and have a greater credit-creation potential than other intermediaries. But this should not preclude, as it apparently did in the past, attempts to use monetary controls to exercise a direct influence on intermediaries. On occasion, the Federal Reserve might well improve the effectiveness of monetary policy by using operations in long-term bonds to affect interest rates, the portfolios of nonbank financial intermediaries, and liquidity positions generally, and by reviving selective credit controls to affect the demand for intermediary credit.

PROBLEM OF VELOCITY. It is surprising that the Federal Reserve's statements and publications paid so little attention in 1951–1959 to the possibility that changes in the velocity of money could seriously complicate, if not frustrate, monetary policy. The official view seemed to be that the combined result of increases in the velocity of money and in the supply of money was an excessive flow of expenditure over much of the postwar period. The drift of prices was upward, and Reserve officials warned repeatedly of inflationary pressures. It is thus hard to escape the feeling that the authorities were too complacent about the extent to which velocity could interfere with the effectiveness of monetary policy.

On the other hand, it must be said that many critics have taken far too pessimistic a view of the implications of velocity for the future effectiveness of monetary policy. The idea that restrictive credit policies will be frustrated automatically and almost inevitably by rising velocity, at least so long as interest rates continue to rise, finds little support in the evidence.

Examination of the data on velocity and interest rates during the postwar period does indeed show a very close positive relation. But examination of the data on a quarterly basis suggests that the velocity-interest rate relation has been shifting during this period, and, most significant from the point of view of the effectiveness of monetary policy, that the shifts have been in the direction of a decreasing responsiveness of velocity to interest rates. In other words, as the postwar period has gone on, it has taken more and more of an increase in the rate on 91-day Treasury bills to stimulate a given rise in velocity. The data thus suggest that velocity may be approaching some sort of a limit. This hypothesis is supported by a review of the annual movements in velocity over the fifty-one years from 1909 to 1959. Viewed in this longer perspective, the postwar increases in velocity suggest a recovery to a previously-known more or less normal level, from the extremely depressed levels to which velocity had been driven during the Depression and World War II by massive money creation and loss of confidence.

Whether or not velocity is actually approaching a limit remains for the future to tell. But the decreasing sensitivity of velocity to interest rate increases is a fact which argues for an increased effectiveness of monetary policy in the future. Contrary to the extremely pessimistic views of some critics of monetary policy, this study suggests that the restrictive effects of increased interest rates and lessened availability of money are less likely to be offset by increased velocity of money in the future than they were in the 1946–1959 years.

LONG-TERM INTEREST RATES AND CAPITAL VALUES. Roosa and his associates at the Federal Reserve Bank of New York argued vigorously for direct central bank influence on long-term interest rates and bond prices on the grounds that higher yields and lower prices on long-term Government securities would increase financial institutions' willingness to hold them, while lower yields and higher prices would increase their willingness to sell. As a result, fluctuations in the prices and yields of long-term Treasury securities could have a significant influence on the willingness of financial institutions not otherwise subject to Federal Reserve policy to extend credit to private borrowers.

A number of critics attacked the Roosa thesis, arguing that substantial changes in long-term interest rates and capital values would demoralize the economy, or that financial institutions actually would be impelled to sell more or buy less Government securities if their yields rose and prices declined. The latter tendency would be strengthened, they asserted, if the spread of yields on alternative investments over yields on Governments increased—as usually happens with respect to corporate bonds in periods of rising interest rates. Thus the effect of central bank influence on long-term interest rates would be either disruptive to the economy, or perverse.

Examination of financial institutions' holdings of long-term Treasury bonds in relation to yields on long-term Treasury bonds tends to support Roosa's view rather than that of his critics. In the first place, it is quite clear that considerable fluctuation in interest rates and bond prices have occurred and have *not* touched off cumulative waves of selling by investors or a collapse of capital values as some of Roosa's critics feared. Moreover, to the extent there is a relationship between institutional holdings and yields of long-term Government bonds it is the one Roosa postulated: sales decrease or purchases increase as yields rise and prices decline. The data also do not support the critics' idea that increases in Treasury bond yields would not attract financial institutions if yields on private loans or investments, such as corporate bonds, increased as much or more. For life insurance companies and mutual savings banks, at least, sales of Government securities have been reduced when their yields rose even though the spread of corporate yields over Treasury yields was increasing. On the other hand, if the data do not support the extreme criticisms of the Roosa doctrine, they also do not justify uncritical faith in it. Roosa clearly overestimated the sensitivity of financial institutions to changes in long-term interest rates.

Among the institutions studied, only life insurance companies and mutual savings banks have clearly been influenced in their willingness to hold Government bonds by fluctuations in their yields and prices, in the way Roosa suggested. Even in their cases, the relationship is relatively loose. And the dealings of commercial banks, corporate pension funds, and fire, marine and casualty insurance companies in long-term Government bonds do not seem to bear any consistent relation to long-term yields and prices. Finally, one attempt to use multiple correlation techniques supported the critics' view that yields on alternative private investments were more important than yields on Treasury bonds for institutions' willingness to hold Treasury bonds, though a refinement of the multiple correlation failed to support this contention.

There is, however, some reason to believe that the failure of the data to support Roosa's thesis more fully might have been due to the failure of the Federal Reserve, during the period studied, to conduct open market operations in long-term Governments, as Roosa had suggested. Both the multiple correlation analysis and the scatter diagrams show clearly that financial institutions were strikingly willing to buy long-term Government bonds on original issue when they were freely available. This suggests that the failure of institutions to respond more to high market yields on Treasury bonds reflected the thinness of the Government bond market which reduced both the availability and the marketability of securities at any given price or yield. Thus if the Federal Reserve had broadened the long-term Government market by dealing actively in it, it is conceivable that institutional interest in the market and responsiveness to price and yield movements might have been appreciably increased.

When all of this is considered, it seems fair to infer that the Federal Reserve could have gained additional influence over the activities of some capital market institutions, specifically, life insurance companies and mutual savings banks, by dealing directly in long-term Treasury bonds to exert active influence on their prices and yields. Moreover, if such operations had broadened the long-term bond market, the responsiveness of financial institutions to yield changes on long-term Treasury bonds might well have been increased. This is not to say that the effects of such operations would have been as powerful as Roosa originally envisaged. But there seems little question that the effects of such a central bank policy would have worked in the right direction and would have reached institutions, the nonbank financial intermediaries, which were largely outside the scope of traditional central bank controls over bank reserve positions. The conclusion is then that a central bank which refused to exert direct influence in the long-term Government bond market was not utilizing its powers for monetary control to the full.

GENERAL CONCLUSIONS OF THE STUDY

The Federal Reserve's conduct of monetary policy from 1951 to 1959 would have been more effective if it had paid more heed to Walter Bagehot's widely quoted aphorism: "Money will not manage itself," [2] and to his warning that "we must not confide too surely in long-established credit, or in firmly rooted traditions of business. We must examine the system on which these great masses of money are manipulated and assure ourselves that it is safe and right." [3]

The Federal Reserve authorities in the 1951–1959 period quite clearly had reservations about the extent to which money should be managed. In a sense they seem to have wished that money *would* manage itself. In part this attitude seemed to reflect a real conviction that the positive management of money is inconsistent with the freedom of the economy. In part it apparently stemmed from a belief that the less the Federal Reserve *appeared* to be managing money, the less opposition its activities would arouse. But these beliefs ignored the facts of contemporary life. Monetary management is the least disruptive form of Government influence over the economy which both public opinion and the complexities of modern society demand. It should be compared not with the absence of any Government control at all, but with a network of direct controls on spending, lending, production, distribution, prices, and wages—all of which would restrict the freedom of the economy infinitely more. Vigorous and effective monetary management is a prerequisite for the continued freedom of the economy, not a limitation on that freedom.

Moreover, it seems clear from the volume of public and political attacks on the Federal Reserve whenever it has imposed credit restraint that its efforts to minimize its responsibility for money conditions have been unsuccessful. Indeed, efforts to suggest that the Federal Reserve has little or nothing to do with the level of interest

[2] Walter Bagehot, *Lombard Street* (London, John Murray, 1915), p. 20.
[3] *Ibid.*, p. 18.

rates, for example, have succeeded only in increasing suspicion about the frankness and good faith of the monetary authorities. It is hard to escape the conclusion that the Federal Reserve would be better advised to assert frankly its duty to *manage* money and to defend its actions on their merits in promoting the national welfare. Education, not confusion, of the public and of political leaders is the only sound way of gaining the public support the central bank needs if it is to be successful.

Furthermore, contrary to Bagehot's second injunction, the Federal Reserve made the mistake of relying uncritically on traditional usages of central banking without paying sufficient attention to whether they were consistent with its acceptance of a wide range of responsibilities, far beyond the ken of any traditional central banker, and with the new and more complex environment in which the Federal Reserve now operates.

The effectiveness of monetary policy suffered on all these counts. It soon became clear that monetary instruments and techniques, which once were adequate, in an older and simpler setting, were only partially effective in a modern economic and financial environment. Moreover, the diversity of tasks the Federal Reserve has assumed have made it increasingly evident that a corresponding variety of monetary control instruments and techniques is required for their successful achievement. Conflicting objectives may pose an insuperable problem under the best of circumstances, but they are far more likely to do so if the central bank restricts itself to only one approach to monetary control.

The moral seems clear that central banks and central bankers require a full complement of instruments, a flexible approach to their problems, and a willingness to treat existing techniques and instruments of policy as tentative and subject to modification as the environment in which they operate changes. Failure to accept this view impaired the effectiveness of monetary policy from 1951 to 1959. Prospects for the future are enhanced by the Federal Reserve's recent willingness to take a more flexible approach to monetary policy and techniques.

BIBLIOGRAPHY

Adams, E. S. Monetary Management. New York, Ronald Press, 1950.

Alhadeff, David. Monopoly and Competition in Banking. Berkeley and Los Angeles, University of California Press, 1954.

Anderson, Clay J. "Monetary Policy—a 1914 Model in a Space-Age Economy." Address before the Conference of Pennsylvania Economists, Pittsburgh, Pennsylvania, June 11, 1959.

Angell, James W. "Appropriate Monetary Policies and Operations in the United States Today," Review of Economics and Statistics, XLII (August, 1960), 247–52.

——. Investment and Business Cycles. New York, McGraw-Hill, 1941.

——. The Behavior of Money. New York, McGraw-Hill, 1936.

——. "The Monetary Standard: Objectives and Limitations," American Economic Review, XLVIII (May, 1958), 76–87.

Arndt, H. W. "The Monetary Theory of Deficit Spending, A Comment on Dr. Clark Warburton's Article," Review of Economics and Statistics, XXVIII (May, 1946), 90–94.

Ascheim, Joseph. "Commercial Banks and Financial Intermediaries: Fallacies and Policy Implications," Journal of Political Economy, LXVII (February, 1959), 59–71.

Beckhart, Benjamin H. Discount Policy of the Federal Reserve System. New York, Holt, 1924.

Birnbaum, Eugene A. "The Growth of Financial Intermediaries as a Factor in the Effectiveness of Monetary Policy," Staff Papers of the International Monetary Fund, VI (November, 1958), 369–83.

Board of Governors of the Federal Reserve System. Consumer Instalment Credit. Washington, 1957.

——. The Federal Reserve System, Purposes and Functions. Washington, 1954.

Bopp, Karl R. "Borrowing from the Federal Reserve Bank—Some Basic Principles," in Federal Reserve Bank of Philadelphia, Business Review, June, 1958, pp. 3–9.

Botha, D. J. A Study in the Theory of Monetary Equilibrium. Leiden, H. E. Stenfert Kroese N.V., 1959.

Burgess, W. Randolph. The Reserve Banks and the Money Market. Revised ed. New York, Harper, 1936.

Burns, Arthur. Prosperity Without Inflation. New York, Fordham University Press, 1957.

Carson, Deane. "Recent Open Market Committee Policy and Techniques," *Quarterly Journal of Economics,* LXIX (August, 1955), 321–42.

"Controversial Issues in Recent Monetary Policy: A Symposium," *Review of Economics and Statistics,* XLII (August, 1960), 245–82.

Culbertson, John M. "A Positive Debt Management Program," *Review of Economics and Statistics,* XLI (May, 1959), 89–98.

——. "Intermediaries and Monetary Theory: A Criticism of Gurley-Shaw Theory," *American Economic Review,* XLVIII (March, 1958), 119–31.

——. "Timing Changes in Monetary Policy," *Journal of Finance,* XIV (May, 1959), 145–60.

Currie, Lauchlin. The Supply and Control of Money in the United States. Cambridge, Harvard University Press, 1934.

Davies, Owen L., ed. Statistical Methods in Research and Production. New York, Hafner, 1957.

Eastburn, David. "Real Estate Credit Controls as a Selective Instrument of Federal Reserve Policy." Unpublished Ph.D. dissertation, University of Pennsylvania, 1957.

——. "The Philosophy of Selective Regulation," in Readings in Money and Banking. Edited by Charles R. Whittlesey. New York, Norton, 1952, pp. 107–14.

Edie, Lionel. The Banks and Prosperity. New York, McGraw-Hill, 1936.

Ellis, Howard S. "The Rediscovery of Money," in Money, Trade, and Economic Growth. Essays in Honor of John Henry Williams. New York, Macmillan, 1951, pp. 253–69.

Fauver, Clarke L., and Ralph A. Young. "Measuring the Impact of Consumer Credit Controls on Spending," *Journal of Finance,* VII (May, 1952), 388–402.

Federal Reserve Bank of Kansas City. "Bank Reactions to Securities Losses," *Monthly Review,* June, 1960, pp. 9–16.

Federal Reserve Bank of New York. "Borrowing from the Fed," *Monthly Review,* 41 (September, 1959), 138–42.

——. "The Significance and Limitation of Free Reserves," *Monthly Review,* 40 (November, 1958), 162–67.

Federal Reserve Bank of St. Louis. "The Discount Mechanism and Monetary Policy," *Monthly Review,* XLII (September, 1960).

Fisher, Irving. The Purchasing Power of Money. New York, Macmillan, 1913.

Fousek, Peter. Foreign Central Banking: The Instruments of Monetary Policy. New York, Federal Reserve Bank of New York, 1957.

Freeman, Louise. "The 'Bills-Only' Policy: An Aspect of the Federal Reserve's Relationship to the United States Government Securities Market." Unpublished Master's thesis, Columbia University, 1957.

Friedman, Milton. A Program for Monetary Stability. New York, Fordham University Press, 1959.

Gaines, Tilford. "Management of the Public Debt." Unpublished Ph.D. dissertation, Columbia University, 1959.

Garvy, George. Deposit Velocity and Its Signifiance. New York, Federal Reserve Bank of New York, 1959.

Gehrels, F., and S. Wiggens. "Interest Rates and Manufacturers' Fixed Investment," *American Economic Review,* XLVII (October, 1957), 79–92.

Goldenweiser, E. A. American Monetary Policy. New York, McGraw-Hill, 1950.

Goldsmith, Raymond W. Financial Intermediaries in the American Economy since 1900. National Bureau of Economic Research. Princeton, Princeton University Press, 1958.

Great Britain, Committee on Finance and Industry. Report. London, 1931.

Great Britain, Committee on the Working of the Monetary System. Memoranda of Evidence. London, 1960.

——. Minutes of Evidence. London, 1960.

——. Report. London, 1959.

Gurley, John G. "The Radcliffe Report and Evidence," *American Economic Review,* L (September, 1960), 672–700.

Gurley, John G., and Edward S. Shaw. "Financial Aspects of Economic Development," *American Economic Review,* XLV (September, 1955), 515–38.

——. "Financial Growth and Monetary Controls." Unpublished paper delivered before the Southern Economic Association, November 17, 1956.

——. "Financial Intermediaries and the Savings-Investment Process," *Journal of Finance,* XI (May, 1956), 257–76.

——. "The Growth of Money and Debt in the United States, 1800–1950," *Review of Economics and Statistics,* XXXIX (August, 1957), 250–62.

Guttentag, Jack M. "Credit Availability, Interest Rates, and Monetary Policy," *Southern Economic Journal,* XXVI (January, 1960), 219–28.

——. "Some Studies in the Post-World War II Residential Construction and Mortgage Markets." Unpublished Ph.D. dissertation, Columbia University, 1958.

Hansen, Alvin. "Bankers and Subsidies," *Review of Economics and Statistics,* XL (February, 1958), 50–51.

——. "Monetary Policy," *Review of Economics and Statistics,* XXXVII (May, 1955), 110–19.

——. The American Economy. New York, McGraw-Hill, 1957.

Hardy, Charles O. Credit Policies of the Federal Reserve System. Washington, The Brookings Institution, 1932.

Harris, Seymour, ed. "A Symposium on Monetary Policy," *Review of Economics and Statistics,* XLII (August, 1960), 245–81.

——. ed. The New Economics. New York, Knopf, 1947.

——. Twenty Years of Federal Reserve Policy. Cambridge, Harvard University Press, 1933.

Harrod, R. F. "Is the Money Supply Important?" *Westminster Bank Review,* November, 1959, pp. 3–7.

Hart, A. G. Defense and the Dollar. New York, Twentieth Century Fund, 1953.

————. "Some Inconsistencies in Debt Management," *Review of Economics and Statistics,* XLII (August, 1960), 257–58.

Hawtrey, R. G. The Art of Central Banking. London, Longmans, Green, 1934.

Hayes, Alfred. "A Breathing Spell for Monetary Policy." Remarks before the Fifty-Seventh Annual Convention of the New Jersey Bankers Association, Atlantic City, New Jersey, May 19, 1960.

————. "Monetary Policy in a Recession." Remarks before the Fifty-Fifth Annual Convention of the New Jersey Bankers Association, Atlantic City, New Jersey, May 22, 1958.

————. Speech before the New York State Bankers Association, January 21, 1957.

Haywood, Charles F. "The Adequacy of Federal Reserve Powers to Discharge Responsibilities," *Journal of Finance,* XIV (May, 1959), 135–44.

Holtrop, M. W. "Theories of the Velocity of Circulation of Money in Earlier Economic Literature," *Economic History,* I (January, 1929), 503–34.

Homan, Paul T., and Fritz Machlup, eds. Financing American Prosperity. New York, Twentieth Century Fund, 1945.

Kaldor, Nicholas. "The Radcliffe Report," *Review of Economics and Statistics,* XLII (February, 1960), 14–19.

Kareken, John H. "Federal Reserve System Discount Policy: an Appraisal," *Banca Nazionale Del Lavoro Quarterly Review,* XII (March, 1959), 103–25.

————. "Post Accord Monetary Developments in the United States," *Banca Nazionale Del Lavoro Quarterly Review,* X (September, 1957), 322–51.

Keynes, John M. A Treatise on Money. New York, Harcourt Brace, 1930.

————. The General Theory of Employment, Interest and Money. New York, Harcourt Brace. 1936.

Klein, Lawrence R. A Textbook of Econometrics. Evanston, Illinois, Peterson, 1953.

Lanston, Aubrey G., and Co. "Address Delivered by Aubrey G. Lanston before the Investment Group of Hartford." Hartford, Connecticut, January 11, 1956.

Lindsay, Robert, and Jack Guttentag. "Financial Intermediaries and the Effectiveness of Monetary Policy." Unpublished paper, 1959.

Luckett, Dudley G. " 'Bills Only': a Critical Appraisal," *Review of Economics and Statistics,* XLII (August, 1960), 301–6.

McKinley, G. W. "The Federal Home Loan Bank System and the Control of Credit," *Journal of Finance,* XII (September, 1957), 319–32.

Maisel, Sherman J. Housebuilding in Transition. Berkeley and Los Angeles, University of California Press, 1953.

Marget, Arthur W. The Theory of Prices. 2 vols. New York, Prentice-Hall, 1938.

Martin, William McChesney. "The Transition to Free Markets," *Federal Reserve Bulletin,* XXXIX (April, 1953), 330–35.

Miller, Ervin. "Monetary Policy in a Changing World," *Quarterly Journal of Economics,* LXX (February, 1956), 23–43.

Minsky, Hyman P. "Central Banking and Money Market Changes," *Quarterly Journal of Economics,* LXXI (May, 1957), 171–87.

O'Leary, James J. "The Effects of Monetary Policies on the Mortgage Market," *Journal of Finance,* XIII (May, 1958), 176–87.

Riefler, Winfield. "Open Market Operations in Long-Term Securities," *Federal Reserve Bulletin,* XLIV (November, 1958), 1260–74.

Rist, Charles. History of Monetary and Credit Theory. New York, Macmillan, 1945.

Ritter, Lawrence. "Income Velocity and Anti-Inflationary Monetary Policy," *American Economic Review,* XLIX (March, 1959), 120–29.

Robertson, Dennis H. "A Squeak from Aunt Sally," *The Banker,* CIX (December, 1959), 718–22.

——. Economic Commentaries. London, Staples Press Ltd., 1956.

Robinson, Roland. The Management of Bank Funds. New York, McGraw-Hill, 1950.

Rodkey, R. G. Legal Reserves in American Banking. Ann Arbor, University of Michigan, 1934.

Roosa, Robert V. "Credit Policy at the Discount Window: a Comment," *Quarterly Journal of Economics,* LXXIII (May, 1959), 333–37.

——. Federal Reserve Operations in the Money and Government Securities Markets. New York, Federal Reserve Bank of New York, 1956.

——. "Interest Rates and the Central Bank," in Money, Trade, and Economic Growth. Essays in Honor of John Henry Williams. New York, Macmillan, 1951, pp. 270–95.

——. "Monetary Policy Again," *Bulletin of the Oxford University Institute of Statistics,* XIV (August, 1952), 253–61.

——. "The Revival of Monetary Policy," *Review of Economics and Statistics,* XXXIII (February, 1951), 29–37.

Rousseas, Stephen W. "Velocity Changes and the Effectiveness of Monetary Policy," *Review of Economics and Statistics,* XLII (February, 1960), 27–36.

Samuelson, Paul. "Recent American Monetary Controversy," *Three Banks Review,* No. 29 (March, 1956), pp. 3–21.

——. "Reflections on Monetary Policy," *Review of Economics and Statistics,* XLII (August, 1960), 263–69.

Saulnier, Raymond J. "An Appraisal of Selective Credit Controls," *American Economic Review,* XLII (May, 1952), 247–63.

Sayers, R. S. Central Banking After Bagehot. London, Oxford University Press, 1957.

——. Modern Banking. 4th and 5th eds. Oxford, The Clarendon Press, 1958 and 1960.

——. "Monetary Thought and Monetary Policy in England," *The Banker,* CX (October, 1960), 671–83.

Scott, Ira O. "Regional Impact of Monetary Policy," *Quarterly Journal of Economics,* LXIX (May, 1955), 269–84.

Selden, Richard T. "Monetary Velocity in the United States," in Studies in the Quantity Theory of Money. Edited by Milton Friedman. Chicago, University of Chicago Press, 1956, pp. 179–257.

Shay, Robert P. "Regulation W: Experiment in Credit Control," *University of Maine Bulletin,* LV (April, 1953), 1–175.

Shaw, Edward S. "Money Supply and Stable Economic Growth," in United States Monetary Policy. New York, American Assembly, Columbia University Press, 1958.

Shelby, Donald. "Some Implications of the Growth of Financial Intermediaries," *Journal of Finance,* XIII (December, 1958), 527–41.

Simmons, Edward C. "A Note on the Revival of Federal Reserve Discount Policy," *Journal of Finance,* XI (December, 1956), 413–21.

——. "Federal Reserve Discount Rate Policy and Member-Bank Borrowing, 1944–50," *Journal of Business of the University of Chicago,* XXV (January, 1952), 18–29.

Smith, Paul. "Response of Consumer Loans to General Credit Conditions," *American Economic Review,* XLVIII (September, 1958), 649–55.

Smith, Warren. "Financial Intermediaries and Monetary Controls," *Quarterly Journal of Economics,* LXXII (November, 1959), 533–53.

——. "Monetary Policy, 1957–1960: An Appraisal," *Review of Economics and Statistics,* XLII (August, 1960), 269–72.

——. "On the Effectiveness of Monetary Policy," *American Economic Review,* XLVI (September, 1956), 588–606.

——. "The Discount Rate as a Credit Control," *Journal of Political Economy,* LXVI (April, 1958), 171–77.

Smithies, Arthur. "Uses of Selective Credit Controls," in United States Monetary Policy. New York, American Assembly, Columbia University, 1958.

Sproul, Allan. "Central Banks and Money Markets." Remarks before the Fifty-First Annual Convention of the New Jersey Bankers Association, Atlantic City, New Jersey, May 6, 1954.

——. "Changing Concepts of Central Banking," in Money, Trade, and Economic Growth. Essays in Honor of John Henry Williams. New York, Macmillan, 1951, pp. 296–325.

——. "Monetary Policy in Periods of Transition." Remarks at the Sixteenth Annual Pacific Northwest Conference on Banking, Pullman, Washington, April 7, 1955.

——. "Reflections of a Central Banker." Remarks before a Joint Luncheon of the American Economic Association and the American Finance Association, New York, December 29, 1955.

Thomas, Woodlief. "The Controversy Over Interest Rates." Address at the Fifteenth Annual Conference for Senior Executives in Mortgage Banking, New York University, New York, January 20, 1960.

Thorn, Richard S. "Nonbank Financial Intermediaries, Credit Expansion, and Monetary Policy," *Staff Papers of the International Monetary Fund,* VI (November, 1958), 369–83.

Thornton, Henry. An Enquiry into the Nature of and Effects of the Paper Credit of Great Britain. Edited by F. A. Hayes. London. G. Allen and Unwin, 1939.

Tobin, James. "Asset Holdings and Spending Decisions," *American Economic Review,* XLII (May, 1952), 109–23.

——. "Liquidity Preference and Monetary Policy," *Review of Economics and Statistics,* XXIX (May, 1947), 124–31.

——. "Monetary Policy and the Management of the Public Debt: The Patman Inquiry," *Review of Economics and Statistics,* XXXV (May, 1953), 118–27.

——. "Towards Improving the Efficiency of the Monetary Mechanism," *Review of Economics and Statistics,* XLII (August, 1960), 76–79.

Turner, R. C. Member Bank Borrowing. Columbus, Ohio, Ohio State University, 1938.

U.S. Congress, Joint Committee on Defense Production. Defense Production Act, Regulation W—Automotive, Hearings. 81st Cong., 2d Sess., 1950.

——. Second Annual Report. 82d Cong., 2d Sess., 1952.

U.S. Congress, Joint Committee on the Economic Report, Subcommittee on Economic Stabilization. United States Monetary Policy: Recent Thinking and Experience, Hearings. 83d Cong., 2d Sess., 1954.

U.S. Congress, Joint Committee on the Economic Report, Subcommittee on General Credit Control and Debt Management. Monetary Policy and the Management of the Public Debt, Replies to Questions and Other Materials. 82d Cong., 2d Sess., 1952.

——. Monetary Policy and the Management of Public Debt, Report. 82d Cong., 2d Sess., 1952.

U.S. Congress, Joint Committee on the Economic Report, Subcommittee on Monetary, Credit, and Fiscal Policies. Monetary, Credit, and Fiscal Policies, Compendium. 81st Cong., 1st Sess., 1949.

——. Monetary, Credit, and Fiscal Policies, Hearings. 81st Cong., 1st Sess., 1949.

——. Monetary, Credit, and Fiscal Policies, Report. 81st Cong., 2d Sess., 1950.

U.S. Congress, Joint Economic Committee. Employment, Growth, and Price Levels, Hearings. 86th Cong., 1st Sess., 1959.

——. Employment, Growth, and Price Levels, Report. 86th Cong., 2d Sess., 1960.

——. Staff Report on Employment, Growth, and Price Levels. 86th Cong., 1st Sess., 1959.

——. Employment, Growth, and Price Levels, Study Paper No. 14: Liquidity and Financial Institutions in the Postwar Period. By John Gurley. 86th Cong., 1st Sess., 1960.

——. A Study of the Dealer Market for Federal Government Securities. 86th Cong., 2d Sess., 1960.

——. The Relationship of Prices to Economic Stability and Growth, Compendium. 85th Cong., 2d Sess., 1958.

U.S. Congress, Joint Economic Committee, Subcommittee on Economic Stabilization, Economic Policy Questionnaire. 85th Cong., 2d Sess., 1958.

——. Monetary Policy: 1955–56, Hearings. 84th Cong., 2d Sess., 1957.

U.S. Executive Office of the President, Bureau of the Budget. Review of the 1956 Budget. August 25, 1955.

U.S. House, Member Bank Reserve Requirements. House Report No. 651. 86th Cong., 1st Sess., 1959.

U.S. House, Committee on Ways and Means. Public Debt Ceiling and Interest Rate Ceiling on Bonds. 86th Cong., 1st Sess., 1959.

United States Monetary Policy. New York, American Assembly, Columbia University, 1958.

U.S. Senate, Committee on Banking and Currency. Defense Production Act Amendments of 1951, Hearings. 82d Cong., 1st Sess., 1951.

U.S. Senate, Committee on Banking and Currency, Subcommittee on Housing. Study of Mortgage Credit, Hearings. 86th Cong., 1st Sess., 1959.

U.S. Senate, Committee on Finance. Investigation of the Financial Condition of the United States, Compendium. 85th Cong., 2d Sess., Vol. 1–7, 1958.

——. Investigation of the Financial Condition of the United States, Hearings. 85th Cong., 1st Sess., 1957.

U.S. Treasury Department and Board of Governors of the Federal Reserve System. Treasury-Federal Reserve Study of the Government Securities Market. 1959–1960.

Walker, Charls. "Discount Policy in the Light of Recent Experience," *Journal of Finance,* XII (May, 1957), 223–37.

Warburton, Clark. "The Secular Trend in Monetary Velocity," *Quarterly Journal of Economics,* LXIII (February, 1949), 86–90.

White, W. H. "Interest Inelasticity of Investment Demand—The Case from Business Attitude Surveys Re-examined," *American Economic Review,* XLVI (September, 1956), 565–87.

Whittlesey, Charles R. "Credit Policy at the Discount Window," *Quarterly Journal of Economics,* LXXIII (May, 1959), 207–16.

——. "Monetary Policy and Economic Change," *Review of Economics and Statistics,* XXXIX (February, 1957), 31–39.

——. "Old and New Ideas on Reserve Requirements," *Journal of Finance,* VIII (May, 1953), 190–95.

Wilson, T., and P. W. S. Andrews, eds. Oxford Studies in the Price Mechanism. Oxford, The Clarendon Press, 1951.

Wold, Herman. Demand Analysis, A Study in Econometrics. New York, Wiley, 1953.

Young, Ralph, and Charles Yager. "The Economics of 'Bills Preferably,' " *Quarterly Journal of Economics,* LXXIV (August, 1960), 341–73.

INDEX